HANDBOOK OF PRACTICAL MICROCOMPUTER TROUBLESHOOTING

HANDBOOK OF PRACTICAL MICROCOMPUTER TROUBLESHOOTING

JOHN D. LENK

Reston Publishing Company, Inc.
A Prentice-Hall Company
Reston, Virginia

Library of Congress Cataloging in Publication Data

Lenk, John D.
Handbook of practical microcomputer troubleshooting.

Includes index.
1. Microcomputers—Maintenance and repair.
I. Title.
TK7888.3.L36 621.3819'58 79-1357
ISBN 0-8359-2757-1

A Prentice-Hall Company
Reston, Virginia 22090

10 9 8 7 6 5 4 3 2 1

Printed in the United States of America

To Irene, the "Sandpiper Lady"
and Mr. Lamb, the "Magic Bunny"

CONTENTS

PREFACE ix

Chapter 1. INTRODUCTION TO MICROCOMPUTER BASICS 1

1–1. Basic Definitions, 1
1–2. Microcomputer Number Systems, 2
1–3. Binary Basics, 3
1–4. Octal Basics, 12
1–5. Hexadecimal Basics, 14
1–6. Binary Codes, 20
1–7. Alphanumeric Codes, 20
1–8. Relationship Between Binary Numbers and Electrical Signals, 22
1–9. Basic Microprocessor/Microcomputer Circuit Functions, 30
1–10. Microprocessor Hardware, 41
1–11. Memory Hardware, 45
1–12. Input/Output Hardware, 54
1–13. Basic Microcomputer System, 56
1–14. System Timing and Synchronization, 65
1–15. Typical Microcomputer System Operation, 67
1–16. Machine Language Versus Assembly Language Programming, 80
1–17. Development of a Microprocessor-Based System, 84

Chapter 2. INTRODUCTION TO PERIPHERAL EQUIPMENT 91

2–1. The Need for Peripheral Equipment, 91
2–2. Electric Typewriter or TTY Terminals, 94
2–3. Video Terminal (Keyboard/CRT), 99

2–4. Paper-Tape Reader and Punch, 102
2–5. Output Printers, 105
2–6. Magnetic Recording Basics, 110
2–7. Tape Recording Basics, 112
2–8. Diskette (Floppy Disk) Recording Basics, 122
2–9. Data Communications, 133

Chapter 3. MICROCOMPUTER TROUBLESHOOTING EQUIPMENT 137

3–1. Safety Precautions in Microcomputer Troubleshooting, 138
3–2. Logic Probe, 140
3–3. Logic Pulser, 143
3–4. Current Tracer, 146
3–5. Logic Clip, 150
3–6. Logic Comparator, 151
3–7. Basic Approach to Microcomputer Troubleshooting, 152
3–8. Hewlett Packard Model 1611A Logic State Analyzer, 162
3–9. Hewlett Packard Model 1610A Logic State Analyzer, 169
3–10. Hewlett Packard Model 1602A Logic State Analyzer, 180
3–11. Tektronix 7D01 Logic Analyzer and DF1 Display Formatter, 183

Chapter 4. TYPICAL MICROCOMPUTER CIRCUITS AND CIRCUIT TROUBLESHOOTING 199

4–1. Heathkit Model H11 Computer System, 200
4–2. Heathkit H11–1 4K Memory Expansion Module, 233
4–3. Heathkit H11–2 Parallel Interface Module, 236
4–4. Heathkit H11–5 Serial Interface Module, 242
4–5. Heathkit Model H9 Video Terminal, 248
4–6. Heathkit Model H10 Paper-Tape Reader/Punch, 292

Chapter 5. OVERALL MICROCOMPUTER TROUBLESHOOTING APPROACHES 307

5–1. Basic Digital IC Troubleshooting Techniques, 307
5–2. Troubleshooting in the Development Stage, 321
5–3. Analyzing Microcomputer Program Flow During Troubleshooting, 334
5–4. Using the Hewlett Packard 1610A Logic State Analyzer, 339
5–5. Using the Tektronix 7D01 Logic Analyzer, 363
5–6. Serial Pattern Recognition Problems, 371

INDEX 383

PREFACE

The purpose of this book is to provide a simplified system of troubleshooting for the many types and models of microcomputers in use. For our purposes, a microcomputer is any computer or control system that uses a *microprocessor*, operating in response to a *stored program of instructions*, as the primary control element. This can include the classic personal computer, which operates with such peripherals as a keyboard, video display, and tape cassette or floppy disk, as well as the many industrial and commercial control systems (industrial process controls, supermarket checkstand computers, video games, and so forth).

While attempts have been made to do so, it is not only impractical, but virtually impossible to cover troubleshooting for all such microcomputers and their related peripheral equipment in one book. Books that dealt with such a vast amount of material have soon been made obsolete by rapid technological advances.

To overcome this problem, we concentrate on *basic approaches to microcomputer troubleshooting*. These approaches can be applied to any microprocessor/stored-program system now being developed, to those that will be manufactured in the future, and to microprocessor-based equipment now in use.

The troubleshooting approaches described here are based on the techniques found in the author's best-selling troubleshooting books: *Handbook of Practical Solid State Troubleshooting, Handbook of Basic Electronic Troubleshooting, Handbook of Simplified Television Service,* and *Handbook of Practical CB Service*.

Chapter 1 starts by describing the basic elements of a microprocessor-based system, Chapter 2 provides similar coverage for peripheral equipment. As is discussed, each of the several different types of circuits involved in microcomputers (power, linear, digital, cathode-ray tube, stored-program, and mechanical control) requires a somewhat different approach to troubleshooting.

Chapter 3 is devoted to test equipment used in servicing microprocessor-based systems. This is particularly important since microcomputer faults are often best located by analyzing test results (response to input signals, presence or absence of pulses and signal levels, step-by-step tracing of instructions and data through each step of the program, etc.). Chapter 3 includes a wide variety of test equipment for practical microcomputer work, and covers basic operating principles and characteristics. The discussions in Chapter 3 describe how the features found on present-day test equipment relate to specific problems in microcomputer service.

Chapter 4 describes the theory of operaton for a cross-section of present-day microcomputer circuits. These include a basic microcomputer system, CRT video terminal, memory expansion module, parallel interface, serial interface, and a peripheral (a paper tape reader/punch). After studying these circuits thoroughly, the reader should have no difficulty in understanding the schematics and block diagrams of any microcomputer. This understanding is essential for logical troubleshooting.

Chapter 5 describes the basic approaches to microcomputer service, or how the basics of Chapters 1 and 2 are combined with the practical use of test equipment discussed in Chapter 3, together with a knowledge of typical circuits covered in Chapter 4, to locate specific faults in various types of microprocessor-based systems. Considerable emphasis is placed on "universal" test, service, and troubleshooting procedures that apply to all microcomputers. The chapter also concentrates on the relationship between software and troubleshooting.

Many professionals have contributed their talent and knowledge to the preparation of this book. The author gratefully acknowledges that the tremendous effort required to make this book such a comprehensive work is impossible for one person, and he wishes to thank all who have contributed directly and indirectly.

Special thanks are due the following: Walter Dennen of RCA Corporaton, Solid State Division; Lothar Stern of Motorola Semiconductors Products, Inc.; J.C. Carsten and Rob Walker of Intel Corporation; Stanley Victor, Jr. of Mostek Corporation; E.S. Huber, Jr. of Texas Instruments Incorporated; Hy Siegel of Radio Shack; Louis Frenzel of Heath Company; Pat Whitty and Wyn Giluck of Tektronix, Inc.; Ross Snyder and Art Pettis of Hewlett-Packard; and Joseph A. Labok of Los Angeles Valley College.

Chapter 1

INTRODUCTION TO MICROCOMPUTER BASICS

This chapter is devoted to the basics of microcomputer operation. It is assumed that the reader has a knowledge of microprocessor-based systems equal to that found in the author's *Handbook of Microprocessors, Microcomputers, and Minicomputers* (1979, Prentice-Hall, Inc., Englewood Cliffs, New Jersey). However, no reference to the above book, or to any other book, is required to understand and use this troubleshooting handbook.

With that in mind, and on the assumption that you may need a refresher, we start with descriptions of a basic microcomputer system. These descriptions are kept to an elementary level since you are interested in troubleshooting (not theory), and so that the descriptions will apply to the greatest number of microcomputer systems.

This introduction provides a summary of, not a complete course, in microcomputer theory. Throughout these discussions, references are made to the remaining chapters, where you will find detailed information on peripherals, microcomputer test equipment, operational theory, software, troubleshooting, and service procedures.

1–1. BASIC DEFINITIONS

A *microprocessor* is an integrated circuit (IC) that performs many of the functions found in a digital computer. A single microprocessor IC is capable of performing all the arithmetic and control functions of a computer. By itself, a typical microprocessor IC does not contain the memories and input/output (I/O) functions of a computer. However, when these functions are provided by additional ICs, a *microcomputer* is formed.

In most systems, a simple microcomputer requires a read-only memory (ROM) to store the computer program or instructions, a random-access memory (RAM) to store temporary data (the information to be acted upon by the computer program), and an I/O IC to make the system compatible with outside or peripheral equipment, such as an interactive video computer terminal, teletype, or line printer. There are some ICs that contain some or all of these functions. In effect, when an IC contains all of the basic functions, the IC is a "computer on a chip." However, this is not the typical case.

Microprocessors are sometimes referred to as *microprocessor units* (MPU) or *control processor units* (CPU) (and CPU can sometimes mean *central processor unit*). As you will soon find out, there is no real standardization in terms for the microprocessor field at this time.

It should also be noted that a microprocessor is not always used in digital computer applications. Instead, the microprocessor is used as a controller. As a matter of interest, the microprocessor was originally developed as the control element for those applications for which digital computer functions (the ability to store and execute a complete program automatically) were required, but for which a computer (even a simple minicomputer) was too large or expensive. Sometimes, the microprocessor is called a *microcontroller* when used in these control applications. The various terms are discussed further throughout the remainder of this chapter.

The term *minicomputer* can be applied to many relatively small and relatively simple computers. A minicomputer often contains many ICs, but not necessarily a microprocessor IC. In this book, we are concerned primarily with microprocessor-based systems, whether they be computers, controllers, video games, or whatever.

1–2. MICROCOMPUTER NUMBER SYSTEMS

The decimal number system is generally used in the world outside the microprocessor. Inside a microprocessor-based system, the *binary* number system is used most often. This is because binary numbers are compatible with pulses used in digital or logic systems. Binary numbers use only two digits, 0 or 1. The zero can be represented by the absence of a pulse, with the 1 being represented by the presence of a pulse (or vice versa in some systems). The pulses are typically about 5 volts (V) in amplitude and a few microseconds (μs) or nanoseconds (ns) in duration; they can be positive or negative without affecting the binary number system (as long as *only two states* exist). In any event, to understand the language of microprocessor-based systems (generally referred to as *machine language*), it becomes necessary to examine number systems in general and the binary number system in particular.

Although microprocessors use binary numbers in the form of pulses, most microcomputer systems use some other form of number system for assembly of computer programs (generally referred to as *assembly language*). This is because binary numbers (although compatible with pulses) are cumbersome when the values are beyond a few digits. Shorthand number systems are used to enter and read out programs and data in a microcomputer system. The most common shorthand number systems used for microcomputer programming are the *octal, hexadecimal* (or *hex*), binary-coded decimal (or BCD), and alphanumeric systems. We discuss each of these systems in the following paragraphs.

1–3. BINARY BASICS

The binary number system uses only two digits, 0 and 1. The *positional weights* or *values* assigned to the digits increase from right to left as in the familiar decimal system. However, with binary, the increase of value is in ascending powers of 2. Thus, the digit at the extreme right (the least significant digit, or LSD) has a weight or value of 2^0, or decimal 1. A digit in the position immediately to the left has a weight of 2^1, or decimal 2. The next digit to the left is equivalent to decimal 4, and so on. This can be shown as follows:

2^7	2^6	2^5	2^4	2^3	2^2	2^1	2^0
128	64	32	16	8	4	2	1
MSD							LSD

When all the above decimal values are added, the total is 255. Thus, an eight-digit binary number can represent decimal numbers from 0 to 255.

1–3.1 Words, Bits, Bytes, and Nibbles

Note that the extreme left digit (the most significant digit, or MSD) has a value of 128. Also note that this combination of eight binary digits is commonly used in microprocessors to form a binary *word*. In computer work, binary digits are referred to as *bits* (a contraction of *bi*nary digi*ts*). The LSD bit is bit zero, or b_0, whereas the MSD is bit seven, or b_7. When eight binary digits are used to form words, the arrangement is known as an 8-bit system. When all 8 bits are used at once, the combination is referred to as a *byte*. Any number less than 8 bits is called a nibble, although in an 8-bit system a nibble is generally considered as 4 bits. Likewise, some computer systems use 4-bit or 16-bit binary words or bytes. Many of the newer microcomputer systems are designed for 16-bit words, but will also accept 8-bit words so as to be compatible with the majority of present-day microcomputer systems.

1–3.2 Binary Number Values

In binary, if the digit is zero, its value is zero. If the digit is 1, its value is determined by its position from the right. For example, to represent the decimal number 83 in binary form, the following combination of zeros and ones can be used:

b_7	b_6	b_5	b_4	b_3	b_2	b_1	b_0	(bit number)
0	1	0	1	0	0	1	1	(binary number)
128	64	32	16	8	4	2	1	(weight or value)
0	+ 64	+ 0	+ 16	+ 0	+ 0	+ 2	+ 1	= decimal 83

which means that 01010011 in 8-bit binary form is 83.

Notc that it is not always necessary to use the full 8 bits to write a binary number. For example, decimal 15 requires only four binary digits, 1111, and need not be written as 00001111 on paper. However, in an 8-bit microprocessor system, all 8 bits must be included by adding the zeros.

1–3.3 Number Identification

Also note that binary number 1011 (which may be interpreted as 8 + 0 + 2 + 1, or decimal 11) is not read as "one thousand eleven" but as "one, zero, one, one." In some computer literature, when binary and decimal numbers are mixed, a number subscript (a 2 for binary, a 10 for decimal) is added to minimize confusion.

For example, 101_{10} is decimal "one hundred and one," whereas 101_2 is binary "one, zero, one," or decimal 5_{10}. In other literature, a letter is added to the number (D for decimal, B for binary) for identification. Two other commonly used number systems, octal and hexadecimal (described in Secs. 1–4 and 1–5, respectively), are identified by number subscripts (8 for octal, 16 for hex, or possibly the letter H for hex) in some literature.

1–3.4 Counting in Binary

The counting method for binary numbers is the same as for the decimal system, except that we use only two digits, 0 and 1. Thus, starting with 0, if we add one count, we get 1. Adding another count, we go back to 0 again, and a carry is added to the next position at the left, producing 10 (decimal 2). Adding another count produces 11 (decimal 3), and if another count is added, we get 100 (decimal 4). The next count produces 101 (decimal 5), and so on. The relationship between binary counting and the operation of an electronic *counter circuit* is described in Sec. 1–9.1.

1–3.5 Binary Fractions

When we come to binary fractions, we use the same rules that we apply to decimal fractions. A binary point (similar to the decimal point) is used to separate the integers (whole numbers) from the fraction. The weight of the digit to the right of the binary point is 2^{-1}, or decimal ½. The next position to the right has a weight of 2^{-2}, or decimal ¼; the next position to the right has a weight of 2^{-3}, or decimal ⅛, and so on. As an example, the binary fraction 0.101 may be interpreted as $0 + \frac{1}{2} + \frac{0}{4} + \frac{1}{8}$, or as $0 + 0.5 + 0 + 0.125$, which is equal to the decimal fraction 0.625.

1–3.6 Signed Binary Numbers

Thus far, we have assumed that all binary numbers are positive. This is the case for *true, natural,* or *pure binary* numbers. However, the *signed binary* system may be used to represent both positive and negative numbers. With signed binary, the extreme left bit of a binary number or word is used to indicate the *sign* of the number, and the remaining bits give the magnitude. The number is positive (+) if the leftmost bit is 0; the number is negative (−) when the leftmost bit is 1.

Using signed binary, when the sign bit changes from 0 to 1, the whole number is negated, and its magnitude is not changed. For example,

$$01100111 = +\ 103 \text{ (decimal)}$$
$$11100111 = -\ 103 \text{ (decimal)}$$

1–3.7 Conversion from Binary to Decimal Numbers

To convert binary numbers to decimal numbers, multiply each binary digit by its positional weight, and add all the products, as is done in Sec. 1–3.2. There are other methods for conversion, but they are generally not any simpler.

1–3.8 Conversion from Decimal to Binary Numbers

A decimal number can be converted into a binary number in many ways. The obvious way is to make up a chart showing the power of 2, as has been done in Sec. 1–3.2, and to then count the necessary number of 1s and 0s to make up the desired decimal number.

For example, assume that the decimal number 33 is to be converted. The number 33 is more than 32 (sixth position from the right in the table of Sec. 1–3.2), but less than 64 (seventh position from the right). This means that you need a combination of six digits (1s or 0s, probably both).

Start with the sixth position, or 32. Since you want number 32, write a 1 in the sixth position. Then move to the fifth position, or 16. Since 32 plus 16 is greater than the desired 33, use a zero for the fifth position. The fourth position is 8, and 8 plus 32 is more than 33, so use a 0 for the fourth position. The same is true of the third position, or 4, and the second position, or 2; so both these positions use a 0. The first (right, or LSD) position is 1, and 1 plus the sixth position (or 32) makes the desired 33, so both these positions require a 1. Thus, the pure binary equivalent of decimal 33 is 100001. If the 8-bit system is used, the binary number will read 00100001 for a decimal 33.

Section 1–3.2 shows the powers of 2 for positions 2^0 through 2^7, or bit 0 through bit 7. Figure 1–1 shows the powers of 2 from 2^8 through 2^{24}, or bit 8 through bit 24.

1–3.9 Binary Addition

Binary addition, like decimal addition, is essentially a counting process. However, binary addition is simpler than decimal addition. There are only four simple rules for binary addition:

$$0 + 0 = 0 \text{ with no carry}$$
$$0 + 1 = 1 \text{ with no carry}$$
$$1 + 0 = 1 \text{ with no carry}$$
$$1 + 1 = 0\text{, with a carry of } 1$$

For example, suppose that we wish to add binary numbers 11101 and 1011:

Binary								Decimal equivalent
	+1	+1	+1	+1			(carry)	
		1	1	1	0	1	(augend)	29
+			1	0	1	1	(addend)	+ 11
	1	0	1	0	0	0	(sum)	40

2^n	n
256	8
512	9
1 024	10
2 048	11
4 096	12
8 192	13
16 384	14
32 768	15
65 536	16
131 072	17
262 144	18
524 288	19
1 048 576	20
2 097 152	21
4 194 304	22
8 388 608	23
16 777 216	24

Fig. 1–1. Powers of 2 from bit 8 through bit 24 (2^8 through 2^{24})

1–3.10 Binary Subtraction

There are also four simple rules for binary subtraction:

$0 - 0 = 0$ with no borrow
$1 - 1 = 0$ with no borrow
$1 - 0 = 1$ with no borrow
$0 - 1 = 1$ with a borrow of 1

For example, to subtract binary 0111 from binary 1001,

Binary		Decimal equivalent
−1 −1	(borrow)	
1 0 0 1	(minuend)	9
−0 1 1 1	(subtrahend)	−7
0 0 1 0	(difference)	2

Note that when the first borrow is subtracted from the 0 of the minuend it leaves a 1, with a borrow from the digit at the left. When the 1 of the subtrahend is subtracted from the resulting 1 of the minuend, the difference is 0 with no borrow.

The above example shows how binary numbers are subtracted on paper. In a microcomputer, subtraction is often done by a combination of addition and complementing, as described in the following section.

1–3.11 Binary Complements

As in the decimal system, binary subtraction can be performed as an addition process using the complement method. There are two types of binary complements, the *1's complement* and the *2's complement.*

One's Complement. The 1's complement of a binary number is found by subtracting each digit of the number from 1, or, more simply, by reversing the digits of the number. Thus, to find the 1's complement of 10101,

```
10101   (binary)
↕↕↕↕↕
01010   (1's complement)
```

Although simple, the 1's complement system has certain problems and is not generally used for microprocessor-based systems. However, the 1's complement number must be found as the first step in finding a 2's complement number.

Two's Complement. The 2's complement system is in general use for microcomputer arithmetic systems. To convert a pure binary number (which is considered to be positive) to its positive equivalent in 2's complement, simply add a zero (or sign bit, as discussed in Sec. 1–3.6) as the next higher significant bit position. For example,

b_7	b_6	b_5	b_4	b_3	b_2	b_1	b_0	
	1	1	1	1	1	1	1	(pure binary 127)
0	1	1	1	1	1	1	1	(+ 127 in 2's complement)
	0	0	0	0	0	0	1	(binary 1)
0	0	0	0	0	0	0	1	(+1 in 2's complement)

To convert a pure binary number (considered to be positive) to its negative equivalent in 2's complement, invert all the bits (that is, find the 1's complement), and then add 1 to the LSD. For example, to convert decimal +37 to negative 2's complement,

```
00100101   =   +37
  invert
11011010
   add 1
--------
11011011   =   −37 in 2's complement
```

Since the positive form of 2's complement is the same as pure binary with a positive sign bit added, the same procedures can be used for conversion. That is, when the negative of a positive 2's complement number is required, the negative is formed by complementing each bit position of the positive representation and then adding 1, as follows:

b_7	b_6	b_5	b_4	b_3	b_2	b_1	b_0	
0	1	1	1	1	1	1	1	(+127 in 2's complement)
1	0	0	0	0	0	0	0	(1's complement)
							1	(add 1)
1	0	0	0	0	0	0	1	(−127 in 2's complement)
0	0	0	0	0	0	0	0	(0 in 2's complement)
1	1	1	1	1	1	1	1	(1's complement)
							1	(add 1)
0	0	0	0	0	0	0	0	(0 is same in either notation)
0	0	0	0	0	0	0	1	(+1 in 2's complement)
1	1	1	1	1	1	1	0	(1's complement)
							1	(add 1)
1	1	1	1	1	1	1	1	(−1 in 2's complement)

Note that although +127 is the largest positive 2's complement number that can be formed with 8 digits, the largest negative 2's complement number is 10000000, or −128. Thus, with 2's complement, an 8-bit byte can represent whole numbers between −128 and +127. Bit 7 can be regarded as a sign bit (if b_7 is 0, the number is +; if b_7 is 1, the number is −):

10000000	11111111	00000000	00000001	01111111
−128	−1	0	+1	+127

1- 3.12 Relationship Between 2's Complement and Signed Binary

Since much of the literature on arithmetic operations in microcomputers presents the information in terms of signed binary numbers (Sec. 1–3.6), the difference between 2's complement and signed binary is of interest. As discussed in Sec. 1–3.6, signed binary number notation also uses the most significant bit as a sign bit (0 for positive, 1 for negative). The remaining bits represent the magnitude as a binary number. For example:

±	64	32	16	8	4	2	1	
b_7	b_6	b_5	b_4	b_3	b_2	b_1	b_0	
1	1	1	1	1	1	1	1	(−127 in signed binary)
1	0	0	0	0	0	0	1	(−1 in signed binary)
0	0	0	0	0	0	0	0	(0 in signed binary)
0	0	0	0	0	0	0	1	(+1 in signed binary)
0	1	1	1	1	1	1	1	(+127 in signed binary)

An 8-bit byte in signed binary represents whole numbers between −127 and +127:

11111111	10000001	00000000	00000001	01111111
←				→
−127	−1	0	+1	+127

Comparing this to the 2's complement representation, the positive numbers are identical and the negative numbers are reversed (−127 in 2's complement is the same as −1 in signed binary, and vice versa). In microcomputers, the difference between the two number systems causes no particular problem, since numerical data are usually converted (automatically) to the correct format when the microcomputer is programmed. That is, the program should provide for the conversion. This is done as follows:

±	64	32	16	8	4	2	1	
b_7	b_6	b_5	b_4	b_3	b_2	b_1	b_0	
1	1	1	1	1	1	1	1	(−127 in signed binary)
1	0	0	0	0	0	0	0	(1's complement except for sign bit)
							1	(add 1)
1	0	0	0	0	0	0	1	(−127 in 2's complement)

1–3.13 Binary Subtraction Using 2's Complement

Section 1–3.10 describes how binary numbers are subtracted on paper. In most microcomputer systems, binary numbers are subtracted by adding the 2's complement of the subtrahend to the minuend, and ignoring the carry bit. This arrangement simplifies circuits in the arithmetic logic unit (ALU) of the microprocessor. For example, assume that decimal 3 is to be subtracted from decimal 10:

On paper				In microcomputer	
00001010	=	(decimal 10)	=	00001010	
−00000011	=	(decimal 3)	=	+11111101	(2's complement)
00000111	=	(decimal 7)	=	00000111	

The final carry bit (ninth bit) that results from adding these two binary numbers is not needed. Thus, the bit is not carried, but is ignored and lost. In an 8-bit microcomputer, the circuits are simply not capable of carrying more than 8 bits, so the ninth bit disappears.

1–3.14 Binary Multiplication

There are three rules for binary multiplication:

$$0 \times 0 = 0$$
$$0 \times 1 = 0$$
$$1 \times 1 = 1$$

The binary multiplication process is simple. If the digit or the multiplier is 0, the partial product is 0. If the multiplier digit is 1, the partial product is the same as the multiplicand. Then the partial products are summed as follows:

Binary							Decimal
	1	0	1	0	1	(multiplicand)	21
×				1	0	(multiplier)	× 2
	0	0	0	0	0	(first partial product)	42
1	0	1	0	1		(second partial product)	
1	0	1	0	1	0	(final product)	

From this, it will be seen that multiplication in binary numbers is a form of addition and shifting (the partial product is shifted to the left for each digit in the multiplier; then the products are added). In a microcomputer system, the addition is done by means of *adder circuits* within the microprocessor, and shifting is done with *shift registers,* also in the microprocessor.

Keep in mind that shift operations are used to multiply binary numbers by powers of 2 (not multiples of 2). A left shift of one bit position multiplies by 2; a left shift of two bit positions multiplies by 4; three-bit positions multiply by 8, and so on. (Similarly, as discussed in Sec. 1–3.15, a right shift of one position divides by 2, (that is, multiplies by one half; a right shift of two positions divides by 4, and so on.)

1–3.15 Binary Division

On paper, binary division is performed in much the same way as decimal long division. The process is much simpler, since there are only two rules in binary division:

$$0 \div 1 = 0$$
$$1 \div 1 = 1$$

Generally, to do division, a microcomputer system reverses the multiplication process. That is, division is a series of subtractions and right shifts to provide partial dividends (as opposed to a series of additions and left shifts to provide partial products for multiplication). The following example illustrates the binary division process, as done on paper.

Binary	Decimal
11	3
$11\sqrt{1001}$	$3\sqrt{9}$
11	9
011	
11	

1–4. OCTAL BASICS

The octal number system uses eight digits from 0 to 7 in ascending order. Conventional (non-microprocessor-based) computers often use octal numbers in their circuits, since octal can provide a shorthand method for bridging the gap between decimal and binary. Microcomputers rarely use octal directly. However, you should have an understanding of octal numbers, since 8 is a power of the binary 2, and the octal number system can be used as an aid in programming and number conversion.

In octal, when a count is added to the largest digit, 7, the count goes back to the start, 0, and a carry is added to the next position to the left. Thus, decimal 8 appears as octal 10 (pronounced "one, zero," not "ten"). The following list shows the octal equivalents of the 10 digits of the decimal system.

Octal	*Decimal*
0	0
1	1
2	2
3	3
4	4
5	5
6	6
7	7
10	8
11	9

As in other systems, the digits of an octal number are arranged in positions of ascending powers, from right to left. The following shows the position weights of the octal system:

Digital position

8^3	8^2	8^1	8^0	8^{-1}	8^{-2}	8^{-3}	Powers of 8
512	64	8	1	$1/8$	$1/64$	$1/512$	Decimal equivalents

Thus, octal number 1305.1 really means $(1 \times 512) + (3 \times 64) + (0 \times 8) + (5 \times 1) + (1 \times 0.125)$, which is equal to 709.125 in the decimal system.

1–4.1 Conversion from Decimal to Octal Numbers

To convert a decimal number to its octal equivalent, divide the decimal number by 8 and record the remainder, even if it is 0, which becomes the LSD of the octal number. Divide the quotient by 8 again and record the remainder of this division, which becomes the next significant octal digit. Continue this process until the quotient becomes 0. The remainder from this division process is the MSD of the octal number. For example, to convert 759_{10} to its octal equivalent,

$$\begin{aligned} 759 \div 8 &= 94 \text{ with remainder 7 (LSD)} \\ 94 \div 8 &= 11 \text{ with remainder 6} \\ 11 \div 8 &= 1 \text{ with remainder 3} \\ 1 \div 8 &= 0 \text{ with remainder 1 (MSD)} \end{aligned}$$

Thus, $759_{10} = 1367_8$.

1–4.2 Conversion from Octal to Decimal Numbers

To convert an octal number to its decimal equivalent, multiply each digit by its positional weight expressed in decimal equivalents and add the products. For example,

$$\begin{aligned} 123_8 &= (1 \times 8^2) + (2 \times 8^1) + (3 \times 8^0) \\ &= (1 \times 64) + (2 \times 8) + (3 \times 1) = 83_{10} \end{aligned}$$

1–4.3 Conversion from Octal to Binary Numbers

To convert an octal number to its binary equivalent, convert each digit of the octal number to the binary equivalent *using three binary digits per octal digit*. Then combine these binary groups in proper order. For example, to convert 377_8 to its binary equivalent,

3 7 7 (octal digits)
011 111 111 (binary equivalents)

Thus, $377_8 = 011111111_2$. As you can see, this grouping of three binary digits will not work for an octal 10 or 11 (decimal 8 and 9, respectively). Also, for three octal digits, it is necessary to use nine binary digits. For these reasons, the octal number system is generally not compatible with the typical 8-bit byte used in microprocessor-based equipment.

1–4.4 Conversion from Binary to Octal Numbers

To convert a binary number to its octal equivalent, divide the digits of the binary number into groups of three, starting from the right. If necessary, fill out the last group (at the left) by placing 0s in front. Then convert each binary group to its octal digit equivalent and combine these digits in proper order. For example, to convert 10110110_2 to its octal equivalent,

Added zero	010	110	110	(binary)
	2	6	6	(octal)

Thus, $10110110_2 = 266_8$.

1–4.5 Conversion of Decimal to Binary Numbers Using Octal Numbers

One way to convert decimal numbers to their binary equivalents, or vice versa, is to use an octal conversion as an intermediary step. This is often done in nonmicroprocessor computers. Using this system, to change a decimal number to binary, first convert the decimal number to its octal equivalent, and then change this octal number to its binary equivalent. The same procedure may be applied in going from binary to decimal numbers. For example, binary 10101 can be handled as

	10	101		(binary)
Added zero	010	101		(octal)
	16	5	= 21	(decimal)

1–5. HEXADECIMAL BASICS

One problem with binary numbers is that they are difficult to manipulate, particularly when large values are involved. The length of a large binary number makes it tedious to write and thus more vulnerable to error. This problem is overcome by use of the octal number system, described in Sec. 1–4, in which three binary digits are represented by one octal digit. The *hexadecimal* number system goes one step further; *each digit represents four binary digits.*

Unlike the base 10 of the decimal numbers, base 2 of binary numbers, or base 8 of octal numbers, the hexadecimal number system uses a *base of 16.* Since the familiar decimal system has only 10 digits or characters (0, 1, . . ., 9), six additional characters are required for the hexadecimal system. The first six letters of the English alphabet (A,B,C,D,E,F) are used. Letter A represents a value of 10, letter B a decimal value of 11, and so on, with letter F representing decimal 15. The following table shows the relationship among the decimal, binary, octal, and hexadecimal number systems.

Decimal	*Pure Binary*	*Octal*	*Hexadecimal*
0	0	0	0
1	1	1	1
2	10	2	2
3	11	3	3
4	100	4	4
5	101	5	5
6	110	6	6
7	111	7	7
8	1000	10	8
9	1001	11	9
10	1010	12	A
11	1011	13	B
12	1100	14	C
13	1101	15	D
14	1110	16	E
15	1111	17	F
16	10000	20	10
17	10001	21	11
18	10010	22	12
25	11001	31	19
26	11010	32	1A
27	11011	33	1B
32	100000	40	20
33	100001	41	21

Note that the carry occurs at 16 in hexadecimal numbers. Additional digits are required when the count goes beyond 16. For example, a decimal 16 is hexadecimal 10 (one, zero), decimal 17 is hexadecimal 11 (one, one), and so on. Thus, it is possible to represent a large decimal number with a hexadecimal number of fewer digits. For example, $FF_{16} = 255_{10}$, and $FFFF_{16} = 65{,}535_{10}$.

1–5.1 Conversion from Hexadecimal to Decimal Numbers

To convert a hexadecimal number to its decimal equivalent (beyond those numbers in the previous table), use the following rules:

1. Multiply the most significant hex digit by 16.

2. Add the next most significant hex digit to the product and multiply the sum by 16.

3. Continue the process (adding, then multiplying) until the least significant hex digit has been added to the last product.

For example, to find the decimal equivalent of hex 3C7,

```
              3  C  7
multiply:    16  |  |
             --  |  |
             48  |  |
add:         12<-┘  |
             --     |
             60     |
multiply:    16     |
             --     |
            960     |
add:          7 <---┘
            ---
            967
```

Thus, $3C7_{16} = 967_{10}$.

This conversion process can be somewhat simplified by means of the table that appears in Figure 1–2. Note that there are six columns in the table. Column 1 represents the LSD of a six-digit hex number, columns 2 through 5 are the next higher order digits, and column 6 is the MSD of the six-digit number.

To convert from hex to decimal simply add the decimal equivalents for each of the hex digits. Using the same number, $3C7_{16}$, find the decimal equivalent of hex 3 in column 3, or 768_{10}. Add this to the decimal equivalents of hex C (in column 2, or 192_{10}) and hex 7 (in column 1, or 7_{10}). Thus, $3C7_{16} = 768 + 192 + 7 = 967_{10}$.

1–5.2 Conversion from Decimal to Hexadecimal Numbers

To convert a decimal number to its hexadecimal equivalent, divide the decimal number by 16, and use the remainder of each division as the hexadecimal number. For example, to find the hex equivalent of decimal 967,

$$
\begin{aligned}
967 \div 16 &= 60 \quad \text{with remainder 7 (LSD)} \\
60 \div 16 &= 3 \quad \text{with remainder 2 (or C)} \\
3 \div 16 &= 0 \quad \text{with remainder 3 (MSD)} \\
&\qquad\qquad\qquad\qquad\qquad\qquad 3\ C\ 7
\end{aligned}
$$

Thus, $967_{10} = 3C7_{16}$.

Again, this conversion can be somewhat simplified by means of Fig. 1–2. To convert from decimal to hex, first find the next lowest decimal number in one of the columns, and note the corresponding hex digit. Then move to the nearest column to the right and find a decimal number that, when added to the previous decimal number, will come nearest to the desired decimal number. Note the corresponding hex digit in this column. Repeat the procedure until the decimal numbers, when added, are equal to the desired decimal number. Note all the corresponding hex digits.

For example, to convert from decimal 4011 to hex using Fig. 1–2, note that 3840_{10} in column 3 is the next lowest decimal number, and that F is the corresponding hex digit. Thus, F is the MSD for our hex equivalent number, and the number will have two more digits. Moving to column 2 (the next column to the right), note that 160_{10}, when added to the 3840_{10} (for a total of 4000), will come nearest to the desired 4011. (If 176_{10} in column 2 is chosen, the total is 4016, and thus higher than the desired 4011). The hex equivalent digit for 160 in column 2 is A. Moving to column 1, note that 11_{10}, when added to the previous 3840 + 160 (which equals 4000), will equal the desired 4011 exactly, and that the hex equivalent digit is B. Thus, $4011_{10} = FAB_{16}$.

1–5.3 Conversion from Hexadecimal to Binary Numbers

To convert a hexadecimal number to its binary equivalent, convert each digit of the hex number to its binary equivalent *using four binary digits per hex digit*. Then combine these binary groups in proper order.

Hexadecimal Columns											
6		5		4		3		2		1	
Hex	Dec	Hex	Dec	Hex	Dec	Hex	Dec	Hex	Dec	Hex	Dec
0	0	0	0	0	0	0	0	0	0	0	0
1	1,048,576	1	65,536	1	4,096	1	256	1	16	1	1
2	2,097,152	2	131,072	2	8,192	2	512	2	32	2	2
3	3,145,728	3	196,608	3	12,288	3	768	3	48	3	3
4	4,194,304	4	262,144	4	16,384	4	1,024	4	64	4	4
5	5,242,880	5	327,680	5	20,480	5	1,280	5	80	5	5
6	6,291,456	6	393,216	6	24,576	6	1,536	6	96	6	6
7	7,340,032	7	458,752	7	28,672	7	1,792	7	112	7	7
8	8,388,608	8	524,288	8	32,768	8	2,048	8	128	8	8
9	9,437,184	9	589,824	9	36,864	9	2,304	9	144	9	9
A	10,485,760	A	655,360	A	40,960	A	2,560	A	160	A	10
B	11,534,336	B	720,896	B	45,056	B	2,816	B	176	B	11
C	12,582,912	C	786,432	C	49,152	C	3,072	C	192	C	12
D	13,631,488	D	851,968	D	53,248	D	3,328	D	208	D	13
E	14,680,064	E	917,504	E	54,344	E	3,584	E	224	E	14
F	15,728,640	F	983,040	F	61,440	F	3,840	F	240	F	15
0 1 2 3		4 5 6 7		0 1 2 3		4 5 6 7		0 1 2 3		4 5 6 7	
Byte				Byte				Byte			

Fig. 1–2. Basic hexadecimal-to-decimal conversion table

For example, to convert $3C7_{16}$ to its binary equivalent,

3	C	7	(hex)
0011	1100	0111	(binary)

Thus, $3C7_{16} = 001111000111_2$.

From this, it can be seen that hex is a very convenient shorthand notation that can be substituted for binary. Most microcomputers use 8-bit bytes, and thus only require two hex digits. That is, the 8-bit byte can be divided into two 4-bit nibbles. The left nibble represents the left (MSD) hex digit, and the right nibble represents the right (LSD) hex digit. For example, 115_{10}, or 01110011_2, can be written

0111	0011
7	3

When an 8-bit byte is involved, the smallest hex number is 00_{16} (00000000_2), and the largest is FF_{16} (11111111_2). Keep in mind that the microcomputer still reads binary numbers only. Hex is the user's shorthand, not the microcomputer's.

1–5.4 Conversion from Binary to Hexadecimal

To convert a binary number to its hex equivalent, divide the digits of the *binary number into groups of four,* starting from the right. If necessary, fill out the last group (at the left) by placing 0s in front. Then convert each binary group to its hex digit equivalent, and combine these digits in proper order. For example, to convert 11011001011_2 to its hex equivalent,

Added zero	0110	1100	1011	(binary)
	6	C	B	(hex)

1–5.5 Manipulating Hexadecimal Numbers

Hexadecimal addition is a form of counting, as in other number systems. However, since the carry function occurs at 16, the carry must be added when the sum of digits is greater than F (decimal 15). For example, to add hex 7 (decimal 7) and hex A (decimal 10), the sum is hex 11 (decimal 17).

Hexadecimal subtraction is similar to other number systems, except that the borrow occurs at 16. Hexadecimal multiplication is similar to decimal multiplication. However, since the base is 16, this must be included when the final product is greater than F (decimal 15). For example, 3 multiplied by 8 is 24 in decimal, but this is represented as 18 in hex. When there is more than one digit in either the multiplier or multiplicand or a hex number, the digits must be handled one at a time, with a shift for each digit. Then the product of the two digits is added. Hex division is done by means of subtraction and shifting, as in other number systems.

From this, it can be seen that manipulating hex numbers on paper is a difficult task, especially for those familiar with decimal. Manipulating hex numbers in a microprocessor is equally complex, but fortunately it never occurs. In microprocessors, all nonbinary numbers (including hex) are converted to binary before they are added, subtracted, multiplied, divided, and so on. Then the number is converted back from binary as necessary. For example, assume that a microcomputer is operated with a terminal that has a hex keyboard and a decimal readout. When a hex key is pressed, the number is generated in hex form, and then converted to binary. The binary number is then manipulated (added, subtracted, etc.) and the result is obtained in binary. This binary result is then converted to decimal for display on the readout.

1–6. BINARY CODES

There are a number of codes based on the binary number system. The simplest form of such coding is when decimal numbers (0 to 9) are converted into binary form using four binary digits or bits. This *four-bit* system is one of the original codes used in early computers. With this system, generally known as *binary-coded decimal* or BCD, decimal 1 is represented by 0001, decimal 2 by 0010, and so on.

When the decimal number has more than one digit, four binary bits are used for each decimal digit. For example, the decimal number 3738 is represented by 16 binary digits, in groups of four, as follows:

3	7	3	8	(decimal)
0011	0111	0011	1000	(BCD)

In a typical 8-bit byte microcomputer, each byte can be thought of as containing two 4-bit BCD numbers. With this interpretation, each byte can represent numbers in the range from 0 to 99 (decimal). This is shown as follows:

2^3	2^2	2^1	2^0	2^3	2^2	2^1	2^0	
b_7	b_6	b_5	b_4	b_3	b_2	b_1	b_0	
0	0	0	0	0	0	0	0	(decimal 0)
0	0	1	1	1	0	0	0	(decimal 38)
1	0	0	1	1	0	0	1	(decimal 99)

There are also many other codes using the binary system, including the 2421, 5421, XS3, reflected gray, 2 out of 5, and biquinary. However, only the BCD is used to any extent. In present-day systems, the trend is to use *only hexadecimal outside* the microcomputer and *binary inside* the system. This is because binary is most compatible with the signal pulses used in microcomputer circuits, and conversion between binary and hex is relatively simple. Also, it is possible to have as many as 256 coded characters with only two hex digits (since each hex digit represents up to 16 possibilities).

1–7. ALPHANUMERIC CODES

Although the 4-bit system is adequate to represent any decimal digit from 0 to 9, additional bits are necessary to represent letters of the alphabet and special characters (such as dollar signs, percent symbols, etc.) that are often required for microcomputer applications. Most microcomputer manufacturers have settled on the U.S. American Standard Code for Information Interchanges, or USASCII, which is now generally written as ASCII (and pronounced "askey"). Although microprocessor circuits are not designed to accommodate ASCII directly, there are adapter circuits (decoders, encoders, code converters) that convert the microprocessor's binary code into ASCII (and vice versa) for interchange of information with the world outside the microcomputer.

ASCII is an 8-bit code and is thus ideally suited for hex representation. (Actually, as discussed in Sec. 1–8.8, only seven digits are required for ASCII, even though it is considered an 8-bit code.) Also, since hex to binary conversion is relatively simple, both on paper and in the electrical circuits, ASCII can be adapted to any microprocessor-based system.

Figure 1–3 shows the conversion between ASCII and hex. To convert from ASCII to hex, select the desired letter, symbol or number,

MOST SIGNIFICANT HEX DIGIT

LEAST SIGNIFICANT HEX DIGIT	0	1	2	3	4	5	6	7
0	NUL	DLE	SP	0	@	P	`	p
1	SOH	DC1	!	1	A	Q	a	q
2	STX	DC2	"	2	B	R	b	r
3	ETX	DC3	#	3	C	S	c	s
4	EOT	DC4	$	4	D	T	d	t
5	ENQ	NAK	%	5	E	U	e	u
6	ACK	SYN	&	6	F	V	f	v
7	BEL	ETB	'	7	G	W	g	w
8	BS	CAN	(	8	H	X	h	x
9	HT	EM	)	9	I	Y	i	y
A	LF	SUB	*	:	J	Z	j	z
B	VT	ESC	+	;	K	[	k	{
C	FF	FS	,	<	L	\	l	¦
D	CR	GS	-	=	M	]	m	}
E	SO	RS	.	>	N	↑	n	~
F	SI	US	/	?	O	←	o	DEL

NOTES:

(1) PARITY BIT IN MOST SIGNIFICANT HEX DIGIT NOT INCLUDED.
(2) CHARACTERS IN COLUMNS 0 AND 1 (AS WELL AS SP AND DEL) ARE NON-PRINTING.
(3) MODEL 33 TELETYPE PRINTS CODES IN COLUMNS 6 AND 7 AS IF THEY WERE COLUMN 4 AND 5 CODES.

Fig. 1–3. ASCII-to-hexadecimal conversion table

then move up vertically to find the hex MSD. Then move horizontally to the left and find the hex LSD. For example, to find the hex code for the letter I, note that I appears in the 4 column of the hex MSD, and in the 9 column of the hex LSD. Thus, hex 49 equals the letter I in ASCII. The hex 49 can then be converted to 0100 1001 in binary, as is generally done inside the microprocessor circuits. The process can be reversed to convert from binary to ASCII. For example, binary 0010 0100 is 24 in hex and $ in ASCII. As an exercise, find the ASCII letters for binary 0100-1100 0100-0101 0100-1110 0100-1011.

Keep in mind that all microprocessor terminals do not use ASCII keyboards or printouts. Thus, although any 8-bit byte in binary can be converted to hex for convenience, the result does not necessarily mean anything in ASCII. Also, when ASCII is used, the ASCII characters are converted to binary for use by the microprocessor, and then converted back to ASCII for use by the terminal. Also, as shown in Fig. 1–3, there are some variations in ASCII-coded devices, but not in the basic format. For example, a model 33 teletype prints codes in MSD columns 6 and 7 as if they were column 4 and 5 codes. Such factors must be considered when interfacing an ASCII terminal with a microprocessor-based system.

1–8. RELATIONSHIP BETWEEN BINARY NUMBERS AND ELECTRICAL SIGNALS

Thus far, we have discussed how binary numbers and words are used on paper. A microprocessor operates with electrical signals (generally pulses) *arranged in binary form*. For example, a microprocessor performs its functions (program counting, addition, subtraction, etc.) in response to *instructions*. Usually, these instructions come from a memory within the system, but they can also come from the outside world via a terminal. A typical microprocessor can perform from 70 to 100 functions (or possibly many more), with each function being determined by a specific instruction.

The instructions are applied to the microprocessor as electrical pulses arranged to form a binary word. Each pulse is applied on a separate electrical line (or wire), as shown in Fig. 1–4, where a basic microprocessor has 8 lines to accommodate an 8-bit binary word or data byte. In this system, which is typical for the great majority of microprocessors the pulses are +5 V in amplitude, and are a few nano seconds or micro seconds in duration. The presence of a pulse indicates a binary 1; the absence of a pulse, or zero volts, indicates a binary 0.

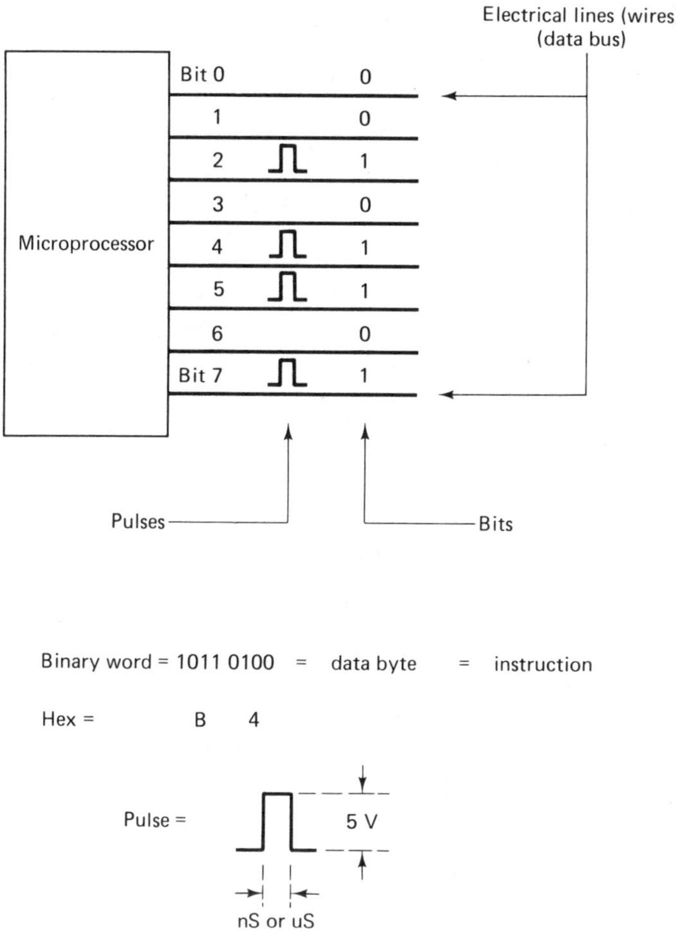

Fig. 1–4. Relationship between binary numbers and electrical signals

Thus, in Fig. 1–4, the microprocessor is receiving a binary 10110100, which can be converted to hex B4 for convenience.

For one microprocessor, this word (B4) may be an instruction to perform addition. For another microprocessor, the same word may mean perform subtraction. For still another microprocessor, the word may be meaningless. Thus, one of the first things you must do to troubleshoot a microprocessor-based system is to *learn all the instructions* (known as the *instruction set*), including the corresponding binary code, hex code, and what is accomplished by the microprocessor when the instruction is received. Microprocessor manufacturers provide information on the instruction set in their user manuals. This is fortunate, since it is a nearly impossible task to remember the entire instruction set of even a simple microprocessor.

1–8.1 Microprocessor Memories and Addresses

Microprocessors also use electrical signals arranged in binary form to communicate with other elements in the systems. Most microprocessors are used with memories (RAMs and ROMs, typically both), which hold data bytes to be manipulated by the microprocessor, and instructions to be followed by the microprocessor during the program. (Data bytes are usually stored or held in the RAM; instructions are usually stored in the ROM.)

Memories are divided into locations called *addresses*. Each address is identified by a number (usually decimal). During a typical microcomputer program, the microprocessor will select each address in a certain order (determined by the program) and "read" the contents of the address. Such contents can be an instruction, data, or a combination of both. Likewise, it is possible to "write" information into memory using electrical signals arranged in binary form.

1–8.2 Buses and Ports

A typical microprocessor/memory arrangement (or a very simple microcomputer) is shown in Fig. 1–5, where a microprocessor is connected to a RAM and a ROM by data and address *buses*. The term *bus* is applied when several electrical lines are used for a common purpose. In our example, the *data bus* has 8 lines (which is typical) and the *address bus* has 8 lines (which is not typical). Generally, the address bus will have as many as 16 lines. The 8-line system is used here for simplicity.

The term *highway* is sometimes used when a bus interconnects many system components. Also, the term *handshake bus* is sometimes used to indicate a bus that interconnects a microprocessor-based system with the outside world.

The term *port* is often applied to the point or terminals at which the bus enters the microprocessor or other IC element. Thus, in Fig. 1–5, there is an address port and a data port.

Buses are generally *bidirectional*. That is, the electrical pulses (representing data bytes, addresses, etc.) can pass in either direction along the bus lines. For example, data bytes can be written into memory from the microprocessor, or read from memory into the microprocessor on the same data bus. Ports may or may not be bidirectional, depending upon design.

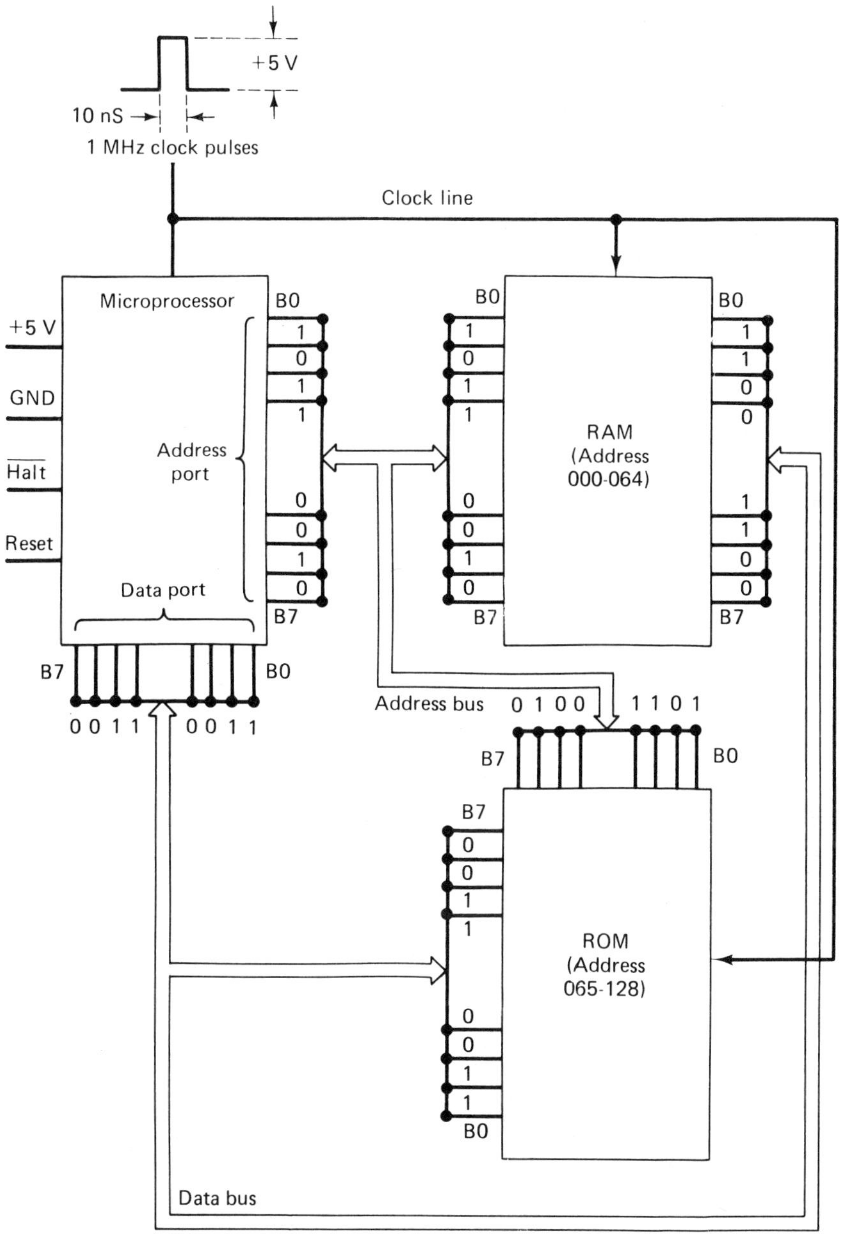

Fig. 1–5. Typical microprocessor/memory arrangement, including data and address buses

1–8.3 Address and Data Buses

Note that in Fig. 1–5 the electrical pulses appearing on the address bus are arranged to produce a binary 01001101, or a decimal 77. Thus, address number 77 is being selected by the microprocessor. Both the ROM and RAM receive the same set of electrical pulses (or binary word), since these pulses appear on the address bus. However, since address 77 is located in the ROM, the contents of the ROM at that address are read back to the microprocessor via the data bus. The pulses on the address bus have no effect on the RAM, and no data are obtained from the RAM. Likewise, the address pulses have no effect on other addresses in the ROM. Only the data at the selected address is read back on the data bus.

In Fig. 1–5, the electrical pulses on the data bus are arranged to form the binary word 00110011, or hex 33. In our microprocessor, hex 33 is an instruction to add the contents of a register within the microprocessor to the contents at some address in the RAM (read out during a previous step in the program).

1–8.4 Debugging Versus Troubleshooting

Keep in mind that the microprocessor responds to the *arrangement* of electrical pulses. It makes no difference where the pulses originate. Thus, if an undesired instruction is stored in memory at some location that is addressed by the microprocessor during a program, that instruction will appear as the corresponding arrangement of electrical pulses on the data bus. The microprocessor will follow the instructions when received, and will thus produce an erroneous result. Probably, the program will come to a complete halt, or will jump to some undesired address. Under these conditions, the program is said to have a *bug* or *bugs*. The process of finding the undesired instruction, removing it, or replacing it at the correct address is known as *debugging*, which applies to finding any fault in a program.

Debugging is not to be confused with *troubleshooting*, which is the term applied to the process of finding electrical or mechanical faults in a microprocessor system. Troubleshooting usually implies that the system once performed the program properly. For example, referring to Fig. 1–5, assume that the electrical line labeled b_0 on the data bus becomes broken (after weeks of operation) at the microprocessor terminal. The b_0 pulse from the ROM still appears on the data bus, but does not reach the microprocessor. Thus, the microprocessor sees zero volts, or binary 0, on terminal b_0. This produces binary word 00110010, or hex 32, instead of the desired binary 00110011, or hex 33. The hex

32 might be meaningless or might be an erroneous instruction. In any event, the microprocessor will not perform the correct function.

It is obvious, then, that a good microcomputer troubleshooter must have a knowledge of the specific program, as well as a knowledge of general programming techniques. A good part of the troubleshooter's time will be spent comparing program listings against actual readout of words or data bytes on address and data buses.

1–8.5 Nature of Pulses

The pulses used by present-day microprocessors are generally compatible with TTL pulses found in logic or digital equipment. (For those not already familiar with the term, TTL means transistor–transistor logic, and is described fully in the author's *Logic Designer's Manual*, 1977, Reston Publishing Company, Inc., Reston, Virginia.) Typically, TTL pulses start at 0 V, rise to near 5 V, then drop back to 0 V, all within a few nano seconds or micro seconds. All the pulses in a given binary word or data byte must arrive at the same time. Thus, all the pulses are said to be transmitted in *parallel* on the bus. All binary information within a microprocessor system is transmitted in parallel form.

This is not always true in the world outside the microprocessor system, where information can also be transmitted in *serial* form. In serial transmission of an 8-bit binary word, 8 pulses (for binary 1) or spaces (for binary 0) are transmitted at regular intervals on a single electrical line (or a pair of lines). This is followed by a long space before the next 8-bit byte is transmitted. Obviously, serial is slower; but it requires only one or two lines, compared to one line for each bit in parallel. Since microprocessors use only parallel within the system, serial data bytes must be converted before they are used with a microprocessor system (and vice versa). This is one of the functions of an I/O device.

1–8.6 Clock and Timer Pulses

The electrical pulses used by the microprocessor, ROM, and RAM are generated by a *clock* or *timer*, which may be part of the microprocessor or can be external. In Fig. 1–5, the clock is external, and is a +5-V pulse of 10-ns duration, at a frequency of 1 megahertz (MHz). The clock circuit is an oscillator that produces pulses of fixed amplitude and duration at regular intervals. One to three megahertz is a typical clock frequency.

The microprocessor, ROM, and RAM do not actually generate the binary pulses, but produce their binary word pulses on the address and data lines *when they receive clock pulses*. It may take many clock pulses to form a binary word. In some cases, the microprocessor, ROM, and RAM must also receive other signals before they will produce the binary word pulses or data bytes. For example, a RAM usually requires a "read" signal, plus the clock pulses, before the contents of an address is read onto the data bus from the RAM. Such control signals are discussed in later paragraphs.

1–8.7 Power Supply and Other Signals

Not all electrical voltages and signals applied to a microprocessor, ROM, or RAM are in pulse form. For example, referring to Fig. 1–5, note that there are two lines into the microprocessor labeled +5 V and GND. These are the power supply lines connected to an external 5-V power supply.

There are also two lines labeled $\overline{\text{HALT}}$ and RESET, respectively. The RESET and $\overline{\text{HALT}}$ lines receive a +5-V signal from various circuits in the system. This signal may be a momentary pulse identical to those on the address and data buses, or it may be a fixed +5 V that remains on the line for some time. When a fixed signal (sometimes called a *level*) is applied, the line is said to be *high* and the function is *turned on*.

For example, if +5 V is applied to the RESET line, the RESET line is high, and all circuits within the microprocessor are reset to zero, regardless of their condition before the line goes high. When the fixed voltage is removed, the RESET line goes low (is at zero volts), and the RESET function is no longer in effect. In most microprocessors, when a reset signal is received, all circuits return to zero and then resume their normal function (counting and so on). Note that in some literature the terms *true* and *false* are used instead of high and low, respectively. Likewise, the binary 1 and 0 are used for high and low in some literature. However, the terms high and low are generally preferred. In some microcomputer literature, such as the circuits described in Chapter 4, the term *asserted* is used when a line is placed in the active condition. For example, when the RESET line receives a +5-V voltage or signal, the RESET function is said to be *asserted*.

An overbar is used on the word $\overline{\text{HALT}}$. This indicates that the $\overline{\text{HALT}}$ operates in the reverse of all other lines. That is, the $\overline{\text{HALT}}$ function is in effect when the line is at 0 V (the normal low condition). When the line is at +5 V (normal high), the $\overline{\text{HALT}}$ function is removed.

In our microprocessor, when the $\overline{\text{HALT}}$ line is at 0 V, all functions within the microprocessor (counting through the program and so on) are stopped, and remain stopped as long as the $\overline{\text{HALT}}$ line remains low. All functions resume normal operation when the $\overline{\text{HALT}}$ line is made high by a +5-V level. If the microprocessor is in the middle of some operation when $\overline{\text{HALT}}$ is applied (by 0 V on the line), the operation will stop, but will continue from the same point when the +5 V is reapplied.

The foregoing illustrates the need to understand *all instructions and control signals* applied to your particular microprocessor. A thorough knowledge of the microprocessor functions and controls is essential for both writing and debugging programs, as well as troubleshooting. For example, should the program inadvertently issue an instruction that removes +5 V from the $\overline{\text{HALT}}$ line, the microprocessor will stop in the middle of the program, possibly in the middle of an instruction. The same condition can be caused if the $\overline{\text{HALT}}$ line is accidentally disconnected from the $\overline{\text{HALT}}$ terminal on the microprocessor, if the $\overline{\text{HALT}}$ line is shorted to ground, or if the $\overline{\text{HALT}}$ line is broken.

1–8.8 Parity Bit Signals

The notes in Fig. 1–3 refer to a *parity bit*. Although the ASCII code is considered to be an 8-bit code, note that the most significant bit is always 0. For example, the highest number required for ASCII is 0111–1111 in binary, or 7F in hex. Thus, the MSB can be 0, or simply omitted, whichever is convenient. This permits the MSB to be used for parity check. The parity system is one of the many codes that has been developed to detect errors that might occur in electronic equipment using binary numbers and signal pulses.

Any complex equipment that operates with the binary counting system is subject to counting errors owing to circuit failure, electrical noise, or some similar occurrence. For example, a defect can reduce the amplitude of a pulse (representing a binary 1) so that it appears as a binary 0 on the line or bus. Likewise, noise on the line or bus can be of equal amplitude to a normal binary 1 pulse. If the noise occurs at a time when a port is being opened to pass what is supposed to be a binary 0, the circuit will react as if a binary 1 is present.

One method for error detecting is known as *parity check*. Parity refers to the quality of being equal, and a parity check is actually an equality checking code. The coding consists of introducing additional bits or pulses into the binary number. The additional bit is known as the parity bit, and may be either a 0 or a 1. The parity bit is chosen to make the number of all bits in the binary group even or odd. If a system is chosen in which the bits in the binary number, plus the parity bit, are even, the system is known as *even parity*. Even parity is in general use. However, odd parity can be used.

As an example of even parity, 7F in hex, or 0111–1111 in binary, requires a 1 as the parity bit. Thus, in the total of 8 bits (7 binary bits, plus the 1 parity bit, or 1111–1111) there will be an even number of 1s.

Error-detection circuits based on the parity system use both *parity generators* and *parity detectors* or *checkers*. The function of a parity generator is to examine the word (or group of binary bits) and calculate the information required for the added parity bit. For example, if there are three 1s in the binary group, and even parity is used, a 1 must be used for the parity bit to make an even number in the *parity word*.

Once the parity bit has been included (a pulse has been added on the appropriate line of the bus), the parity word (binary bits, plus parity bit) can be examined after any transmission, or at any point in the system, to determine if a failure or error has occurred. A parity-detection circuit or parity checker examines the parity word to see if the desired odd or even parity still exists (say, after passing through several ICs in a microcomputer system). If an error has occurred, the system control can be informed by means of a signal that the system is not functioning properly. Parity circuits are often used with peripheral equipment such as tape recorders and magnetic disks, as discussed in Chapter 2.

1–9. BASIC MICROPROCESSOR/MICROCOMPUTER CIRCUIT FUNCTIONS

Most circuit elements of a microcomputer system are in integrated-circuit (IC) form. Possible exceptions are the interconnecting buses, wiring, and a few external switches, gates, readouts, keyboards, and so on. In any event, the microprocessor, ROM, RAM, and I/O devices are all ICs. Thus, you do not have access to the circuit elements, nor can you change them in the way that they function. Also, it is not necessary that you understand every detail of the internal circuits to effectively use and troubleshoot microcomputers. That is, you do not need to know that diodes are interconnected to form flip-flops, and that flip-flops are interconnected to form registers and counters. However, you must know what registers and counters are and how (in basic terms) they operate.

As an example, a typical microprocessor instruction (found in the user manual) might say that a hex 33, or binary 00110011, applied to the data bus will cause the microprocessor to "add the contents of register A to register B, and increment (advance) the program counter by 1.'' All basic circuits found in microprocessor literature are described in the following paragraphs of this section. If you want more detailed descriptions of such circuits, see *Logic Designer's Manual*, which is referenced in Sec. 1–8.5.

1–9.1 Counters, Registers, Accumulators, and Pointers

For our purposes, counters, registers, accumulators, and pointers are all circuits used to hold and manipulate binary numbers in electrical (pulse or level) form. As such, these circuits have one stage for each binary bit to be held or manipulated. Thus, an 8-bit counter/register has 8 stages. Generally, flip-flop (FF) stages are used. An FF stage can be in only one of two electrical states, 1 or 0. If you measured the instantaneous state of a particular stage, you would find it at +5 V if the stage is to represent a 1, and at 0 V for binary 0. (Except in certain troubleshooting situations, it is not necessary to actually measure the states of counter/register stages. However, this concept may help you to understand the operation of counters and registers.)

In a microprocessor, the purpose of a counter is to count events (such as steps of a program, a sequence of addresses selected, etc.). This is usually done by counting pulses. Counters are sometimes used as *pointers*, in that they point to another event or location. For example, a typical *program counter* counts each step of the program, and then advances to the next address to be used in the program. Thus, the counter *points* to the next step of the program. Note that, when a counter, register, or other circuit in a microprocessor system is used solely or primarily for one purpose, it is said to be *dedicated*. For example, a microprocessor counter used only to count program steps is referred to as a dedicated program counter.

A microprocessor register is similar to a counter, except that the primary function of a register is to hold the binary numbers (or words) so that they can be manipulated. Registers are often used to hold some binary number taken from a particular address in memory so that that number may be added to another number in memory. Likewise, one register can hold a binary number that is to be added to another binary number in another register. When a register is used primarily for arithmetic operations, the word *accumulator* is often applied.

Serial Operation of Counter/Registers. Microprocessor manufacturers use many methods or symbols to represent counters and registers. One of the most common methods is shown in Fig. 1–6, which illustrates operation of a typical counter used to count serial pulses. Assume that the circuit is used as a program counter, and that it receives one pulse

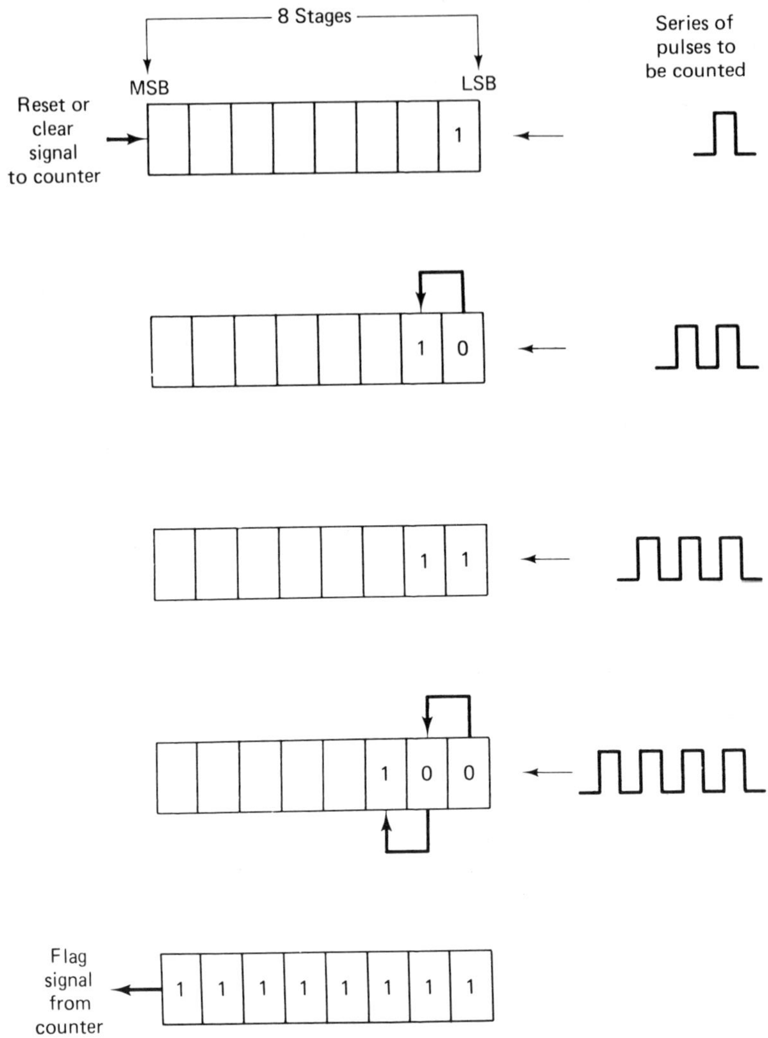

Fig. 1–6. Operation of a typical counter or register used to count serial pulses

for each step in the program. That is, the counter is to be *incremented* (or advanced) for each pulse representing a step. (When each step or pulse removes one count, the counter is said to be *decremented*.)

Initially, all stages are *reset* or *cleared* to low, binary 0, or 0 V by a reset signal. In serial operation, the first or LSB stage operates on the pulses to be counted. All other stages receive a pulse from the stage ahead. As each pulse to be counted is applied, the stage representing the LSB is changed from 0 to 1 (0 V to +5 V). When the next pulse arrives, the first stage returns back to 0 V (binary 0), and sends a signal to the next stage, which moves to binary 1. This process continues until all pulses are counted.

If there are four pulses, as shown in Fig. 1–6, the third stage moves to 1 and the first two stages are at 0. All remaining stages are at 0. The counter indicates a binary 00000100 (decimal 4), which corresponds to the number of pulses applied and, in turn, to the number of steps in the program accomplished thus far. In this way, the instantaneous count corresponds to the program step just accomplished, or to be accomplished next, depending upon design.

When all stages are moved by sufficient pulses to 1 (the binary count is 11111111, decimal 127), the counter is full. Generally, the counter then sends a *flag* or signal to other circuits indicating the full count. This flag can be used for any number of functions. For example, the flag could be used to halt or reset operation of the microprocessor if the program has only 127 steps. Or the flag can be used as the first pulse to the LSB of another counter (to accommodate a 16-bit word). It should be noted that flag signals do not always indicate a full count. The term *flag* can be applied to any signal that indicates that a particular condition has occurred (full count, error, request for further information, etc.).

Parallel Operation of Counter/Registers. Counters and registers can also be designed to receive information in parallel form, as shown in Fig. 1–7. Here all the stages are set simultaneously by pulses in binary word 01100100 (decimal 100). That is, bits 2, 5, and 6 receive

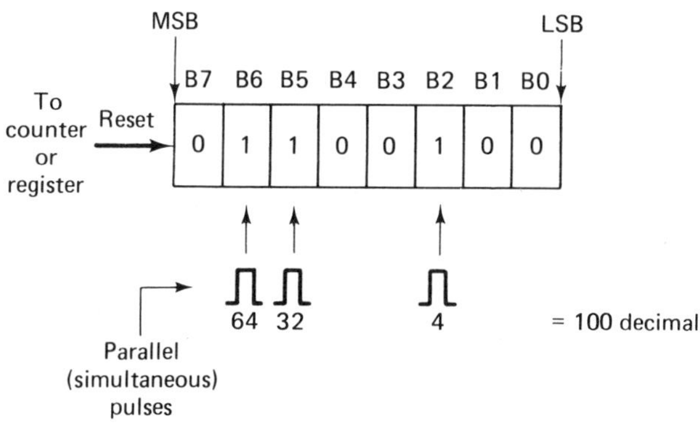

Fig. 1–7. Operation of a typical counter or register used to count (or receive) parallel pulses

+5-V pulses, and all other bits remain at 0 V. Sometimes, the terms *load* or *dump* are used when data bytes are so applied to a counter or register. Typically a counter/register will hold the data byte (all stages remain at the selected stage) until the register is cleared (reset to zero), or until another set of pulses forming a data byte is applied (or the power is removed).

Initializing Counter/Registers. The ability to be set by both parallel and serial pulses makes it possible to *initialize* counters and registers (although the term initialize is usually applied to counters). It is not always desired that all counts start from zero or that all counts go through every step in the count. For example, assume that the count is to start at the seventh step in a program. This could be done by applying +5-V pulses to bits 1, 2, and 3 simultaneously, as shown in Fig. 1–8. Then the first serial pulse to be counted moves bit 1 to 0, which in turn moves bit 2 to 0, bit 3 to 0, and bit 4 to 1.

Shifting Counter/Registers. The contents of counters and registers can also be shifted by an appropriate signal. That is, the contents of each stage in the counter or register are shifted by one position to the right or left by a shift signal applied to all stages simultaneously. The effects of a left shift are shown in Fig. 1–9, where a register is holding the binary word 00001000 (decimal 8). Bit 3 is at binary 1, and all remaining bits are at 0.

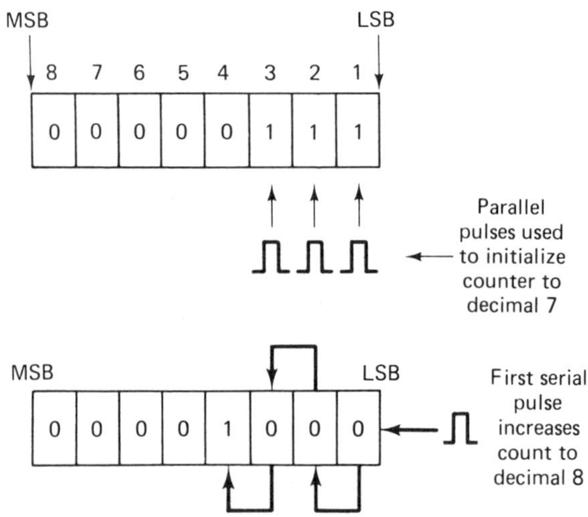

Fig. 1–8. Operation of a typical counter or register initialized to decimal 7 by parallel pulses, and increased to decimal 8 by first serial pulse

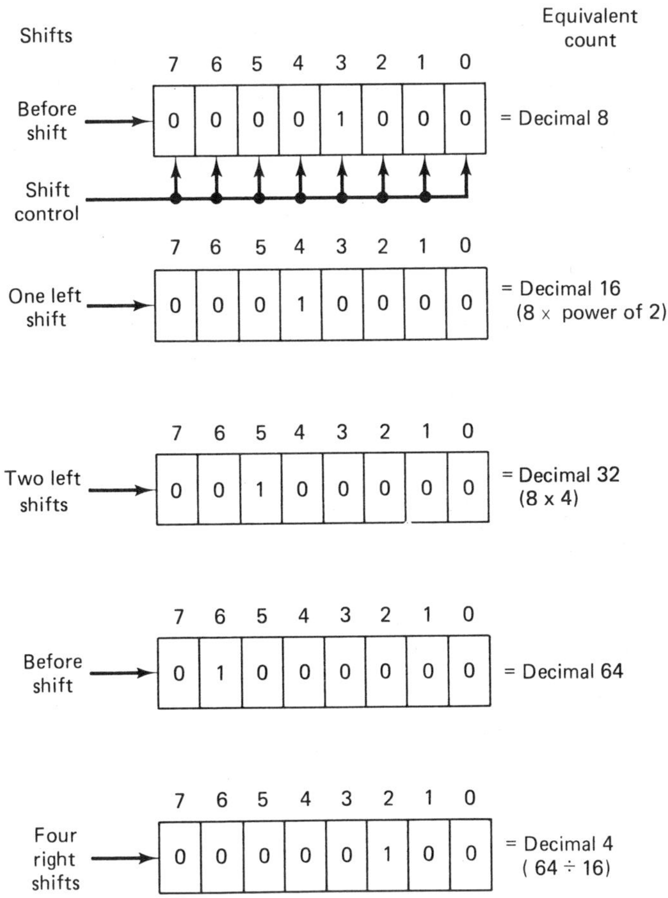

Fig. 1–9. Effects of left and right shifts on counters and registers

During the shift, the contents of bit 0 move to bit 1, bit 1 to bit 2, and so on. After the shift, bit 0 remains at binary 0, since there is no new pulse entering bit 0. Bit 4 is at binary 1, since this was the state of bit 3 before the shift. All other bits are at 0, since 0 was the stage of corresponding stages to the right (before the shift).

As a result of the shift, the binary number is changed from 00001000 to 00010000, or from decimal 8 to decimal 16. Thus, *one left shift multiplies the number by the power of 2*. If there are two shifts to the left, the binary number is changed to 00100000, decimal 32 (or the same as multiplying by 4). Three left shifts produce 01000000, decimal 64 (multiplication by 8). Registers can also be shifted to the right, which results in division by the powers of 2. This is also shown in Fig. 1–9, where a register is shifted four places to the right for a division by 16. That is, binary 01000000 (decimal 64) is shifted to binary 00000100 (decimal 4); 64 divided by 16 is 4.

1–9.2 Decoders, Encoders, and Multiplexers

The terms decoder, encoder, and multiplexer are often interchanged in microprocessor literature. In a strict sense, a *decoder* converts from one code or numbering system to another, such as from hex to decimal. The term *encoder* is generally applied when an uncoded value is converted to coded form, such as when an analog voltage is converted to binary. Equally strictly applied, a *multiplexer* (or MUX) is a data selector and/or distributor. However, in microprocessor literature, the terms are generally applied to any circuit that converts data from one form to another.

For example, one microprocessor contains a circuit (designated by the manufacturer as a multiplexer) that converts 16 lines of information from a register into 8 lines suitable for an 8-line address bus. Another microprocomputer system contains a decoder in each ROM that makes it possible to select one of 128 memory addresses with an 8-bit word supplied on an 8-bit address bus.

The symbol for such decoders and multiplexers is usually a box with the appropriate number of lines in and out, as shown in Fig. 1–10.

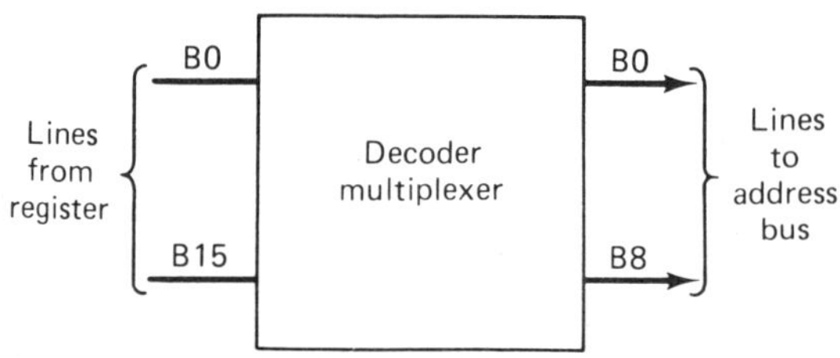

Fig. 1–10. Basic decoder/multiplexer symbol

1–9.3 Buffers, Drivers, and Latches

Buffers, drivers, and latches are also terms often interchanged in microprocessor literature A *buffer* can be considered as any circuit between two other circuits that serves to isolate the circuits under certain conditions and to connect the circuits under other conditions. A buffer circuit between an internal register and the data bus (at the data

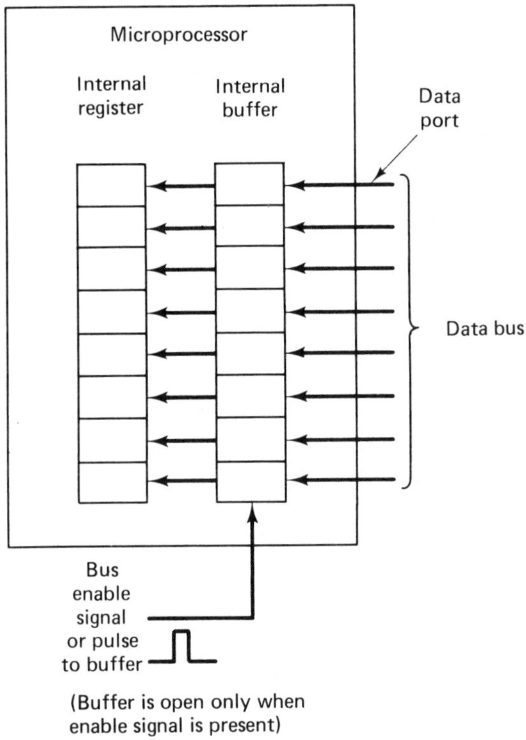

Fig. 1–11. Buffer circuit between an internal register and the data bus

port) is a classic example, as shown in Fig. 1–11. Here the buffer can be switched on or off by a *bus enable* signal or pulse. (This same signal may also be known as an *enable*, *select*, or *strobe* signal.)

When the enable signal is present, the buffer will pass data, instructions, or whatever combination is on the data bus to the register within the microprocessor. When the enable signal is removed, the buffer will prevent passage of data. This feature is necessary, for example, when the register is holding old data not yet processed, but there are new data on the bus. The buffer closes the data port until the register is ready to accept new data.

This raises the obvious problem of what happens when the new data are momentary. In such cases, the buffer has a *latch* function that permits each bit in the buffer to be latched to 1 or 0 by the data pulses. The latched data word is held in the buffer until the register is ready to accept new data.

Three-State Buffers. Typically, buffers are three-state devices, with one stage for each bit to be handled. The stages can be in one of three states: *in*, *out*, or at a *high-impedance* level. This high-impedance level or state makes it appear that the circuit is closed to the passage of data. Some buffers also include a *driver* function, particularly when the buffer is going to feed many devices simultaneously via a bus. The output of a register or counter may be sufficient to drive one other register, but not many registers or devices. Thus, the buffer includes a driver function that amplifies the drive capability.

1–9.4 Matrix

The term *matrix* is generally applied to the memory circuits within the RAM or ROM, but is also applied by some manufacturers to a group of registers in the microprocessor. A typical memory matrix is divided into sections or locations, with each section identified by an *address*, as shown in Fig. 1–12. In turn, the addresses are divided into a number of stages, with one stage for each bit to be held in memory. Thus, each address in an 8-bit memory will have 8 bits. The number of addresses in a memory matrix depends on use. Generally, the number is based on the powers of 2, since the addresses are selected by a number system based on binary (such as hex).

A typical ROM matrix will have 128 addresses, each with 8 bits, and will be described as a 128 by 8 matrix. A typical RAM matrix can

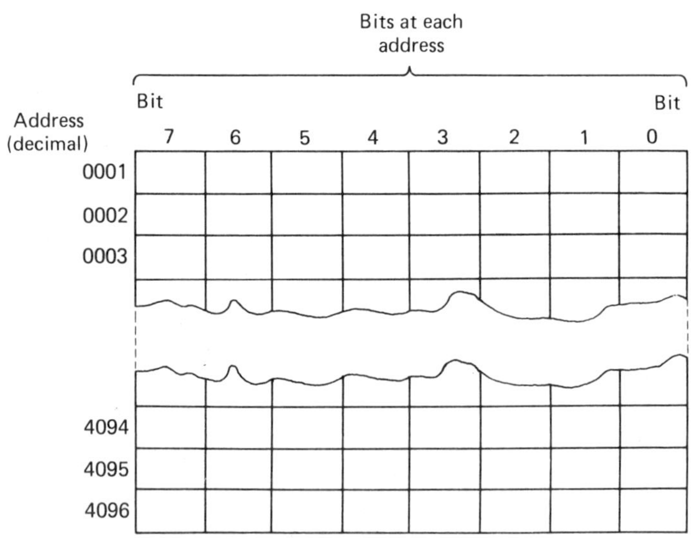

Fig. 1–12. Typical 4096 by 8 memory matrix

have 512, 1024, or 4096 addresses (or possibly more). Sometimes a 1024 by 8 memory matrix is described as a *1K memory*, since there are approximately 1000 addresses available. A 4096 by 8 memory matrix is likewise called a 4K memory.

Matrix Vectors. The addresses within a matrix are selected by some form of *vector* or *intersect* system, as shown in Fig. 1–13. The

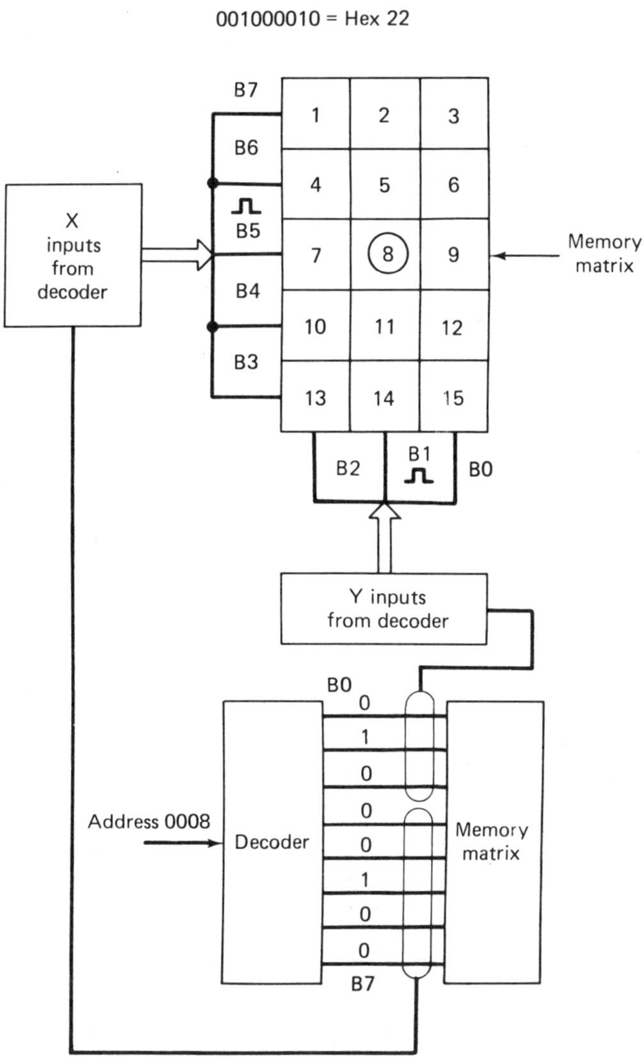

Fig. 1–13. Vector system for selecting one address in a 15-address memory matrix

memory address to be read in or out is selected when a combination of two appropriate bit lines has a +5-V pulse present (is at binary 1). Only one of the *X* lines and one of the *Y* lines can be binary 1 at any given time. All other lines are at binary 0. This action is controlled by some form of decoder or multiplexer, as discussed in Sec. 1–9.2.

As an example, assume that address 8 is to be selected. The desired decimal 8 is converted to hex 22 (0010 0010) by a decoder/multiplexer. This causes bits b_1 and b_5 to receive pulses (+5 V or binary 1). All remaining bit lines are at binary 0 (zero volts). Thus, the address (number 8) at the intersection or vector of the two lines is selected. Keep in mind that there are *8 bits in each address*, and that each of the 8 bits is fed back to the microprocessor or other destination on a bus (usually the data bus).

1–9.5 Arithmetic Logic Unit

Virtually all microprocessors have an arithmetic logic unit or ALU (although it may not be called an ALU). The ALU performs the arithmetic and logic operation on the data bytes. The symbol for an ALU is generally a simple box with lines in or out. Sometimes the box will contain a hint as to the functions being performed by the ALU. However, these functions are usually described only in the microprocessor instruction set.

As a minimum, the ALU has an adder circuit that is capable of combining the contents of two registers in accordance with the logic of binary arithmetic (Sec. 1–3.9). This adder/register combination permits the microprocessor to perform arithmetic manipulations on the data obtained from memory and other inputs. Using only the basic adder, a skilled programmer can write routines that will subtract, multiply, and divide, giving the microprocessor system complete arithmetic capabilities. However, most ALUs provide other built-in functions, including Boolean algebra, logic operations, and shift capabilities.

The ALU is generally capable of producing flag bits (as described in Sec. 1–9.1) that specify certain conditions arising in the course of arithmetic and logic operations. It is possible to program *jumps* that are conditionally dependent on the status of one or more flags. For example, the program may be designed to jump to a special routine if the carry bit is not following an additional instruction.

1–9.6 Control Circuitry or Logic

All microprocessors have some form of control or logic circuit (or circuits). As in the case of the ALU, the symbol for the control circuit is usually a simple box with lines and arrows leading in and out.

Generally, the halt, reset, interrupt, initialize, start, and similar lines are shown going into the control logic box symbol. This is because the control logic is the primary functional circuit or unit within the microprocessor. Using clock inputs, the control logic maintains the proper sequence of events required for any processing task.

For example, after a microprocessor instruction is taken (or *fetched*) from memory and decoded, the control logic issues the appropriate signals (to the microprocessor and to such external units as the ROM, RAM, and I/O) for initiating the proper processing action (such as a write signal to write data into memory and a read signal to read data from memory).

One function found in most microprocessor control logic circuits is the capability of responding to an *interrupt* signal or *service request* (say, from an external video terminal, disk, or tape reader). An interrupt request causes the control logic to temporarily interrupt the program execution, jump to a special routine to service the interrupting device, and then automatically return to the main program.

1–10. MICROPROCESSOR HARDWARE

The term *hardware* applied to a microprocessor or any other element in a microcomputer refers to the physical components, wiring, and so on. This contrasts with the term *software,* which applies to programs, instructions, and so on. Some microprocessor manufacturers also use the term *firmware* to describe something between hardware and software. For example, when instructions (software) are permanently programmed into a ROM (hardware), the result is firmware.

The microprocessor of one manufacturer will have little in common with the microprocessor of another manufacturer, with the possible exception of outward physical appearance. Compare the two microprocessors shown in Fig. 1–14. Both are 40-lead, duel-in-line (DIP) IC packages. Both are about 2 in. long and ½ in. wide. Now compare this to the terminal assignment diagrams of Fig. 1–15. Although both have

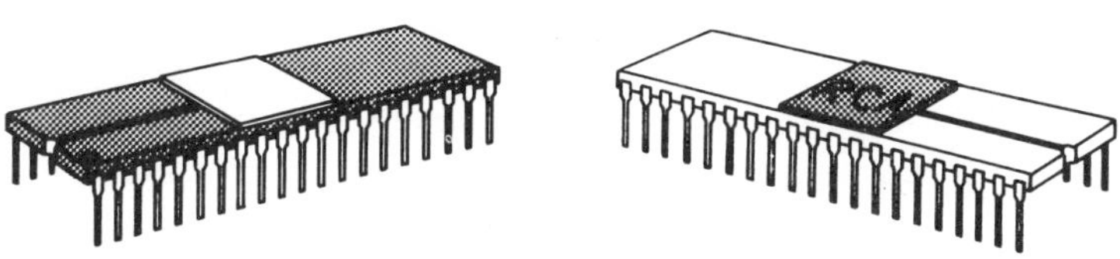

Fig. 1–14. RCA and Motorola microprocessors in 40-lead dual-in-line (DIP) IC packages

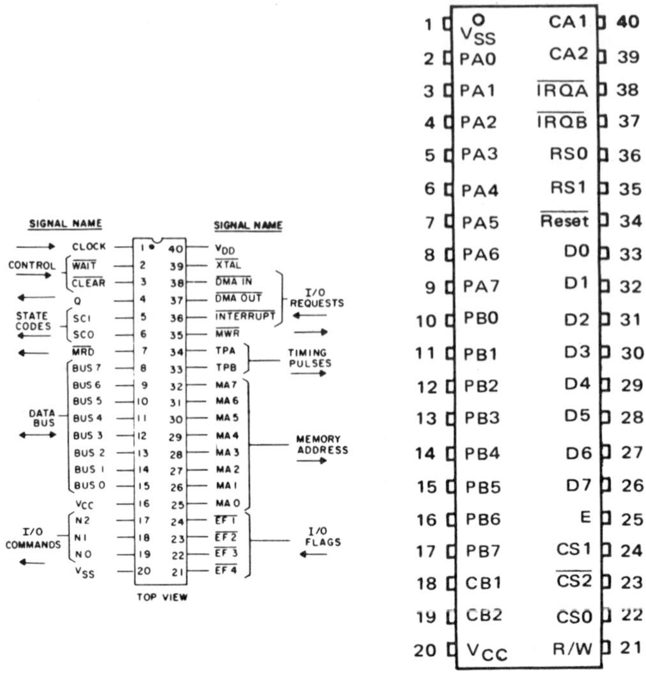

Fig. 1–15. Typical microprocessor terminal assignment diagrams

40 leads (also known as *pins* or *terminals*), the terminals are used for entirely different purposes.

For example, the RCA microprocessor has 8 data lines to a data bus and 8 memory lines to an address bus, whereas the Motorola unit has 8 data lines (D) and 16 address lines (PA and PB). From this, it can be seen that you must have all available data on a particular microprocessor (and the other hardware) to troubleshoot the system effectively. Fortunately, such information is available in manufacturer's data. However, the format used to show the internal arrangement of microprocessors will vary from manufacturer to manufacturer. The following paragraphs of this section deal with these differences in format, and introduce you to the internal functions of typical microprocessors.

1–10.1 Microprocessor Architecture

The term *architecture* is most accurately applied to the arrangement of counters, registers, ALUs, and so on, within the microprocessor. However, some manufacturers apply the term architecture to the entire system arrangement.

There are two commonly used methods to show architecture. The *block diagram* of Fig. 1–16 shows all the internal registers, counters,

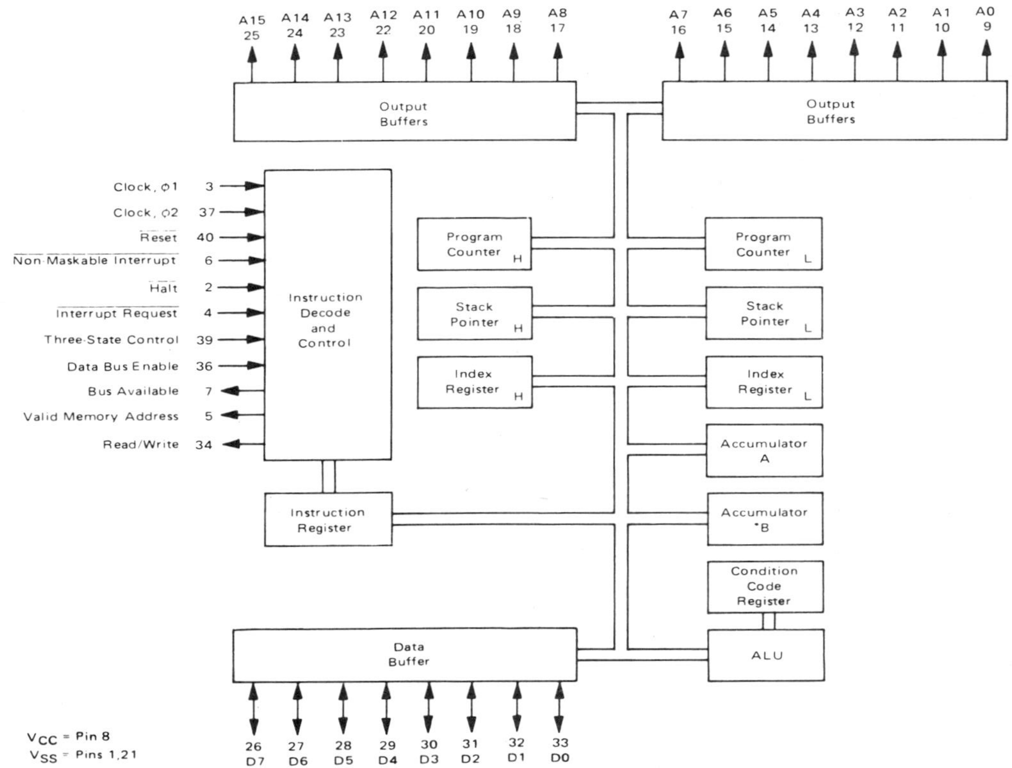

Fig. 1–16. Motorola M6800 microprocessor, block diagram

and so on, of the Motorola 6800 microprocessor of Figs. 1–14 and 1–15. Compare this to the *program model* of Fig. 1–17, which shows only accumulator, register, counter, and pointers. Obviously, the information shown in Fig. 1–17 is suitable for programming only. The information in Fig. 1–16 is required for design and troubleshooting, since each line to and from the microprocessor is identified by function or destination and pin number. For example, address line A_{15} is connected at terminal 25, and so on. Compare this to the block diagram of Fig. 1–18, which shows the architecture of the RCA CDP1802 microprocessor, also shown in Figs. 1–14 and 1–15.

Note that none of these diagrams shows how the microprocessor accomplishes its functions (in the same sense that a television set block diagram shows the functions of the set's circuits). This is typical for microprocessor literature. You must consult the instruction set to find out what the microprocessor will do in response to commands. You will probably never know how the microprocessor accomplishes this response (nor do you need to know for troubleshooting purposes).

We shall not go into any detail here concerning the operation of these microprocessors. Operation of similar units is covered in Chapter 4.

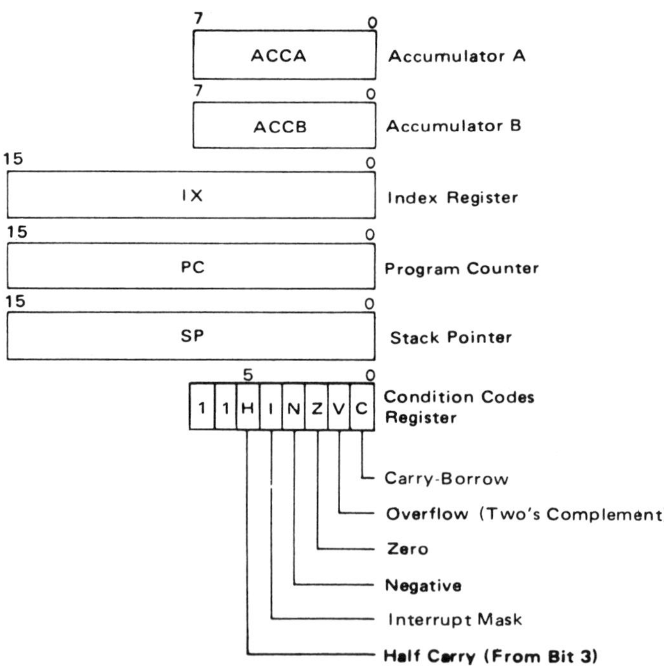

Fig. 1–17. Motorola M6800 microprocessor, program model

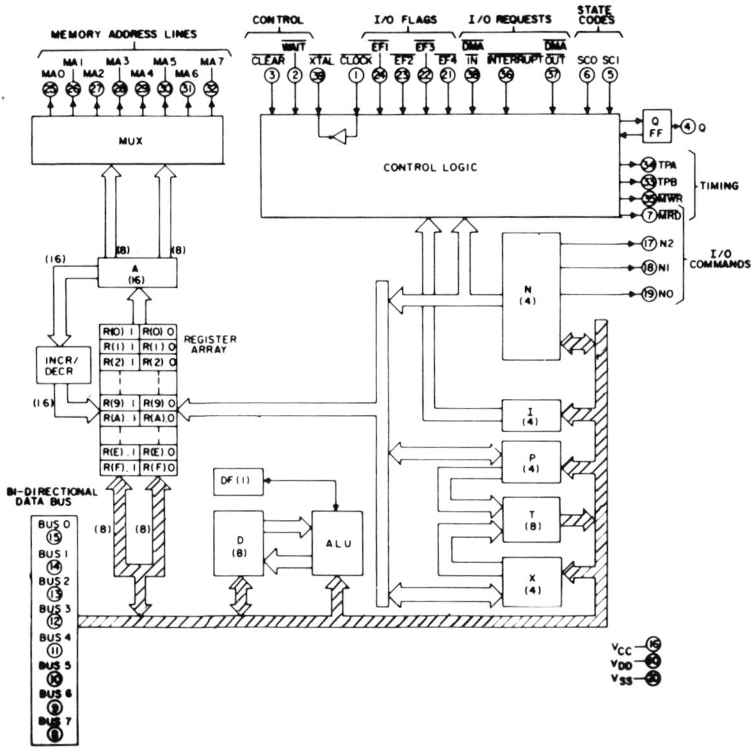

Fig. 1–18. RCA CDP1802 microprocessor, block diagram

1–11. MEMORY HARDWARE

Two types of memory units are used in microprocessor-based systems: the RAM and ROM. Generally, each of these memories is contained in a separate IC package. However, in some systems one of the memories or both are contained in the same IC package as the microprocessor. Such arrangements are discussed in appropriate chapters. For now, we shall consider the more typical case where there is a separate ROM and RAM in individual IC packages (or several ROMs and RAMs in separate packages).

1–11.1 RAM Circuits

Figure 1–19 shows the package, pin-assignment diagram, and functional block diagram of a typical RAM. This unit is described by the manufacturer as a 128 by 8 static RAM. This means that the matrix

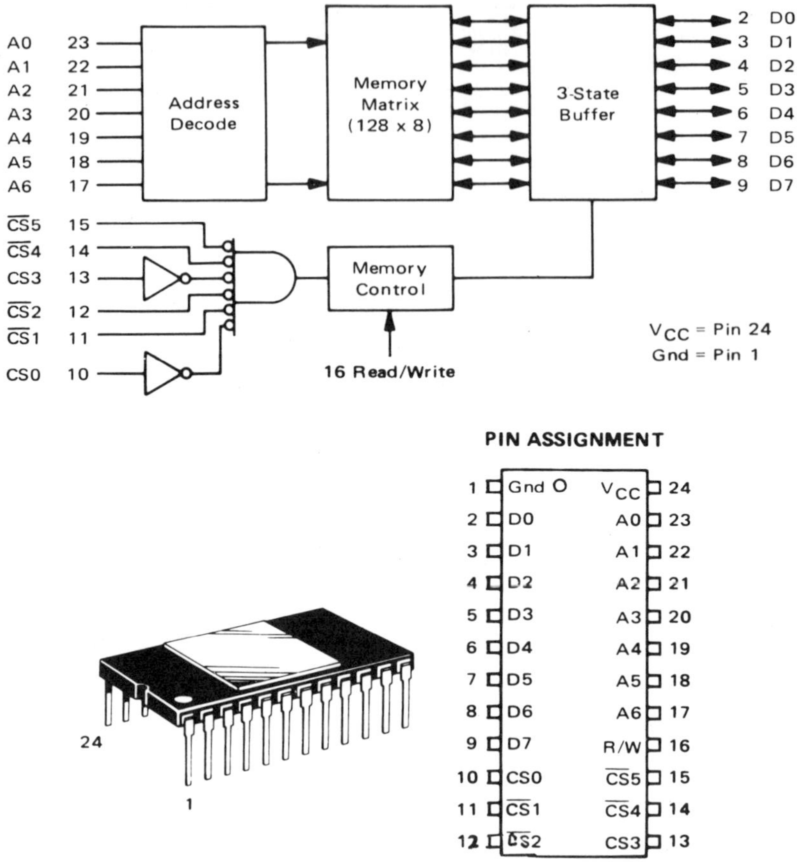

Fig. 1–19. Motorola 128 by 8 static RAM

has 128 addresses, each with 8 bits. Thus, 8-bit bytes can be read into, or out of, 128 locations. The data bytes appear on the data lines D_0 through D_7, usually connected to a data bus. The data byte is read into the matrix if the buffer is in the *in* state, and is read out when the buffer is in the *out* state. The data lines are disconnected from the matrix if the buffer is in the *high-impedance* state.

Buffer State Control. The buffer state is controlled by two factors: (1) the read/write signal at pin 16, and (2) the control signals at pins 10 through 15. If any one of the control signals (called *chip-select inputs*) is absent, the buffer remains in the high-impedance state, and no data pass between the matrix and the data lines. Thus, it is possible to shut off the memory from the microprocessor system by controlling only one of 6 lines or inputs.

Note that some of the chip-select inputs are *active high* (turn on when the line is at binary 1), whereas others are *active low* (turn on when the line is at binary 0). Active lows are indicated by the overbars. This arrangement permits one memory IC to be turned on, with other memories to be turned off, by the same signal on the same address line.

When all the chip-select imputs are present (all active highs are at 1, all active lows are at 0), the buffer can be placed in the read (data into the matrix) or write (data from the matrix to the data line) condition by a signal on the read/write line.

Address Selection. The address to be read in or out is selected by an address decoder, which, in turn, is controlled by binary word on the address bus (lines A_0 through A_6). In certain systems, part of the address lines is connected to some of the chip-select inputs. This is done where there may be several memories, all connected to the address and data buses. For example, assume that a 128 by 8 RAM is used on the same data and address buses with a 1024 by 8 ROM, as shown in Fig. 1–20. Usually, the RAM will be assigned to lower-number addresses (say from 0000 to 0127, in decimal) with the ROM containing the higher-number addresses (say from 49,152 to 50,175, in decimal).

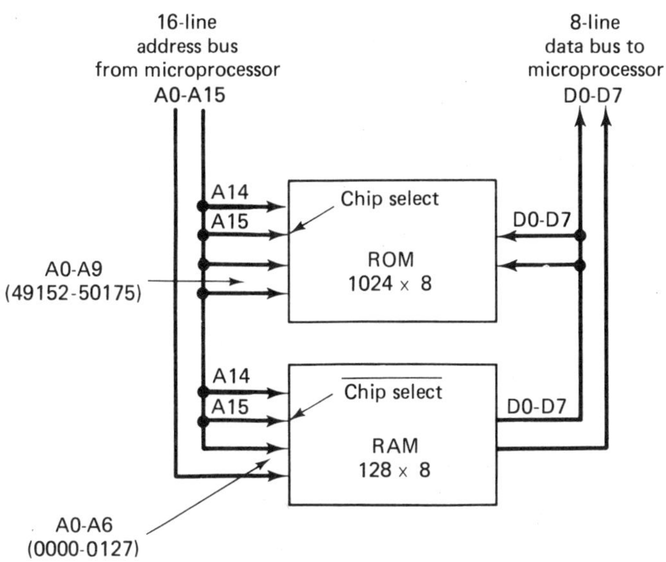

Fig. 1–20. Typical address and data bus arrangement where one address line (A_{15}) is used for chip select

When the highest address line A_{15} is at 1, the ROM is made active. When A_{15} is at 0, the RAM is active.

Keep in mind that the use of address line signals to control memory ICs does not occur in all systems. For example, Fig. 1–21 shows the block diagram of a 32-word by 8-bit static RAM, together with the operational modes of the buffer. The buffer between the matrix (shown as an *array*) and the data bus are controlled by the $\overline{\text{MWR}}$, $\overline{\text{MRD}}$, and $\overline{\text{CS}}$ lines. Since all these lines are identified with an overbar, they are active low, as indicated by the operational-mode table.

As an example, assume that the $\overline{\text{CS}}$ and $\overline{\text{MRD}}$ lines are at binary 0, and the state of the $\overline{\text{MWR}}$ line is undetermined (the *don't care* state.) Under these conditions, the output of each bit in the selected address is passed through the buffer to the data bus. If the bit is high, the corresponding data line is high, and vice versa. If the $\overline{\text{CS}}$ and MWR lines are 0, and the $\overline{\text{MRD}}$ line is 1, the state of each line in the data bus is read into the corresponding bit of the selected address. If the $\overline{\text{CS}}$ line

OPERATIONAL MODES

Function	$\overline{\text{CS}}$	$\overline{\text{MRD}}$	$\overline{\text{MWR}}$	Data Pins Status
READ	0	0	X	Output: High/ Low Dependent on Data
WRITE	0	1	0	Input, Output Disabled
Not Selected	1	X	X	Output Disabled High-Impedance State
Standby	0	1	1	

Logic 1 = High Logic 0 = Low X = Don't Care

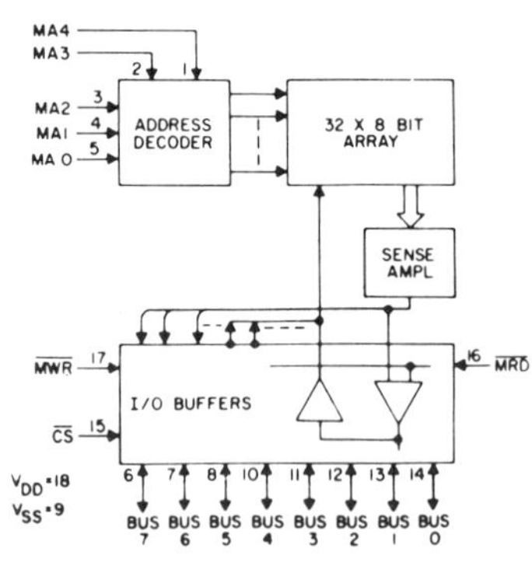

Fig. 1–21. RCA 32 by 8 static RAM, functional diagram

is 1, the buffer is in the high-impedance state, and no data pass between the array and data bus, no matter what the state of the $\overline{\text{MRD}}$ and $\overline{\text{MWR}}$ lines. This same high-impedance condition (no input, no output) can be produced with the $\overline{\text{MRD}}$ and $\overline{\text{MWR}}$ lines both at 1 simultaneously. From this, it can be seen that there is no common method to control RAM hardware during the read/write function.

1–11.2 Static Versus Dynamic RAMs

In a typical *dynamic* RAM, information is stored as an electrical charge on the gate capacitance of a MOS (metal oxide semiconductor) transistor. Since these transistors have some leakage, the charge is removed in time, even with the power applied. Thus, the information (binary 0 or 1 for each bit at each address) is lost in time if the charge is not periodically *refreshed.* There are many ways to refresh a dynamic RAM. However, the circuitry is complex and usually involves circuits outside the RAM IC. The main advantage of a dynamic RAM are high-speed operation and low power consumption.

In a typical *static* RAM, each bit of information is stored on a flip-flop or latch. Static RAMs do not require refreshing, and are thus far less complex than dynamic RAMs of the same capacity. However, static RAMs are slower and consume more power.

1–11.3 Volatile RAMs

Most present-day semiconductor RAMs are *volatile.* That is, all information is lost when the power is removed. This problem can be avoided by using a battery-maintained power supply during standby operation conditions. Dynamic RAMs are often used for battery operation, since they draw less power than static RAMs. Also, there is a form of static RAM, the CMOS (complementary MOS) RAM, that draws lower power and is suitable for battery operation. For a thorough discussion of MOS devices, including RAMs, see the author's *Manual for MOS Users* (1975, Reston Publishing Company, Inc., Reston, Virginia).

1–11.4 ROM Circuits

The term ROM is applied to a wide range of devices in which fixed two-state information is stored for later use. Usually, the ROM is housed in a separate IC package containing a matrix of addressed locations. In a ROM, each bit in each address is *permanently set* to binary 1 or 0. ROMs are generally used to hold the program of microprocessor instructions and possibly other data constants, such as routines and tables. Unlike the RAM, the ROM is nonvolatile (the memory remains after power is removed), and the write function does not exist for a ROM.

Figure 1–22 shows the functional block diagram of a typical ROM. This unit is described by the manufacturer as a 1024 by 8 ROM, which means that the matrix has 1024 addresses, each with 8 bits. Thus, 8-bit binary words or bytes can be read out of 1024 locations. The bytes appear on the data lines D_0 through D_7 connected to the data bus.

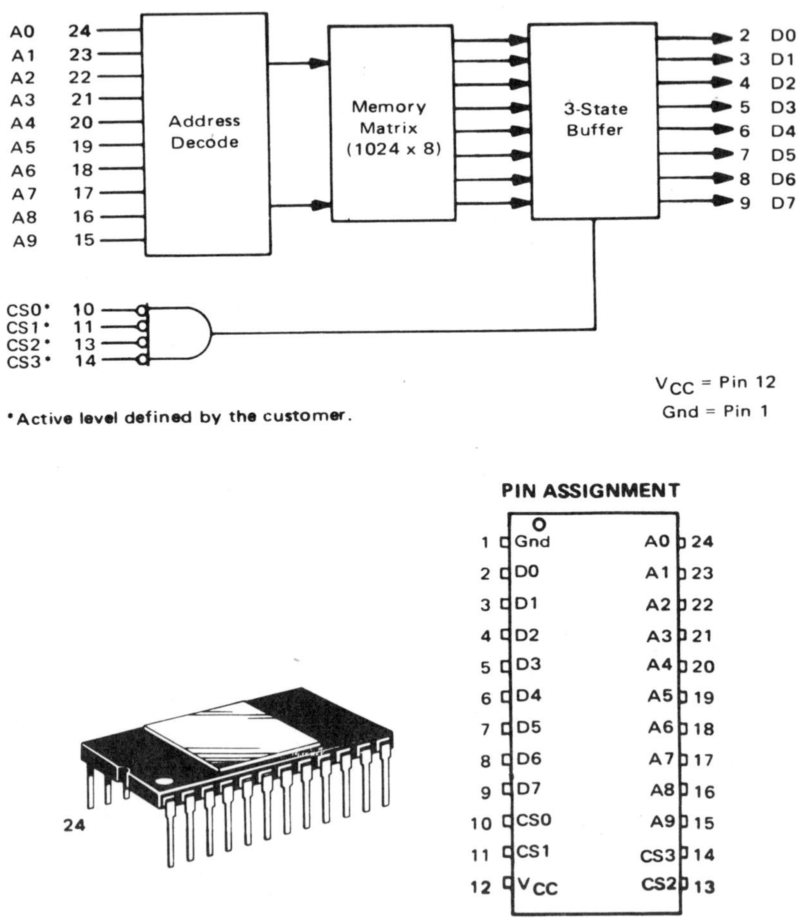

Fig. 1–22. Motorola 1024 by 8 ROM

Although the buffer is three-state, only the high-impedance and output lines are used.

When all chip-select (CS) inputs are available, the permanent information stored at the selected address is passed to the data bus. When one or more of the chip-select inputs are absent, the buffer remains in the high-impedance state, and no data pass from the matrix to the data bus. Thus, it is possible to shut off the ROM from the system by controlling *only one* of the four lines or inputs.

Note that the user can define whether the chip-select inputs are active high or active low. Also note that the user must define the binary word to be stored at each address. Generally, the user defines the desired contents of the ROM by means of IBM cards or punched paper tape when the ROMs are ordered from the manufacturer. The manufacturer then programs the ROMs (sets in the binary bit pattern at each address), usually by means of a mask for the final metallization step in IC manufacture. This process is generally used when a large number of ROMs are required (typically 300 or more), but can be used for smaller numbers. As in the case of the RAM, the address to be read out of the ROM is selected by an address decoder which, in turn, is controlled by the binary word on the address bus (lines A_0 through A_9).

There are two obvious problems with this method of custom ROM manufacture. First, the cost of the metallization mask (used for all the ROMs of a given program) is quite high. Thus, if only a few ROMs are needed, the cost per ROM is equally high. More important, the user rarely (if ever) knows the exact programming required for a ROM until after the program has been tested and debugged. That is, you do not know what binary word is to be located at which address until you have written the program, tested it, and found that the program works under all circumstances. There are several ways to overcome this problem, including the use of PROMs (programmable ROMs), EPROMs (erasable, ultraviolet, PROMs), EAROMs (electrically alterable ROMs), and RMMs (read mostly memories), all of which are described in the following paragraphs.

1–11.5 PROM Circuit

A PROM is shipped by the manufactueer with all bits at each address blank (or at binary 0, in most cases). The user then programs each bit at each address by means of an electrical current. Typically, when current is applied to a bit, a nichrome wire is "fused" or opened by the current, making that bit assume the electrical characteristics of a binary 1. Bits to be at binary 0 are left untouched. The program in the PROM is then permanent and irreversible.

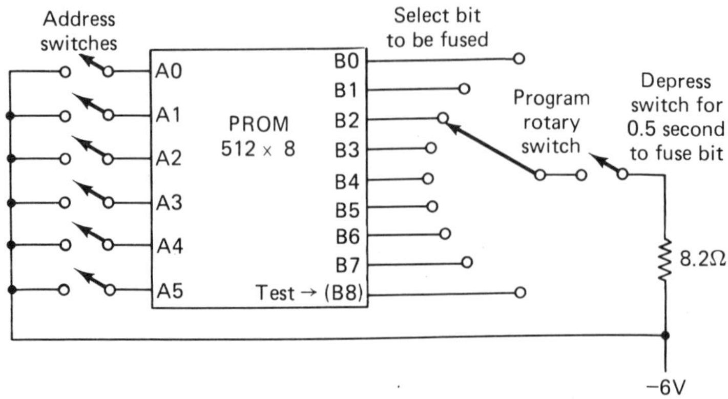

Fig. 1–23. Basic PROM programming circuit

The programming can be used with simple switches and a voltage source, as shown in Fig. 1–23. In this circuit, the address switches are set to produce the binary word at the address terminals of the PROM (switches closed to provide 5 V for each binary 1, switches open for a 0). With the proper address selected, the rotary programming switch is set to each bit requiring a binary 1, in turn, and the fusing switch is pressed for about 1 second to fuse the nichrome wire with the PROM. This process is very time consuming and tedious. Also, if a mistake is made on even one bit in one address, the entire PROM is made useless for that program. Automatic and semiautomatic PROM programming devices are available to overcome this problem.

1–11.6 EPROM Circuits

Even though it is possible to program a large number of PROMs with automatic equipment rather quickly, there is still the problem of testing and debugging before a final program is obtained for the ROM. This problem is overcome by means of an EPROM, in which information is stored as a charge in a MOSFET (metal oxide semiconductor field-effect transistor). Such EPROMs can be erased by flooding the IC with ultraviolet radiation. Once erased, new information can be programmed into the PROM in the normal manner. The erasure and reprogramming process can be repeated as many times as required.

As shown in Fig. 1–24, an EPROM package is provided with a transparent lid, which allows the memory content to be erased with ultraviolet (UV) light. For proper erasure, the semiconductor chip within the IC package must be exposed to strong UV light for a few minutes; thus there is no danger of the program being erased acciden-

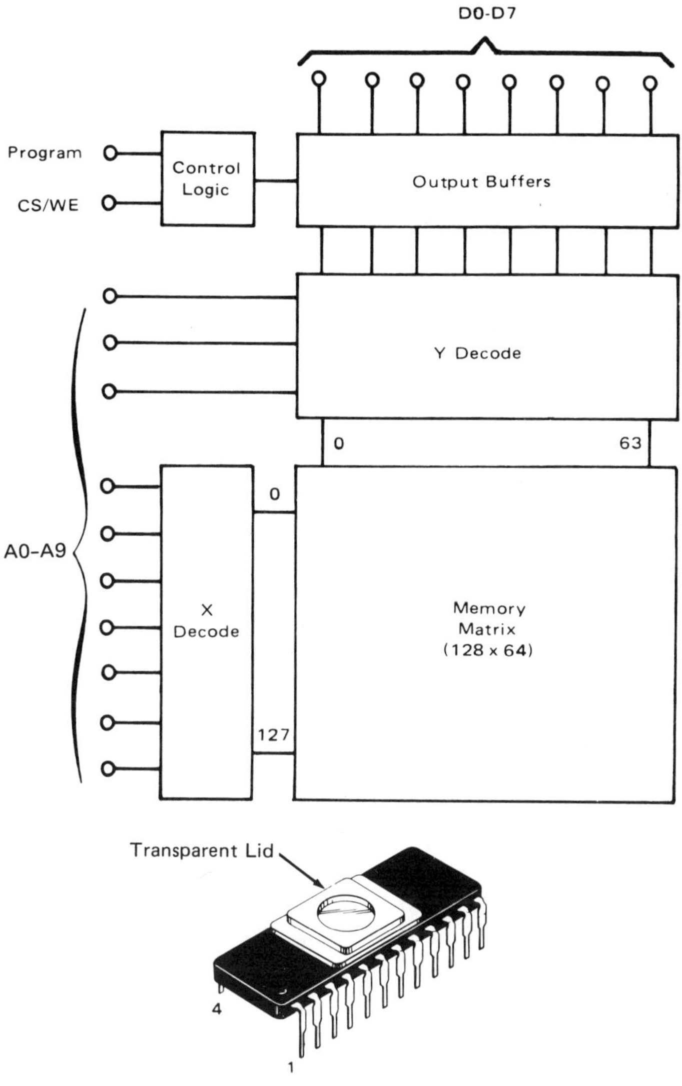

Fig. 1–24. Motorola 1024 by 8 alterable (ultraviolet) ROM

tally. Even exposure to direct sunlight will not produce erasure for several days.

Typical UV Erasure Procedure. The typical erasure procedure for a UV EPROM is exposure to shortwave ultraviolet light, which has a wavelength of 2530 Å (angstrom units). The integrated dose (i.e., UV light intensity times exposure time) for erasure should be a minimum of 15 watts per second per square centimeter (W-s/cm^2). The erasure time with this dosage is approximately 15 to 20 min using an ultraviolet lamp with a 12,000 μW/cm^2 power rating. The EPROM should be placed within 1 in. of the lamp tubes during erasure. Some lamps have a filter on their tubes, which should be removed before erasure.

Except for the erasure feature, a typical EPROM is similar to a ROM in function, as shown by the block diagram of Fig. 1–24. In addition to the usual address inputs, data outputs, decoders and buffers, an EPROM usually has a "program" input line. An appropriate signal on the program line permits information to be programmed into the selected address.

1–11.7 EAROM and RMM Circuits

These devices are a form of erasable PROM, but use electrical currents instead of UV light for erasure. The programming is similar to that of the EPROM, but the erasure is a slow process and requires special circuits. For these reasons EPROMs are generally used for microprocessor-based systems, rather than EAROMs and RMMs. However, this trend could change in future.

1–12. INPUT/OUTPUT HARDWARE

The microprocessor and memories described in Sec. 1–10 and 1–11 can be connected to form a simple and almost-complete microcomputer. The missing element is an input/output device between the microcomputer hardware and the outside world, or peripherals. Without some input/output hardware, the transfer of data between the outside world and the microcomputer would be impossible.

Assume, for example, that a basic microcomputer (microprocessor, ROM, and RAM) is used with a conventional video terminal (keyboard and Cathode-ray tube, CRT, video display), and that the data lines of the video terminal are connected to the microcomputer data buses. Information to be processed is typed on the keyboard and transmitted directly to the microcomputer data lines. After processing, the data bytes are returned directly to the video display. There are three basic problems with such an arrangement.

First, data bytes from the keyboard can appear simultaneously with data from the selected memory. Second, the video terminal and microcomputer have no way of telling each other that they are ready to transmit data or receive data. Third, there is no synchronization of timing between the microcomputer and video terminal. That is, the microcomputer and video terminal clocks may be operating at different frequencies, phase relationships, and so on.

Another problem is created if the peripheral operates with serial data, rather than the parallel data required for the microcomputer. And there is always the problem of *interfacing* electronic devices (different devices operating at different voltage levels, impedances, etc.). These and other problems are overcome by means of an input/output IC. Most microprocessor manufacturers supply one or more I/O ICs for their systems. Typically, there is one I/O device for interfacing with parallel peripherals and another for serial peripherals.

1–12.1 Typical Parallel I/O IC

Figure 1–25 is the block diagram of a basic parallel I/O IC. The circuit is described as an 8-bit input/output port, and consists essentially of an 8-bit register and 8-bit buffers, together with the control elements. The MODE control is used to program the device as an input port or output port. The MODE control is 0 for input and 1 for output.

Input Port. When used as an input port, information is passed into the 8-bit register when pulses on the clock line are high. The clock also sets the service request (SR/SE) circuit and latches the data in the register. The SR output can be used to signal or flag the microprocessor that there are data from the peripheral ready for processing. The CS1 and CS2 inputs are used to control the three-state buffers. The buffers are enabled when the CS1 and CS2 lines are high. This also resets the SR circuits (to flag the microprocessor that the data bytes have been passed).

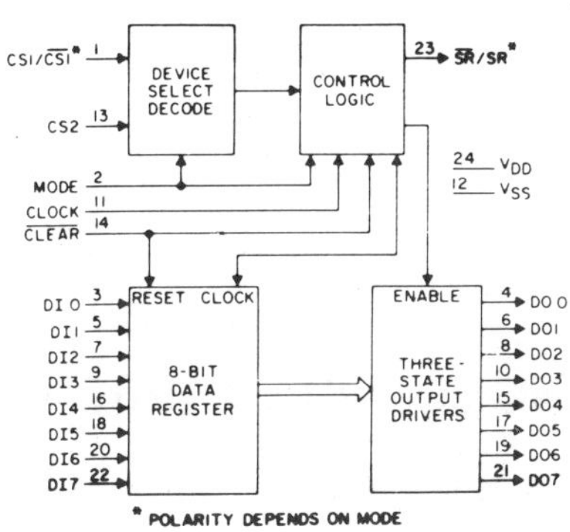

Fig. 1–25. RCA COSMAC 8-bit I/O port

Output Port. When used as an output port, the buffers are enabled at all times, and information is passed into the 8-bit register (if CS1, CS2, and the clock are all high). The service-request SR signal is generated when CS1 and CS2 are swinging low, and remains until the clock swings low. Stated another way, SR is generated when CS1 and CS2 go from 1 to 0, and remains until the clock line goes to 0.

Clear Signal. A CLEAR signal is provided for resetting the register and the service-request circuit. The CLEAR function operates in both the input- and output-port modes.

From these descriptions, it can be seen that the circuit of Fig. 1–25 provides the basic I/O functions. Using the video terminal example of Sec. 1–12, a data byte from the keyboard can be held in the register until the microprocessor is ready to accept new data. This condition is signaled or flagged to the microprocessor by the SR line. Then the buffers are enabled by the microprocessor, and the data byte is passed to the microcomputer system. The buffers are set to the high-impedance state, and the registers are reset.

After processing the microcomputer system, the data byte is placed in the registers, and this condition is flagged to the video terminal by the SR line. When the video terminal is ready to accept data for display on the CRT, the buffers are enabled by the video terminal, the byte is passed to the CRT display, the buffers are again returned to the high-impedance state, and the registers and SR line are reset.

1–12.2 Serial I/O IC

Operation of a serial I/O circuit is generally far more complex than that of the basic parallel I/O circuit just described. In addition to all the control, timing, and data-transfer functions, a serial I/O must also convert from parallel to serial, and vice versa, for each exchange of information between the peripheral microcomputer system. Because of this complexity, and because serial operation of a microcomputer system is often closely related to operation of the peripheral, the discussions of serial operation are covered in Chapter 2 (peripherals) and Chapter 4 (operation of microcomputer circuits).

1–13. BASIC MICROCOMPUTER SYSTEM

Now that we have covered basic microcomputer hardware (microprocessor, RAM, ROM, and I/O ICs) and the circuits within these

ICs, we are ready to describe a simple, yet complete, microprocessor system.

Figure 1–26 is the block diagram of an elementary microcomputer system. This is the theoretical minimum system configuration of the Motorola M6800 family. Such a system could be used with two parallel peripherals. The circuits shown in Fig. 1–26 provide for control of the I/O devices, transfer of data or control information between I/O and memory, movement of data bytes between different memory locations, and interpretation of data bytes stored in memory. The system consists of a microprocessor, ROM, RAM, and I/O (called a PIA, or peripheral interface adapter). All these devices can be interfaced directly without external components. However, the external components required (besides a power supply and wiring) are a two-phase clock signal source and a reset switch or control.

1–13.1 System Functions

The major function performed by the system of Fig. 1–26 include the following:

1. Control of peripheral devices such as video terminals, tape/card readers, printers, and the like.
2. Transfer of data and/or control information between the peripheral devices and memory.
3. Movement of data bytes between different memory locations.
4. Interpretation or modification of bytes stored in memory.

In such a system, the microprocessor can, for example, control the entry of data bytes from an input keyboard and store them in predetermined memory locations. The microprocessor can then perform specified arithmetic operations using the stored bytes and transfer the results to an output display or printing device.

1–13.2 Typical Peripherals

Typical system input peripheral devices may include simple switches, paper-tape/card readers, magnetic-tape disk devices, relays, modems, analog-to-digital (A/D) converters, photodetectors, and other computers. Output peripherals may include lights, relays, CRT, light-emitting diodes (LED), liquid crystal devices (LCD), digital-to-analog (D/A) converters, modems, printers, and other computers. Typical peripherals used with microcomputers are discussed in Chapter 2.

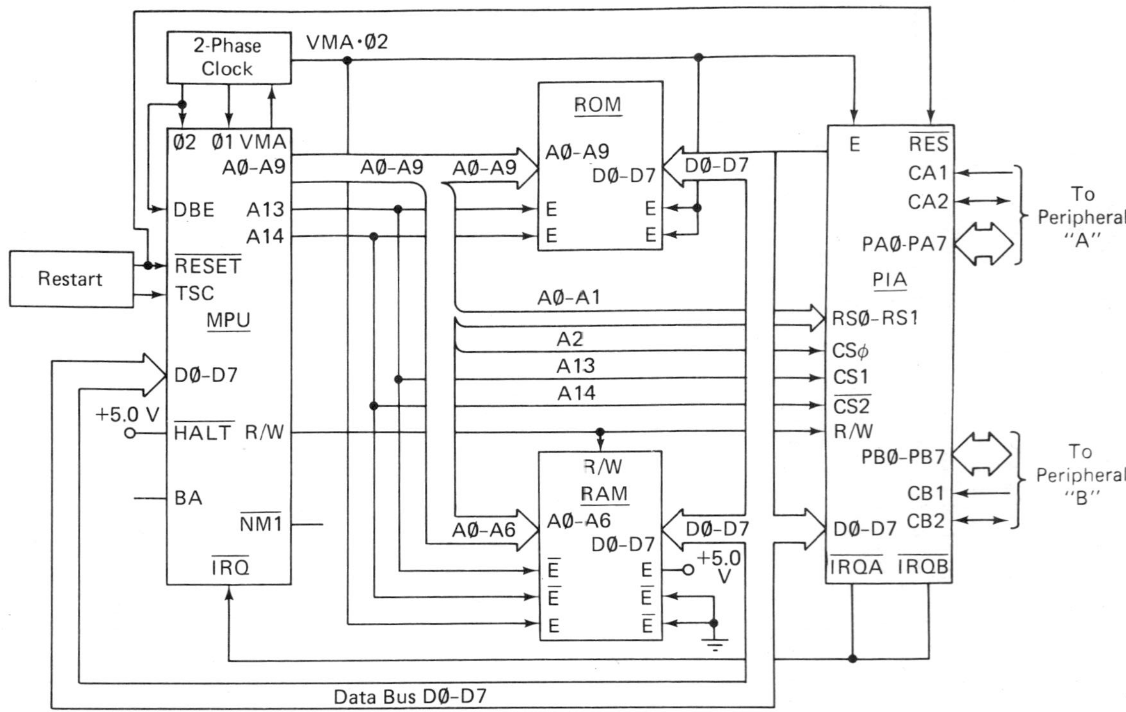

Fig. 1–26. Theoretical minimum system configuration for M6800 family

1–13.3 System Memory and Data Bus

The system memory can be any combination of RAM and ROM up to 65,535 bytes. ROM is used for permanent storage of programs, tables, and other types of fixed data. RAM is required for general-purpose computer systems that have frequent program changes. RAM is also required for temporary storage of variable data. The type of memory and required storage capacity are determined by the specific application of the system. Bytes are transferred between peripheral devices, memory, and the microprocessor by means of a common, bidirectional, 8-bit data bus.

1–13.4 Microprocessor Interface Lines

The microprocessor input/output is broken into three groups: (1) the bus interface lines, (2) the bus control lines, and (3) the microprocessor control lines.

Microprocessor Address Bus Lines (A0 to A15). Sixteen pins are used for the address bus. The outputs are three-state bus drivers. When the output is turned off, it is essentially an open circuit. This permits the microprocessor to be used in DMA (direct-memory address) applications. Putting TSC (three-state control, Sec. 1–13.7) in its high state forces the address bus and R/W (read/write) lines to go into the three-state mode.

Microprocessor Data Bus Lines (D0 to D7). Eight pins are used for the data bus, which is bidirectional, and transfers data to and from the memory and peripheral devices. The three-state drivers can be put into the three-state mode by forcing DBE (data bus enable, Sec. 1–13.7) low.

Microprocessor Clock Inputs, Phases 1 and 2. Two pins are used for a two-phase nonoverlapping clock.

Microprocessor Read/Write Line (R/W). The read/write line is an output that signals the peripheral and memory devices whether the microprocessor is in a read (high) or write (low) state. The normal standby state of this signal is read (high). Three-state control going high will turn read/write to the high-impedance state. Also, when the microprocessor is halted, the R/W line will be in the high-impedance state.

Microprocessor Valid Memory Address Line (VMA). This output indicates to the peripherals that there is a valid address on the address bus. In normal operation, this signal should be used for enabling the RAM and the PIA. The VMA signal is active high. The output buffer of VMA is not three-state.

Microprocessor Interrupt Request Line ($\overline{\text{IRQ}}$). This level-sensitive input requests that an *interrupt sequence* be generated within the microprocessor when $\overline{\text{IRQ}}$ is low. The microprocessor will wait until it completes the current instruction that is being executed before it recognizes the request. At this time, if the interrupt mask bit in the condition code register is not set, the microprocessor will begin an interrupt sequence.

The contents of the index register, program counter, accumulators, and condition code registers are stored away on a *stack* (a group of memory addresses), and the interrupt mask bit is set so that further interrupts may occur. At the end of the cycle, a 16-bit address will be placed on the address bus that points to vectoring address, which is located in memory locations FFF8 and FFF9. An address located at these locations causes the microprocessor to jump to an interrupt routine in memory.

The $\overline{\text{Halt}}$ line must be in the high state for interrupts to be serviced; interrupts will be latched internally while $\overline{\text{Halt}}$ is low. The wired-OR capability of the $\overline{\text{IRQ}}$ input requires a 3-kilohm (kΩ) minimum external resistor to V_{CC}.

1–13.5 PIA and Memory Interface Lines

The peripheral and memory interface lines are the data bus (D0 to D7), the address inputs, the register selects (RS0 to RS1), chip selects, R/W, the enable E, and interrupt request ($\overline{\text{IRQ}}$). A description of these follows.

Data Bus (D0 to D7). The peripheral data bus lines are bidirectional and capable of transferring data to and from the microprocessor and memory. The drivers are three-state input/output buffers.

Address Inputs (A0 to A15). Sixteen address lines are available for addressing peripherals and memories. Seven are used for addressing the internal locations of the RAM, and 10 are used for addressing internal locations of the ROM. The address inputs are high impedance.

Register Selects (RS0 to RS1). Register-select inputs on the PIA are essentially the same as address inputs to the RAM and ROM. Bus address lines are tied directly to the register-select inputs in a minimum system configuration.

There are six locations within the PIA accessible to the microprocessor data bus: two peripheral registers (A and B), two data direction registers (A and B), and two control registers (A and B). Selection of these locations is controlled by the RS0 and RS1 inputs, together with CRA-2/CRB-2 in the control register, as follows:

		Control Register		
RS1	*RS0*	*CRA-2*	*CRB-2*	*Location Selected*
0	0	1	×	Peripheral register A
0	0	0	×	Data direction register A
0	1	×	×	Control register A
1	0	×	1	Peripheral register B
1	0	×	0	Data direction register B
1	1	×	×	Control register B

× means "don't care."

Chip Selects (CS0 to CS5). Chip selects on the PIA and memory devices are used to distinguish one device from another. The number of chip selects available varies from three on the PIA to six on the RAM. The chip selects may tie directly to the microprocessor address bus and VMA line in a minimum system configuration. Chip-select lines are high-impedance inputs. The PIA and memory are enabled to various combinations of *true* and *not true* chip selects.

Read/Write (R/W). The read/write is a high-impedance input that is used to control the direction of data flow through the microprocessor data bus interface. When R/W is high (microprocessor read cycle), the PIA and memory data bus drivers are turned on, and the selected location is read. When R/W is low, the data bus drivers are turned off, and the microprocessor writes into the selected location.

Enable (E). The enable input E is the PIA and memory enable signal. The E input is a high-impedance input that enables the PIA and memory output data buffers. One of the chip selects is used for the E enable on the RAM and ROM.

Peripheral Interrupt Request (IRQA and IRQB). The only difference between the special function I/O device (PIA) and memories from a system consideration is that the PIA has interrupt outputs that are used as a request for servicing.

$\overline{\text{IRQA}}$ and IRQB from the PIA are ORed to the system $\overline{\text{IRQ}}$ line. Since the PIA may be used to detect incoming interrupt signals on any of its control lines, this connection must be made in order to initiate the interrupt sequence at the microprocessor. The $\overline{\text{IRQ}}$ will be pulled down by the PIA following detection of a pulse on any control line that has been enabled as a system interrupt. $\overline{\text{IRQ}}$ will be held low until the interrupt is serviced. Thus, no interrupts will be lost to the system even if the interrupt mask is set at the microprocessor.

1–13.6 PIA to Peripheral Interface Lines

The PIA provides two 8-bit bidirectional data buses and four interrupt/control lines for interfacing to peripheral devices.

Section A Peripheral Data (PA0 to PA7). Each of the peripheral data lines can be programmed to act as an input or output. This is done by setting a 1 in the corresponding data direction register bit for those lines that are to be outputs. A 0 in the bit of the data direction register causes the corresponding peripheral data line to act as an input. During a microprocessor "read peripheral data operation," the data on peripheral lines programmed to act as inputs appear directly on the corresponding microprocessor data bus lines. In the input mode, the internal pull-up resistor on these lines represents a maximum of one standard TTL load.

The data in output register A will appear on the data lines that are programmed to be outputs. A 1 written into the register will cause a high on the corresponding data line; a 0 results in a low. Data bytes in the output register may be read by a microprocessor "read peripheral data A" operation when the corresponding lines are programmed as outputs. These data bytes will be read properly if the voltage on the peripheral data lines is greater than 2 V for a 1 output, and less than 0.8 V for a 0 output. Loading the output lines such that the voltage on these lines does not reach full voltage causes the data transferred to the microprocessor on a read operation to differ from that contained in the respective bit of output register A.

Section B Peripheral Data (PB0 to PB7). The peripheral data lines in the B section of the PIA can be programmed to act as either inputs or outputs in a similar manner to PA0 to PA7. However, the output buffers driving these lines differ from those driving lines PA0 to PA7. The PB lines have three-state capability, allowing them to enter a high-impedance state when the peripheral data line is used as an input. In addition, data on the peripheral data lines PB0 to PB7 will be read properly from these lines programmed as outputs even if the voltages are below 2 V (for a high). As outputs, the PB lines are compatible with standard TTL, and may also be used as a source of up to 1 milliampere (mA) at 1.5 V to directly drive the base of a transistor switch.

Interrupt Input (CA1 to CB1). Peripheral input lines CA1 and CB1 are input-only lines that set the interrupt flags of the control registers. The active transition for these signals is also programmed by the two control registers.

Peripheral Control (CA2). The peripheral control line CA2 can be programmed to act as an interrupt control or as a peripheral control output. As an output, this line is compatible with standard TTL. As an input, the internal pull-up resistor on this line represents one standard TTL load. The function of this signal line is programmed with control register A.

Peripheral Control (CB2). Peripheral control line CB2 may also be programmed to act as an interrupt input or peripheral control input. As an input, this line has high input impedance and is compatible with standard TTL. As an output, CB2 is compatible with standard TTL, and may also be used as a source of up to 1 mA at 1.5 V to directly drive the base of a transistor switch. This line is programmed by control register B.

1–13.7 Microprocessor Controls

In addition to 72 instructions entered on the data bus and the bus control lines, the microprocessor has the six additional control lines shown in Fig. 1–26. Two of the control lines, $\overline{\text{Reset}}$ and DBE (data bus enable) are used for all systems. The remaining control lines, $\overline{\text{NMI}}$ (nonmaskable interrupt), $\overline{\text{Halt}}$, BA (bus available), and TSC (three-state control), can be used to increase flexibility.

$\overline{\text{Reset}}$. The $\overline{\text{Reset}}$ input is used to reset and start the microprocessor from a power-down condition resulting from power failure or initial start-up. Reset input can also be used to reinitialize the microprocessor at any time after start-up.

If a high level is detected on $\overline{\text{Reset}}$, this will signal the microprocessor to begin the reset sequence, during which the contents of the last two locations (FFFE and FFFF) in memory will be loaded into the program counter to point to the beginning of the reset routine. During the reset routine, the interrupt mask bit is set and must be cleared under program control before the microprocessor can be interrupted by $\overline{\text{IRQ}}$. While $\overline{\text{Reset}}$ is low (assuming that a minimum of eight clock cycles has occurred), the microprocessor output signals will be in the following states: VMA = low, BA = low, data bus = high impedance, R/W = high (the read state), and the address bus will contain the reset address FFFE.

Nonmaskable Interrupt ($\overline{\text{NMI}}$). The microprocessor is capable of handling two types of interrupts: maskable ($\overline{\text{IRQ}}$) and nonmaskable ($\overline{\text{NMI}}$). $\overline{\text{IRQ}}$ is maskable by the interrupt mask bit (bit I) in the condition code register. $\overline{\text{NMI}}$ is nonmaskable. That is, an interrupt signal on the $\overline{\text{NMI}}$ line produces an interrupt without regard to other conditions.

$\overline{\text{Halt}}$ and Single-Instruction Execution. The $\overline{\text{Halt}}$ line provides an input to the microprocessor to allow control of the program execution by an outside source. If $\overline{\text{Halt}}$ is high, the microprocessor will execute the instructions. If $\overline{\text{Halt}}$ is low, the microprocessor will go to a halted or idle mode. A response signal of BA (bus available) provides an indication of the current status of the microprocessor. When BA is low, the microprocessor is in the process of executing the control program. If BA is high, the microprocessor bus is halted and all internal activity has stopped.

When BA is high, the address bus, data bus, and R/W line will be in a high-impedance state, effectively removing the microprocessor from the system bus. VMA is forced low so that the floating system bus will not activate any device on the bus that is enabled by VMA.

While the microprocessor is halted, all program activity is stopped, and if either an $\overline{\text{NMI}}$ or $\overline{\text{IRQ}}$ interrupt occurs, it will be latched into the microprocessor and acted on as soon as the microprocessor is taken out of the halted mode. If a $\overline{\text{Reset}}$ command occurs while the microprocessor is halted, the following states occur: VMA = low, BA = low, data bus = high impedance, R/W = high (read state), and the address bus will contain address FFFE as long as $\overline{\text{Reset}}$ is low. As soon as the $\overline{\text{Halt}}$ line goes high, the microprocessor will go to locations FFFE and FFFF for the address of the reset routine.

Three-State Control (TSC). When the TSC line is at 1, the address bus and the R/W line are placed in a high-impedance state. VMA and BA are forced low whenever TSC = 1 to prevent false reads or writes on any device enabled by VMA. While TSC is held at 1, the phase 1 and phase 2 clocks must be held high and low, respectively, in order to delay program execution (this is required because of the bus lines being in an indeterminate state). Since the microprocessor is a dynamic device, the phase 1 clock can be stopped for a maximum time PWΦH (pulse width phase high) without destroying data within the microprocessor. TSC can then be used in a short direct-memory-access (DMA) application.

Bus Available (BA). The BA signal will normally be in the low state. When activated, BA will go to the high state, indicating that the microprocessor has stopped and that the address bus is available. This will occur if the $\overline{\text{Halt}}$ line is in the low state, or if the microprocessor is in the wait state as a result of a wait instruction. At such time, all three-state output drivers will go to their off state, and other outputs will go to their normally inactive level. The microprocessor is removed from the wait state by the occurrence of a maskable interrupt (when bit I in the CRR goes to 0) or a nonmaskable interrupt (by a signal on the $\overline{\text{NMI}}$ line). Note that, if TSC is high, BA will be low.

Data Bus Enable (DBE). The DBE is a three-state control signal for the microprocessor data bus and will enable the bus drivers when in the high state. This input is TTL compatible. However, in normal operation, DBE is driven by the phase 2 clock. During a microprocessor read cycle, the data bus drivers will be disabled internally. When it is desirable that another device control the data bus, such as in DMA applications, DBE should be held low.

1–14. SYSTEM TIMING AND SYNCHRONIZATION

It is obvious that all the system functions described in Sec. 1–13 and shown in Fig. 1–26 must be synchronized as to time. For example, if a data byte is to be entered into memory at a particular address, that (and only that) data byte must be on the data bus when the desired address byte is on the address bus. If the two bytes (data and address) are not synchronized exactly as to time, the data byte will be entered at the wrong address (or will not be entered at any address). This problem is overcome by timing within the microprocessor. Registers are opened and closed at exact time intervals to accomplish the desired results.

System timing is primarily a function of the microprocessor. As in the case of microprocessor instructions, *you cannot change* the time relationships or operating cycles of the microprocessor. However, you can change system speed. The system speed, or operating frequency, is determined by the crystal or other clock pulses. If a 1-MHz crystal is used, the clock pulses will be approximately 1 μs; with a 3-MHz crystal, the clock pulses will be about one-third of this, or about 333 ns, and so on. However, if it takes eight clock pulses to complete a certain function or instruction, at some speed, it will take eight clock pulses to complete the same function at any other speed.

The time relationships and synchronization are shown by *timing diagrams* such as Fig. 1–27 (which happens to be a basic timing diagram of the RCA COSMAC microcomputer family). The clock pulses are shown at the top and bottom of the diagram. There are two sets of eight clock pulses. Thus, each clock pulse represents one bit in an 8-bit byte. Some functions are accomplished within the first byte; other functions

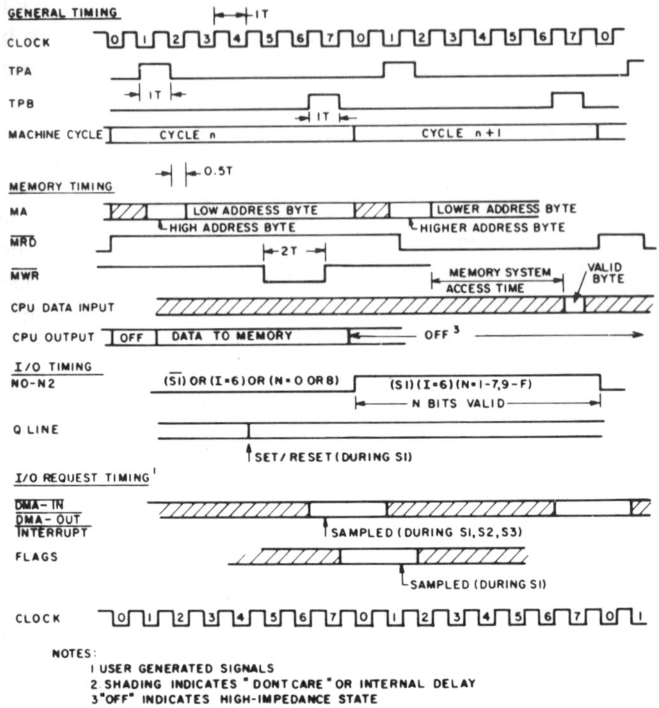

Fig. 1–27. Timing diagram for basic RCA COSMAC microcomputer system

require two bytes (a few functions may even require three bytes). Note that there is no reference to operating speed on the clock pulse, but that one clock cycle is shown as a time interval 1T (at clock pulse 3 on the top line). This is known as a *clock period*. If the clock frequency (set by the crystal or other external clock pulse source) is 1 MHz, the time interval or clock period 1T is about 1μs.

From a programming standpoint, the timing intervals and relationships are not that critical. It is generally more important that the programmer know that it takes one or two bytes to accomplish a given function or instruction. However, from a *design or troubleshooting standpoint, timing synchronization is critical*. For example, as discussed in Chapter 5, one of the standard troubleshooting techniques for microprocessor-based systems is to display the microprocessor signal pulses (as many as possible) on an oscilloscope or logic analyzer. In effect, the timing diagram of Fig. 1–27 (or a significant portion of it) is displayed on a scope. Then the time relationships are compared.

To further illustrate this point, note that the timing pulses TPA and TPB (sent from the microprocessor to control the peripherals and I/O circuits) occur at 8-bit (one byte) intervals. However, TPB occurs 5½ bits (or 5½ cycles) after TPA. If either TPA or TPB is absent or abnormal (wrong time relationship; say, 3 bits apart instead of 5½), this will pinpoint a fault in the system.

To troubleshoot a microprocessor-based system, it is essential that you understand the time relationships of the microprocessor, just as you must understand the instruction set. Such timing information is found in microcomputer literature, generally in the form of diagrams such as Fig. 1–27. It is not uncommon to have several timing diagrams, one for each major function or group of functions. For these reasons, we shall not go into a full discussion of timing here. However, one point of interest should be noted on Fig. 1–27. Each *machine cycle* consists of eight clock pulses (or a full 8-bit byte), and each instruction or function requires two or three bytes (or two or three machine cycles, whichever term is used by the microprocessor manufacturer). This relationship among clock bits, machine cycles, and instruction or function timing is common to many microprocessors.

1–15. TYPICAL MICROCOMPUTER SYSTEM OPERATION

Before going into the circuits of specific microcomputers, discussed in Chapter 4, let us consider a microprocessor and related IC equipment operating as a "typical" microcomputer. The difficulty is that there are many different types of microcomputers. As you will discover, there is no real standardization in hardware, software, or microcomputer system configurations.

Since it would be difficult for anyone (even experienced technicians and engineers) not already familiar with computers of some type (standard, mini, or micro) to immediately grasp the operation of any microcomputer described in Chapter 4, we shall consider a generalized and simplified microcomputer, one that never has nor ever will be designed. Nevertheless, this microcomputer contains the basic principles upon which all microprocessor-based systems operate. Once you understand how this simplified microcomputer operates, you will be in a better position to consider the more sophisticated and realistic systems described throughout this book. Borrowing a technique used by microcomputer manufacturers, we shall call our system the LENKMICROCOMP (LENK MICRO COMPuter).

1–15.1 Microcomputer System Hardware

Our microcomputer consists of a microprocessor, a 128 by 8 RAM, a 1024 by 8 ROM, and an I/O device. The RAM, ROM, and I/O are all in IC form, and are similar to the devices shown in Figs. 1–19, 1–22, and 1–25, respectively. The microprocessor is of special design, but it contains the usual registers, accumulators, counters, pointers, decoders, multiplexers, buffers, drivers, latches, ALU, and control circuitry described in Sec. 1–9.

As is typical, the registers are used as temporary storage locations for data bytes or words, such as the accumulators in the ALU section where the mathematical operations are performed. The counters are used to tally various items of information, such as commands (instructions) and locations (addresses) in the memory where the information can be found. Decoders translate the instructions to electrical signals (pulses) for executing these commands and for translating addresses to electrical signals, permitting the microprocessor to locate the required information and transfer it to the appropriate destinations. Interconnecting all these elements are electronic and logic circuits (buffers, drivers, latches, flip-flops) to direct the signals along the appropriate paths.

1–15.2 Peripheral Equipment

In most microcomputers, there must be some means for direct human-to-machine communication. The only exceptions to this are when the microcomputer system is used for control or processing of information to and from other electronic devices (such as when a microprocessor-based system is used in industrial control). Human-to-machine communication is usually the job of peripheral equipment. As discussed in Chapter 2, there are many peripheral devices available for use with microcomputer systems.

For simplicity, we have chosen a manually operated keyboard device. This keyboard permits the operator to enter information into any location in memory or to insert extra instructions. Our keyboard is in the form of a typewriter (similar to a teletype or TTY instrument). With this arrangement, the typewriter can both insert and print out information. As an alternative, we can use a video terminal; information is inserted by the keyboard and read out by the CRT video display.

The information fed to the microcomputer from the peripheral keyboard falls into two general categories. There are the *data bytes* (consisting of numbers, alphabetic letters, symbols, or combinations of all three that are to be processed), and the *instruction bytes* (the commands indicating how the data bytes are to be processed). Since the microcomputer's language is composed of binary numbers (in electrical pulse form), all information to be used must first be converted to numbers (or combinations of letters and numbers), and these numbers then converted to binary numbers.

In the LENKMICROCOMP keyboard, the conversion is done with a decoder. The keyboard decoder converts letters, numbers, and symbols from the keyboard into an ASCII code, which appears at the keyboard output in the form of an 8-bit binary word or byte. This byte is in parallel form, and is applied to the microcomputer's 8-bit I/O IC. As an example, assume that the letter A on the keyboard is pressed. This is converted to a hex 41 by the keyboard decoder, and appears as binary 01000001 at the I/O terminals.

1–15.3 Microcomputer Program

Microcomputers solve problems in a step-by-step manner. Since the microcomputer cannot think by itself (contrary to popular opinion), a *program* must be prepared that breaks the problem down into a series of sequential, logical, and simple steps. This is the task of the programmer. An extended discussion of the art of programming (and it is an art, not a science) is not intended for this book, you, the reader, must have some understanding (preferably a very detailed understanding) of the program if you are to learn microprocessor troubleshooting. For example, as discussed in Chapter 5, the usual first step in troubleshooting a microcomputer is to operate the system through its normal program, and note any abnormalities in operation, sequence, or failure to perform a given step.

Since there are many variations among microprocessors, programs are specifically developed for the particular microprocessor used in the microcomputer. The troubleshooter must know the microprocessor language and the manner in which the microprocessor operates. In short, you must know the instruction set! The program that we shall consider here is for our hypothetical, general-purpose microcomputer, the LENKMICROCOMP.

1–15.4 The Basic Program

As an example of how a program may be prepared for the microcomputer, let us consider how far a freely falling body will fall in 5 s. The equation for this problem is $d = gt^2/2$, where d is the distance in feet, t is the time in seconds, and g is the acceleration due to gravity (32 ft/s for each second of fall).

The programmer analyzes the problem and breaks it down into a sequential series of logical steps. The programmer then draws up a *flow chart* that diagrams the sequence of steps to be taken in solving the problem. Such a flow chart is shown in Fig. 1–28.

Although the flow chart helps the programmer to analyze the problem, the microcomputer cannot use the flow chart as is. The microprocessor has its own language (machine language) based on binary numbers, not alphabetic letters or words. Accordingly, the flow chart must be converted to a program or set of step-by-step instructions (in machine language) that the microprocessor can follow.

This conversion process is known as *assembly* and is discussed in Sec. 1–17. Some microprocessor manufacturers provide software programs, known as *assemblers*, that aid in the conversion process.

There are many ways in which manufacturers identify their instructions. First, some manufacturers call their instructions *operation codes* (or simply *op codes*). In some cases, each op code or instruction is identified by a binary number. This is the same binary number applied to the data inputs of the microprocessor to initiate an instruction or function, as discussed in Sec. 1–8. However, as discussed in Sec. 1–17, machine language programming (using binary numbers) is very laborious and subject to error, except for very simple, short programs.

Most microprocessor manufacturers identify the instructions by

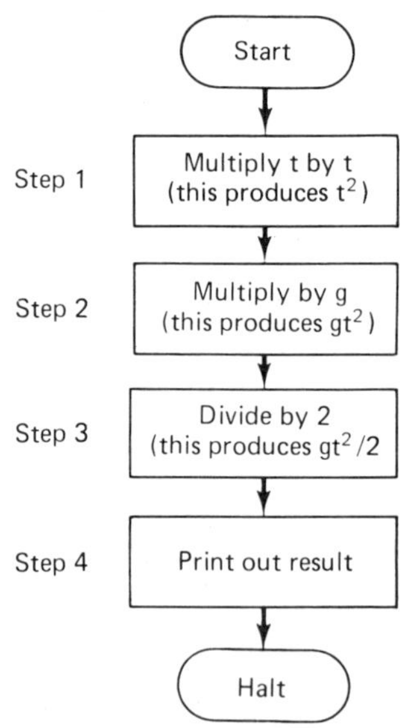

Fig. 1–28. Basic flow chart for falling-body problem

an alphabetic abbreviation or *mnemonic*, by a numeric abbreviation (usually in hex), and by an assembly code or statement. Examples of such identification for our LENKMICROCOMP are shown in Fig. 1–29. Note that the assembly code or statement is used for the convenience of the programmer when writing a program. However, only the numeric portion is used by the microprocessor (in binary form). Hex is used as shorthand for the binary number.

Both the numbers representing the instructions and the numbers that constitute data are stored in the memory at particular addresses. Each instruction or data byte is stored at a separate address. The programmer must keep a record of the address of each instruction or data byte. Then, if the programmer wishes the microcomputer to obtain any specific instruction or data byte, the address is put on the address bus by the program, and the instruction or data byte at that address appears on the data bus.

Arrangement of Instruction Addresses. There are several methods for arranging the instruction addresses in memory. Since the instructions follow in sequence, the address of the instructions may also be in sequential order. Thus, instruction 1 may be stored at address 0001, as an example. Then instruction 2 can be stored at address 0002, instruction 3 at address 0003, and so forth.

Before the start of operation, the address of instruction 1 (0001) is placed in a *program counter* register within the microprocessor. Then, as the microprocessor executes instruction 1, a signal is sent to the program counter, advancing the count by 1. The number in the program counter is now 0002, which is the address of instruction 2.

Alphabetic (Mnemonic) Representation	Numerical Representation		Meaning of Instruction
	Hex	Binary	
CAD	3A	0011 1010	Clear accumulator and add
ADD	3B	0011 1011	Add
SUB	3C	0011 1100	Subtract
MUL	3D	0011 1101	Multiply
DIV	3E	0011 1110	Divide
STO	3F	0011 1111	Store
PRT	7A	0111 1010	Print
HLT	00	0000 0000	Halt

Fig. 1–29. Typical op codes for the LENKMICROCOMP

The microprocessor obtains the address of the second instruction from the program counter (i.e., the number in the program counter appears on the address bus). As the microprocessor executes instruction 2, the program counter advances to 0003, which is the address of instruction 3. This process continues as long as there are instructions to be carried out. The final instruction directs the microprocessor to stop.

Keep in mind that the instructions are *permanently* programmed into the ROM at the indicated addresses. Neither the instructions nor the order in which they appear can be altered (unless the ROM is erasable). An erasable or alterable ROM is used during development of the program. When the program is debugged and the desired order of instructions is determined, a ROM is permanently programmed to that order.

Arrangement of Data Addresses. There are several methods for arranging the data bytes in memory. One method is to store both the instruction and data bytes at each address. When the microprocessor is directed to that address (i.e., when that address word appears on the address bus), the microprocessor will find both the op code indicating an instruction and the data to be acted upon. This is sometimes called *direct addressing*. Another method (known as *indirect addressing*) is to store each data byte at any address that is unoccupied and available. Using this system, each step of the program requires two machine cycles, one for instructions and one for data. Some microprocessors require three machine cycles for each program step. Usually, the first cycle is for the op code or instruction, with the remaining two cycles for data. Keep in mind that data bytes are *temporarily programmed* into the RAM at the desired addresses. In our case, the data bytes are entered at the peripheral typewriter keyboard.

Note that, with any of the systems for instruction and data addressing, the program does not contain the actual data, but the address at which the data bytes are stored. For example, if the programmer wishes the microprocessor to add a certain number, the programmer indicates to the microprocessor the instruction for addition (the addition instruction word appears on the data bus), and gives the address of the data byte number to be added (the data byte address word appears on the address bus). The microprocessor will then obtain the data byte at the selected address and add it to whatever number appears in the microprocessor arithmetic register or accumulator.

Example of Programming. As an example, let us program the falling-body problem using the flow chart of Fig. 1–28 and the instructions or op codes of Fig. 1–29. The data values involved are as follows:

1. t, the time in seconds that the body is falling.
2. g, the acceleration in feet per second of fall due to gravity.
3. Two, the number by which gt^2 is divided.

As previously indicated, $t = 5$ and $g = 32$.

These data bytes may be stored at any unoccupied address in the memory. For example, the data byte for t (5) can be stored at address 1001, data byte g (32) at address 1030, and data byte 2 at address 1201. The program listing will then appear as shown in Fig. 1–30.

The method of listing the program illustrated in Fig. 1–3 is often called an *assembly listing,* since it shows the program in assembly language (hex op codes, mnemonics, explanations, etc.) rather than in machine language (binary numbers). The differences in program listing methods are discussed further in Secs. 1–16 and 1–17.

Initially, the program counter is set to instruction address 0001 by a signal from the peripheral typewriter keyboard (via the keyboard

Instruction Address	Program stored in Computer: Operation Code	Data Address	Explanation
0001	3A	1001	CAD (clear and add). Erase any number remaining in the accumulator from a previous operation. Bring the contents of address 1001(t) to the accumulator.
0002	3D	1001	MUL (multiply). Multiply the number in the accumulator by the number at address 1001. (The result is t^2.)
0003	3D	1030	MUL (multiply). Multiply the number in the accumulator by the number at address 1030 (g). (The result is gt^2.)
0004	3E	1201	DIV (divide). Divide the number in the accumulator by the number at address 1201 (2). (The result is $gt^2/2$.)
0005	3F	2001	STO (Store). Store the number in the accumulator at address 2001.
0006	7A	2001	PRT (print). Print out data stored at address 2001.
0007	00		HLT. The microcomputer is directed to halt.

Fig. 1–30. LENKMICROCOMP program for falling-body problem

decoder, I/O IC, and data bus and/or control lines). The instruction at that address (which happens to be op code 3A) tells the microprocessor to clear the accumulator to zero, and then add the number found at data address 1001 (which is decimal 5, or t).

In some microprocessors, this operation can be accomplished in one machine cycle, since part of the byte at address 0001 is the op code (3A) and part is the address (1001) at which the data to be addressed resides. This second part of the byte is described as the *operand* in some microprocessor literature (since the second part is to be operated on by the instruction or op code).

In our microprocessor, the operation is accomplished in two machine cycles (one for the op code and one for the data or operand address). However, the program counter in our microprocessor advances only one step (to instruction address 0002), even though two machine cycles are required.

The instruction at address 0002 (which is op code 3D) tells the microprocessor to multiply the number in the accumulator by the number found at data address 1001. This is the same data address used in the previous step, and contains a data byte equal to decimal 5. The result in the accumulator is now 5×5, or 25, or t^2. Again, two machine cycles are used (one for instruction and one for data), and the program counter advances to instruction address 0003.

The instruction at address 0003 (again op code 3D) tells the microprocessor to multiply the number in the accumulator by the number found at data address 1030 (which is decimal 32, or g). The result in the accumulator is now 25×32, or decimal 800, or gt^2, and the program counter advances to instruction address 0004.

The instruction at address 0004 (now op code 3E) tells the microprocessor to divide the number in the accumulator by the number found at data address 1201 (which is decimal 2). The result is now $gt^2/2$, or decimal 400, which is the answer to our problem (the body will fall 400 ft in 5 s). The program counter advances to instruction address 0005.

The instruction at address 0005 (now op code 3F) tells the microprocessor to store the number appearing in the accumulator at address 2001. The program counter advances to instruction address 0006, which tells the microprocessor to print out the result at address 2001 on the peripheral typewriter (via the data bus, I/O IC, and keyboard decoder). The operator thus has a permanent record of the answer. In the case of a video terminal, the answer appears on the CRT screen or display. After the printout, the program counter advances to instruction address 0007, which directs the microprocessor to halt.

1–15.5 Special Program Instructions

In addition to the routing instructions for our LENKMICROCOMP system, typical examples of which are shown in Fig. 1–29, there are a number of instructions that help make the microcomputer a flexible, decision-making machine. These are the *branch* instructions (also known as jump, skip, or transfer instructions) shown in Fig. 1–31. These instructions direct the microcomputer to leave the main program at some designated point and, under proper conditions, branch or jump to some other designated point in the program. This is sometimes known as a branch or subroutine *call*.

For example, assume that op code 20 and address 0033 appear at a certain point of the program, say at instruction address 0011. The instruction (op code 20) tells the microprocessor to leave the main program at this point and branch or jump to address 0033. However, the program counter first increments by 1 to address 0012. The contents of the program counter (0012) are then put into an address in an unoccupied area of memory, usually called the *stack*. The stack thus saves the address of the instruction to be executed after the branch routine is completed.

With the address of the next step in the main program safely stored in memory, the program counter goes to the address specified by the branch instruction (0033 in our case). After the instruction at 0033 is performed, the microprocessor follows, in sequence, instructions at addresses 0034,0035, and so on, until the last address of the branch instruction is reached. This last address usually contains an instruction to return to the main program. Such an instruction need specify no address. When the microprocessor receives a return instruction, the microprocessor replaces the current contents of the program counter with the address stored in the stack (0012). This causes the microprocessor to resume execution of the original program at the point immediately following the original branch instruction.

Alphabetic (Mnemonic) Representation	Numerical Representation		Meaning of Instruction
	Hex	Binary	
BRA	20	0010 0000	Branch, unconditionally
BRN	21	0010 0001	Branch, on negative
BRP	22	0010 0010	Branch, on positive

Fig. 1–31. Branch op codes for the LENKMICROCOMP

Conditional and Unconditional Branches. The preceding is an example of an *unconditional branch* instruction. The other two branch instructions shown in Fig. 1–30, BRN (op code 21) and BRP (op code 22), are examples of *conditional branch* instructions. If, for example, op code 21 and address 0033 appear in the program, it means that, if the number in a certain counter or register is negative, the microprocessor must branch to address 0033, perform the instruction, and proceed (in sequence) from there. If the number is not negative, the microprocessor is to ignore the branch instruction and proceed with the original program. The BRP instruction is the same as the BRN, except that branching is to occur if the number is positive. Otherwise, the branch instruction is ignored.

1–15.6 Microcomputer Operation Cycle

Once the program has been entered (or *loaded*) into memory (instructions permanently programmed into ROM, data bytes temporarily entered into RAM via the peripheral typewriter), the microcomputer is ready to go automatically through the program cycle. Each cycle has two alternate phases: the *instruction* phase (or instruction *fetch* as it may be called), and the *execution* phase. After these two phases have been completed, the cycle is repeated. The duration of each phase is determined by a fixed number of clock pulses. Typically, there are eight clock pulses per machine cycle. Each phase may require one or more machine cycles.

The combined fetch and execution of a single instruction is referred to as an *instruction cycle*. The portion of a cycle identified with a clearly defined activity is called a *state*. The interval between clock pulses is referred to as a *clock period,* as discussed in Sec. 1–14. Typically one or more clock periods are necessary for the completion of a state, and there are several states in a cycle. The flow diagram of the LENKMICROCOMP operation cycle is shown in Fig. 1–32.

Instruction or Fetch Phase. The first instruction fetch is initiated by a start command. In our case, this command is initiated by the peripheral typewriter. The start command sets the first instruction address (0001) into the *program counter.* The instruction phase of the operation cycle starts when this address is transferred to the *address register.*

Note that, as information is transferred from one storage location to another, the information is not erased from the original location unless specifically so ordered. Thus, in our example, the address of the first instruction word appears in both the program counter and address

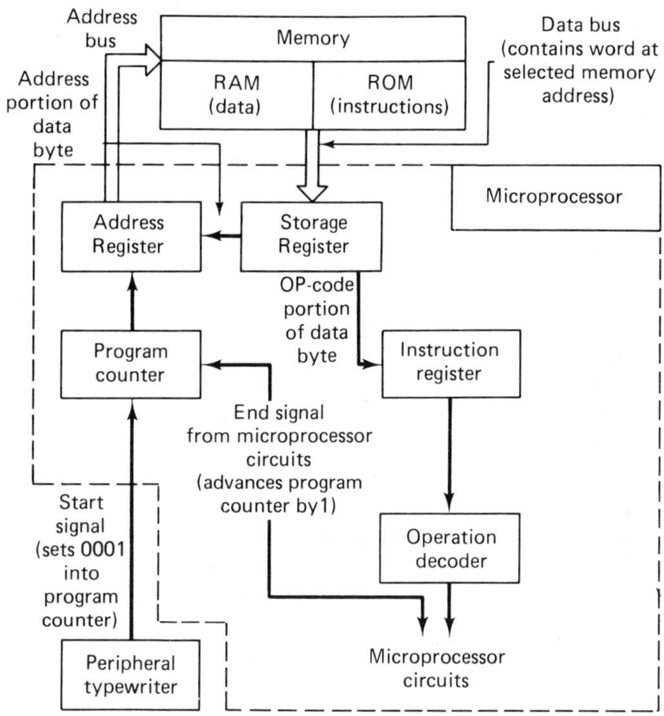

Fig. 1–32. Flow diagram of LENKMICROCOMP operation cycle

register. On the other hand, when new information is placed in a storage location, any previous information stored at that location is first erased. (Generally, registers and counters are cleared to zero before the new information is applied.)

The output of the address register is applied to memory via the address bus. The word at the selected address in memory is transferred to the *storage register* via the data bus. From the storage register, the op code portion of the word is transferred to the *instruction register.* Here the word is decoded by the operation decoder, and the microprocessor circuits perform the indicated instruction. Also from the storage register, the portion of the word that contains the address of the data to be used is transferred to the address register, first erasing the information previously stored there. This completes the instruction phase of the cycle.

Execution Phase. The execution phase starts when the data address placed in the address register during the instruction phase is applied to memory via the address bus. The data word at the selected address in memory is transferred to the storage register via the data bus. The data byte is then processed in accordance with the instruction (still in the instruction register). When the processing is finished, an *end signal* or *processing complete* signal advances the program counter by 1 (to 0002 in our case). The program counter now contains the address of the next instruction, and the instruction fetch or phase can start.

This completes the execution phase of the operation cycle. The cycle is repeated over and over again, the instruction phase alternating with the execution phase for each cycle, until the entire program is complete.

In the case of a branch operation, the op code portion of the instruction word is that of the branch instruction, and the operand portion is the address of the next instruction to be followed if branching is to take place. Under such conditions, this address is placed in the program counter, replacing the address already there, as described in Sec. 1–15.5. The microcomputer will then follow the branch program until a return to the original program is instructed.

We have just described the complete operation cycle of the LENKMICROCOMP. Different microcomputers may have different methods for going through the cycle, but the basic principles of operation are essentially the same for all microcomputers.

1–15.7 Subroutines, Libraries, and Nesting

Practically every instruction to the microprocessor involves a routine series of steps. Thus, to add two 8-bit numbers, for example, the LSD must be added first. If there is a carry, the carry must be added to the next significant bits. Then these bits must be added. If there is another carry, this carry must also be added to the MSD, and then they must be added. Although this series of calculations is complete within itself, the series may only be part of a larger program.

Since the microprocessor can only follow instructions, this routine series of steps must be included in the program. However, to save the user's time, this series of steps is listed in the microprocessor literature. Such listings or general-purpose sets of instructions are called *libraries, routines,* or *subroutines*. Often, the term *libraries* is given to a group of routines.

A typical subroutine might include all the steps necessary to find square root, sines, cosines, logarithms, and so on. If these types of calculations are repeated throughout the program, the programmer may prepare a special program for each of them and store the program in memory. Usually, subroutines are handled as a branch or jump. Then, when the programmer calls for a routine, the microprocessor is given the branch op code and the address of the first branch instruction, as discussed in Sec. 1–15.5.

Subroutines are often *nested*. That is, one subroutine calls a second subroutine. The second may call a third, and so on. This is acceptable, as long as the microcomputer has enough capacity to store the necessary return addresses, and the microprocessor is capable of doing so. The maximum depth of nesting is determined by the depth of the stack (or reserve memory). If the stack has space for storing three return addresses, then three levels of subroutines may be accommodated.

1–15.8 Interrupts

Most microprocessors have some provision for interrupts. Generally, interrupts are used for communications with peripheral equipment. For example, assume that the LENKMICROCOMP is processing a large volume of data, portions of which are to be printed on the peripheral typewriter. The microcomputer can produce one 8-bit data byte output (or one alphabet character) for each machine cycle, but it may take the typewriter the equivalent of several machine cycles (or several dozen) to actually print out the character specified by the data byte. The microprocessor could then remain idle, waiting until the typewriter can accept the next data byte.

If the microprocessor is capable of interrupts, the microprocessor can output a data byte, and then return to data processing. When the typewriter is again ready to accept the next data byte, the typewriter can request an interrupt. When the microprocessor acknowledges the interrupt, the main program is suspended, and the microprocessor automatically branches to a routine that will output the next data byte. (This is known as *servicing* the peripheral device, or servicing the interrupt.) After the data byte is delivered to the typewriter and the corresponding character is printed, the microprocessor continues with main program execution. Note that this is, in principle, quite similar to a branch or subroutine call, except that the jump is initiated externally (by the typewriter) rather than by the program.

There are more complex interrupt schemes, particularly when several peripherals must share the same microprocessor. Usually, such interrupts involve assigning priority levels (*prioritizing* the peripherals). One approach (called the *polled* method) is for the microprocessor to check each peripheral, in turn, on a given priority basis, for a service request. The polled method is generally wasteful, since part of the main program is used up whether the peripherals want service or not. It is generally more efficient for the microprocessor to stop only when the peripheral sends an interrupt. The peripherals can still be assigned priorities. For example, if peripheral A is first priority and B is second priority, A will be serviced before B if both peripherals make a service request simultaneously. B will be serviced first only if A is not making a request.

1–16. MACHINE LANGUAGE VERSUS ASSEMBLY LANGUAGE PROGRAMMING

A microprocessor may be programmed by writing a sequence of instructions in binary code that the microprocessor can interpret directly. For example, referring back to Fig. 1–29, the instruction for addition is binary 00111011. If this byte is programmed into memory, and then appears on the data bus when the microprocessor data port is open, the microprocessor will add (probably the contents of one register to another). This is *machine language programming,* and is useful only where the program to be written is short.

At best, writing a program in machine language is a tedious task and subject to many errors. The task of writing a program can be speeded up and errors minimized when hex is used instead of binary (both hex and binary are shown in Fig. 1–29). However, hex coding has two major limitations.

First, hex coding is not self-documenting. That is, the code itself does not give any indication in human terms of the operation to be performed. The user must learn each code or constantly use a *program reference card or sheet* to convert.

Second, hex coding is *absolute.* That is, the program will work only when stored at a specific location in memory. This is because branch or jump instructions in the program reference specific addresses elsewhere in the program. Consider the example shown in Fig. 1–33, which is the listing of an eight-step program written in machine code (but in hex format). Steps 0007 and 0008 of Fig. 1–33 make reference to step (or address) 0004. If the program is moved for some reason, step 0008 must be changed to refer to the new address of step 0004.

1–16.1 Assembly Language

The problems just discussed can be overcome by writing the program in *assembly language* in which alphanumeric symbols are used to represent machine language codes, branch addresses, and so on. For example, the instruction to increment the contents of register 0 becomes

Step Number	Machine Code (Hex Format)	Explanation
0	1011 1000	Load decimal 32 in
1	0010 0000	register R0
2	1011 1010	Load decimal 5 in
3	0000 0101	register R2
4	0000 1001	Load Port 1 to accumulator
5	1111 0000	Transfer contents of accumulator to register addressed by register 0
6	0001 1000	Increment R0 by 1
7	1110 1010	Decrement register 2
8	0000 0100	by 1, if result is zero continue to step 9, if not go to step 4
9	---	
10	---	

Fig. 1–33. Basic eight-step program written in machine code arranged in hex format

INC R0 instead of hex 18, giving the user the meaning of the instructions at a glance. Our example program of Fig. 1–33 can then be written in assembly language as shown in Fig. 1–34.

The use of assembly language makes it much easier to write a program, but it results in a program that is useless to the microprocessor (which operates only with binary numbers). One way to overcome this problem is to write the program in assembly language, but include the hex code (as shown in Fig. 1–34). Then when you enter the program

Step Number	Hex Code		Assembly Code
0	B8		MOV R0, #32
1	20		
2	BA		MOV R2, #05
3	05		
4	09	INP:	IN A, P1
5	F0		MOV @R0, A
6	18		INC R0
7	EA		DJNZ R2, INP
8	04		

Fig. 1–34. Basic eight-step program written in assembly language, but including hex code

into the microcomputer, it is relatively easy to convert from hex to binary. Of course, this requires that you *remember both the hex code and the assembly code* for each instruction of the microprocessor. While it is not a bad idea for you to learn all the hex codes, it does require more remembering (or looking up) on your part, and thus increases the chance for error.

A more convenient method is to *assemble* programs using an *assembler,* which is a program that converts from one code to another. In our case, the assembler converts from a verbal-type assembly code to binary numbers. In practice, the assembler program is entered into another microcomputer (or any computer or computer-like device); you write the program for your microcomputer on paper (known as the *source program*), and then you enter your microcomputer program into the other computer (known as a *host* computer), which prints out a program (usually on paper tape or disks) in binary form. This program is known as the *object program;* it can be entered directly into your microcomputer from the paper tape reader or disk.

When a different computer is used for assembly, the program is known as a *cross-assembler.* It is also possible to use *time-sharing* services for assembly, and there are special devices and equipment developed by manufacturers for assembly of their microcomputer programs.

1–16.2 Typical Assembly or Source Code

The first statement in Fig. 1–34 can be verbalized as follows: move to register 0 the decimal number 32. Move instructions should always be structured such that the destination is first, and the source is second. The sign "#" indicates that the source is "immediate" data (or data contained in the following byte of memory). In this case, the data byte is specified as decimal 32. Some assemblers will accept hex (or even binary) notation. Note that the assembly code of Fig. 1–34 is based on the INTEL MCS-48 system (described in the author's *Handbook of Microprocessors, Microcomputers, and Minicomputers).* It is essential that you learn the assembly codes and language of your particular microprocessor system, just as you must learn the instruction set.

The input instruction INA,P1 has the same form as a MOV instruction, indicating that the contents of port 1 are to be transferred to the accumulator. In front of the input instruction is an *address label* INP. This label allows the program to be written in a form independent of its final location in program memory, since the branch instructions at the end of the program can refer to this label, rather than to a specific address. This is a very important advantage of assembly language programs over machine language,since instructions can be added or deleted throughout the program during debugging, without requiring that any jump address be changed.

The next instruction, MOV @R0,A, can be verbalized as "move to the data memory location addressed by R0 the contents of the accumulator." The @ sign indicates an indirect operation whereby the contents of either register 0 or register 1 act as a pointer to the data memory location to be operated on.

The last instruction is a "decrement and jump if not zero" instruction, which acts in combination with the specified register as a *loop counter.* (A *loop* is a sequence of instructions in which the last instruction is a jump or return back to the first instruction.) In this case, register 2 is loaded with 5 initially, and then decremented by 1 each time the loop is executed. If the result of the decrement is not zero, the program jumps to INP and executes another input operation. The fifth time through the loop the result is zero, and execution goes to whatever routine follows the DJNZ instruction.

Advanced Assemblers. In addition to the normal features provided by assemblers, more advanced assemblers offer such advantages as *evaluation of expressions* at assembly time, *conditional assembly,* and *macro* capability.

Evaluation of Expressions. Certain assemblers allow the use of arithmetic expressions and multiple symbols in the operand portion of the instructions. For example, the assembler for the INTEL MCS-48 accepts instructions such as ADD A, # ALFA*BETA/2.

ALFA and BETA are two previously defined symbols. At assembly time, the expression ALFA*BETA/2 will be evaluated and the resulting number (which is the average of ALFA and BETA) is treated as immediate data, and designated as the second byte of the ADD immediate instruction. This expression allows the immediate data of this instruction to be defined in a single statement, and eliminates the need for a third symbol equal to ALFA*BETA/2.

Conditional Assembly. Conditional assembly allows the programmer to select only certain portions of the assembly language (source) program for conversion to machine (object) code at assembly. This allows various debugging routines to be included in the program during development. Using conditional assembly, these routines can be left out when the final assembly is done. Conditional assembly also allows several versions of one basic program to be generated by selecting various portions of a larger program at assembly time.

Macro Assembly. A macro instruction is essentially a symbol that is recognized by the assembler to represent a specific sequence of several standard instructions. A macro is a shorthand way of generating the same sequence of instructions at several locations in a program without having to rewrite the sequence each time that it is used. For example, a typical macro instruction might be one that performs a subtract operation. Some microprocessors do not have a single instruction that performs subtraction but require several instructions such as the following:

COMP A (complement the accumulator)

ADD A REG (add the contents of register to accumulator)

COMP A (complement the accumulator)

This routine subtracts a register from the accumulator and leaves the result in the accumulator. The sequence can be defined as a macro with the name SUB, and can specify a register by number (such as register 1, 2, 3, etc.). To subtract register 3 from the accumulator, the programmer writes SUB R3, and the assembler will automatically insert the three instructions, with R3 substituted for REG.

Once the assembly language source code is written, it can be converted to a machine-executable object code (in binary form) by passing the source code through the assembler program.

1–17. DEVELOPMENT OF A MICROPROCESSOR-BASED SYSTEM

Although debugging, rather than troubleshooting, is more often required during development of a microprocessor-based system, a troubleshooter should have a basic knowledge of the typical development cycle. Of course, the exact procedures for development of a "typical" microcomputer are different for each case, and depend on such factors as what support equipment, and design aids (simulators, emulators,etc.) and support software (assembler programs, debug programs, etc.) are available from the manufacturer of the microprocessor.

Those systems that include a very complete line of hardware, software, design aids, and so on, are said to be *pervasive*. When a particular item of hardware or software is very effective (for assembly, debugging, testing, troubleshooting, etc.), it is said to be a *powerful* tool. Here we shall consider a typical microprocessor-based system development approach.

1–17.1 Learning the Microprocessor and System Components

The first step in developing any microprocessor-based system is to become familiar with the microprocessor and all of the system components. Most microprocessor manufacturers also produce a line of compatible system components such as RAMs, ROMs, and I/O units. The microprocessor is the most important component, and the learning process should start there. As a minimum, you must learn all the microprocessor instructions, since the entire system compatibility is based on what the microprocessor can and cannot do. Next learn the capabilities and limitations of the other system components (how many bits and addresses in the ROM and RAM, how many data and control lines available in the I/O IC, etc.). This sort of information is given in the manufacturer's user manuals and/or data sheets.

1–17.2 Hardware Characteristics

Do not overlook the hardware aspect of the microprocessor and other components. For example, what power supplies are required? What is the power dissipation for each IC in the system? What are the operating and storage temperature ranges? How many ROMs, RAMs, and I/Os can be driven by one microprocessor? How long does it take to process each instruction? (This will tell you how long it will take to process an entire program.) This sort of information is given in design manuals and/or data sheets.

1–17.3 Manufacturer's Training Courses

Some microprocessor manufacturers sponsor training courses or programs for their systems. Generally, these are 2- or 3-day sessions held at the manufacturer's facilities or at selected cities (or at customer's facilities for large groups). If you have access to such programs, you should take advantage of them, since they will provide hands-on experience. Also, you will have all information and literature for a particular microprocessor system at your fingertips. These training courses are especially helpful for those with no previous computer experience whatsoever.

1–17.4 Writing Sample Programs

Once you are familiar with the microprocessor and related system components (either through self-instruction or manufacturer's training), the next step is to gain a better feel for what a microprocessor can do in your own applications by writing several exercise programs that perform basic functions. For example, in a typical microprocessor program, you may require such things as I/O routines,delays, counting functions, look-up tables, arithemetic functions, and logical operations.

Once you have made up routines to solve these functions, you can retain the programs to serve as a set of building blocks for future applications. For example, when you have developed a routine for subtraction that is compatible with your particular microprocessor, you can use the same routine for all future programs.

1–17.5 Defining System Functions with a Flow Chart

A flow chart, similar to that shown in Fig. 1–28, is probably the simplest method of defining the functions to be accomplished by a program. Thus, when you think you thoroughly understand your microprocessor, the system functions to be implemented by a program can be defined using the flow-chart method. Of course, the flow chart must include all the functions to be accomplished and the sequence in which the microprocessor must execute these functions. Once the system application is flow charted, you can identify and analyze all the critical time-related functions, and then write a sample program to verify that performance requirements can be met.

Keep in mind that there are usually many, many ways to accomplish the same overall system function, using the same microprocessor, but with different programs. Of course, each program will have a different number of steps. Generally, the shortest program is the most desirable for obvious reasons. Short programs require the least amount of memory (and thus require a minimum of ROM/RAM ICs), resulting in the fastest system and minimizing the chance for error.

1–17.6 Defining Hardware Configuration

When you have defined the system function with a flow chart and written a sample or trial program, the next step involves defining the hardware required to implement the function. For example, input/output capability must be defined in terms of number of inputs, number of outputs, bidirectional lines, latching or nonlatching I/O, output drive capabilites, and so on. Likewise, the number of words of RAM storage required for intermediate results and data storage must be determined. (Some systems require a battery backup to maintain the RAM data in case of power failure.)

Amount of Program Memory. Typically, the most difficult hardware parameter to define is the amount of memory needed to store the program. (Program memory is stored in the ROM.) Although previously written exercise programs will make this "guesstimate" more accurate, a generous amount of breathing room should be allowed in program memory until coding is complete and the exact requirements are known.

Keep in mind that it may be possible to eliminate a few program steps (develop a new, shorter program) to match available memory hardware. Also, there may be hardware to replace programs. For example, many special functions such as serial communications or keyboard/display interfaces, may be implemented with programs. However, there may be compatible I/O IC that will do the same job. As a trade-off, it may be more advantageous to use these ICs rather than the programs, particularly where such functions place a severe load on the microprocessor in terms of time or program memory. In simple terms, it may be more advantageous to use a special-purpose I/O IC, rather than a longer program (which slows down system performance and requires a larger memory). Such factors should always be considered when defining microprocessor hardware.

1–17.7 Writing the Program Code

Once the system function and hardware have been defined, the next step is to convert the program to a machine code that is suitable for the microprocessor. (This is sometimes known as *generating the code*.) An experienced programmer/designer is often able to generate the code during the same time that the hardware is being defined and assembled (printed-circuit card layout, power supply, etc.). Then the trial program can be entered in memory and tested for bugs immediately.

There are several options available when it is time to write the program machine code. Unfortunately, not everyone has all these options available to them. Obviously, the designer/programmer with a complete set of manufacturer's design aids (both hardware and software) has an advantage over the student/hobbyist who has nothing but minimum hardware and possibly some data sheets. Of course, designer/programmers need every advantage, since they do not have the luxury of making many mistakes over an infinite period of time, as does the student/hobbyist.

There are two basic approaches for writing the program code: hardware and software.

1–17.8 Basic Hardware Approach

The most primitive approach to program codes is to write each step in machine language (binary code), and enter each step in memory using machine language. (This is the approach most common for the student/hobbyist.) As an example, once a trial program has been written and the binary code for each step determined (possibly using hex as shorthand), the program can be entered (programmed) into an erasable or alterable PROM using a basic circuit similar to that of Fig. 1–23. Then the hardware (microprocessor, ROM, RAM, I/O, keyboard/display, etc.) is interconnected in "breadboard" (experimental) form, power is applied, and the program is tested for bugs.

The PROM can be erased and reprogrammed as necessary until the program is free of bugs. Then the erasable PROM can be replaced by a permanent PROM, which is programmed using the desired (bug-free) program. The final ROM is connected in the system, and the program is given a final test. At this point, you have a complete, functioning microprocessor-based sytem or microcomputer.

1–17.9 Sophisticated Hardware Approach

The basic hardware approach described in Sec. 1–17.8 is slow, tedious, and generally inefficient, except for very simple programs (and is the system followed by the average student/hobbyist). Most major microprocessor manufacturers provide design aid hardware to simplify and speed up development of a microprocessor-based system. Such hardware includes *simulators, emulators,* and *evaluation kits*. Some of these design aids also include software or are a combination of software and hardware.

A typical hardware design aid includes a microprocessor, ROM, RAM, and I/O, as well as some form of keyboard/display to enter and read out programs. All these devices are interconnected on a board or chassis, possibly using plug-in PC (printed circuit) boards and ICs. In effect, a complete microprocessor-based system (including a keyboard/display), interconnecting wiring, and power supply are provided, using compatible ICs of the same manufacturer. The hardware is supplied with a user's manual, which includes operating instructions and sample programs. The advantage of such a system is obvious. You can develop a complete, functioning system (including the programs to meet your application needs) without having to assemble various hardware components on a trial-and-error basis. Once you have the designed system and the debugged programs, you can order the exact hardware from the manufacturer, including how you want the ROM programmed.

1–17.10 Software Design Aid Approach

There are about as many software design aids for microprocessor systems as there are microprocessor manufacturers. All these design aids use some form of assembler (or possibly a macroassembler) as described in Sec. 1–16.1. In some cases, the assembler is used in conjunction with the manufacturer's design aid hardware. That is, you can write the program in assembly language, enter the program in the design aid hardware, and end up with a machine language program (usually on paper tape or magnetic disks). In other cases, the software is designed for use with in-house computers. (The assembler is actually a cross-assembler used with a host computer; Sec. 1–16.1.) In other cases, the assembler is used with time-sharing computer systems.

1–17.11 Production of a Microprocessor-Based System

Once you have a working program, a preproduction phase usually follows in which several prototype systems (possibly with microprocessors of different manufacturers) are evaluated in simulated situations or in actual field operation. During this period, the use of an erasable ROM allows quick alteration of the program when problems (bugs) or suggested changes arise. Depending upon the magnitude and number of future changes anticipated, the first production units may be shipped with an erasable PROM. However, for maximum cost reduction potential in high-volume applications, a custom ROM (programmed at the factory by the manufacturer) is usually necessary. This is an easy transition if two conditons are met: (1) the custom ROM must be compatible in electrical terminal configuration (pin-for-pin) and in machine code, and (2) you must have retained a paper tape of the program in machine code (as you will if you follow the hardware and/or software approaches of Secs. 1–17.9 and 1–17.10). Generally, you can ship the paper tape to the ROM manufacturer along with your order.

Chapter 2

INTRODUCTION TO PERIPHERAL EQUIPMENT

This chapter is devoted entirely to the peripheral equipment used with microcomputers. Such equipment is essentially the same as for larger, conventional computers and minicomputers. As one example, a typical microcomputer can be operated with a video terminal (keyboard and display CRT) or with an electric typewriter or TTY. Likewise, a microcomputer can be used with the console-type magnetic tape recorders (or, more likely, with magnetic disks and tape casettes) for high-volume storage of data. Of course, this requires suitable I/O devices or software programs (or a combination of both) that match the peripheral characteristics to those of the microcomputer.

As in the case of Chapter 1, this chapter serves as a refresher for those already familiar with computer basics. However, the descriptions in this chapter are kept to an elementary level, since you are interested in practical troubleshooting (not theory), and so that the descriptions will apply to the greatest number of microcomputer systems. More detailed descriptions of peripheral circuits are discussed in Chapter 4.

2–1. THE NEED FOR PERIPHERAL EQUIPMENT

The primary function of peripheral equipment is to translate human instructions and data into microcomputer language (binary data bytes) and microcomputer language into a form suitable for readout. In effect, the peripheral equipment (in conjunction with the I/O IC) reconciles the "outer world" with the microcomputer.

There are two major reasons for this reconciliation or translation. First, the outer world rarely expresses anything in binary data bytes. (Generally, the outer world uses numbers, letter, words, etc.) However, the microcomputer always uses binary data bytes (usually in pulse form). Second, the microcomputer operates at extremely high speeds when compared to the outer world. For example, in the fraction of a second that it takes to strike a key of an input typewriter, a microcomputer can perform hundreds or thousands of operations.

2–1.1 Peripherals in Data Processing

To take advantage of available microcomputer speed when used in data-processing applications, the information to be processed is prepared in advance and stored. Common storage forms include paper tape, punch cards, and magnetic tape, drums, or disks. The basic relationship between a data-processing microcomputer and peripheral devices is shown in Fig. 2–1.

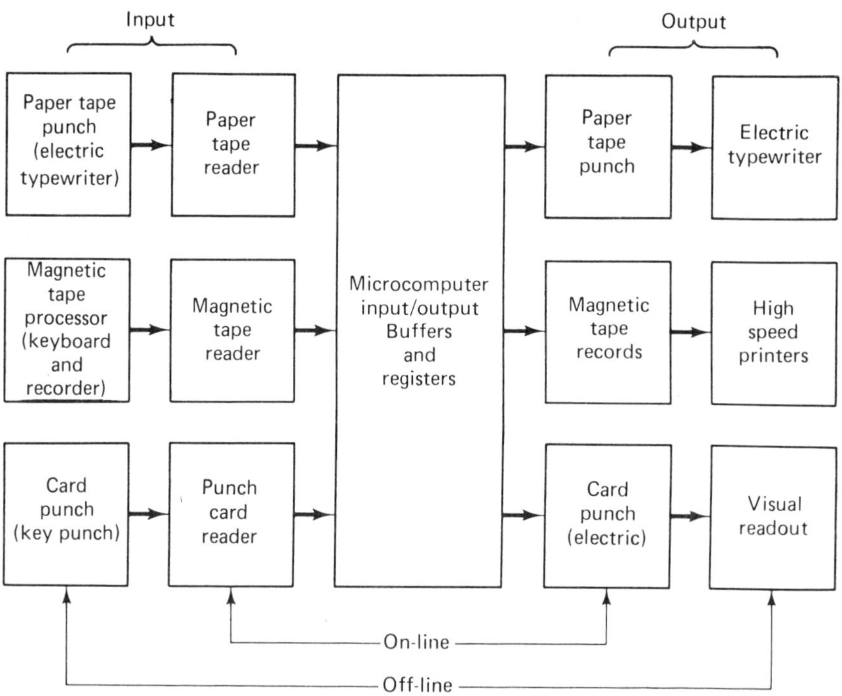

Fig. 2–1. Basic relationship between the microcomputer and input/output accessories in data-processing applications

Note that the terms *on line* and *off line* are used to indicate *direct* and *indirect* connection to the microcomputer. For example, a paper-tape punch that is operated by an electric typewriter is an off-line device for indirect input. The paper-tape reader that converts holes in the paper tape into pulses applied to the microcomputer is an on-line device for direct input. Information is put into the off-line devices by human operators. The on-line devices then automatically convert the information into data bytes (in pulse form) for application to the microcomputer. On-line devices require only that the human operator load the tapes or cards and turn on the unit.

With a data-processing system such as the one shown in Fig. 2–1, the microcomputer does not have to wait for the operator to type out messages, since the microcomputer can read directly from the tapes or cards. Large quantities of tapes or cards can be made in advance by many operators handling different problems on separate typewriters. The microcomputer can look at all the tapes or cards from the appropriate reader. After processing, the microcomputer directs the on-line tape or card punch (or magnetic recorder) to store the processed data. The tapes or cards containing the processed data are then read out on output printers or typewriters (or other visual display devices).

These output readout devices are not as fast as the microcomputer. However, the devices are very fast in comparison to human operators and have a chance of keeping pace, since many microcomputer calculations require repeated steps.

2–1.2 Peripherals in Real-Time Processing

Not all microcomputers are used for data processing. In fact, most high-volume data-processing systems still use larger computers and minicomputers. Many microcomputers operate on a real-time basis in which the microcomputer stands ready to solve problems presented by the human operator. When human operators must command a microcomputer, a manual keyboard (as found on an electric typewriter or TTY) is the simplest and most common form of input/output device. The commands are typed and applied directly to the microcomputer (in the form of data bytes). The processed output signals from the microcomputer then "type out" the answers on the same keyboard.

2–1.3 Peripherals in Process Control Applications

Many microcomputers receive continuously changing inputs and produce corresponding readouts. Microcomputers used to monitor (and control) industrial processes are an example. There are generally no off-line devices with such systems. Instead, these microcomputers receive inputs from *transducers* that convert such factors as process temperature, flow rate, and volume into electrical voltages. The voltages, which are *analogs* of the temperature, flow, and volume, are converted into data bytes by an *analog-to-digital* circuit (which is a form of decoder). The automatic readout from the microcomputer, in addition to providing a permanent record on a typewriter or printer, is also used to control the industrial process. At the microcomputer output, the data bytes are converted to a corresponding electrical voltage by a *digital-to-analog* circuit (another form of decoder). The output electrical voltages are then applied to control voltages, switches, valves, and so on, as needed to control the industrial process.

2–2. ELECTRIC TYPEWRITER OR TTY TERMINALS

Electric typewriters and TTYs provide both input and output for a microcomputer. Generally, the same I/O IC is used for both input and output functions.

2–2.1 Basic Input Circuit

Figure 2–2 shows the input relationship between a peripheral typewriter or TTY and a typical microcomputer. With any peripheral typewriter system, there must be circuits between the keyboard and the microcomputer input that (1) convert the data instructions into bytes that are compatible with the microcomputer circuits, and (2) store the bytes until they can be entered into the microcomputer circuits without disrupting normal operation. This process is sometimes referred to as a *service routine*.

The conversion is done by a decoder circuit, while the storage and timing is done by registers and buffers, as discussed in Chapter 1. The present design trend is to include the register and buffer functions in the I/O IC of the microcomputer, with the decoder function in the typewriter.

Note that the data bytes are transmitted in both parallel and serial form from the peripheral to the microcomputer. The parallel method is the fastest and requires the simplest I/O circuit in the microcomputer. However, TTY terminals generally transmit their data bytes over a *single* telephone line (or a pair of lines). Typically, eight lines, plus any control, flag, service request, or interrupt lines, are required for an 8-bit parallel system. Thus, TTYs (and all serial data transmission devices) require a special serial I/O IC (often called an *asynchronous* or *universal* I/O).

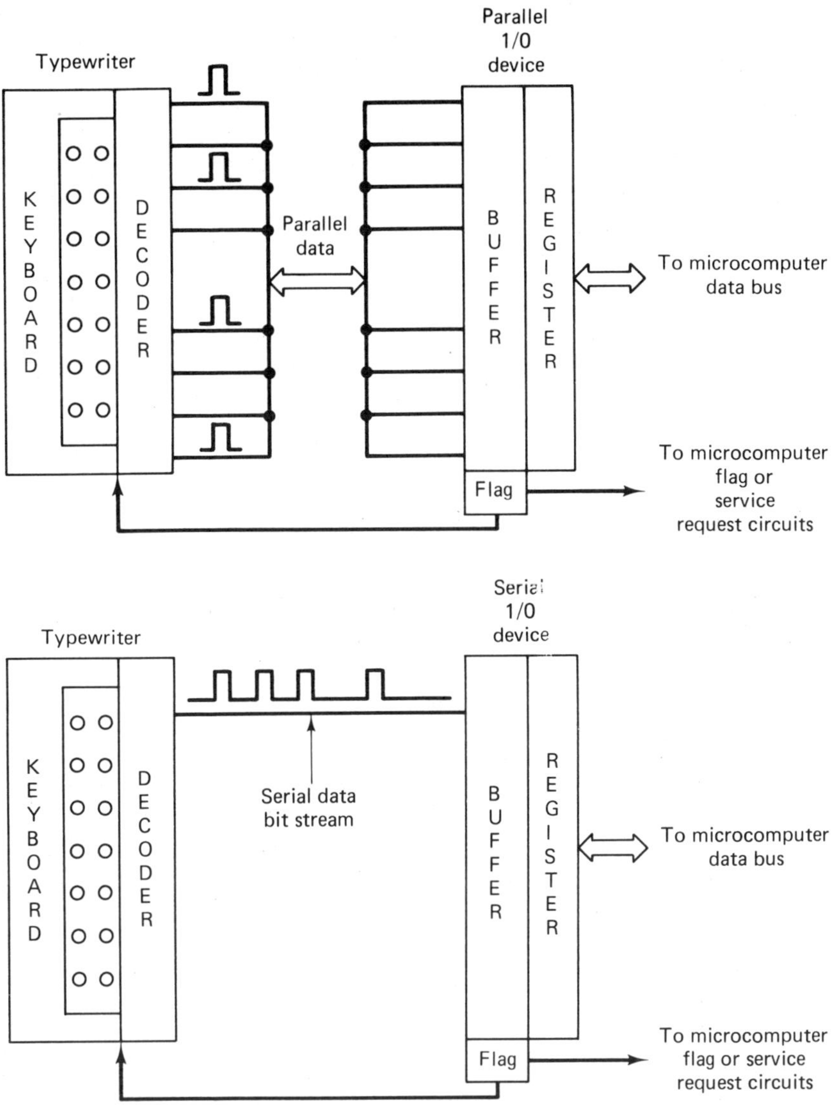

Fig. 2–2. Input relationship between a peripheral typewriter and a microcomputer for both serial and parallel operation

Serial Data Transmission. It is conventional to transmit serial data in a fixed format similar to that shown in Fig. 2–3. When a user strikes a key on the TTY keyboard (an M for example), the information denoting that character is converted to its ASCII code (4D in hex) and appears at the TTY output as a *serial data bit stream*. Note that each

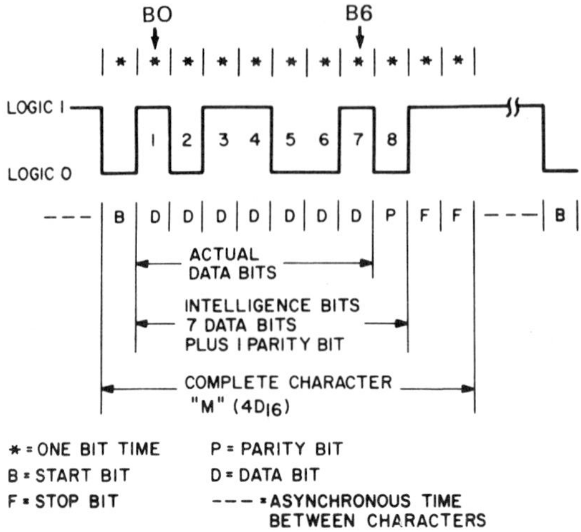

Fig. 2–3. TTY serial data transmission format (showing character M)

of the character data bits (b_0 through b_6) is identified on Fig. 2–3. The character (letter M in this case) is framed by a start bit B and two stop bits FF. By convention (or *protocol*), two stop bits are used for data transmitted at 10 characters per second, and one stop bit for higher data-transmission rates.

A parity bit P is also shown in Fig. 2–3. (Parity and its relation to the ASCII code are discussed in Sec. 1–8.8.) The parity bit is a 1 only if the seven data bits contain an odd number of 1s. Hence the total number of 1s in the eight intelligence bits (seven data bits plus one parity bit) is always an even number. This convention is called the *even parity option* for ASCII-coded data transmission (which is in general use for TTYs and most of the serial data-transmission devices). Since there are four bits (an even number) in the ASCII code for the letter M, the parity bit is a 0 in Fig. 2–3.

Input Timing Sequence. With either serial or parallel transmission, the data/instructions must pass from the typewriter to the microcomputer circuit in a precisely timed sequence. As shown in Fig. 2–2, the decoder output is applied to a register/buffer combination. The buffer is opened and closed by pulses or control signals from the microcomputer, in response to *service requests* (also called flags, interrupts, etc.) from the typewriter. This reconciles the high speed of the microcomputer with the slow speed of the typewriter. For example, assume that the buffer can be opened and closed 10,000 times per second, and that it takes 1 s for the typewriter key to be pressed and released. No matter at what time the data byte from the keyboard starts and stops, the buffer/register has thousands of times to read in, store, and read out the data byte to the microcomputer.

This combination of service-request signals and timing signals is necessary to prevent undesired conflict between the typewriter and microcomputer circuits. Assume, for example, that the microcomputer is performing a series of mathematical calculations on data bytes previously entered by the keyboard, and that the operator starts to enter more data. In the normal sequence, a service request is sent by the typewritier. (In practice, a service request is sent for each data byte, or each time a typewriter key is struck.) The service request indicates to the microcomputer that there is new information to be entered into the buffer. If old information in the buffer is reset to zero, and new data are entered and then read out to the microcomputer.

Now assume that the microcomputer is not ready to accept new information (previous data bytes are still being processed). Then the buffer accepts the new data, but does not pass them to the microcomputer until the circuits are ready. Keep in mind that, since the microcomputer operates at such a high speed, the operator does not have to "wait" until the computer is finished before striking the next key.

2–2.2 Basic Output Circuit

Microcomputer output circuits are essentially the reverse of input circuits. The output circuits to an electric typewriter or TTY must (1) convert the processed data bytes into a form (usually numbers, letters, words, etc.) that is compatible with the typewriter keys, and (2) synchronize the high-speed microprocessor output with that of the lower-speed typewriter.

As in the case of input, the conversion is done by a decoder circuit (usually within the typewriter), whereas the synchronization is done by the I/O buffer/register, which operates in response to a combination of microcomputer and typewriter signals.

Figure 2–4 shows the output relationship between a peripheral typewriter or TTY and a typical microcomputer. In the readout mode, the keys are operated by electrical voltages from the decoder. When the buffer/register is opened, the data byte is applied to the decoder which, in turn, applies this operating voltage to the appropriate typewriter key. This causes the appropriate key to strike and print out the corresponding character (number, letter, symbol, etc.).

In the normal sequence, a service request is sent by the typewriter. This indicates to the microcomputer that the keyboard is ready to receive data from the buffer. The register is set to zero, the new data

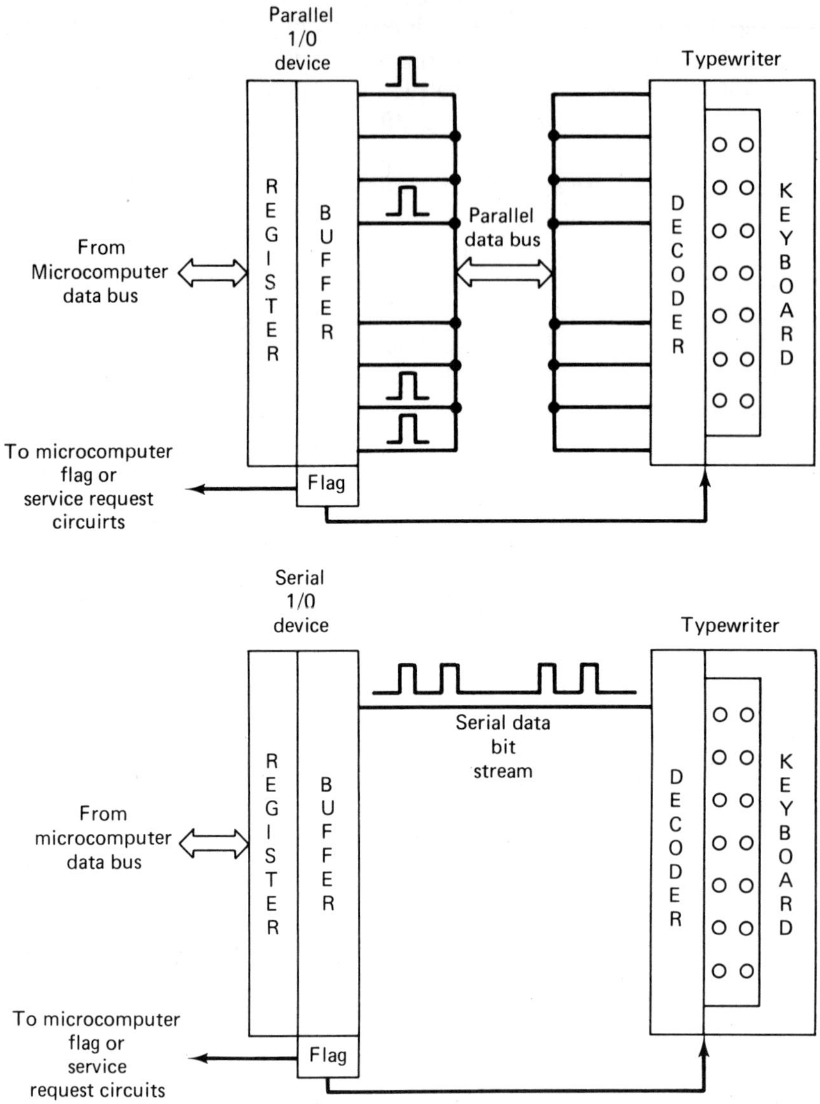

Fig. 2–4. Output relationship between a peripheral typewriter and a microcomputer for both serial and parallel operation

byte is entered from the microcomputer, the buffer is opened, and the data byte is passed to the decoder. In turn, the decoder operates the corresponding key.

It is obvious that the microcomputer can solve problems faster than the keyboard can type them out. This means that two conditions must occur. First, the output buffer must be held in the existing state long enough for the key to be struck. Second, the normal routine of the microcomputer must be interrupted so that the answers to several problems are not computed while the output buffer is held open. In actual practice, the interruption occurs at some convenient point in the microcomputer operation (usually at the end of a timing cycle).

2–3. VIDEO TERMINAL (KEYBOARD/CRT)

The video terminal can be used as an input/output device for microcomputers, particularly in inquiry/response situations where information is required for immediate use. Unless the CRT portion of the video terminal is attached to a printing device, no permanent record of displayed data is kept.

As shown in Fig. 2–5, the video terminal is essentially a cathode-ray tube or CRT (complete with high-voltage power supply and vertical/horizontal sweep circuits, similar to those used in television sets and oscilloscopes) plus a keyboard. Information is displayed on the face of the CRT immediately after it is received from the microcomputer or entered from the keyboard.

The input function of the video terminal is accomplished by the keyboard in a manner similar to that described for the basic input circuit (Sec. 2–2.1). That is, the keyboard output is converted into data bytes (in machine language suitable for the microcomputer) by a decoder (which is generally part of the video terminal).

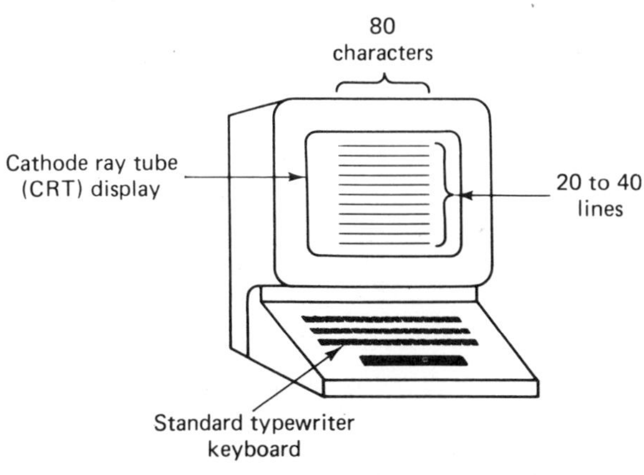

Fig. 2–5. Typical video terminal (CRT display/keyboard)

The output function is performed by the CRT. The horizontal and vertical sweep deflection circuits of the CRT are standard. The electron beam is swept across the CRT face several hundred (or thousand) times per second. Typically, the deflecting circuits sweep out 20 or 40 rows or horizontal lines of characters (letters, numbers, or symbols), with each line divided into 80 spaces (for 80 characters).

There are many systems used to produce the characters. Most video terminals use some type of *character generator,* usually in IC form. Such character generators are a form of decoder, and convert binary data bytes into electrical voltages that alter or manipulate the CRT electron beam as necessary to trace out characters on the screen.

2–3.1 Typical Character-Generator Operation

Figure 2–6 shows how one character generator operates. With this system, the characters are produced by modulating the CRT electron beam intensity with timing pulses that occur at precise intervals as the beam passes a given point on the CRT face. Pulse timing is controlled by outputs from the character generator.

The relationship of timing pulses to the horizontal and vertical deflection voltages is synchronized by master timing pulses. In the example shown, two vertical sweeps are required for each character. Thus, to produce 80 characters across one line, the master pulses must trigger 160 vertical sweeps for each horizontal sweep.

The master pulses are applied to a gate that is controlled (to modulate the electron beam) by operation of the character generator. In turn, the character generator receives input from the microcomputer output (usually from the I/O IC). In the absence of output from the character generator, no pulses pass to the CRT, the screen is blanked, and no characters appear, even though the vertical and horizontal deflection voltages are available. When there is a data byte at the microcomputer output, this data byte is applied to the character generator, unblanking the screen at appropriate points on the vertical and horizontal sweeps.

The relationships of the vertical and horizontal deflection voltages, together with the blanking and unblanking (modulation), are shown in Fig. 2–6b. The heavy lines on the vertical and horizontal sweeps indicate when the CRT is unblanked and producing a character (the numeral 8 in this case). For example, to form the upper-right side of the numeral 8 (arbitrarily labeled at time interval 1), the upper vertical deflection plate goes negative, causing the beam to move down. During the same time interval 1, the right horizontal plate also goes slightly negative, causing the beam to move slightly to the left. The beam is

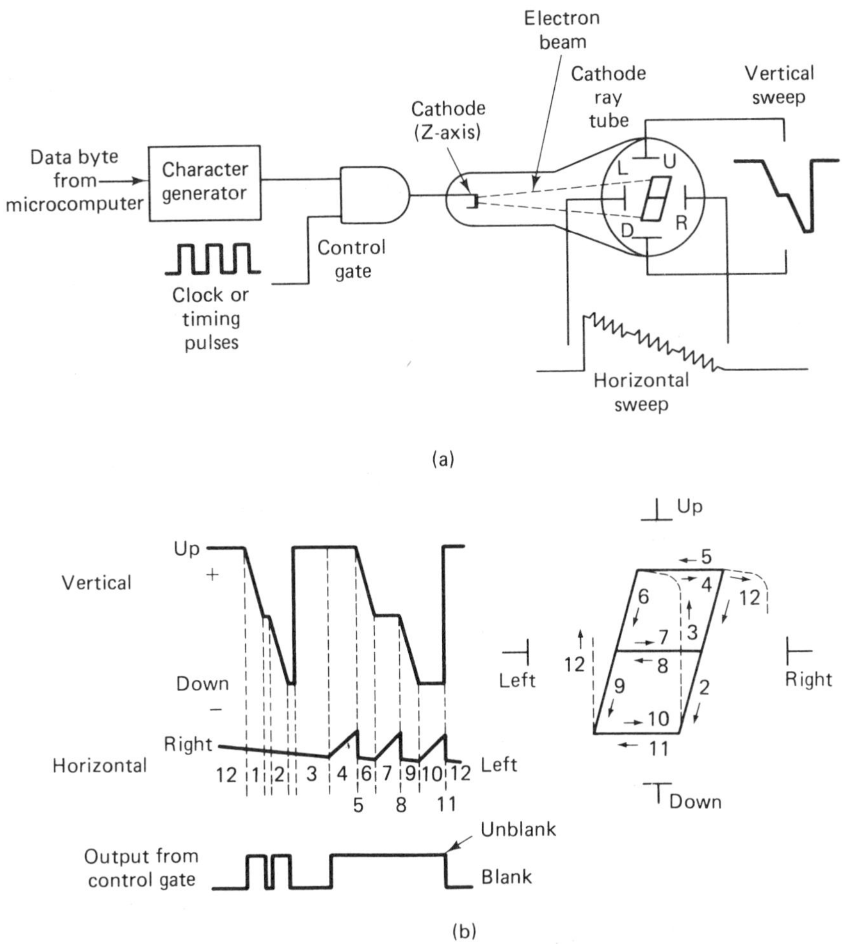

Fig. 2–6. How visual display is formed on video terminal

unbalanced during time interval 1, so the upper-right portion of the 8 is traced out.

The remaining segments of the numeral 8 can be traced out by comparing the status of the horizontal and vertical sweep voltages and the blanking condition for all time intervals during a complete character cycle (two vertical sweeps). Note that neither the vertical nor the horizontal sweep is perfectly linear.

In all video terminal systems, the persistence of the CRT screen is fairly short. This is necessary so that the readout is removed in a reasonable period of time (to permit new data bytes to be read in).

Some video terminals contain storage registers that permit the displayed characters to be retained (or *refreshed*) on the screen until the operator clears the readout.

2–4. PAPER-TAPE READER AND PUNCH

A paper-tape reader provides for direct input to a microcomputer by reading prepunched data in paper (or thin metallic) tape. A paper-tape punch provides a permanently recorded output from a microcomputer by punching output information in the paper. Often the two functions are combined in a single instrument. One common use for a paper-tape instrument is to convert a microcomputer program into machine language. For example, a program can be entered into a computer (host computer, time-sharing computer, support simulator, etc.) using assembly language and an assembler. The output from this computer is a program in machine language that is punched into paper tape. The punched paper-tape program is then read into the microcomputer in machine language.

It should be noted that paper-tape machines are generally useful in computer/data processing applications, and were in use long before microcomputers. For example, recording on paper tape is often done with machines that punch data received directly from a typewriter or keypunch or over telephone lines. Paper-tape reader outputs can sometimes be used to drive typewriters directly or over telephone lines.

2–4.1 Paper-Tape Reader

As shown in Fig. 2–7, information stored on paper tape is recorded in patterns of round punched holes located in parallel tracks (or channels) along the length of the tape. A character is represented by a combination of punches across the width of the tape. Paper tapes vary in width according to the number of channels that they contain. Typically, paper tapes have either five or eight channels.

Paper-tape systems are ideally suited to the binary (or two-state) system used in microcomputers, since the basic indication of paper tape is either "hole" or "no hole." Two methods of sensing the binary bits are shown in Fig. 2–7.

In the system of Fig. 2–7a, wire brushes complete a circuit through the tape holes to a metal plate underneath the tape. As the tape is drawn across the plate, the brushes either complete the circuit through a hole (producing an output pulse) or fail to complete the circuit where there is no hole (producing no output pulse). Generally, an output pulse (hole)

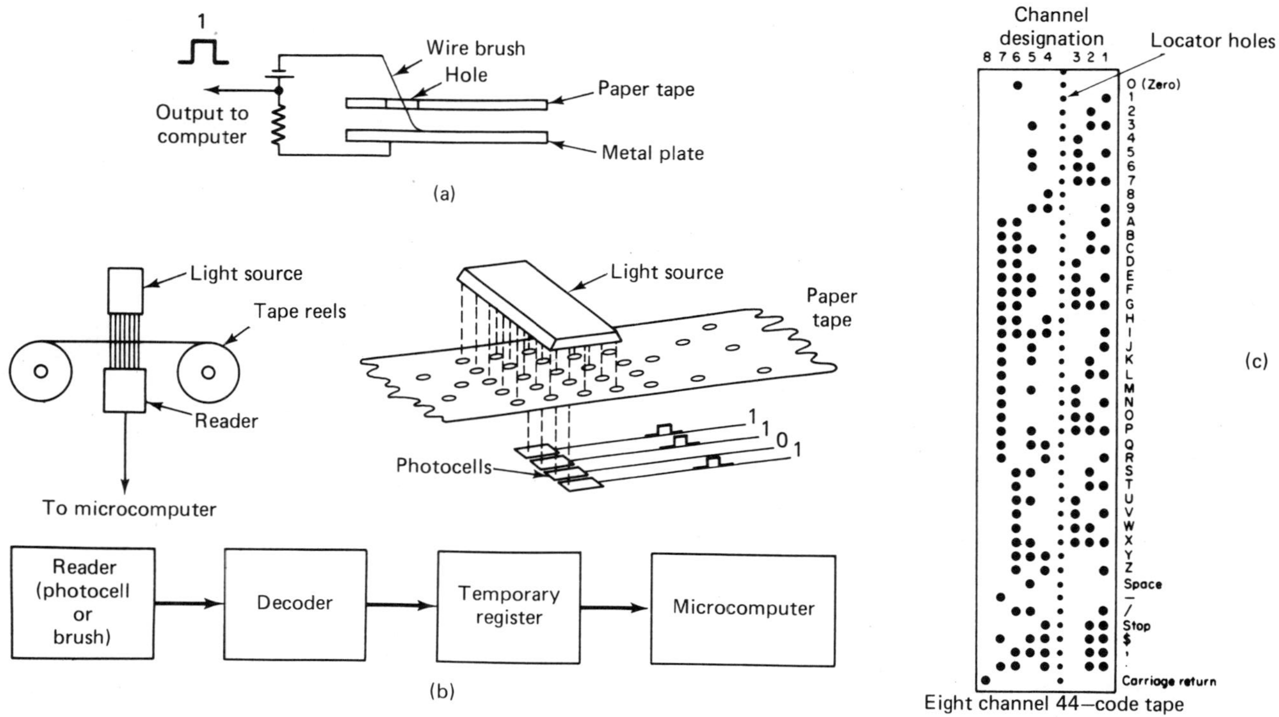

Fig. 2–7. Basic paper-tape reader circuits

represents a binary 1, whereas no output pulse (no hole) represents a 0. Note that one brush is used for each track or channel of holes.

In the system of Fig. 2–7b, a light source is placed on one side of the paper tape, with photocells located on the opposite side. One photocell is used for each track or channel of holes. As the tape moves, the light strikes a photocell whenever there is a hole, producing an output or binary 1. No output (binary 0) is produced when there is no hole, since the light cannot pass to the corresponding photocell.

The holes in the paper tape can be located only at predetermined sites, as shown in Fig. 2–7c. Each set of holes across the tape represents one character. A series of characters makes up a word. Locator holes guide the tape through the reader and hold the tape in proper position for reading. At each character, the tape is stopped momentarily for reading, after which the character is stored in a temporary register. The use of this temporary register between the reader and the microcomputer input buffer compensates for the difference in speeds of the reader and microcomputer. In some systems, the temporary register is part of the microcomputer I/O IC.

If the paper tape is not punched in machine language (typically, an 8–bit binary data byte), a decoder is required between the tape reader and microcomputer input. The decoder converts the five- or eight-channel output from the reader into a format (machine language) suitable for the microcomputer.

2–4.2 Paper-Tape Punch

When paper tape is used at the microcomputer output, the holes are produced by solenoid-operated metal punches on the paper-tape punch. One punch is used for each track or channel, as shown in Fig. 2–8. The output from the microcomputer is applied through a decoder to the punch solenoids. (If the paper tape is to be punched in machine language, the decoder can be omitted.) The decoder converts the processed information from machine language into a five- or eight-channel code, as applicable.

The paper tape is driven past the punches by the same gear mechanism used in reading the tape. There is one locator hole on the tape for each *frame* (or set of holes across the width). As the frame is pulled into position below the punches, a service-request signal is sent to the microcomputer. If a data byte is available at the microcomputer output, the service request permits the I/O buffer to be opened so that the data byte is passed to the punch solenoids. If there is no data byte available, the tape drive is stopped until new information is available. Thus, the microcomputer output is synchronized with the timing of the tape punch. Of course, under normal circumstances the microcomputer

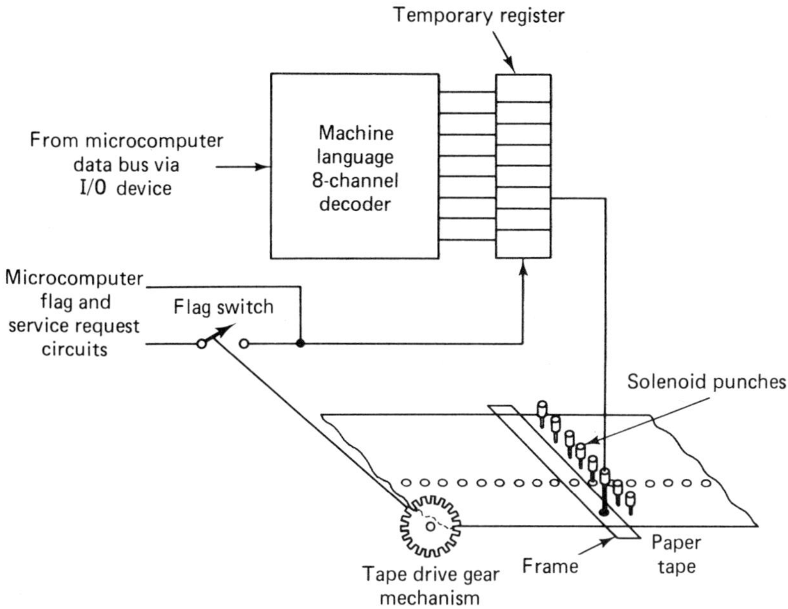

Fig. 2–8. Basic paper-tape punch circuits

will produce outputs faster than they can be punched by the tape unit. For this reason, a temporary register is often used between the microcomputer and tape unit. In some cases, the temporary register is part of the I/O IC.

2–5. OUTPUT PRINTERS

When there is a limited amount of information to be read out of a microcomputer, the electric typewriter is the most convenient and is most commonly used. Such printers are sometimes known as console, message, or supervisory printers. Long rolls of paper are put into the typewriter carriage to record both the entry of data (by the operator at the keyboard) and the readout of processed data.

When high-speed readout is required or a large quantity of information is to be read out, various forms of printers are used. Note that many of these printers were used with electromechanical data-processing equipment long before computers of any kind were invented. With a typewriter, only one letter can be typed at a time. Likewise, the up and down movement of type bars in a typewriter is far too slow for computers. Output printers overcome these problems.

There are two basic types of printers:

1. *Line-at-a-time printers,* which print all characters on a give line simultaneously.

2. *Character-at-a-time printers,* which print each character serially, a position at a time, similar to the way a typewriter prints (but at much higher speeds).

No matter what printer is used, the printer receives signals from a decoder, or character generator, which converts data from the microcomputer into a form that is compatible with the printer. In some printers, a character generator similar to that described for the video terminal (Sec. 2–3) is used to convert machine language to characters. No matter what system is used, the microcomputer output buffer is synchronized with the output printer by service-request signals, as discussed in Secs. 2–2 through 2–4. That is, the printer sends a service-request signal to the microcomputer when the printer is ready to accept the next data byte (or character).

2–5.1 Line-at-a-Time Printers

Line-at-a-time printers include *bar* or *gang printers,* as well as *wheel, drum,* or *chain printers,* and *electrostatic printers*. Because of the great variety, we shall limit our discussion to the drum printer.

Drum-Printer Basics. A drum printer uses a solid cylindrical drum around which characters are embossed, as shown in Fig. 2–9. The drum rotates at a constant speed. As the A row passes the line to be printed, hammers behind the paper strike the paper against the drum, causing one or more As to be printed. As the B row moves into place, any print position requiring the letter B is printed in the same manner. One complete revolution of the drum is required to print each line.

The Seiko printer, shown in Fig. 2–10, has a continually rotating print drum mechanism that uses what is referred to as the *flying printer* technique. The print drum and the ratchet shaft are geared together and rotate continuously in the direction shown. During a nonprint condition, the right end of the trigger level is held away from the ratchet by the trigger level spring. In the nonprinting condition, the trigger magnet is not actuated and the hammers are lifted upward to a neutral position by the hammer lever springs.

When actuated, the trigger magnet actuating lever forces the opposite end of the trigger level against the ratchet. During its next rotation, the ratchet engages the right end of the trigger lever, causing a downward motion to the right end of the hammer. The hammer thus strikes through the inked ribbon printer, causing the character then under the hammer to be printed.

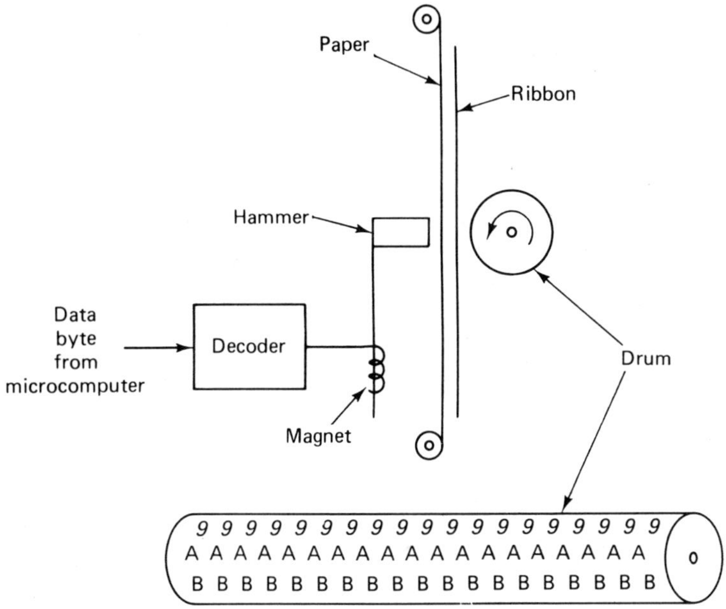

Fig. 2–9. Basic drum printer

Any of 42 characters (alphanumeric plus special characters such as $ and *) are printed in a 21-column format. Each column position has a complete character set spaced evenly around the drum. Because of a 42:1 gear ratio, the ratchet rotates 42 times for each complete drum rotation. Thus, each character of the set is positioned under a print hammer once during every rotation of the drum.

The decoders and control circuitry actuate the hammers at just the right time in response to timing signals generated electromagnetically by means of ferrite chips or magnets and detecting heads, as shown. The timing signals or pulses are generated each time a ferrite magnet passes a detecting head. (The basics of magnetics are discussed in Sec. 2–6.) Rotation of the ratchet shaft generates signals TP and TL for each of the 42 characters. TP provides timing for energizing the trigger magnets, TL for deenergizing. A reset signal R is generated by each complete rotation of the drum. The resulting waveform for a complete drum rotation is shown in Fig. 2–10.

2–5.2 Character-at-a-Time Printers

The *teletype printer* prints one character at a time in a manner similar to that of an electric typewriter. However, all the type is placed on a square block rather than on individual hammers The type block

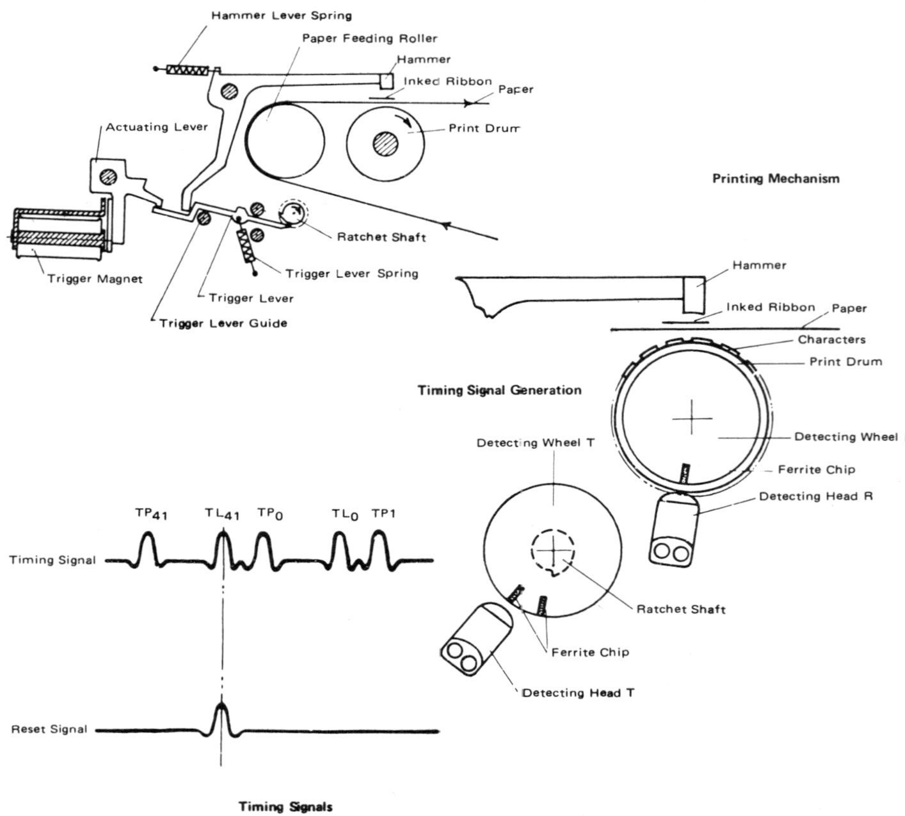

Fig. 2–10. Seiko printing mechanism, timing signal generation, and timing signals

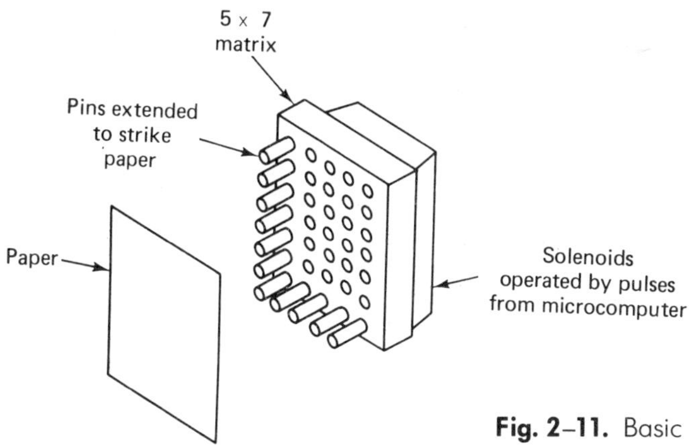

Fig. 2–11. Basic matrix printer

moves from left to right, positioning the proper character at each print position. As the block stops at each position, a hammer strikes the proper character from behind. The character is depressed against an inked ribbon, which, in turn, imprints the character on the paper. Typical teletype-printer speed is about 8 lines per minute.

The *matrix printer* consists of pins placed in a 5 by 7 matrix printer, as shown in Fig. 2–11. The characters are formed when the appropriate pins strike against the paper. (In some matrix printers, the pins burn spots onto the paper. However, this burning technique is not in general use.) The pins are selected by pulses from the decoder. Some matrix printers are capable of printing about 700 to 800 lines per minute, making the unit comparable in speed to most line-at-a-time printers.

A typical microcomputer line printer is shown in Fig. 2–12. This

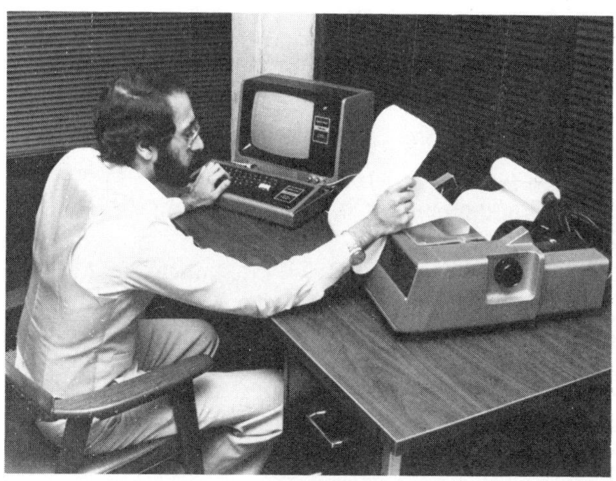

Fig. 2–12. Radio Shack TRS-80 line printer

Fig. 2–13. Radio Shack TRS-80 screen printer, shown with tape casette, keyboard, and CRT

is the line printer used with the Radio Shack TRS–80 microcomputer system. The unit prints from 60 to 110 characters per second using a 5 by 7 impact dot matrix. Character density is adjustable from 10 to 16.5 characters per inch. Roll paper up to 9.8 in. wide may be used. A *screen printer,* shown in Fig. 2–13 along with a tape casette, keyboard, and CRT, is also available with the TRS-80 microcomputer. This screen printer prints 2200 characters per second using electrostatic printing techniques. Whatever is shown on the entire video screen (including graphics) is printed on 4-in. wide paper.

2–6. MAGNETIC RECORDING BASICS

Magnetic tape, drums, disks, and ferrite core memories all operate on the principles of *eletromagnetism*. Therefore, we shall review electromagnetism as it applies to microprocessor memory or data storage.

As shown in Fig. 2–14, current through a coil creates a magnetic field. If a metal capable of being magnetized is placed in this field, the metal will become magnetized in one direction. If current flow is reversed, the metal will be magnetized in the opposite direction. As shown in Fig. 2–15, if metal is magnetized in one direction and an opposite magnetizing current is applied to change the direction of magnetism, the changing magnetic field produces (or induces) a current

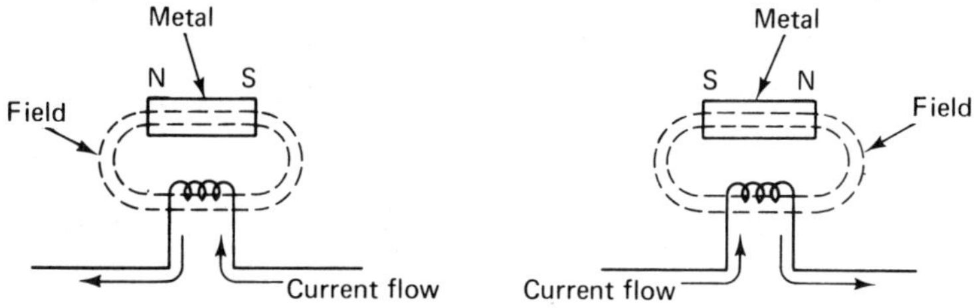

Fig. 2–14. Basic principles of magnetic storage showing metal magnetized in opposite directions by opposite currents

in another conductor (in or near the field). However, if the magnetizing current is applied so as not to change the direction of magnetism, there is no change in the magnetic field and no induced voltage. Thus, the magnetized metal has a "memory" and is ideally suited to the two-state binary numbers (1 or 0) used in microcomputers.

There are two ways in which these magnetic principles can be used. In the case of magnetic tapes, drums, and disks, the *presence* or *absence* of magnetism is used to indicate the binary state. Generally, the presence of magnetism indicates a binary 1, whereas a binary 0 is indicated by the absence of magnetism.

In the case of ferrite cores, the *direction* of magnetism is used to indicate the state (1 or 0). Note that ferrite memories are not generally used with microcomputers, but are often used with larger, conventional computers.

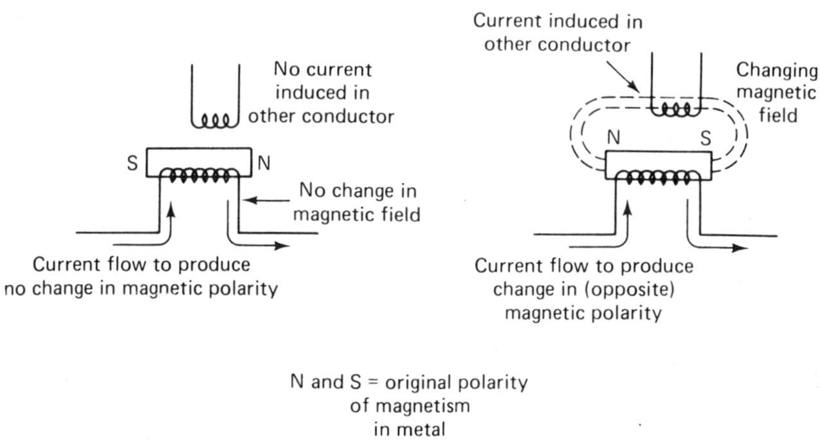

Fig. 2–15. Basic principles of magnetic storage or memory showing effect of currents on previously magnetized metal storage elements

2–7. TAPE RECORDING BASICS

Magnetic-tape recorders are often used with microcomputers as an external data-storage device. These recorders provide high-speed readin and readout of data. The most common type of magnetic-tape recorder used with microcomputers is the cassette recorder, such as shown in Fig. 2–13. However, microcomputers can also be used with the reel-to-reel tape recorders normally associated with larger, conventional computers. Both the cassette and reel-to-reel recorders used with microcomputers are similar to those used in home entertainment units. That is, both computer and home entertainment units have tape transports, record and playback heads (called write and read heads), and amplifiers. However, the detailed characteristics of the two systems are quite different.

2–7.1 Tape Recorder Amplifier Characteristics

The amplifiers used in microcomputer recorders do not require the high fidelity of entertainment units, because microcomputer recorders operate with binary information (bits and bytes of data) rather than voice or music. Data bytes are recorded (written) and played back (read) on a present or absent basis (in most cases). Often, a binary 1 is represented by the presence of a magnetic field on the tape (sometimes known as a *magnetic spot*), whereas the absence of a field represents 0. In other systems, the direction of the magnetic field (north or south, + or −, etc.) represents a 1 or 0.

Because of the on/off method of recording, microcomputer tape recorders generally do not have the supersonic bias signal applied to the tape for linearity, as is the case in other recorders where high fidelity is required. However, microcomputer recording systems often use a fixed dc bias to place the tape in a condition to be magnetized by the data bytes.

2–7.2 Tape Characteristics

The tapes used in microcomputer reel-to-reel recorders are generally longer than those of home units; 2400 or 3600 ft is standard. The cassette tapes used with microcomputers are generally the same as for entertainment units. Although early magnetic tapes were made of metal, all popular tapes are now made of plastic coated on one side with metal oxide. The oxide can easily be magnetized and retains its magnetisim indefinitely. The data bits are placed across the width of the tape in parallel tracks running along the entire length. Figure 2–16 shows the recording format for a typical cassette tape used with microcomputers.

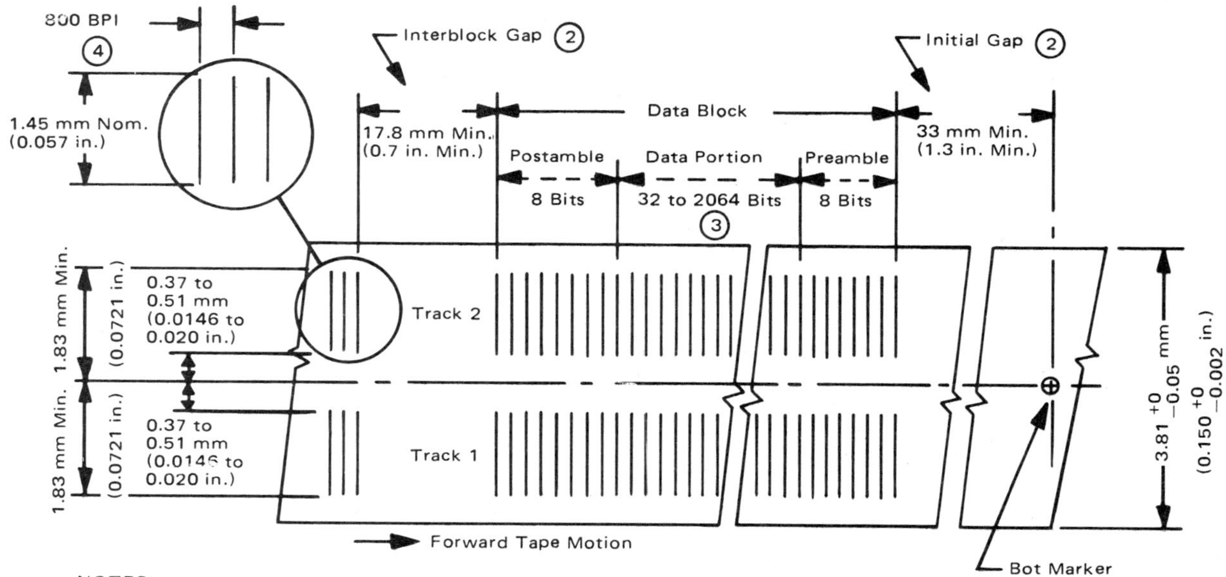

NOTES:

1 Tape is shown with oxide side out.

(2) Tape is fully saturated in the erase direction in the interblock gap and the initial gap.

(3) The last 2 characters (16 bits) of the data portion is the Cyclic Redundancy Check (CRC).

(4) Shown without phase flux reversals that may exist between data bits.

Fig. 2–16. Recording format for 800 BPI (bytes per inch) cassette tape

2–7.3 Tape-Coding Systems

The pattern of the magnetized spots across the width and along the length of the tape is a coded representation of the data stored on it. Several codes are used, as is the case with paper tape. If some code other than machine language has been used to record data on the tape, a decoder is required between the tape reader and the microcomputer input. Likewise, the output from the microcomputer is applied through a decoder to the tape recorder during record or write operation (unless the data bytes are to be recorded in machine language). Figure 2–17 shows a type recording format using the ASCII code. Note that there are eight channels on one track. Seven of the channels are used for the 7-bit ASCII code, and the eighth channel is used for a parity bit (discussed in Sec. 1–7). Thus, the eight channels provide for one character (letter, number, or symbol) across the width of the tape. In Fig. 2–17, each dash or short line represents a binary 1. The absence of a dash represents a binary 0.

The data bytes (representing characters) are recorded serially as the tape passes by the read/write heads. This is shown in Fig. 2–18, which illustrates 1 bit (on one channel) of four successive data bytes. A magnetic field (or spot) is impressed on the tape (representing a binary 1 bit) as current (in the form of pulses) passes through the write winding. (In some systems, one head is used for both read and write. In other recording systems, separate read and write heads are used.) In the absence of current, no spot is impressed on the tape. During the

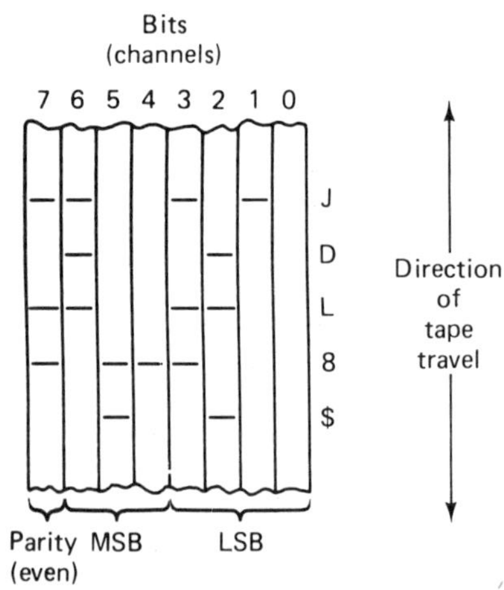

Fig. 2–17. Typical tape recording format for ASCII code with eight channels on one track

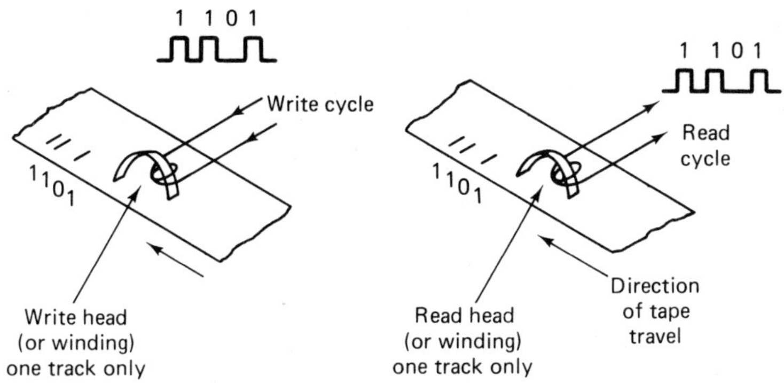

Fig. 2–18. Read and write cycles of magnetic tape showing one bit (on one channel) of four successive data bytes

read operation, as the tape is passed across the head by the tape transport, the presence of a moving magnetic spot produces current in the read head (for a binary 1 bit). No current is produced when there is no spot on the tape passing the head (binary 0 bit).

The system shown in Fig. 2–18 uses the return-to-zero (RZ) format. Although there are many ways in which pulses can be used to represent the 1 and 0 bits, there are only three ways in common use. These are the RZ, NRZL (non-return-to-zero-level), and NRZM (non-return-to-zero-mark) formats. Figure 2–19 shows the relationship of the three formats.

In the RZ format, a 1 bit is represented by a pulse of some definite width (usually a ½-bit width) that returns to the zero signal level. A 0 bit is represented by a zero-level signal.

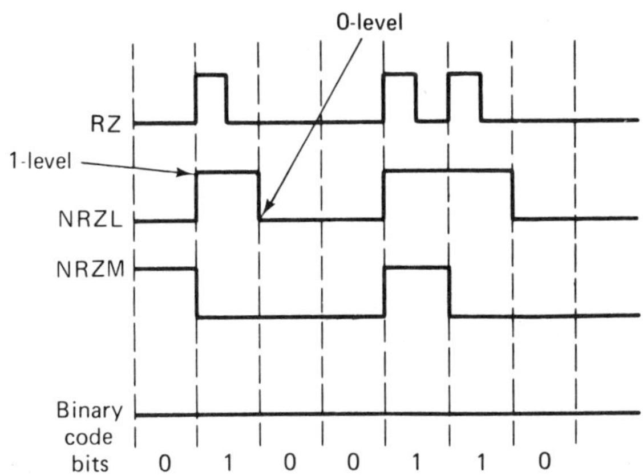

Fig. 2–19. Relationship of RZ, NRZL, and NRZM data bit recording formats

In the NRZL format, a 1 bit is one signal level, and a 0 bit is another signal level. These levels can be 5 V, 10 V, or any other selected value, provided that the 1 and 0 levels are entirely different and predetermined.

In the NRZM format, the level of the waveform has no meaning. A 1 bit is represented by a *change in level* (either higher or lower); a 0 bit is represented by no change in level.

In tape recording, the RZ format is the least efficient for storing the most information on a given area of tape. That is, the RZ format provides the lowest amount of *pulse packing* or *pulse density.* Pulse packing is a measure of how dense the pulse recording is (how close together the information is recorded). The higher the pulse density, the less amount of tape will be needed for storing data. With the RZ method, the pulse current returns to 0 between bits and remains at 0 for a 0 bit. (In some RZ systems, the pulse current returns to 0 between bits, but changes direction for a 1 or 0 bit.)

Pulse density can be increased by use of the NRZL or NRZM formats of Fig. 2–20. In the NRZL format (Fig. 2–20c), the direction of magnetism changes only when switching from a 0 to a 1 or from a 1 to a 0. In NRZM (Figure 2–20b), the magnetism changes direction only when it is necessary to store a 1.

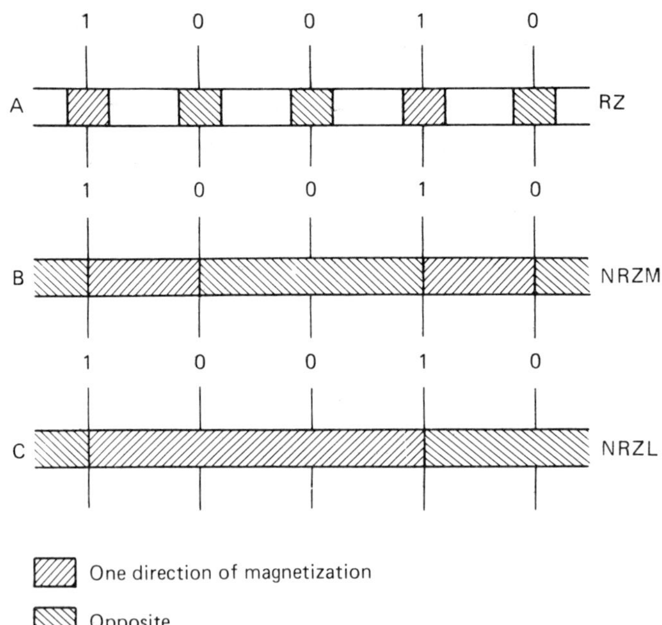

Fig. 2–20. Changes in directions of magnetization for RZ, NRZL, and NRZM data bit recording formats

2–7.4 Tape Control Systems

Another difference between the home entertainment and computer tape systems is in the method of starting and stopping. Unlike an audio tape that moves slowly and need not be stopped, computer tape often moves at fast speeds. For a cassette using the format of Fig. 2–16, the tape moves at a speed of 100 in./s when searching for data, and 15 in./s when reading or writing data. Because the microcomputer must pinpoint specific data (at a selected address or block on the tape), the tape control system must be able to stop the tape at the proper point with no lost motion.

Reading and writing on tape is performed on the tape unit at a constant speed. The *transfer rate* of information to and from tape depends largely on two factors: (1) the actual movement of tape across the read/write heads, and (2) the number of characters or data bytes that can be stored on an inch of tape (packing density). For example, assume a tape movement speed of 15 in./s and a density of 800 bytes/in. At these rates, the character (or byte) transfer rate is 12,000/s.

2–7.5 Storing Data Records on Tape

Information is usually written on tape in groups (called *data blocks*) as shown in Fig. 2–16. In normal operation, information continues to be written on the tape until a flag or control signal is received from the microcomputer. This stops the tape drive. Some tape systems used a fixed number of characters in each block, but variable-length blocks are more common. Actual length is determined primarily by the storage capacity of the microcomputer.

As shown in Fig. 2–16, there are *interblock gaps* between data blocks. (In some systems, the gaps are known as *interrecord gaps*, or IRGs.) These gaps are produced when the tape continues to be driven, but no information is written on the tape. The use of interblock gaps permits the tape drive to accelerate and decelerate when starting or stopping without failing to read or write the desired information. In some tape systems, when an interblock gap is encountered during the read operation, the tape drive stops at about the center of the gap. The remaining half of the gap is used upon acceleration before the next record is read. A new read command from the microcomputer starts the tape drive again.

2–7.6 Safety and Accuracy of Tape Records

Many safeguards must be taken to preserve data stored on microcomputer tapes Obviously, the information can be destroyed if an erase signal is accidentally applied to the tape unit heads or if new information is written on top of old information.

A common safeguard on large, reel-to-reel tape transport systems to prevent accidental overwriting of tape is a safety indicator in the form of a plastic ring. When installed on a groove around the hub of a tape reel, the ring indicates that the tape may be used to store new information. The ring is removed when the writing of new information is to be prevented. This accounts for the term *no-ring, no-write* used by many computer operators and programmers.

The tape transport of a typical cassette recorder contains two microswitches, one to sense the presence of a tape cassette in place, and the other to see if the *write protect tab* (sometimes called the *file protect tab*) is removed. If the cassette tab is removed, the tape is *write-protected,* and circuits within the cassette disable the write circuits. Signals from these switches or sensors are available at the interface, and the microcomputer must check them prior to issuing any "motion" commands to the tape transport.

Just as important, but perhaps not as obvious, there must be some system to ensure that the data bytes are recorded accurately. There are three main concerns in recording data bytes. First, *all the bits* must be recorded. Second, the bits must be readable. Third, the bits must be recorded in correct order, both horizontally and vertically on the tape. Several systems are used to ensure these conditions.

Dual Recording. Where reliability is particularly important (such as when real-time data bytes are being recorded on a one-time-only basis), dual recording systems can be used. In such systems, each data byte is written twice in each frame across the width of the tape by two sets of heads, amplifiers, and so on. Of course, this requires twice the number of channels and tracks. Note that there are two eight-channel tracks on the format of Fig. 2–16.

Constant-Check Read/Write. Some systems provide a constant check (for readability) of data bytes being recorded. (These systems are sometimes known as *dual-gap* read/write arrangements.) All characters or data bytes written on tape are immediately read by a separate head (or winding) adjacent to the write head. Both readability and accuracy can be checked in this way.

A basic constant-check system is shown in Fig. 2–21. In this system, information in the microcomputer output register is amplified and written onto the tape by a write head. Only one bit is shown in Fig. 2–21. The circuit is repeated (amplifiers, heads, etc.) for each bit in the register. As the tape moves, the bit is read out immediately, amplified, and applied to another readout register. Each bit in the readout register is using a comparator circuit.

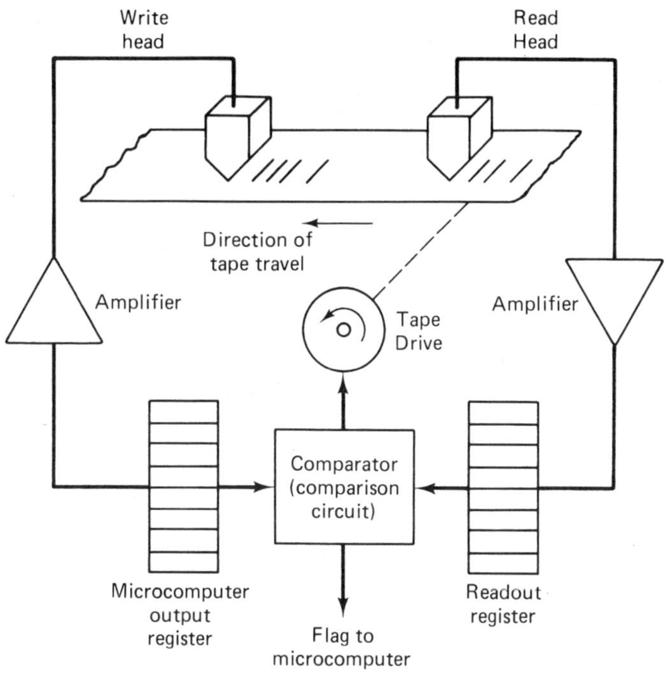

Fig. 2–21. Basic constant-check (dual-gap) read/write magnetic tape recording system

The recording operation continues as long as the recorded bits are readable and in agreement with the bits in the output register. If there is any inequality between the two registers, the comparison circuit stops the tape drive and sends a flag to the microcomputer. In some systems, the tape drive is reversed, and the bit is rewritten at the appropriate location on the tape.

Parity and Cyclic Redundancy Check (CRC) Circuits. When dual recording and constant-check systems are not practical, parity and CRC circuits can be used to check the accuracy of bits on the tape.

Parity circuits use the parity system described in Sec. 1–8.8, and provide a check of individual characters (data bytes) across the track. Such systems are sometimes known as *vertical check* or *vertical parity* schemes. A basic vertical parity system is shown in Fig. 2–22. In this system, one channel of an eight-channel track is reserved for vertical, even-parity check. A 1 bit is added to make an even number of 1 bits across the width of the tape. In the case of data bytes 2 and 3, both normally use an even number of 1 bits. Thus, no parity bit is added. Data bytes 1 and 4 use an odd number of 1s (three 1s). Thus, a parity bit is added to both data bytes 1 and 4. The amplified output of the read

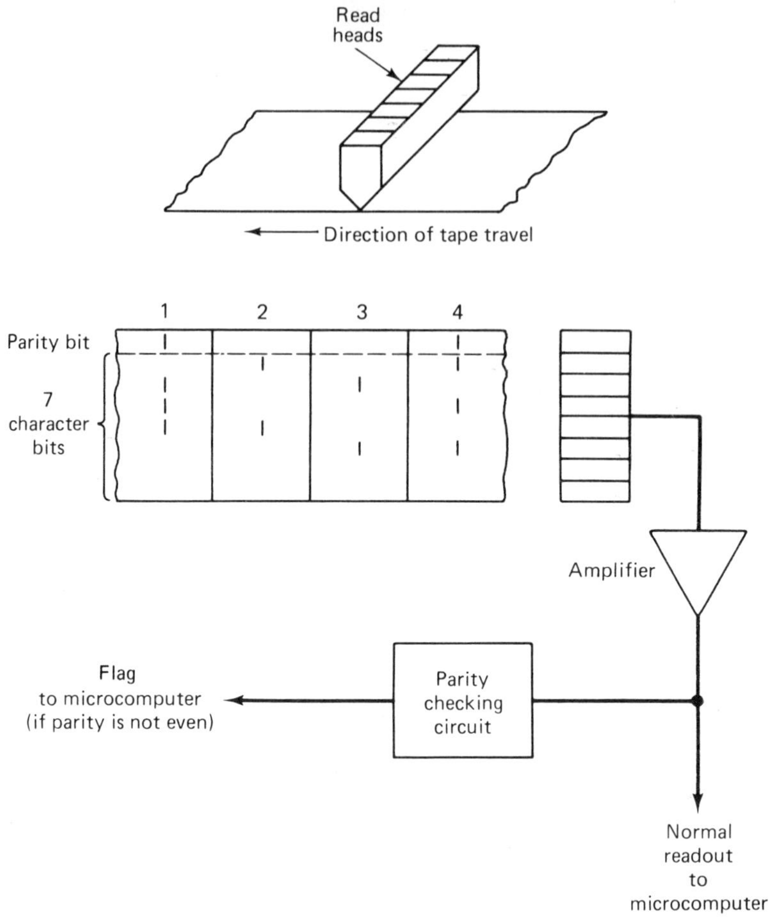

Fig. 2–22. Basic vertical parity system for magnetic tape recording control

heads applied to the microcomputer is also applied to the parity checking circuit. If the input to the parity checking circuit is even, operation continues as normal. If the parity checker receives an odd number of bits (due to recording failure, tape failure, etc.), a flag is sent to the microcomputer.

CRC circuits provide a check of a complete data block, and are thus sometimes referred to as a *horizontal parity* or *horizontal check system*. As shown in Fig. 2–16, the last two bytes or characters of the data portion in the data block are called the CRC bytes. These two CRC bytes are generated by circuits that count all the data bits, starting with bit 0 of the first data byte in the block (sometimes known as the address byte), and ending with the last bit of the last data byte (excluding the CRC bytes). When the data block is read back from the tape, the data bits (from bit 0 of the address or first data byte to the last bit of the second CRC byte) are divided by the CRC number. The remainder should be zero if all the data bits have been properly recorded and played back. A nonzero remainder indicates an error within the data read back. This nonzero remainder can be used to stop the tape drive, send a flag to the microprocessor, and so on.

Preamble and Postamble Bits. As shown in Fig. 2–16, there are 8 preamble and postamble bits at opposite ends of the data portion of each data block. These are 8-bit patterns or bytes of alternating 1s and 0s. (This is sometimes known as a *checkerboard.*) In some systems, the preamble and postamble bits are used to establish the data rate during data recovery or read operation. In such systems, the tape drive operates at high speeds during gaps, and then slows to a fixed rate when data bytes are recorded or read. The preamble and postamble bits permit the system to lock onto (or synchronize with) the desired rate during read operation.

2–7.7 Locating Data on Tape Records

Since tape has no physical markings, some means must be used to locate data at a specific point on the tape. This is true for both read and write.

In the system of Fig. 2–16, reflective markers (usually silver-coated foil) are attached to the tape at the beginning and end of the tape. These are the beginning-of-tape (BOT) and end-of-tape (EOT) markers. Only the BOT marker is shown in Fig. 2–16. A photocell is mounted near the tape and picks up light from the reflective marker. A change in light on the photocell stops the tape drive at the marker until a new read or write command is given to the cassette.

Although physical markings can be used for the beginning and end of a tape, specific information at any point between the markings must be identified by means of an *electronic address,* similar to the addresses in ROMs and RAMs. Several addressing systems are used. In one of the most common, the first character or data byte in the data portion of the data block represents the address for that block. A very simplified version of such a system is illustrated in Fig. 2–23.

As shown, each data block is identified by a three-digit decimal number (from 000 to 255). The read heads are connected through amplifiers and gates to the microcomputer input. When the gates are opened, the information being read is fed into the microcomputer. The gates are opened upon command from a comparator circuit. This comparator compares the data in the address-selection register with data in the readout register. The address-selection register is set to the desired address (data block 233 in Fig. 2–23) by the microcomputer,

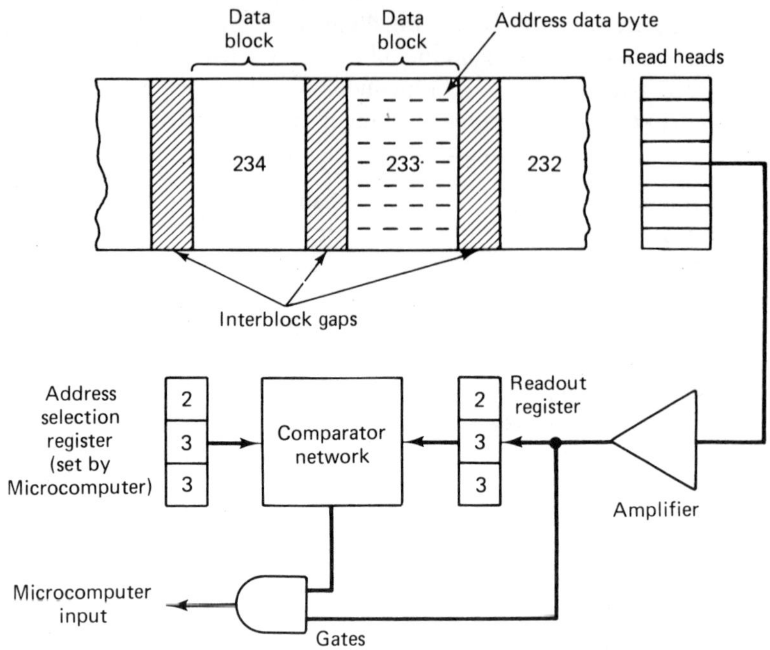

Fig. 2–23. Basic circuit for locating data on magnetic tape records

and the tape drive is started at high speed (or search speed). When the tape is at the desired address (data block 233), the read out register indicates 233, and the comparator opens the gates. As the tape continues to move, the information in the 233 data block is read into the microcomputer. The tape stops at the end of the block or goes to a new address, as determined by the address-selection register.

Of course, the circuit of Fig. 2–23 is oversimplified for illustration purposes. In practice, the tape drive and address-selection circuits move the tape from address to address, stopping, reversing, and again moving forward at high speeds.

2–8. DISKETTE (FLOPPY DISK) RECORDING BASICS

The floppy disk is the most commonly used magnetic storage device for microcomputers. The floppy disk itself (also known as a *diskette*) is a removable magnetic storage media that is permanently contained in a paper envelope. A *diskette drive* is a low-cost peripheral that performs the electromechanical and read/write functions necessary to record and recover data on the diskette. Figure 2–24 shows a typical diskette and drive mechanism. The diskette is similar to the 45-rpm

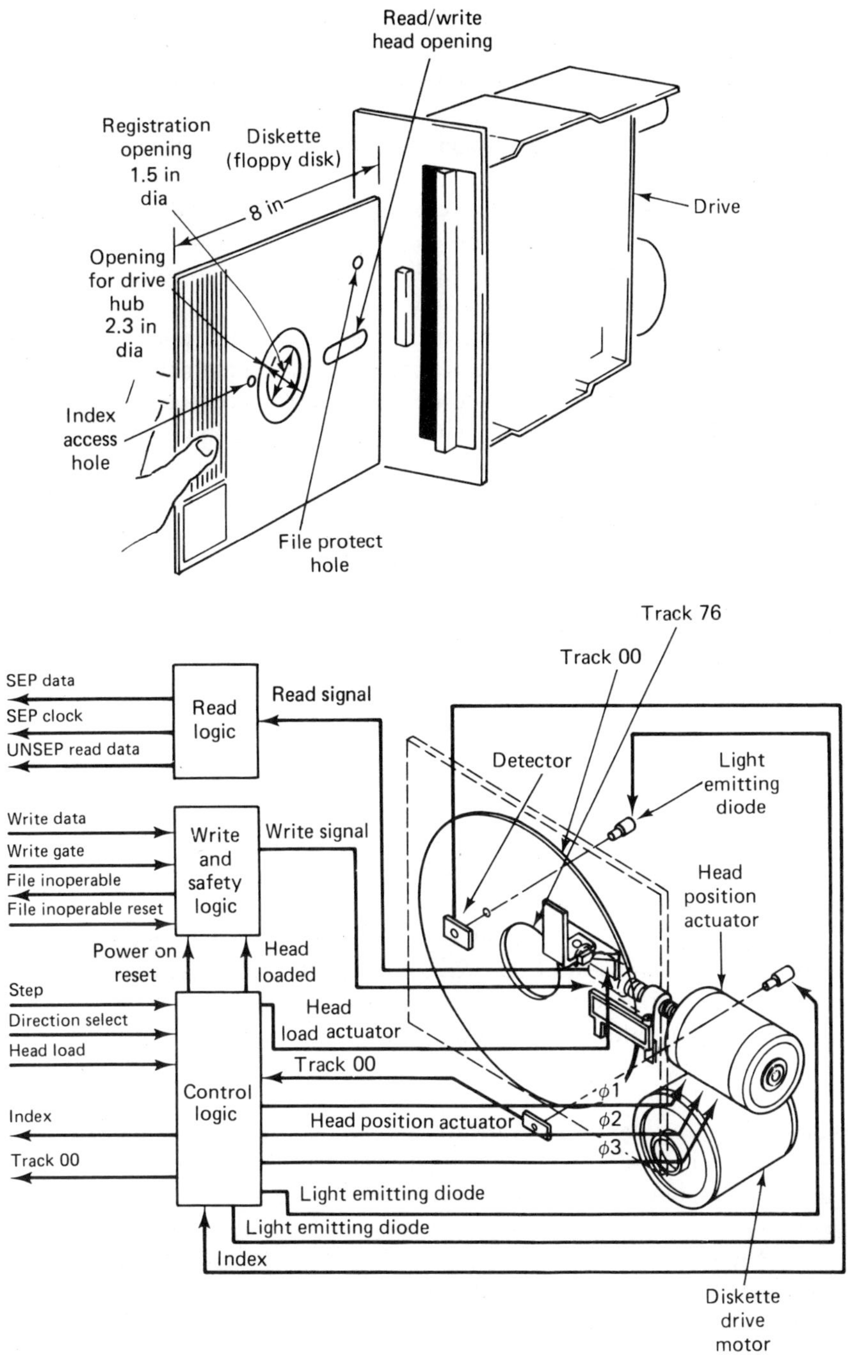

Fig. 2–24. Typical diskette (floppy disk) and drive

record. However, the diskette rotates at a speed of 360 rpm typically and the data bytes are stored magnetically on concentric tracks over the face of the diskette.

Data are recorded serially on the diskette. Usually, because of the high serial data rates, it is necessary to use special circuits for the serial/parallel conversion, data recovery, and data error checking when interfacing a diskette and a microcomputer system. The hardware that performs this function is often called a *formatter.* The formatter also serves as a buffer between the microcomputer and the diskette, as shown in Fig. 2–25. The formatter combines with the microcomputer to control the diskette drive, and sometimes the combination is called a *floppy disk controller.* As used here, the term "controller" includes not only the system hardware, but also those microcomputer programs that directly or indirectly control the diskette drive. The program routines for the diskette are often referred to as floppy disk (or diskette) *drivers* or *control modules*.

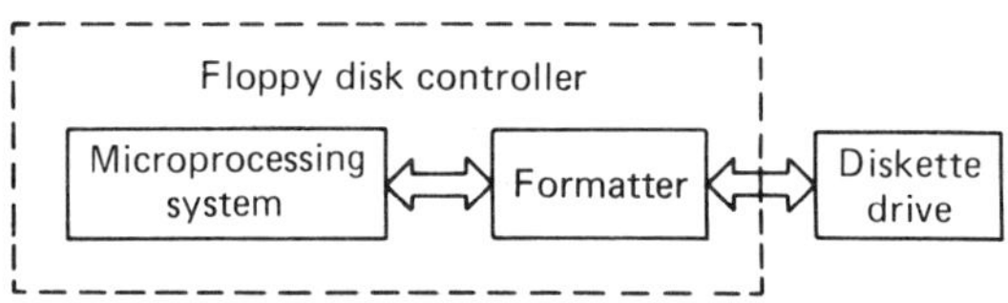

Fig. 2–25. Relationship between microprocessor system and diskette

2–8.1 Interfacing Diskettes with Microcomputers

Several considerations must be made when interfacing diskettes with microprocessors. We shall not discuss all of them, since they are essentially the problem of the system designer. However, two considerations are worth mentioning in relation to troubleshooting.

Some diskette drives are designed for *daisy-chain* interfacing in which some of the interconnecting lines are shared and some are dedicated. Other drives use the *radial* interface in which all the interconnecting lines are dedicated. Both interfacing techniques are shown in Fig. 2–26. Each technique has its advantages. The radical interface isolates (or buffers) each drive, whereas the daisy-chain interface requires less system hardware.

No matter what interfacing system is used, the microcomputer is, in effect, busy all the time when used with a diskette. This is due to the high data rates involved. It also means that no other microcomputer peripherals can be serviced while in a diskette read or write operation. This is true provided that the transfer of data is controlled by the

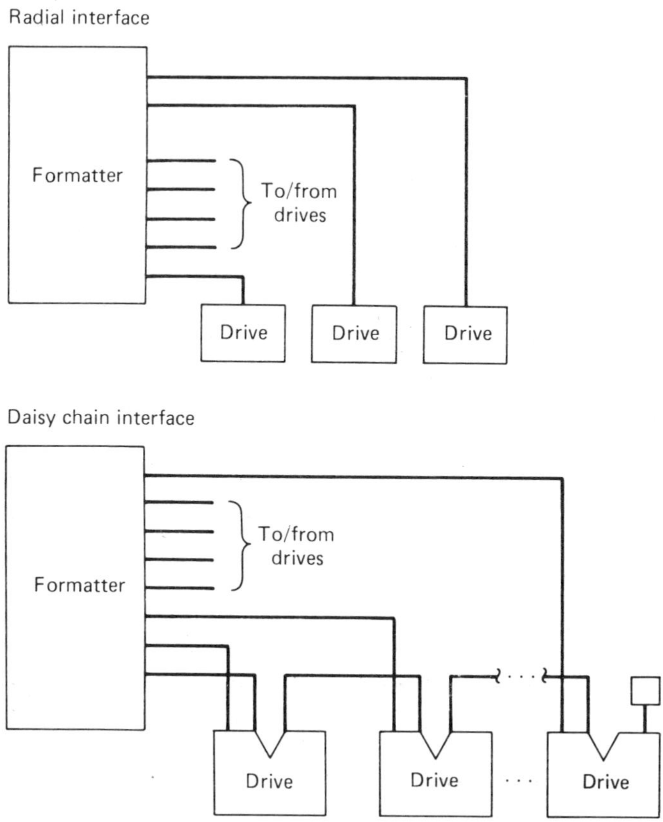

Fig. 2–26. Basic arrangements for radial and daisy-chain interfacing formats

microcomputer and not via some type of direct memory access (DMA) hardware. Since no other peripherals can be serviced, interrupts generated by the other system elements must be disabled during diskette read or write operations. Allowances must be made in the system design to permit 100 percent system dedication to the diskette during read or write operation.

2–8.2 Seek and Restore Operations

Information is transferred to and from the diskette by read/write heads in a manner similar to that described in Sec. 2–7 for magnetic tape recording. (However, data bytes are stored serially on a diskette, whereas most tape cassettes use parallel recording of the data bytes.) One function of the diskette drive is to position the read/write head over the appropriate track where the data bytes are to be recorded or read. This function is sometimes referred to as a *seek and restore* operation.

The diskette records data on 77 circular tracks numbered 00 to 76. In order to access a certain record, the read/write head must first be locked in position at the track that contains that record. The operation that performs the head movement function is called a *seek operation.* For the diskette, a seek is executed by stepping the head one track at a time. The timing between steps is controlled from an interval timer.

The *restore operation* is similar to the seek operation. The main difference between seek and restore is that a restore operation always moves the read/write head to track 00. After the seek operation is completed, the only way to verify that the proper track has been accessed is to read the track address magnetically recorded on the track (in a manner similar to that for tape, as described in Sec. 2–7.7). When track 00 is accessed, the diskette drive usually generates a track 00 signal status signal for flag. As shown in Fig. 2–24, the track 00 signal is often developed by an electromechanical sensor (such as a light-emitting diode, or LED, and a photocell). In some drives, a similar sensor detects when the diskette is at an index or start position.

2–8.3 Data Access Time

A primary reason to use a diskette for storage instead of another type of magnetic device, such as a tape cassette, is improved data access time. By definition, access time includes the following:

Seek time, or the time for the read/write head positioner to move from its present location to the newly specified location (typically 10 m/s track).

Settle time, or the time for the positioner to settle onto a new track (typically 10 ms from the last step pulse).

Latency time, or the time required for the diskette to rotate to the desired position (typically 83.3 ms, average).

The diskette spins at a fixed rate of 167 ms/revolution. On the average, the data will be one-half of a revolution, or 83.3 ms, away from the head. This is known as *average latency time.*

2–8.4 Typical Diskette Specifications

A typical diskette system records and reads data at 250K bits/s or 4μs/bit. When used with a typical 8-bit parallel microcomputer, the data rate is 250÷8 = 31.25K bytes/s, or 32 μs/b.

A single (typical) diskette has a capacity of 2,050,048 bits, or 256,256 bytes on the 77 tracks There are 26 sectors on each track and 128 bytes on each sector. Track recording formats are discussed further in Sec. 2–8.6

2–8.5 Functional Description of a Typical Diskette Drive

The diskette drive shown in Fig. 2–24 consists of read/write and control electronics, drive mechanism, read/write head, track positioning mechanism, and the removable diskette. These components perform the following functions: interpret and generate control signals, move read/write head to the selected track, read and write data. The relationship and interface signals for the internal functions of the drive are shown in Fig. 2–24.

General Operation. The head positioning actuator positions the read/write head to the desired track on the diskette. The head load actuator loads the diskette against the read/write head, and data may then be recorded or read from the diskette. The head position actuator, which consists of an electrical stepping motor and lead screw, positions the lead screw clockwise or counterclockwise in 15° increments. A 15° rotation of the lead screw moves the read/write head one track position. The microprocessor system increments the stepping motor to the desired track.

The diskette drive motor rotates the spindle at 360 rpm through a belt-drive system. Fifty or sixty-hertz power is accommodated by changing the drive pulley. A registration hub centered on the face of the spindle positions the diskette. A clamp that moves in conjunction with the latch handle fixes the diskette to the registration hub.

The read/write head is in direct contact with the diskette. The head surface has been designed to obtain maximum signal transfer to and from the magnetic surface of the diskette with minimum head/diskette wear. The read/write head is mounted on a carriage that is located on the head position actuator lead screw, as shown in Fig. 2–27. The diskette is held in a plane perpendicular to the read/write head by a platen located on the base casting. The precise registration assures perfect compliance with the read/write head. The diskette is loaded against the head with a load pad actuated by the head load solenoid.

Signal Interface. The signal interface between the diskette drive and the microcomputer consists of lines required to control the drive and to transfer data to and from the drive. All lines in the signal interface are digital in nature (the signals are in pulse form), and either provide signals to the drive (input) or provide signals to the microcomputer (output).

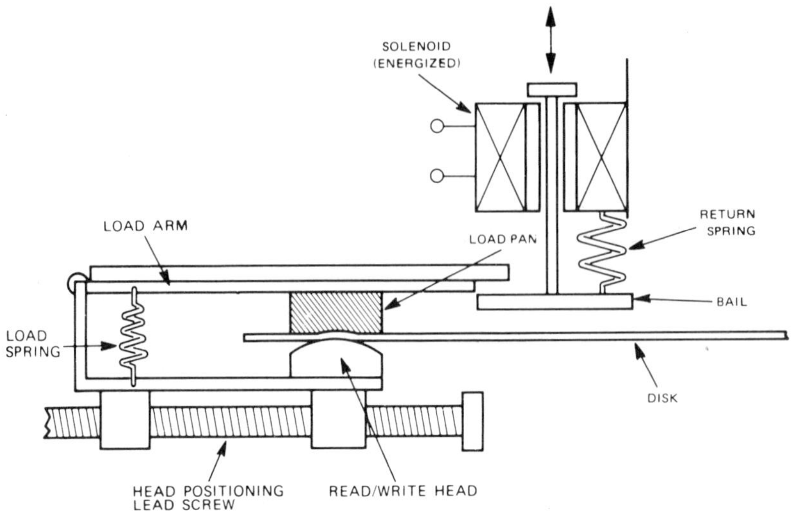

Fig. 2–27. Head load and carriage assembly

Input. There are six input signal lines:

Direction select defines the direction of motion of the read/write head when the *step* line is pulsed. An open circuit or binary 1 defines the direction as out, and if a pulse is applied to the step line, the read/write head will move away from the center of the diskette (toward track 00). Conversely, if the direction-select input is shorted to ground, or a binary 0 is applied, the direction of motion is defined as in, and if a pulse is applied to the step line, the read/write head will move toward the center of the diskette (toward track 76).

Step input is a control signal that causes the read/write head to move with the direction of motion defined by the direction-select line. The access motion is initiated on each binary 0 to binary 1 transition of the step input signal.

Load head is a control signal to an actuator that allows the diskette to be moved into contact with the read/write head. A binary 1 deactivates the head load actuator and causes a bail to lift the pressure pad from the diskette. This removes the load from the diskette and read/write head. A binary 0 level on the load head line activates the head loan actuator, and allows the pressure pad to bring the diskette into contact with the read/write head with the proper contact pressure.

File inoperable reset provides a direct reset for the file inoperable output signal. The file inoperable condition is reset when a binary 0 is applied to the file inoperable reset line.

Write gate controls the writing of data on the diskette. A binary 1 on the write gate line turns off the write function. A binary 0 enables the write function and disables the stepping circuitry.

Write data provides the data to be written on diskette.

Output. There are six output signal lines:

Track 00 indicates when the read/write head is positioned at track zero (the outermost data track).

File inoperable is the output of the data safety circuitry, and is at a binary 0 level when a condition that jeopardizes data integrity has occurred.

Index is a signal provided by the diskette drive once each revolution (166.67ms) to indicate the beginning of the track. Normally, the index signal is at binary 1 and makes the transition to 0 level for a period of 1.7 ms once each revolution.

Separated data is the interface line over which read data are sent to the microcomputer. The signals written on the diskette (using a frequency modulation system) are demodulated by the drive electronics, and are converted to data pulses. The data pulses (representing the data bytes on the diskette) are sent over the separated data line. Normally, the separated data signal is at binary 1, and each data bit recorded on the diskette causes the signal to make the transition to a 0 level for 200 μs.

Separated clock provides the microcomputer with the clock bits recorded on the diskette. The levels and timing are identical to the separated data line except that a separated clock pulse occurs each 4 ns. The recording formats are discussed in Sec. 2–8.6.

Unseparated read data provides raw data (clock and data bits together) to the microcomputer.

2–8.6 Diskette Recording Formats

The format of the data recorded on the diskette is totally a function of the microcomputer. Data bytes are recorded on the diskette using frequency modulation as the recording mode. Each data bit recorded has an associated clock bit recorded with it. Data bits written on and read back from the diskette take the form shown in Fig. 2–28. The clock bits and data bits (if present) are interleaved in the form of *bit cells*. By definition, a bit cell is the period between the leading edge of one clock bit and the leading edge of the next clock bit.

Figure 2–29 illustrates the relationship of the bits within a byte. Figure 2–30 illustrates the relationship of bytes for read and write data.

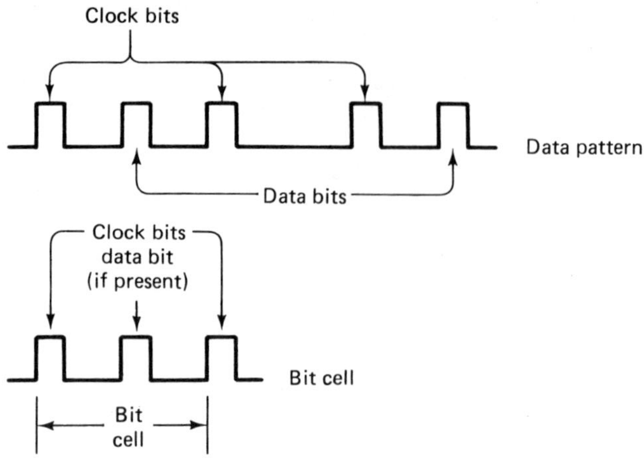

Fig. 2–28. Basic diskette data bit recording format showing formation of a bit cell

A *data byte,* when referring to serial data being written onto or read from a diskette drive, is defined as 8 consecutive bit cells. The MSB cell is defined as bit cell 0, and the LSB cell is defined as bit cell 7. When reference is made to a specific data bit (such as data bit 3), it is with respect to the corresponding bit cell (bit cell 3).

During a write operation, bit cell 0 of each byte is transferred to the diskette drive first, with bit cell 7 being transferred last. Correspondingly, the most significant byte of data is transferred to the diskette first, and the least significant byte last. When data bytes are being read back from the drive, bit cell 0 of each byte is transferred first, with bit cell 7 last. As with reading, the most significant byte is transferred first from the drive to the microcomputer.

Track Formats. Each of the 77 tracks (0 through 76) may be formatted in numerous ways, dependent upon the microcomputer. The

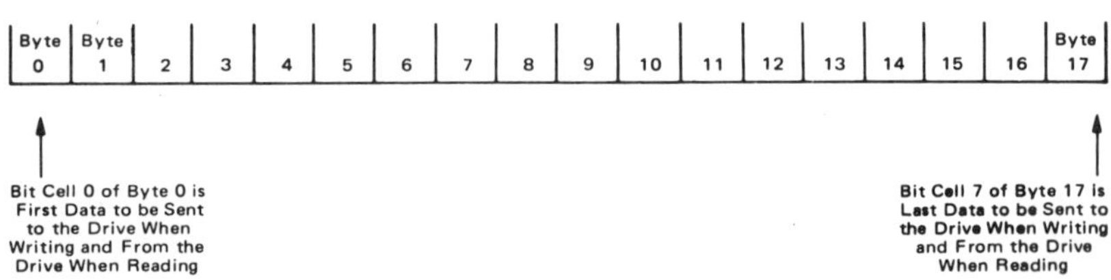

Fig. 2–29. Relationship of bits within a data byte as recorded on a diskette (floppy disk)

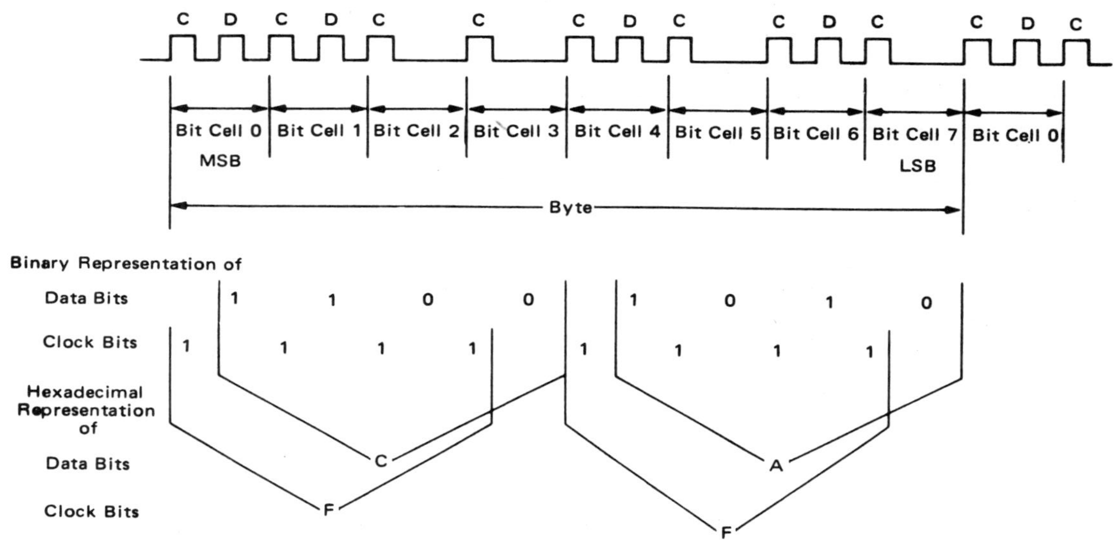

Fig. 2–30. Relationship of bytes for read and write data as recorded on a diskette (floppy disk)

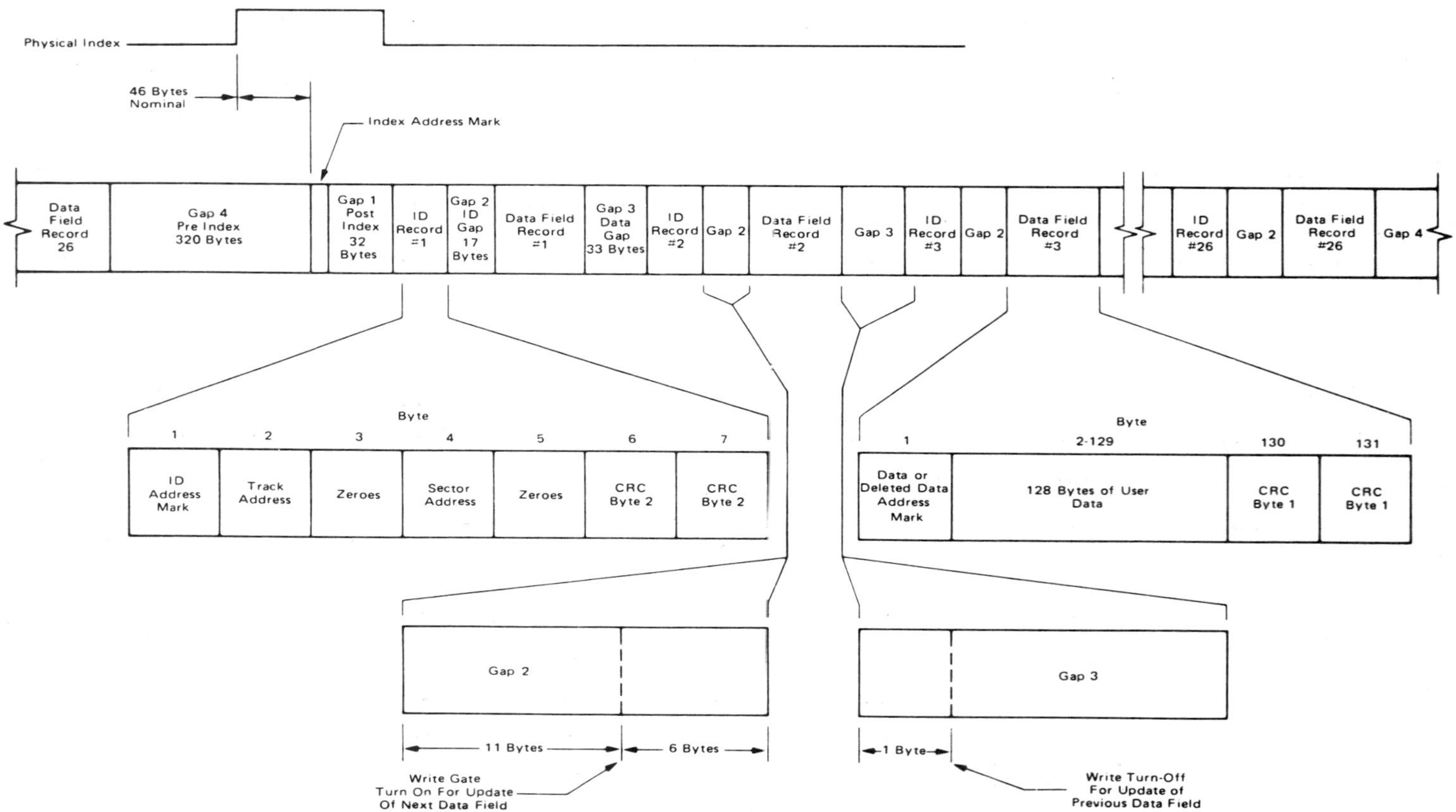

Fig. 2–31. Diskette index recording format with soft sectoring

diskette drive shown in Fig. 2–24 uses either *index recording* or *sector recording*.

Figure 2–31 shows a typical *index recording format*. With index recording, the microcomputer may record one long record or several smaller records. Each track is started by a physical index pulse, and then each record is preceded by a unique recorded identifier. This type of recording is called *soft sectoring*.

With *sector recording* the microcomputer may record up to 32 sectors (or records) per track. (Some systems use 26 sectors per track.) Each track is started by a physical (or mechanical) index pulse, and each sector is started by a physical sector pulse. This type of recording is called *hard sectoring*.

Keep in mind that the recording format is controlled primarily by the microcomputer. However the choice between hard and soft sectoring is set by the diskette drive. For soft sectoring (index recording), only one index hole is required for the diskette, as shown in Fig. 2–24. For hard sectoring (sector recording), one hold is required for each sector (typically 32 or 26 holes).

Because of the great variety of formats available, we shall not discuss them further here. However, it should be noted that diskette recordings generally include some feature to ensure the safety and accuracy of records. As in the case for tape recordings, discussed in Sec. 2–7.6, diskette recordings generally use a form of CRC (cyclic redundancy check).

For example, when using the format of Fig. 2–31, each field written on the diskette is appended with two CRC bytes. These two CRC bytes are generated by circuits that count all the data bits, starting with bit 0 of the address mark and ending with bit 7 of the last byte within a field (excluding the CRC bytes). When a field is read back from the diskette, the data bits (from bit 0 of the address mark to bit 7 of the second CRC byte) are divided by the CRC number. A nonzero remainder indicates an error bit in the data read back; a remainder of zero indicates that the data bytes have been read back correctly (since the CRC bytes contain the necessary number of bits to make a zero, when added to the data bits, and then divided by the CRC number). The nonzero (error) indication can be used to stop the drive, send a flag to the microcomputer, and so forth.

2–9. DATA COMMUNICATIONS

Data communications is the transmission of data from one point to another. For example, the data from one microcomputer can be transmitted to another microcomputer in the same building, in the same

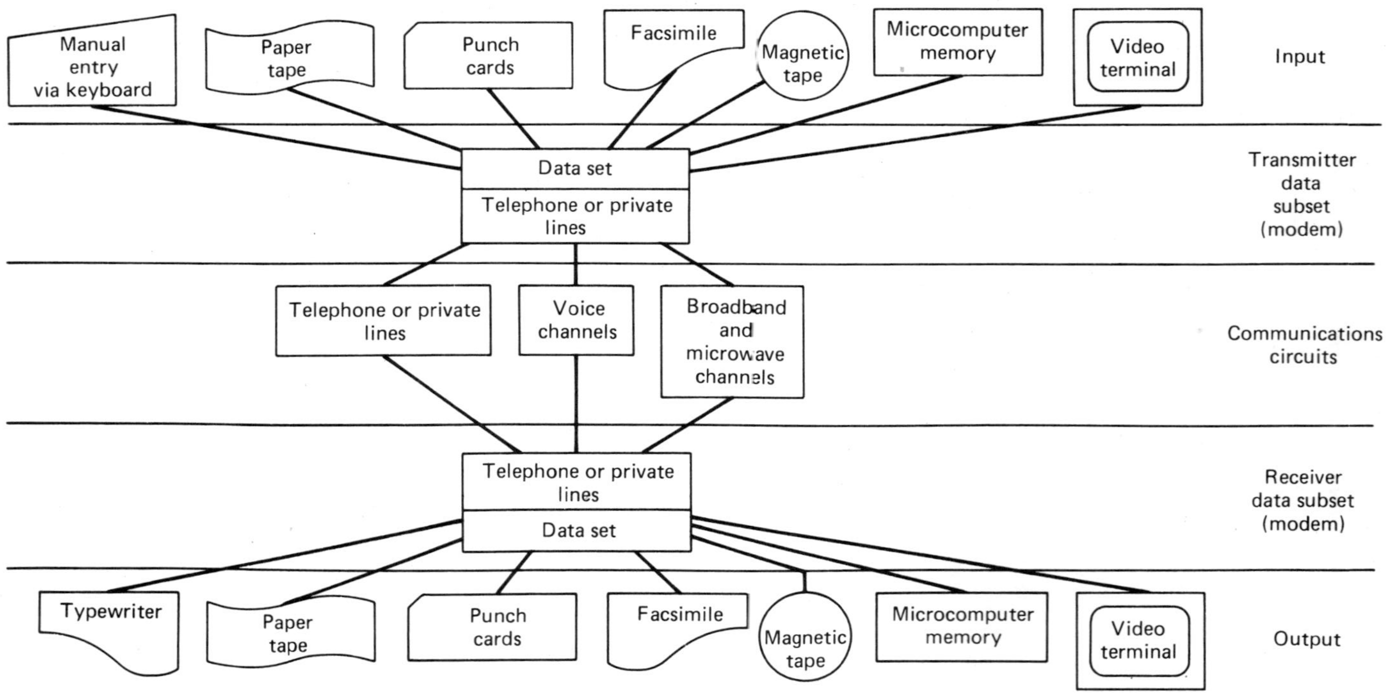

Fig. 2–32. Data-transmission (communication) systems in common use

city, or to a city across the country. Likewise, a central computer can serve several users on a *time-sharing* basis, with each user at a different remote location.

At present, most data-transmission systems use the telephone and teletype lines already available. This requires the translation of microcomputer information (generally in the form of pulses) into a form suitable for transmission across telephone lines. A *data set* and/or a *modem* are the devices used to perform the translation. In most modems, the pulses are used to modulate an audio tone (or tones) that can be transmitted over the lines. At the receiving end, the audio tones are demodulated and converted back to pulses by the modem. Both serial and parallel transmission methods can be used. However, serial is the most popular, since only a single line (or pair of lines) is required.

Many data-communications systems in present use include a standard telephone, in addition to circuits for modulation and demodulation of the pulses. This permits operators to communicate before and after the transmission of data. In a typical situation, the operator will dial a number, putting the operator in touch with operators at opposite ends of the line. After making the necessary arrangements, data can be transmitted back and forth between the locations via the modems and lines.

Any of the input/output units described thus far can be used as terminal devices in association with the data set or modem. The video terminal described in Sec. 2–3 is one of the most popular terminal devices. For example, a time-sharing user can have a visual display unit and a data set or modem at an office location connected by telephone lines to a computer at some remote point. The input and output of the visual display unit are connected through the data set or modem to the telephone lines. With this arrangement, the video terminal is (in effect) connected directly to the microcomputer.

Figure 2–32 summarizes the data-transmission systems in common use. Because these systems are essentially the same for microcomputers and conventional (larger) computers, we shall not discuss them in any detail. The only major difference between the microcomputer and conventional computer data communications is in the interface adapters (or I/O circuits) used between the microcomputer and the communications system.

Chapter 3

MICROCOMPUTER TROUBLESHOOTING EQUIPMENT

The test or service equipment used in microcomputer troubleshooting is basically the same as that used in other fields of digital electronics. That is, most procedures are performed using conventional meters (including high voltage meters for measurement of video terminal CRT voltages), multitrace oscilloscopes (for measurement of pulses on data and address buses, clock and other control lines, etc.), and assorted clips, patchcords, power supplies, and handtools. Theoretically, all microcomputer troubleshooting problems can be solved using such instruments. However, there are some specialized test instruments that greatly simplify microcomputer service (just as they do for any programmed, digital device composed mostly of ICs). Such specialized equipment inludes probes, pulsers, current tracers, logic clips, comparators, and logic analyzers. We shall concentrate on this specialized equipment throughout this chapter. Chapter 5 describes troubleshooting approaches using the equipment covered here.

It is not the purpose of this chapter to promote one type of troubleshooting equipment over another (or one manufacturer over another). Instead, the chapter is devoted to the basic operating principles or features of troubleshooting instrument types in common use. Each type of troubleshooting equipment is discussed in turn. You may then select the type of equipment best suited to your own needs and pocketbook.

Although complicated theory has been avoided, the following discusssions cover the way each type of equipment is used in microcomputer troubleshooting, and what signals or characteristics are to be expected from each. They also describe how the features and outputs found on present-day test equipment relate to specific problems in microcomputer service. Specific techniques for using the equipment in troubleshooting situations are discussed in Chapter 5.

A thorough study of this chapter will familiarize you with the basic principles and operating procedures for typical equipment used in general microcomputer troubleshooting. It is assumed that you will take the time to become equally familiar with the principles and operating controls for any particular test/service equipment that you use. Such information is contained in the user's manuals for the particular equipment.

It is absolutely essential that you become thoroughly familiar with your own particular equipment. No amount of textbook instruction will make you an expert in operating test equipment; it takes actual practice.

It is strongly recommended that you establish a routine operating procedure, or sequence of operation, for each item of troubleshooting equipment. This approach will save time and familiarize you with the capabilities and limitations of your own equipment, thus minimizing the possibility of false conclusions based on unknown operating conditions.

3–1. SAFETY PRECAUTIONS IN MICROCOMPUTER TROUBLESHOOTING

In addition to a routine operating procedure, certain precautions must be observed during operation of any electronic test equipment. Many of these precautions are the same for all types of test equipment; others are unique to special test instruments, such as meters, oscilloscopes, and probes. Some of the precautions are designed to prevent damage to the test equipment or to the circuit where the troubleshooting operation is being performed. Others are meant to prevent injury to you. Where applicable, special safety precautions are included throughout this book.

The following general safety precautions should be studied thoroughly and then compared to any specific precautions called for in the test equipment literature.

1. The most hazardous element in microcomputer troubleshooting is the high voltages used for the CRT of video terminals. Typically, the anode of a CRT requires about 1000 V/in. Thus, a 9-in. CRT requires about 9000 V for the anode. It is essential that the anode voltage (and the related power supply) be measured with a properly

shielded, *high-voltage probe* (similar to those used in television service, see the author's *Handbook of Simplified TV Service,* 1977, Prentice-Hall, Inc., Englewood Cliffs, New Jersey).

2. The next most hazardous problem arises from the fact that a microcomputer usually operates from 115-V line power. This voltage is sufficient to cause death. Even though the voltage is usually dropped to about 5 or 6 V for use by the ICs, the power supply circuits still operate at the line voltage.

3. Many troubleshooting instruments are housed in metal cases. These cases are connected to ground of the internal circuit. For proper operation, the ground terminal of the instrument should always be connected to the ground of the microcomputer being serviced. Make certain that the chassis or housing of the microcomputer being serviced is not connected to either side of the power line or to any potential above ground. If there is any doubt, connect the microcomputer being serviced to the power line through an *isolation transformer.*

4. Remember that there is always danger in servicing microcomputers that operate at hazardous voltages (such as the high voltage used for the CRT), especially as you pull off the microcomputer cover and reconnect the power cord. Always make some effort to familiarize yourself with the microcomputer before servicing it, bearing in mind that high voltages may appear at *unexpected points in a defective microcomputer.*

5. It is good practice to remove power before connecting test leads to high-voltage points. It is preferable to make all service connections with the power removed. If this is impractical, be especially careful to avoid accidental contact with circuits and objects that are grounded. Keep in mind that even low-voltage circuits may present a problem. For example, a screwdriver dropped across a 5-V line can cause enough current to burn out a major portion of the microcomputer, possibly beyond repair. Of course, this problem is nothing compared to the possible injury to yourself. Working with one hand away from the microcomputer and standing on a properly insulated floor lessens the danger of electrical shock.

6. Capacitors may store a charge large enough to be hazardous. Discharge filter capacitors before attaching test leads.

7. Remember that leads with broken insulation offer the additional hazard of high voltages appearing at exposed points along the leads. Check test leads for frayed or broken insulation before working with them.

8. To lessen the danger of accidental shock, disconnect test leads immediately after the test is completed.

9. Remember that the risk of severe shock is only one of the possible hazards. Even a minor shock or burn can place you in danger of more serious risks, such as a bad fall or contact with a higher voltage source.

10. The experienced service technician is continuously on guard against injury and does not work on hazardous circuits unless another person is available to assist in case of accident.

11. Even if you have considerable experience with the test equipment used in troubleshooting, always study the service literature of any instrument with which you are not thoroughly familiar.

12. Use only shielded leads and probes. Never allow your fingers to slip down to the meter probe tip when the probe is in contact with a "hot" circuit.

13. Avoid vibration and mechanical shock. Most electronic test equipment is delicate.

14. Study the circuit being serviced before making any test connections. Try to match the capabilities of the instrument to the circuit being serviced.

3–2. LOGIC PROBE

Figure 3–1(a) shows a typical logic probe. Such probes will detect and indicate high and low (1 or 0) logic levels, as well as intermediate or "bad" logic levels, including an open circuit, on a single line of a microcomputer circuit. For example, the probe can be connected to one of the address or data bus lines (or the clock line, chip-select line, etc.), and will indicate the state (0, 1, or high-impedance) of that line.

A logic level indicator lamp, near the probe tip, gives an immediate indication of the logic states, either static or dynamic, existing in the circuit under test when the probe is touched to the circuit or line. Figure 3–1(b) shows how the logic level indicator lamp responds to voltage levels and pulses for a typical microcomputer line. The indicator lamp can give any of four indications: (1) off, (2) dim (about half brilliance), (3) bright (full brilliance), or (4) flashing on and off. The lamp is normally in its dim state, and must be driven to one of the other three states by voltage levels at the probe tip. The lamp is bright for inputs at or above the 1 state and off for inputs at or below 0. The lamp

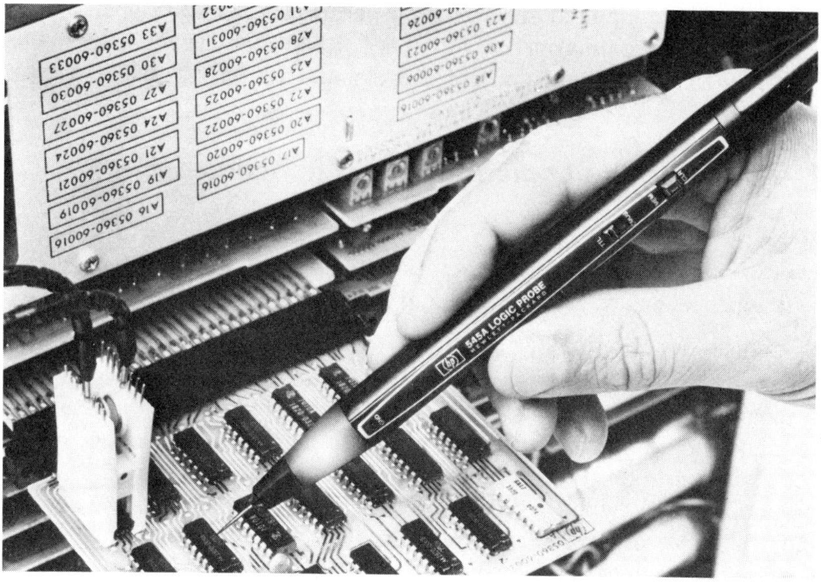

(a)

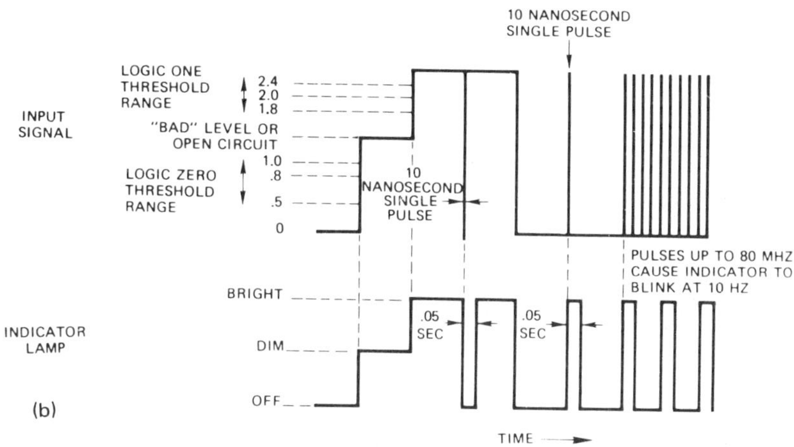

(b)

Fig. 3–1. (a) Hewlett Packard 545A logic probe; (b) TTL logic level lamp indications with probe input voltage levels (5-V power supply)

is dim for voltages between the 1 and 0 states and for open circuits. Pulsating inputs cause the lamp to flash at about a 10-Hz rate.

The logic probe is particularly effective when used with the logic pulser described in Sec. 3–3. For example, the logic pulser can be used to simulate the input to an element in the microcomputer (such as the clock input to the microprocessor, RAM, ROM, or I/O), while the logic probe is touching the output of the element to sense activity of the element.

3–2.1 Using the Logic Probe in Microcomputers

The following paragraphs provide brief descriptions of how the logic probe can be used for troubleshooting. More detailed procedures and approaches are given in Chapter 5.

Probe Power Supply. The logic probe can be powered from the microcomputer power supply or from a regulated dc power supply. If a separate power supply is used, the power supply and microcomputer grounds should be connected together. The power supply voltage range for TTL operation (typical for most microcomputers) is 4.5 to 15 V. A ground wire (provided with the probe) may be connected just behind the probe indicator window. The ground wire is a convenient means of connecting grounds when using external regulated power supplies. The ground wire also improves pulse width sensitivity and noise immunity. However, use of the ground wire is optional and is not required for all applications.

Pulse Detection. The logic probe is ideal for detecting short-duration and low-repetition-rate pulses that would be difficult to observe on an oscilloscope. Typically, positive pulses to $\geqslant$10 ns or more in width trigger the indicator on for $\geqslant$50 ms. Negative pulses cause the indicator to go off momentarily.

Troubleshooting. The bad-level feature of the logic probe is useful for testing three-state logic outputs. The logic HIGH and logic LOW states are detected as described under pulse detection. The third state found in many microcomputer circuits (high-impedance output) is detected as an open-circuit (or bad-level) condition, which leaves the probe indicator dim. The bad-level indication is also useful for detecting floating or unconnected TTL inputs, which look like a bad level to the logic probe.

Basic Probe Techniques. Several logic circuit analysis techniques are useful with the logic probe (as discussed in Chapter 5). One technique is to run the microcomputer under test at its normal clock rate while monitoring for various control signals, such as reset, halt, memory read, flag, or clock. Questions such as "is there a clock signal" or "is there a memory read signal" are quickly resolved by noting if the probe indicator is flashing on and off, indicating that pulse train activity is present. For example, if there is no flashing indication when the probe is connected to the clock line, there is no clock pulse. Or if the probe indicator does not flash when connected to a memory read line, the microcomputer is probably stuck somewhere in the program (since the memory read line is usually pulsed at each step of the program to open the RAM or ROM at each address).

Another useful technique is to replace the normal clock signal with a very slow clock signal from a pulse generator, or to *single step* the clock input with a pulse generator similar to the logic pulser described in Sec. 3–3. This allows changes in logic signals to occur at a rate slow enough that they can be observed on a *real-time basis*. (This basic single-stepping technique is discussed in Sec. 3–7, as well as Chapter 5.) Real-time analysis,coupled with the ability to inject logic level pulses anywhere in the microcomputer with a logic pulser and the means to detect logic state changes with the logic probe, contributes to rapid troubleshooting and fault finding in the control lines. Unfortunately, logic probes are not as valuable when trying to locate faults in multiple-line circuits, such as the data and address buses.

3–3. LOGIC PULSER

Figure 3–2 shows a typical logic pulser. Such pulsers are hand-held logic generators used for injecting controlled pulses into digital logic circuits such as microcomputers. The electronics are housed in a

Fig. 3–2. Hewlett Packard 10526T logic pulser shown with 10525T logic probe

hand-held probe. Automatic pulse control is provided for TTL and many other logic families. Thus, the logic pulses are compatible with most microcomputers. Pulse amplitude depends on the logic supply voltage (3 to 18V), which is also the supply voltage for the logic pulser.

Pulse current and pulse width depend on the load being pulsed. The frequency and number of pulses generated by the pulser are controlled by operation of a push-slide switch on the pulser probe. A flashing LED indicator located in the tip indicates the output mode.

The logic pulser generates pulses as programmed by the fingertip push-slide switch. The pulser is programmed by pushing the switch once for each single-pulse output, or a specific number of times for continuous pulse streams or pulse bursts at selected frequencies. The pulses are also applied to an LED indicator on the pulser tip. (The pulses applied to the LED indicator are slowed down for visibility.)

Pressing the switch automatically drives an IC output or input from low to high (0 to 1) or from high to low (1 to 0). The high source and sink current capability of the pulser can override IC output points, originally in either the 0 or 1 state. The nominal 10-μs pulse width is long enough for even slow CMOS circuits to accept, but heavy circuit loads (such as TTL drivers) result in narrower pulses that limit the amount of energy delivered to the device under test.

The pulser output is three state. In the off state, the pulser's high output impedance ensures that circuit operation is unaffected by probing until the pulser switch is pressed. Pulses can be injected while the circuit is operating, and no disconnects are needed. Some probes have a multipin kit or accessory that provide up to four pulses simultaneously (say to simulate 4 bits of an 8-bit word on a data or address bus).

3–3.1 Using the Logic Pulser in Microcomputers

The following paragraphs provide brief descriptions of how the logic pulser can be used for troubleshooting. More detailed procedures and approaches are given in Chapter 5.

Logic pulsers are generally used with other instruments, such as with the logic probe (Sec. 3–2) and current tracer (Sec. 3–4) in microcomputer troubleshooting. The pulser can also be used with the logic clip (Sec. 3–5) and logic comparator (Sec. 3–6) for general digital electronics troubleshooting. However, as discussed in Secs. 3–5 and 3–6, clips and comparators have limited use in most microcomputers since they are generally limited to 16-pin ICs (thus eliminating the typical microprocessors, ROM, RAM, and I/O IC).

Logic Gate Testing. A logic gate may be tested by pulsing the gate's input, while monitoring the output with a logic probe (Sec. 3–2),

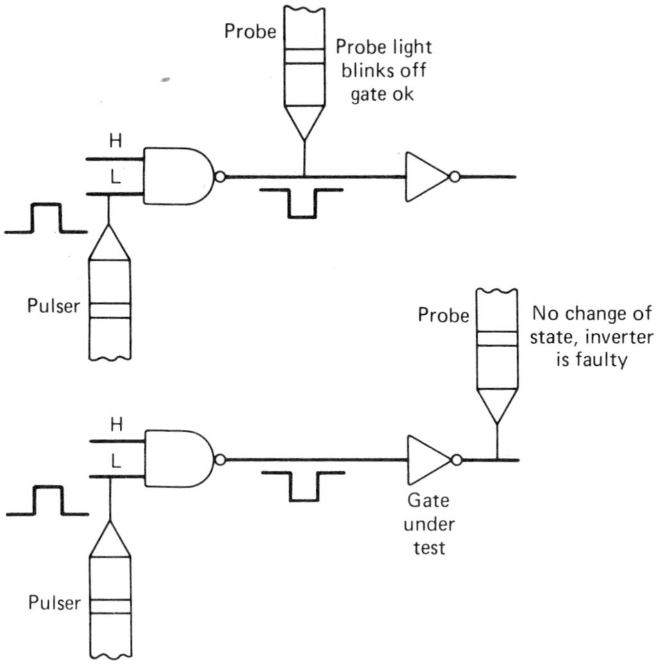

Fig. 3–3. Logic gate testing with probe and pulser

as shown in Fig. 3–3. The logic pulser generates a pulse opposite to the state of the input line and can change the gate output state. This assumes that the output of the gate is not clamped in its state by another input (such as a high on the other input of an OR gate).

If the pulse is not detected at the output, pulse the output line as shown in Fig. 3–4. If the output is not shorted to V_{cc} or common return, the logic probe should indicate a pulse opposite to its original indication.

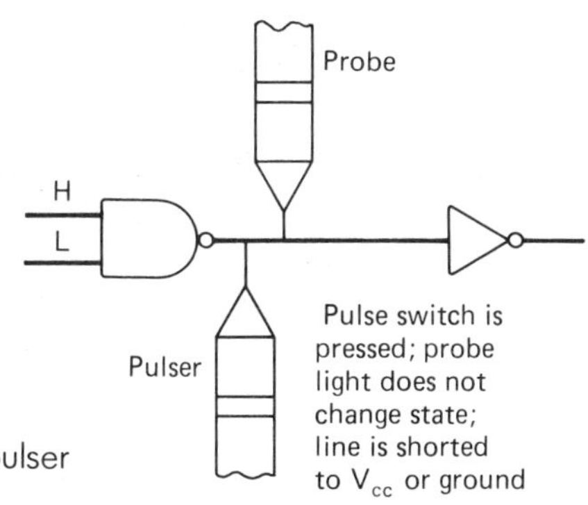

Fig. 3–4. Testing for shorts with pulser and probe

If not, check for external shorts (solder bridges and the like) before removing the IC. Shorts at the inputs and outputs are best located by means of the current tracer described in Sec. 3–4.

3–4. CURRENT TRACER

Figure 3–5 shows a typical current tracer. Such current tracers are hand-held probes that enable the precise localization of low-impendance faults in electrical systems (including typical microcomputer printed-circuit wiring). The probe senses the magnetic field generated by a pulsing current internal to the circuit or by current pulses supplied by an external stimulus such as the logic pulser (Sec. 3–3). Indication of the presence of current pulses is provided by the lighting of the indicator lamp near the current tracer tip. Adjustment of probe sensitivity over the 1-mA to 1-A range is provided by a SENSITIVITY control near the indicator. The probe is self-contained and requires <75 mA at 4.5 to 18 V from any convenient source.

3–4.1 Using the Current Tracer in Microcomputers

The following paragraphs provide brief descriptions of how the current tracer can be used for troubleshooting. More detailed procedures and approaches are given in Chapter 5.

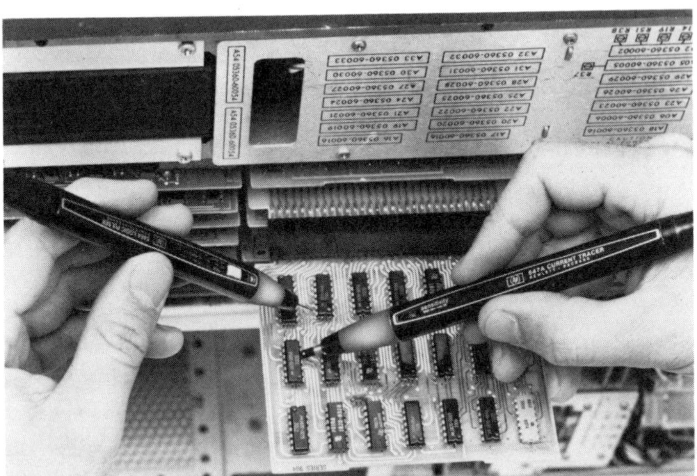

Fig. 3–5. Hewlett Packard 547A current tracer shown with 546A logic pulser

The current tracer operates on the principle that whatever is driving a low-impedance fault node or point must be delivering the majority of the current. Tracing the path of this current leads directly to the fault. Problems that are compatible with this method are the following:

1. Shorted inputs of ICs.
2. Solder bridges on printed-circuit boards.
3. Shorted conductors in cables.
4. Shorts in voltage distribution networks (such as V_{CC}-to-ground shorts).
5. Stuck data or address buses, including three state buses.
6. Stuck wired-AND structures.

Basic Current Tracer Operation. Use of the current tracer is indicated when conventional troubleshooting reveals a low-impedance fault (such as a short). The operator aligns the mark on the current tracer tip along the length of the printed-circuit trace at the driver, and adjusts the sensitivity controls until the indicator lamp just lights. The current tracer is then moved along the trace (line) or placed directly on the terminal points (IC pins), while observing the indicator light. This method of following the path of the current leads directly to the fault responsible for the abnormal current flow. If the driving point does not provide pulse stimulation, the terminal may be driven externally by using a logic pulser (Sec. 3–3) at the driving point. The following paragraphs describe troubleshooting techniques for some of the more common problems.

Wired-AND Problems. One of the most difficult problems in troubleshooting ICs of any type is a stuck wired-AND circuit. (If you are not familiar with such terms as wired-AND, logic gates, and open-collector gates, you should make a thorough study of basic logic circuits before going too far into microcomputer troubleshooting. The author's *Logic Designer's Manual,* 1977, Reston Publishing Company, Inc., Reston, Virginia, provides such a study.) Typically, one of the open-collector gates connected in the wired-AND mode may still continue sinking current after it has been turned off. The current tracer provides an easy method of identifying the faulty gate. (Of course, if the gate is located in an IC, the entire IC must be replaced. However, you have still located the problem.)

Referring to Fig. 3–6, place the current tracer on the gate side of the pull-up resistor. Align the mark on the tracer tip along the length of the printed-circuit trace (line) and adjust the tracer's sensitivity control

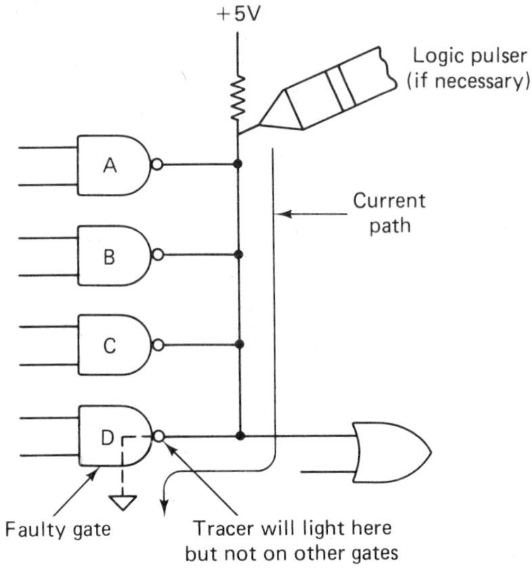

Fig. 3–6. Locating wired-AND problems with a current tracer

until the indicator is just fully lighted. If the indicator will not light, use a logic pulser to excite the line as shown. Place the tracer tip on the output pin of each gate; only the faulty gate (or pin) will cause the indicator to light.

Gate-to-Gate Faults. When a low-impedance fault (short, full, or partial) exists between two gates, the current tracer and logic pulser combine to quickly pinpoint the defect. In Fig. 3–7, the output of gate A is shorted to ground. Place the pulser midway between the two gates, and place the current tracer tip on the pulser pin as shown. Pulse the line and adjust the current tracer sensitivity control until the indicator just lights. First place the current tracer tip next to gate A, and then gate B, while continuing to pulse the line. The tracer will light only on the gate A side, since gate A (the defect in this example) is sinking the majority of the current. If the tracer does not light when placed between the pulser and gate A, look for a short on the line between the pulser and gate B.

Solder Bridge/Cable Problems. When checking printed-circuit traces (lines) that may be shorted by solder bridges or other means, start the current tracer at the driver and follow the trace. Figure 3–8 shows an example of an incorrect current path due to a solder bridge. As the tracer probe follows the trace from gate A toward gate B, the indicator remains lighted until it passes the bridge. This is an indication

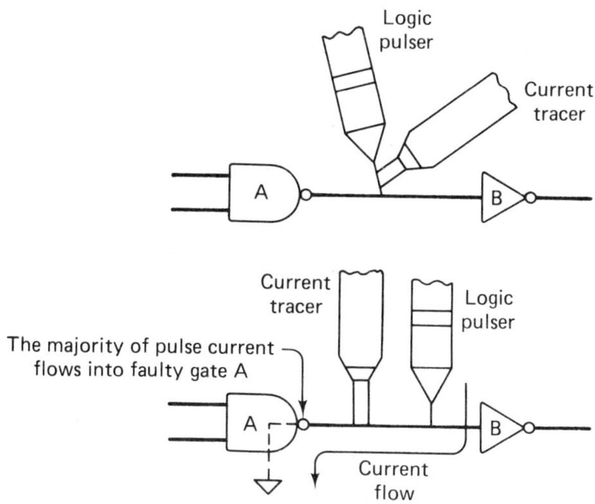

Fig. 3–7. Locating gate-to-gate faults with a current tracer

that the current has found some path other than the trace. Visually inspect this area for solder splashes and the like. These principles also apply when troubleshooting shorted cable assemblies.

Multiple Gate Inputs. Another type of IC arrangement is the one-output, multiple-input configuration. Figure 3–9 shows this type of circuit being pulsed by a signal on the input of gate A. In this case, place the current tracer tip on the output pin of gate A and adjust the sensitivity control until the indicator light just comes on. Then check the input pins of gates B through E. If one of the input pins is shorted, that pin will be the only one to light the indicator.

Should the tracer fail to light when placed next to the output of

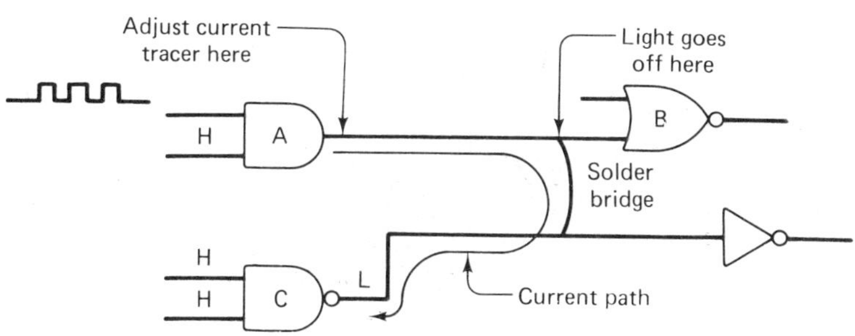

Fig. 3–8. Locating solder bridges in printed-circuit lines with a current tracer

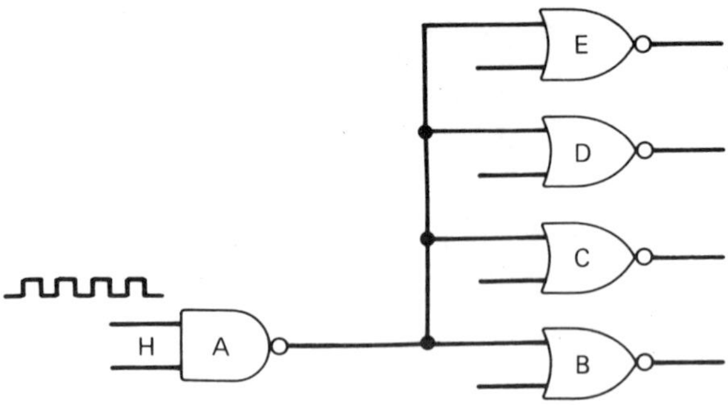

Fig. 3–9. Checking multiple-gate inputs with a current tracer

gate A, it is a good indication that the problem exists in gate A. To be sure that this is true, use the current tracer in the manner described under gate-to-gate faults. If the circuit has no input signal, use a logic pulser.

3–5. LOGIC CLIP

Figure 3–10 shows a typical logic clip. Such clips are designed for logic-level determination only on ICs using TTL and DTL circuits. Generally, clips can test flip-flops, gates, counters, buffers, adders, shift

Fig. 3–10. Hewlett Packard 548A logic clip

registers, and the like, but will not test ICs with nonstandard input levels or expandable gates. Clips will instantly and continuously show the logic levels (0 or 1) at all pins of a dual-in-line IC. All 16 input pins are electrically buffered to minimize loading on any circuit being tested.

Sixteen LEDs are the high and low (0 or 1) logic-level indicators. No power supply connections need be made, since the clip powers itself from the circuit under test by automatically locating the V_{CC} and ground pins of the IC.

In use, you squeeze the thick end of the clip to spread the contacts, and place the clip on the IC to be tested. The LEDs on top of the clip will indicate the logic levels at each connected IC pin. The clip may be turned in either direction.

3–5.1 Using the Logic Clip in Microcomputers

At present, logic clips are of little value in microcomputer work since a typical clip will accommodate only 16-pin ICs. Generally, a microprocessor has 40 pins, and 24 pins is standard for most ROMs, RAMs, and I/Os. However, there may be 40- and 24-pin clips in the future. Also, in some microcomputers, there may be a 16-pin IC that has access to the data and address buses.

If a logic clip could have access to both buses, the clip could be used for a *program trace* function, using *single stepping,* as described in Sec. 3–7. In such a case, the logic clip serves to read out the data word at each address. However, at this writing, the *logic analyzer* is the most practical instrument for making a rapid, thorough program trace.

3–6. LOGIC COMPARATOR

Figure 3–11 shows a typical logic comparator. Such comparators clip onto 16-pin ICs and, through a comparison scheme, instantly display any logic state differences between the test IC and a reference IC. Logic differences are identified to the specific pin or pins of the IC with the comparator's display of 16 LEDs. A lighted LED corresponds to a logic difference.

In use, the IC to be tested is first identified. A reference board with a good IC of the same type is then inserted in the comparator. The comparator is clipped onto the IC in question, and an immediate indication is given if the test IC operates differently from the reference IC. Even very brief dynamic errors are detected, stretched, and displayed.

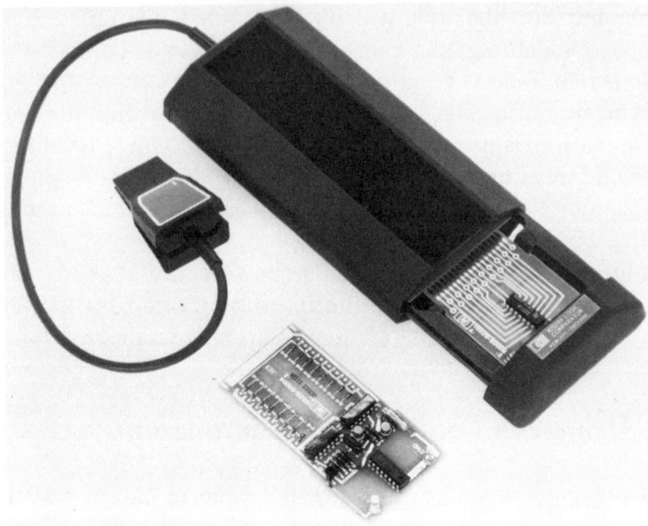

Fig. 3–11. Hewlett Packard 10529A logic comparator

The comparator operates by connecting the test and reference IC inputs in parallel. Thus, the reference IC sees the same signals that are inputs to the test IC. The outputs of the two ICs are compared, and any difference in outputs greater than 200 ns in duration indicates a failure. A failure on an input pin, such as an internal short, will appear as a failure on the IC driving the failed IC. Thus, a failure indication actually pinpoints the malfunctioning pin.

3–6.1 Using the Logic Comparator in Microcomputers

As in the case of the logic clip (Sec. 3–5), logic comparators are presently limited to 16-pin ICs, and are thus of little value in microcomputer work. However, 40- and 24-pin comparators may be developed in the future.

3–7. BASIC APPROACH TO MICROCOMPUTER TROUBLESHOOTING

A microcomputer is a solid-state, digital, programmed device. Thus, all the troubleshooting techniques that apply to such devices also apply to the microcomputer. For example, most microprocessor-based system failures can be solved using multitrace oscilloscopes, as well as logic probes, logic pulsers, and current tracers. However, there is one instrument that can be used most effectively in microcomputers. This instrument is called the *logic analyzer* or *logic state analyzer.* The following paragraphs describe the basics involved when the logic analyzer is used with microprocessor systems. The remaining sections of this chapter describe the operation and use of state-of-the-art logic analyzers. Specific applications for analyzers in microcomputer troubleshooting are discussed in Chapter 5.

3–7.1 Basic Microcomputer Troubleshooting

The classic approach for troubleshooting any programmed device is to monitor some significant system function (such as the data and address buses), go through each step in the program, and compare the results with the program listing for each address and step. This is sometimes known as a *program trace* or, more simply, a *trace* function. One technique for this procedure is called *single stepping.* With the single-stepping approach, you remove the normal clock pulses and replace them with single, one-at-a-time pulses obtained from a logic pulser, switch, or push button. This permits you to examine and compare the data at each address with that shown in the program.

For example, assume that each of the eight lines on the data bus could be connected to a multitrace oscilloscope so that the bit on each line appears as a pulse on a corresponding trace. A pulse on the trace indicates a binary 1, whereas the absence of a pulse indicates a binary 0 on that line. A simplified version of such a test setup is shown in Fig. 3–12.

The test is started by applying a single pulse to the reset or clear line. Then sufficient single pulses are applied to the clock line until address number 1 (0001) appears on the address bus. Now assume that the program listing shows that a hex 7F (binary 0111-1111) data byte should be on the data bus at address 0001, but that the oscilloscope traces show binary 0011-1111. Obviously, the wrong instruction will be applied to the microprocessor, and the system will malfunction. This could be caused by a broken line on the data bus, by a defect in memory, by the absence of a memory read pulse, by a memory read pulse that appears at the wrong time (opens the memory data buffer too soon or too late), or by several other possible causes. However, you have isolated the problem and determined where in the program the problem occurs.

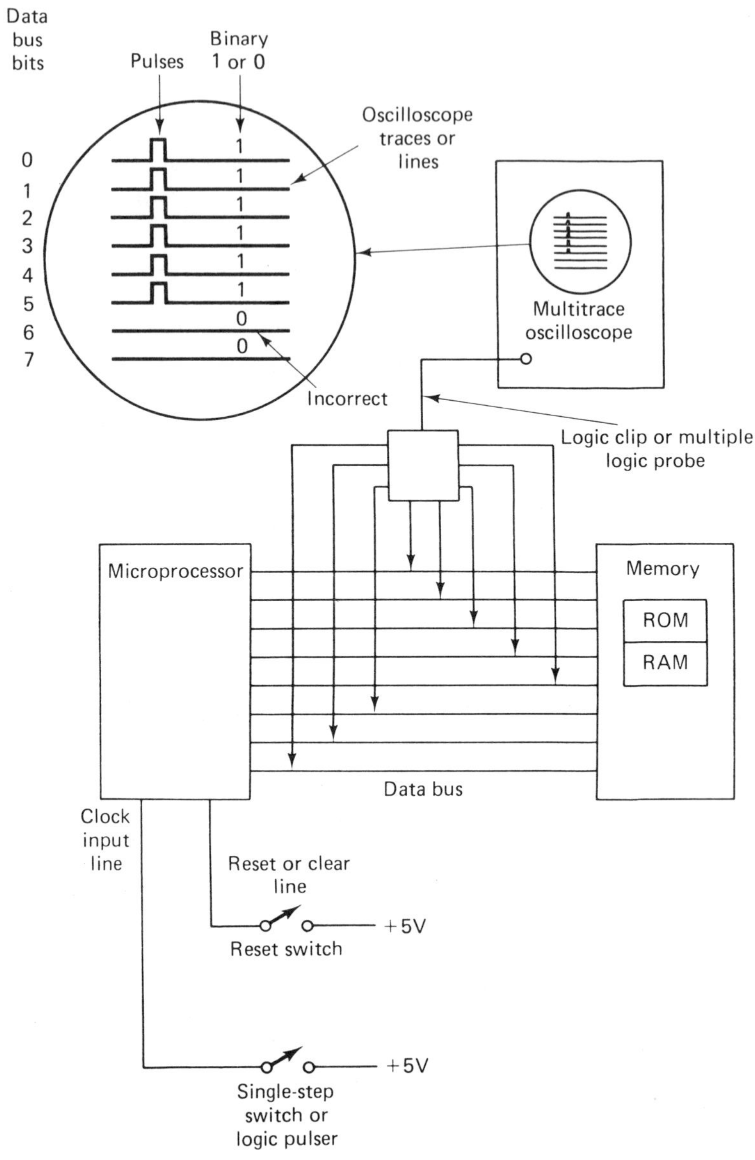

Fig. 3–12. Basic microprocessor troubleshooting approach using multitrace oscilloscope and single stepping

3–7.2 Timing Problems

If the problem appears to be one of timing, the oscilloscope can be used to check the time relationship of the related pulses. For example, the oscilloscope can be connected to the data bus, address bus, and read line as shown in Fig. 3–13. The oscilloscope then shows the *time relationships* among the pulses on these lines.

In the simplified example of Fig. 3–13, the read pulse must hold the memory data buffer closed until the selected address pulses appear on the address bus (sometimes known as the *valid address* point), must

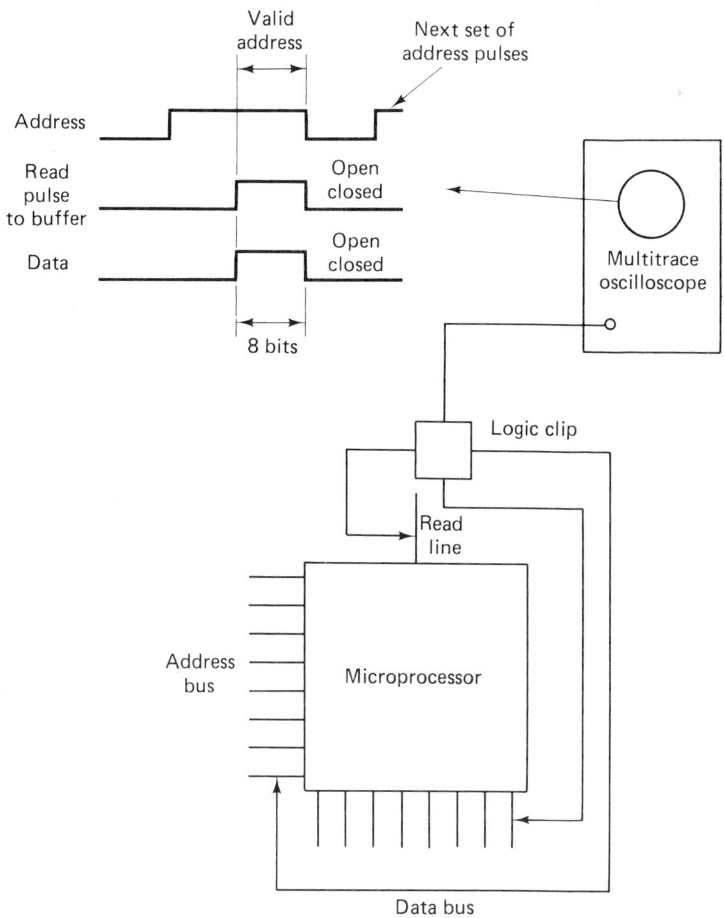

Fig. 3–13. Basic microprocessor troubleshooting approach for timing problems

hold the buffer open just long enough for all 8 data bits to appear on the data bus, and then must close the buffer until the next address is applied. In a practical case, the entire timing diagram (discussed in Sec. 1–14 and shown in Fig. 1–27) can be duplicated on a multitrace oscilloscope.

3–7.3 Logic Analyzer

Although single stepping and a check of system timing can pinpoint many microcomputer problems, there are two obvious problems. First, present-day multitrace oscilloscopes do not have enough traces to accommodate all the lines in data and address buses simultaneously. Second, and more important, a typical data byte is 8 bits, and thus requires 8 clock pulses, or 8 one-at-a-time pushes of the single-step button. Since all program steps require at least one byte (and often two or three bytes, possibly 24 bits), you must push that button many times if the malfunction occurs at step 3333 of the program! This means that you must spend endless hours comparing program lists against binary readouts at addresses. (If you are already familiar with troubleshooting of any programmed device, you know that the most time-consuming part of the task is in making such comparisons.)

The logic analyzer overcomes this basic problem by permitting you to select the data at a particular address for display. The logic analyzer will then run through the program at near the normal system speed (a fraction of a second) and display the selected data at the desired *breakpoint* or between two breakpoints in the program.

Figure 3–14 shows a typical logic analyzer display. (This happens to be the display of the logic analyzer described in Sec. 3–9.) A logic analyzer is essentially a multitrace oscilloscope combined with electrical circuits (generally microcprocessor based) to produce special displays. The electronic circuits that produce these displays are sometimes known as *formatters*. The logic analyzer shown in Fig. 3–14 is operated by a keyboard. Other logic analyzers use switches and controls rather than a keyboard. No matter what control system is used, logic analyzers have three basic types of displays.

3–7.4 Timing Display

The multitrace feature of the logic analyzer can be used to reproduce *timing diagrams* in a manner similar to that of a conventional multitrace oscilloscope. Figure 3–15 shows a typical timing diagram display as produced on a logic analyzer. This is sometimes known as a *time-domain* display, and is not found on all logic analyzers.

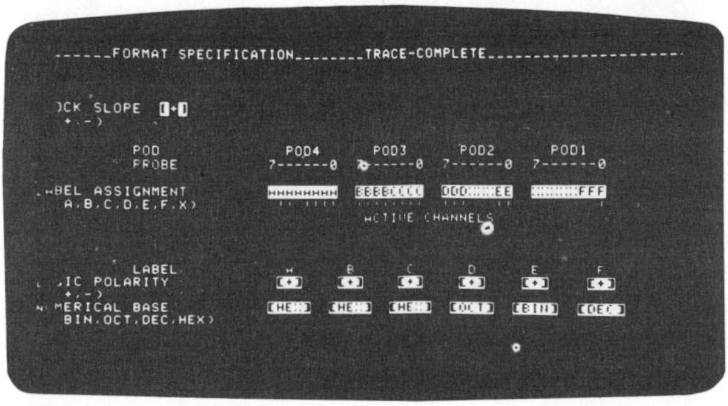

Fig. 3–14. Typical display of Hewlett Packard 1610A logic analyzer

3–7.5 Tabular Data Display

The data display format of the logic analyzer (sometimes called the *data domain* format or display) is used to display data bytes (as they appear on the data and/or address buses) in binary form. In effect, the bytes appear as they would on paper (1s and 0s, rather than the presence or absence of pulses). Figure 3–16 shows that several data

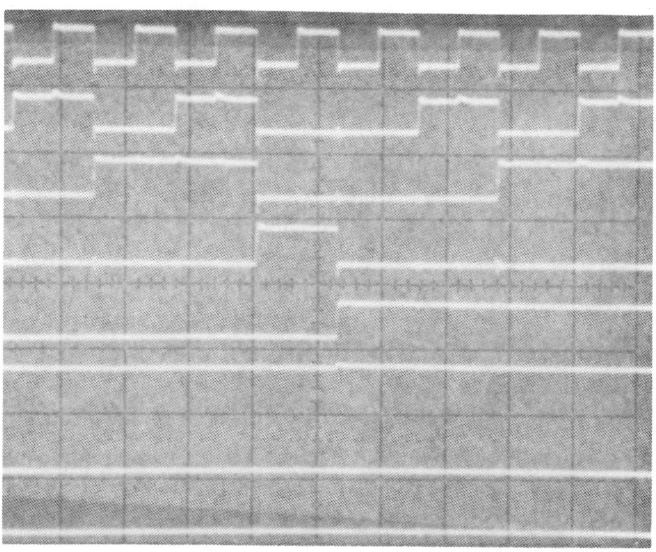

Fig. 3–15. Typical timing diagram (time domain) display as produced on a logic analyzer

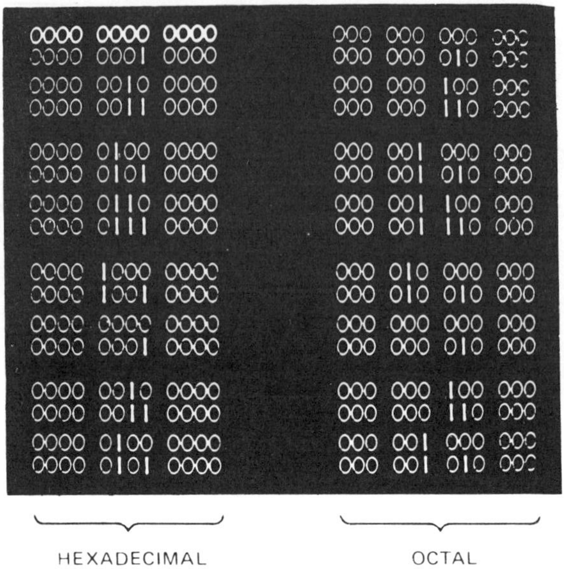

Fig. 3–16. Typical tabular data (data domain) display as produced on a logic analyzer

bytes can be displayed simultaneously. This makes it possible to check the data words before and after a selected point (breakpoint) in the program. With some logic analyzers, the selected data word is indicated by extra brightness of the display. In Fig. 3–16, the top data word is the selected word (the breakpoint starts at this word and continues for 16 steps or words).

To use the tabular data format, you connect the logic analyzer to the data and/or address buses by means of multiple logic probes supplied with the analyzer (usually a cable-probe kit or accessory). Then you select a particular data word and/or address breakpoint from the program listing by means of the logic analyzer controls (keyboard or switches), and start the program. The microcomputer then runs through the complete program, but only the desired portion of the program is displayed.

Figure 3–17 shows a comparison of a typical program listing versus a logic analyzer display. In this example, note that both the address and data bytes are shown for 16 steps of the program. Compare this tabular display with that of the timing display (Fig. 3–15). Even those readers not familiar with troubleshooting will quickly realize the advantages of a tabular display for microcomputer troubleshooting and for debugging. Keep in mind that the program can be operated at near

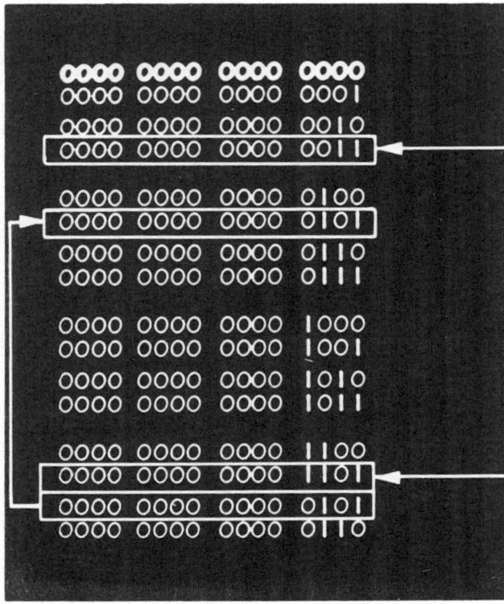

ADDRESS	MACHINE FORMAT INSTRUCTION	FUNCTION
0000	70	Clear Accumulator
0001	B0	Output Port 00 ◄ one byte from ACC
0002	B1	Output Port 01 ◄ one byte from ACC
0003	B8	Output Port 08 ◄ one byte from ACC
0004	B9	Output Port 09 ◄ one byte from ACC
0005	0B	Load ISAR from ACC
0006	70	Clear Accumulator
0007	5C	Load Scratch Pad Register 'C' ◄ ACC
0008	0A	Load Accumulator from ISAR
0009	58	Load Register 8 from ACC
000A	24	Add Immediate
000B	41	41 to Accumulator
000C	81	If result of previous step is positive
000D	F8	Branch to Address 0005
		Loop is continued until all F8 Scratch Pad Registers Clear
000E	20	Load Immediate and
000F	0C	Call Subroutine Direct

Fig. 3–17. Comparison of a typical program listing versus a logic analyzer tabular data display

its normal speed, and can be examined on a line-by-line basis, 16 lines at a time. The next 16 lines can be selected by the simple setting of a switch or touch of a key. Compare this with single stepping through the entire program.

3–7.6 Mapping Display

Another display unique to logic analyzers is the mapping display or mapping *signature*. There is some disagreement among microcomputer wizards as to the value of mapping. For this reason, many state-of-the-art analyzers omit the mapping feature. Other analyzers substitute a *graph* or special tabular display for mapping. It is not our purpose to resolve the mapping controversy here, but to describe the what, where, and why of mapping in logic analyzers.

A mapping display is formed by connecting the MSB bits of a data word to the vertical deflection circuits of the logic analyzer (those circuits that cause vertical deflection of the oscilloscope trace), while the LSB bits are connected to the horizontal deflection circuits. This produces a series of dots as shown in Fig. 3–18. In the mapping mode, the display is an array of 256 dots instead of a table of 1s and 0s. Each dot represents one possible combination of the 16 input lines so that any input is represented by an illuminated dot. An input of all 0s (or 00 00 in hex) is at the upper-left corner of the display, whereas an input of all 1s (or FF FF in hex) is at the lower right. The dots are interconnected

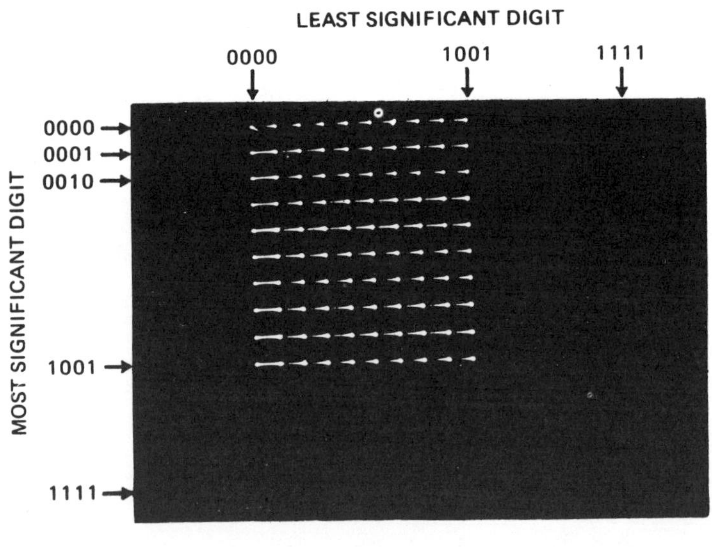

Fig. 3–18. Typical mapping display as produced on a logic analyzer

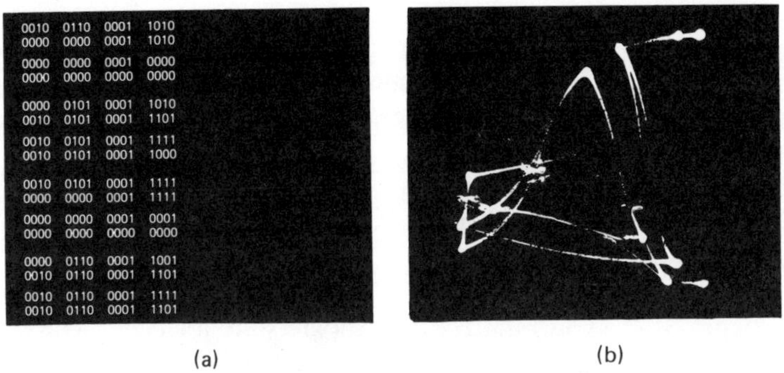

Fig. 3–19. Comparison of tabular display and mapping display as produced on a logic analyzer

so that the sequence of data changes can be observed. The interconnecting line gets brighter as it moves toward a new point, thereby showing the direction of data flow.

When the mapping display is used to monitor a microcomputer program, or a portion of a program, the display assumes a unique pattern or *signature*. Once you have learned to recognize the patterns for a particular microcomputer, it is relatively easy to tell at a glance if the program is proceeding normally. Compare the table and map display of Fig. 3–19. The same data bytes (16 words, 16 bits per word) are in tabular form in Fig. 3–19a, and plotted in a map format in Fig. 3–19b.

Some logic analyzers are provided with a *cursor* function to help locate specific points in the mapping display. Generally, the cursor is a bright circle that can be manipulated over the display by the analyzer controls. In use, the cursor is positioned over an area of interest on the map, and the address or data word is read out on the analyzer controls. For example, as shown in Fig. 3–20, the cursor is positioned over the desired area on the top line of the mapping display.

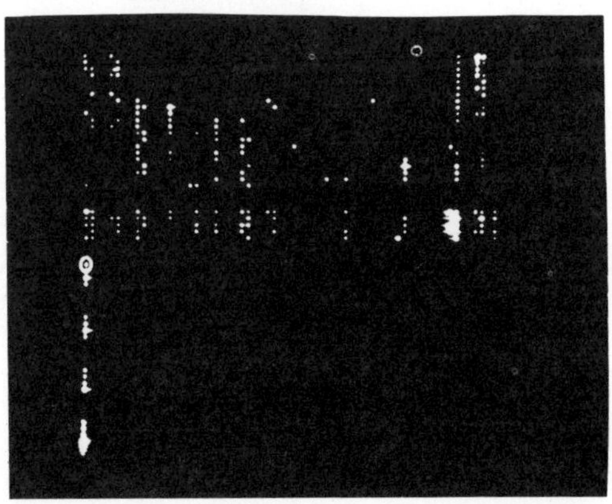

Fig. 3–20. Using the cursor function of a logic analyzer mapping display to locate a malfunction in a program

Keep in mind that the examples given here are very elementary. Logic analyzers, in the hands of experienced operators, are very powerful tools for testing, debugging, troubleshooting, and analyzing all forms of data-manipulating equipment, not just microprocessors.

3–8. HEWLETT PACKARD MODEL 1611A LOGIC STATE ANALYZER

Figure 3–21 shows the HP1611A logic state analyzer. The instrument is keyboard controlled and provides a tabular display. The 1611A is dedicated to the design and troubleshooting of any microprocessor-based system, not only for microcomputers. For ease of use, a special probe offers two methods of connection to 40-pin microprocessors, a 40-pin clip and a 40-pin connector for interfacing with microprocessors in sockets.

Measurements of microcomputer activity are displayed on the analyzer's CRT screen in selectable mnemonic or absolute codes of the *microprocessor's own instruction set.* The display is divided into three distinct fields of address, data, and external information. The events and activities displayed in the address and data fields are collected directly from the system microprocessor's address and data buses. Additional bits of binary information are gathered by auxiliary probes for display of activity on control or other functional lines (such as reset, halt, or memory read).

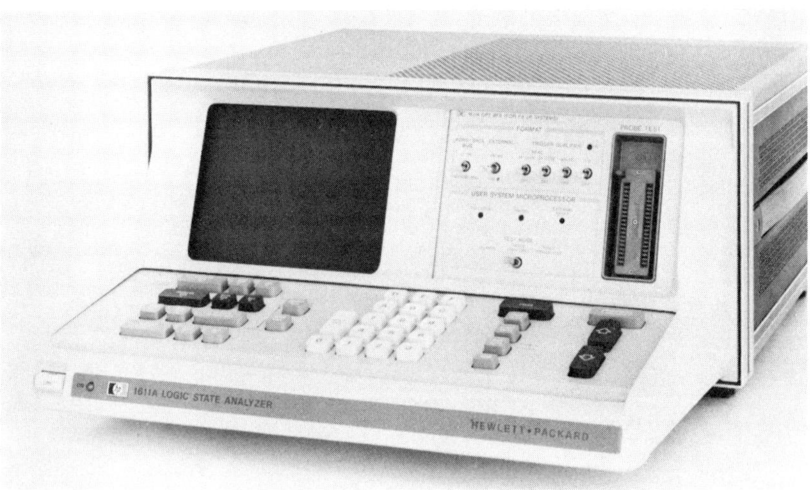

Fig. 3–21. Hewlett Packard 1611A logic state analyzer

With unique *relational-triggering capabilities,* the analyzer permits the framing of a real-time *data window* around virtually any event or set of related events, or any desired sequence of system operations. The analyzer also accurately measures execution time or counts selected events between two keyboard selected events. At a desired point, defined from a keyboard entry, the analyzer can be commanded to halt microprocessor operation. Then, if desired, the analyzer can control the transactions that follow in single or multiple keyed steps. Keyboard entry of address or data bus trigger words (to establish breakpoints) may be entered in either octal or hex notation, and the external trigger information is entered in binary.

For increased confidence of the instrument's operation, the analyzer performs a self-test during the turn-on period, and indicates the results on the CRT. The microprocessor probe data-gathering circuits may also be checked by connecting the probe to the front panel probe test socket with the test results displayed on the CRT.

The following paragraphs provide a brief description of analyzer functions, configurations, and accessories.

3–8.1 Probes

Connection to the microcomputer under test is through multiconductor cables and external probes, shown in Fig. 3–22. When the microcomputer is readily accessible, a 40-pin clip makes the connection, or a plug-in connector may be inserted in the microprocessor socket and the microprocessor then relocated to the probe body. The low profile of the plug-in connector eliminates the need for extender boards to maintain normal system operation.

Eight external miniature probes permit connections in the system external to the microprocessor bus for tracing related events or for additional trigger qualifications (such as reset, halt, and memory read).

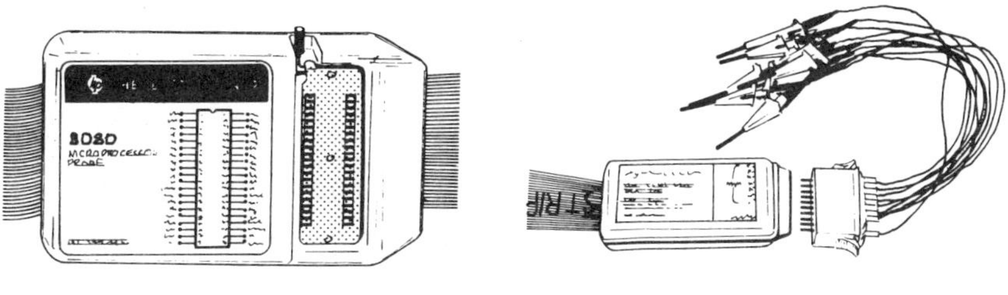

Fig. 3–22. Multiconductor cables, clip, and probes for the 1611A

3–8.2 Configuration with Personality Modules

The analyzer is configured to the characteristics of a particular microprocessor by means of a front-panel *personality* module or option. Upon initial order, the analyzer is specified to fit a particular microprocessor. Option 068 for the 6800 microprocessor system and option 080 for the 8080 microprocessor system are the initial sections.

All the specialization is contained within two printed circuit boards, a removable section of front panel (Fig. 3–21), and the dedicated microprocessor probe (Fig. 3–22). Thus, if another configuration is desired after initial purchase, the parts that determine the analyzer's personality can be ordered separately, and easily exchanged in about 15 minutes.

3–8.3 Data Entry

The desired address, data, and external triggering parameters are entered directly in octal or hex notation with the keyboard controls. This permits both software-and hardware-oriented personnel to work in the format that they are most comfortable with, and not have to worry about conversions among formats.

3–8.4 Trace

The program trace functions are specified by keyboard entries that determine the conditions that must be met for a trigger to occur. Triggering can occur at virtually any point in the program. The program trace specification (trigger points) may simply be the appearance in the data stream of a specified address or a specified data word, or the occurrence of a specified combination of 1s, 0s, or don't cares (often indicated in a program by an $\times$) on the eight external probes. Likewise, triggering can occur for any combination of address, data, and external probe conditions.

3–8.5 Triggering

Entries into the address, data, or external fields are accomplished by first pressing the desired key to open the proper data field, and then entering data with the entry keys. When the trigger conditions are met, a 64-transaction sequence is stored for display. The trigger can be selected to occur at the beginning of the sequence to display events following the trace point, or it may be at the end to display events from 1 to 63 memory transactions preceding the trace point, or the trace

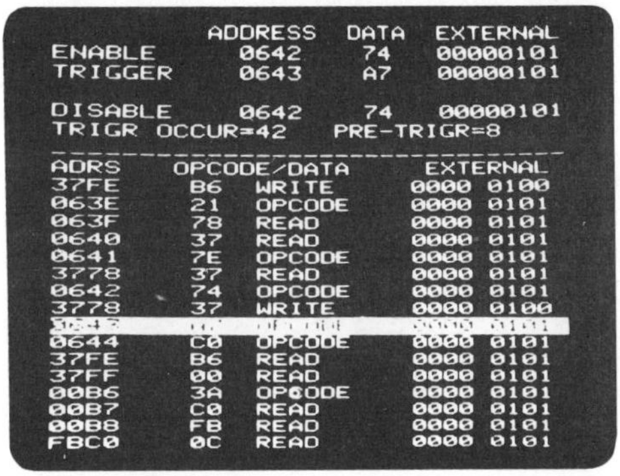

Fig. 3–23. Display showing trigger parameters in alphanumeric format along with data collected

point may be set anywhere in between to display both before and after events. Digital delay of from 1 to 65,472 memory transactions moves the trace point to display information after the desired trigger point occurs.

3–8.6 Display

The analyzer CRT screen displays alphanumeric information about the keyboard entries, as well as the first 16 lines of captured data. This is shown in Fig. 3–23, where triggering parameters (entered through the keyboard) are displayed in alphanumeric format (above the dashed line), along with the data collected (below the dashed line). In the example of Fig. 3–23, the trigger word or combination of conditions occurs when the address is 0643, with data A7, and external conditions (obtained through the external probes) are 00000101. Note that the trigger word is highlighted on the display, as shown in Fig. 3–23, to make it easy to identify. Also note that other information concerning trigger conditions is displayed above the dashed line, such as the trigger enable and disable functions at address 0643, data 74, and external 00000101.

It is possible to view the entire record of captured data by pressing a *roll key* that permits the data in memory to move past the viewing window. In Fig. 3–24, the data words have rolled up seven lines from the position shown in Fig. 3–23. The data may be displayed in either hex or octal, as shown in Figs. 3–24 and 3–25, respectively. Likewise, an absolute/mnemonic key converts the readout to match the microprocessor manufacturer's programming manual. For example, as shown in

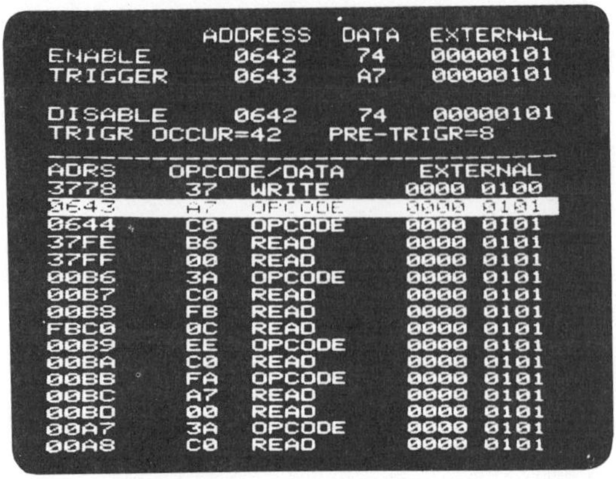

Fig. 3–24. Display showing data words rolled up seven lines

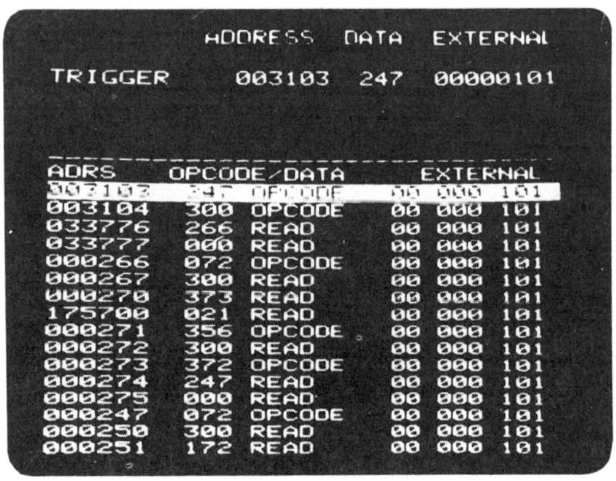

Fig. 3–25. Display showing data words in octal format

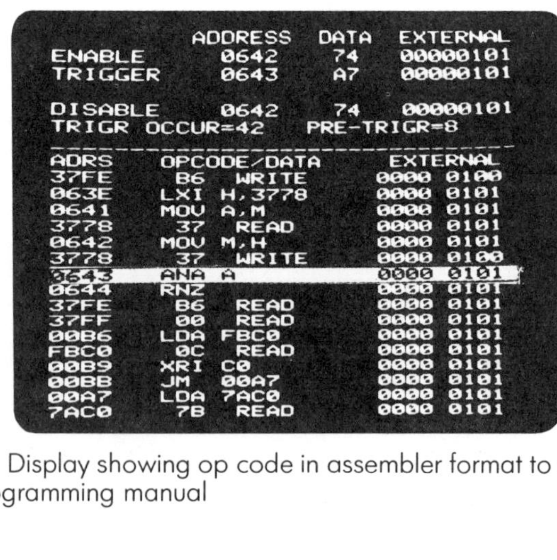

Fig. 3–26. Display showing op code in assembler format to match microprocessor programming manual

Fig. 3–26, the op code may be displayed in a familiar assembler format using mnemonic notation.

3–8.7 Trigger Specification

In addition to a simple trigger point, *ranges of addresses* may be defined. That is, the trigger specification may be selected to include or exclude ranges of addresses. The ranges are determined by selecting the greater-than and lesser-than limits and the desired address word, as shown in Fig. 3–27. In this example, the trace point, address 3779, is the first occurrence of an address between the selected limits ≥ 0100 and ≤ 4000.

Any or all of the trigger specifications can be further modified by requiring a predetermined pass count of up to 256 trigger occurrences before a trace begins. Also, trigger enable and disable conditions can be specified that establish the boundary conditions in which the selected trigger search may be allowed. This *windowed triggering* permits the analyzer to search for a trigger word in a limited portion of a microcomputer's program execution. For example, address, data, and external words may be entered to define a trigger enable event that inhibits trigger arming until the enable event is encountered. Similarly, a three-

```
                ADDRESS     DATA     EXTERNAL

TRIGGER         < = 4000
                > = 0100
                                PRE-TRIGR=5


ADDRS           OPCODE/DATA         EXTERNAL
00AA            MOV B,A             0000 0101
00AB            LXI H,3779          0000 0101
00AE            XRA M               0000 0101
3779             7B  READ           0000 0101
00AF            RRC                 0000 0101
00B0            JC   0599           0000 0101
00B3            CALL 063E           0000 0101
37FF            00   WRITE          0000 0100
37FE            B6   WRITE          0000 0100
063E            LXI H,3778          0000 0101
0641            MOV A,M             0000 0101
3778             37  READ           0000 0101
0642            MOV M,H             0000 0101
3778             37  WRITE          0000 0100
0643            ANA A               0000 0101
0644            RNZ                 0000 0101
```

Fig. 3–27. Display format showing ranges of addresses

field trigger disable event may be selected to disarm the trigger search. This causes the analyzer to look for a valid trigger only between the enable and disable points.

3–8.8 Execute Functions

The execute keys permit selection of desired analyzer operations as defined by the trace specification limits previously inserted. The following paragraphs describe some typical examples.

Trace. Pressing the *trace* key provides a display of successive transactions of program as executed in real time referenced to the selected trace specification.

Selective Trace. Instead of requesting a list of successive transactions, the *trace trigger* key calls for a selective trace of only the occasions when the selected trigger conditions are met. This provides a listing of selected events, which may be all transactions to a particular address, memory writes or reads to a range of addresses, or virtually any desired events. Selective trace permits discarding of all transactions not relevant to the desired measurement, which eliminates the need for expensive, cumbersome bulk memories.

Timing. Instead of analytically determining loop times or time spent in nested loops, the analyzer's *time interval mode* may be used to directly measure execution time. The timing measurement is set up by simply specifying the enable and disable conditions, which directly measures loop or interrupt times rather than the difficult and sometimes impossible methods of calculating these times from software listings.

For example, to determine the total loop execution time, the loop start address is used for both the enable and disable event, which includes any or all nested loops in the total time. In Fig. 3–28, the result of the measurement is directly displayed as 163 μs. This means that a total time of 163 μs is used in executing the loop through address 0642.

Counting. By using a method similar to that for timing, the number of trigger events between the enable and disable trigger points may be displayed. As shown in Fig. 3–29, the readout is direct when the *count trigger* function is selected. The events counted are those satisfying the trigger specification. For instance, if it is desired to count the number of times a particular nested subroutine is called, its entry address can be the trigger event counted between enable and disable events. In the example of Fig. 3–29, three trigger events (writes to memory defined by 0 in the LSB of the external field) occurred in the loop accessed at address 0642.

```
                 ADDRESS    DATA    EXTERNAL
ENABLE            0642
TRIGGER           XXXX               XXXXXXX0

DISABLE           0642

-----------------------------------------

ADRS    OPCODE/DATA                  EXTERNAL



      TIME =           163 MICROSECONDS
```

Fig. 3–28. Display format showing time interval mode

3–8.9 Trigger Outputs

Once a fault is found in the actual software execution on the hardware, another form of analysis instrument, usually an oscilloscope, is often required to pinpoint the problem. The analyzer trigger outputs are stable with respect to the microcomputer clock, so an oscilloscope can be used for critical timing measurements. Trace point outputs are also available if needed to generate interrupt signals or for added *clock-stopper* circuits in other parts of the system under test.

3–9. HEWLETT PACKARD MODEL 1610A LOGIC STATE ANALYZER

Figure 3–30 shows the HP1610A logic state analyzer. The instrument is keyboard controlled, provides a tabular display and graph display, and offers general-purpose measurements in microprocessor-

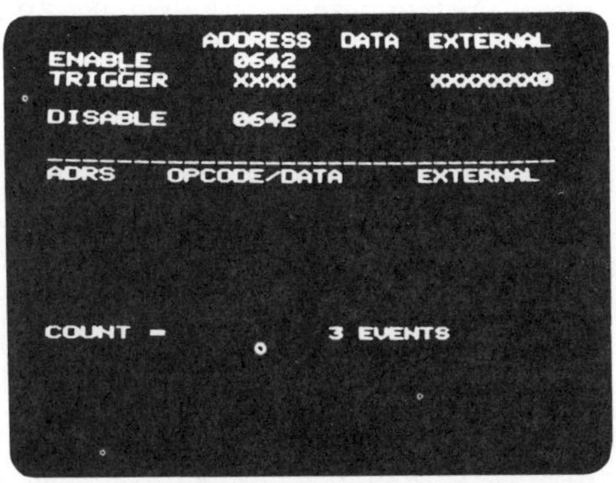

Fig. 3–29. Display showing the counting function

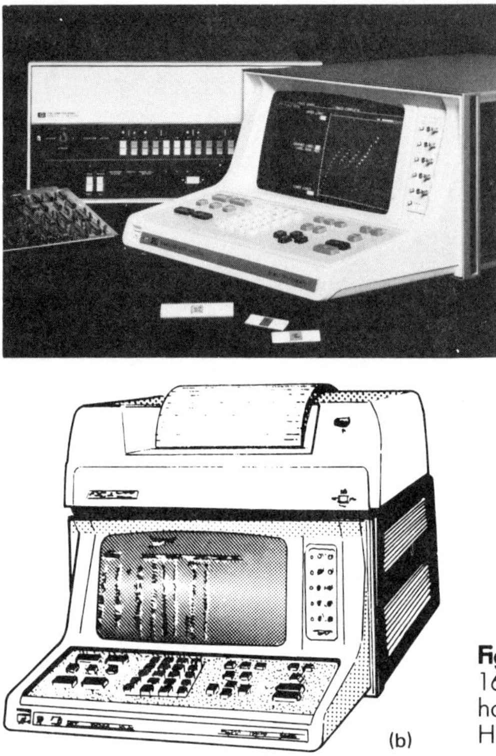

Fig. 3–30. (a) Hewlett Packard 1610A logic state analyzer; (b) hard copy printer option for HP1610A

based systems, minicomputers, or virtually any digital circuit (not just microcomputers). The 1610A synchronously performs real-time trace and count measurement up to 10MHz with powerful triggering capabilities on words up to 32 bits wide, to allow you to capture the data of interest.

Measurements of system activity are displayed on the analyzer's CRT screen in selectable hex, octal, binary, or decimal codes. Setup for measurement is aided with the format and trace specification *menus,* which indicate the test parameters that you are to enter. The events and activity that are captured and displayed from the system are gathered at clock transitions after the analyzer locates the specified trace position and then captures 64 words of data.

The displayed trace may be a *simple breakpoint,* with the trace position at the beginning, end, or center of the captured data, or in a *state sequence* where one to seven words must be found in a specified order before data are captured. This state sequence permits you to directly locate sections of branched, looped, or nested loops of state flow. A selective trace of from one to seven words may be OR-specified, which allows only the words of interest to be captured and eliminates data that are not necessary for your measurement.

A *count measurement* capability allows you to perform a time or state count on all 64 traced states in either absolute or relative modes. With the count measurement you can determine how much time a program spends in loops and servicing interrupts, as well as the time between program steps. This measurement is performed simultaneously with the trace, and all 64 words traced are assigned a count record, which is displayed as positive or negative time in relation to the location of the trace position (absolute mode). In the relative mode, each count record is displayed in relation to the previously acquired state.

One complete measurement, including format and trace specifications, may be internally stored to be recalled at a later time or for use in a *trace compare* mode. When a trace compare mode is selected, the display presents an exclusive-OR tabular listing of the *differences between* the current and stored measurements. The trace compare mode may also be used to direct the analyzer to continuously rerun a measurement until the current and stored measurements are equal, or not equal, and the analyzer automatically halts and retains the current measurement.

The analyzer includes a trace graph to provide a display of *data magnitude versus time sequence* for all 64 words in memory. Each dot representing a word is given a vertical displacement corresponding to its magnitude and is positioned horizontaly in the order of its occurrence. The result is a waveform analogous to oscilloscope displays, and offers a quick overview of program operation. The trace graph function is, in effect, a form of mapping.

For increased confidence of the instrument's operation, there are self-tests for the keyboard, ROM/RAM, display, a trace test that includes all probe pods, an interrupt test, and a printer test.

Hard copy of both the format and trace specifications, as well as the trace list and trace compare, can be obtained by adding an accessory printer to the basic instrument (Fig. 3–30). Rear panel printer outputs are included in the analyzer for direct interfacing.

3–9.1 Probes

Input data are sensed through 32 high-impedance probes at rates up to 10 MHz (see Fig. 3–31). Data probes are separated into four 8-bit pods for easier connection to a system, with a fifth probe pod for connecting to a clock source. To make it easier for connecting to different systems, the front section of each probe may be disconnected

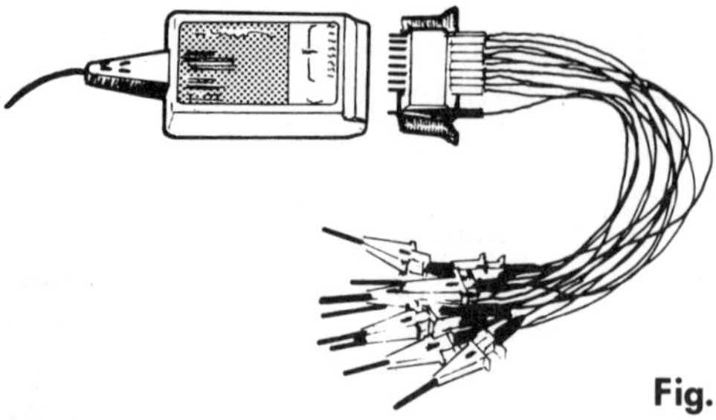

Fig. 3–31. Data probes for 1610A

from its pod. This allows the individual probe leads for each probe pod to be wired to connectors for specific systems. Additional probe lead kits as well as probe tips are available separately as accessories.

3–9.2 Data Entry

Entries are made via an entry keyboard. The entry location is indicated by a blinking cursor on the CRT screen. Entry fields are multiple choice, with the desired test parameter selected by using a field select key. As an example of the multiple choice, the data may be entered on positive or negative edges of the clock signal. Trace specifications are entered through the keyboard directly in octal, hex, binary, or decimal notation, which permits working with a familiar format without worrying about base conversions.

3–9.3 Menus

The displays that are called up by a keyboard command are referred to as menus because they include the selections for setting up test parameters and labeling of test results. These menus include *format specification, trace specification, trace list, trace compare,* and *trace graph*.

Format Specification. The formatting capabilities allow you to separate the 32 input data channels into the desired test parameters. This allows those data bits that act as a unit to be assigned to one of six labels (for example, 16 bits of address bus assigned as A, and 8 bits of data bus assigned as D). This labeling capability then permits all trace specifications to be assigned as a unit rather than on individual lines. Figure 3–32 shows a typical format specification menu. Each assigned label may be independently defined in positive or negative logic, as well as with different bases of binary, octal, decimal, or hex. The allowed selections are defined on-screen to minimize front-panel controls. An-

```
-------------FORMAT SPECIFICATION-----------STORE COMPLETE-------------

CLOCK SLOPE        +
  (+,-)

                  POD         POD4        POD3        POD2        POD1
                  PROBE     7------0    7------0    7------0    7------0

LABEL ASSIGNMENT            AAAAAAAA    AAAAAAAA    DDDDDDDD    EXXXXCCC
(A,B,C,D,E,F,X)              !! !       !!!!!!!!    !!!!!!!

                  LABEL        A           C           D           E
LOGIC POLARITY
(+,-)                          +           +           +           -

NUMERICAL BASE                HEX         BIN         OCT         DEC
(BIN,OCT,DEC,HEX)
```

Fig. 3–32. Typical format specification menu

other feature of this menu is that active channels are shown as exclamation marks for a quick overview of system activity.

Trace Specification. After the format specifications have been defined, the trace specification menu is called up and the measurement parameters are entered. Figure 3–33 shows a trace specification menu, resulting from the format specification in Fig. 3–32. Figure 3–33 shows the labels with their numerical bases (A in hex, C in binary, D in octal, E in decimal, etc.), making it easier to enter test parameters. The blinking cursor indicates where the specification is to be entered. In Fig. 3–33, the cursor is in the trace position field, which means that start, center, or end could be selected by using the field select key.

```
--------TRACE SPECIFICATION----------------STORE COMPLETE--------

                LABLE     A      C     D     E        OCCUR
                BASE     HEX    BIN   OCT   DEC        DEC

[START]         TRACE    XXXX   XXX   XXX   X         00001

TRACE

    [ALL STATES]

COUNT  [OFF]
```

Fig. 3–33. Trace specification menu

The trace measurement may be in a sequence from one to seven words that must be found in the specified order. The ability to select a sequence of words allows you to locate sections of branched, looped, or nested loops during a program run. To further qualify the sequence, each word in a sequence may be specified to occur from 1 to 65,536 times, so you can capture the *n*th pass of a loop beginning at a given word. Figure 3–34 shows a typical trace specification for defining a test sequence that will capture a nested loop as well as only selected states in the loop. With the trace specification shown in Fig. 3–34, the analyzer will find, in sequence, the first occurrence of $28B7_{16}$, the ninth occurrence of $28AE_{16}$, and the eight occurrence of $28A5_{16}$, and start a trace on the seventh occurrence of 2841_{16}. The analyzer will then trace the range of states within $284X_{16}$, $285X_{16}$, and $286X_{16}$.

A sequence restart state capability is available so that the search for a given sequence will be restarted if the sequence is not satisfied before or upon locating the restart word condition. A selective trace of from one to seven words may be OR-specified for collection. By collecting only the words of interest, you eliminate the clutter of unnecessary words, which makes it easier to analyze the displayed information. To further condense the display to only the desired portion of the program, one trace occurrence may be specified to occur from 1

```
----------TRACE SPECIFICATION---------EXCHANGE COMPLETE------


                   LABEL          A       C      D     E        OCCUR
                   BASE          HEX     BIN    OCT   DEC        DEC

FIND IN SEQUENCE                 28B7    XXX    XXX    X        00001
                   THEN          28AE    XXX    XXX    X        00009
                   THEN          28A5    XXX    XXX    X        00008
[START]          TRACE           2841    XXX    XXX    X        00007

SEQ RESTART    [OFF]


TRACE
 [ONLY STATE]                    284X    XXX    2XX    X        00001
           OR                    285X    XXX    XXX    X
           OR                    286X    XXX    XXX    X


COUNT   [OFF]
```

Fig. 3–34. Typical trace specification for defining a test sequence that will capture a nested loop as well as only selected states in the loop

to 65,536 times, which allows the *n*th occurrence of a word to be captured.

Trace List. When the trace key is pressed, the analyzer searches for the word sequence defined in the trace specification. As the data are captured, they are displayed on the CRT along with a line number and alphabetically formatted into the assigned labels and their numerical base. Figure 3–35 shows a trace list of data collected as defined by the trace specification of Fig. 3–34. The analyzer displays the label and numerical bases for fast data interpretation, as well as the sequence requirements and resulting state flow. The display contains 20 words, and roll keys permit you to view the entire 64-word listing. To make it easier to locate the trace position, which may be selected to start, be in the center, or end of a trace, start is spelled out on the display as shown in Fig. 3–35. Any count information is also presented adjacent to each word.

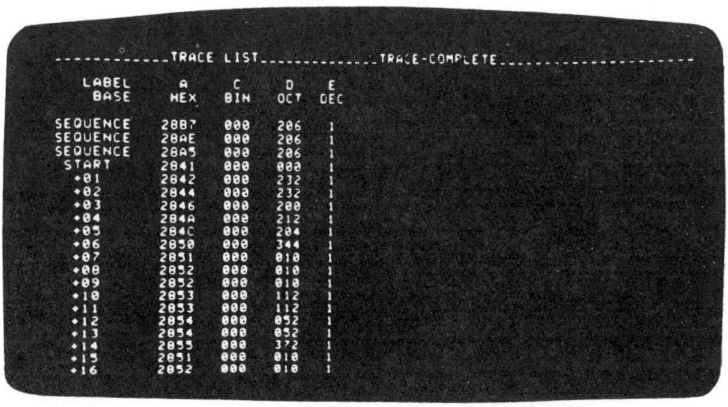

Fig. 3–35. Trace list of data collected as defined by the trace specification in Fig. 3–34

A *count states* specification can be defined in the trace specification so that a trace list will count states, as shown in Fig. 3–36. The count measurement may be specified to be either *time* or *state* (word) count for all 64 words in memory. Furthermore, the count may be in either absolute or relative mode. The absolute mode gives you the time or count between the trace position and a selected word; the relative mode presents the time or count between each consecutively acquired state. This allows you to directly determine the time spent in loops, interrupts, or program time between steps.

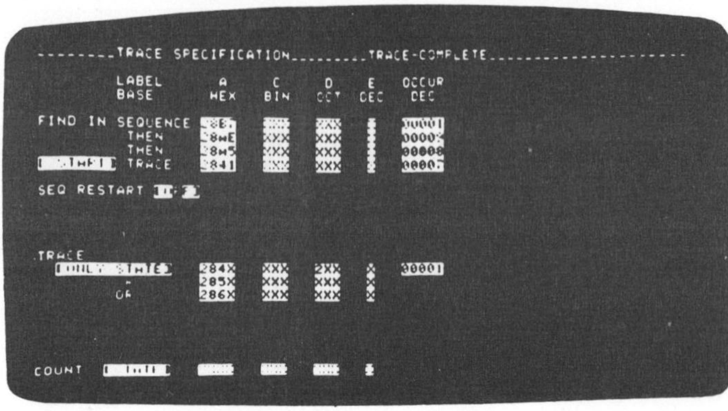

Fig. 3–36. Trace specification formatted so that the trace list will count states

Figure 3–37 shows a trace list (absolute mode) resulting from the trace specification in Fig. 3–36, and shows the number of states (in decimal) that occurred prior to and following the trace start. Notice that negative signs indicate states occurring prior to the start state, and positive signs indicate states occurring after the start state.

Figure 3–38 shows time in the relative mode, which is the elapsed real time between each state and the previously acquired state.

Trace Graph. Figure 3–39 is a trace graph that may be selected to give a view of all 64 states in analyzer memory. The data bytes to be

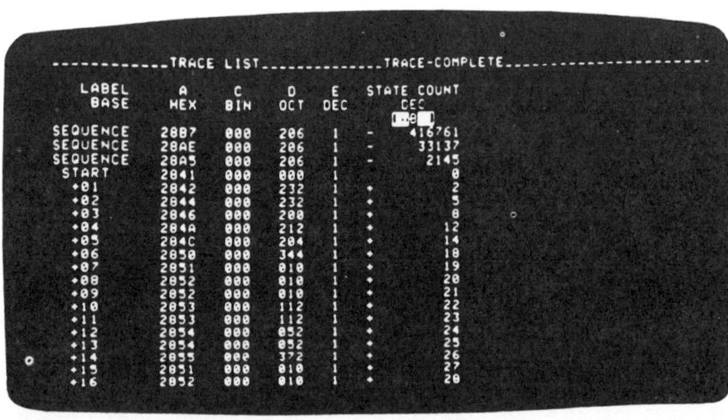

Fig. 3–37. Trace list (absolute mode) resulting from the trace specification in Fig. 3–36, showing the number of states (in decimal) that occurred prior to and following the trace start

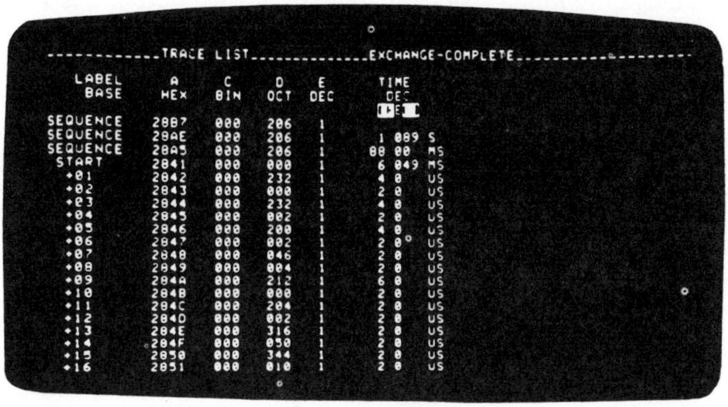

Fig. 3–38. Display showing time (in the relative mode) that is the elapsed read time between each state and the previously acquired state

graphed are selected by label with the base displayed on screen. Each dot's vertical position is determined by its absolute numerical value, and its horizontal position is determined by its time sequence and occurrence. Settable upper and lower limits on the graph make it easy to see the level of memory in which the program is operating. The example of Fig. 3–39, which is a graph of a label of the trace list in Fig. 3–36, shows that the program is looping prior to branching to a higher level in the program.

Scaling of the vertical displacement is controlled by specifying the upper and lower limits in the same numerical base as the data. By being

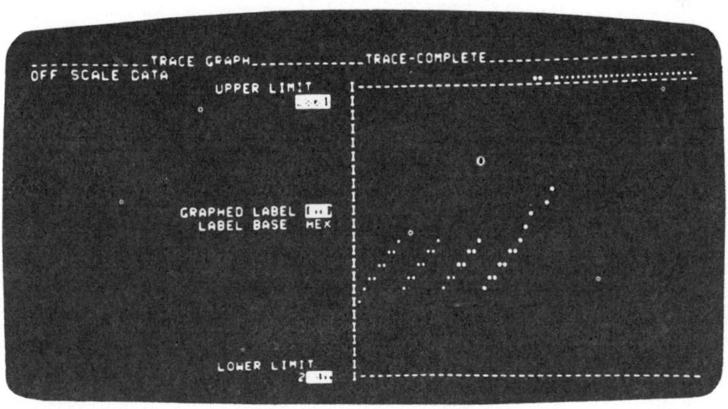

Fig. 3–39. Trace graph of a label of the trace list shown in Fig. 3–36

able to change the limits, you can magnify any section of a graph to full scale for detailed examination. To make it easier to pinpoint data of interest, 20 dots corresponding to the lines viewed in the trace list are intensified. The intensified section may be rolled to points of interest in the graph, which then allows their absolute value to be read by switching to the trace list. The trace list of Fig. 3–40, called from the graph of Fig. 3–39, shows the program completing a loop (states 2851_{16} through 2855_{16}) prior to branching to a higher memory.

Trace Compare. One complete trace measurement including format and specification may be stored internally, which allows comparison between a current and stored measurement. The current and stored measurement may be interchanged, which allows you to quickly review the stored measurements, as well as their specifications. Figure 3–41 shows the analyzer stopping data acquisition when the active data are not equal to the stored data at state +06.

The trace compare is actually an exclusive-OR tabular listing of the differences between the current and stored measurements. The listing is formatted and rolled as a trace list, with identical bits displayed as zeros and different bits displayed as nonzeros. For example, in octal,

---------TRACE LIST------------TRACE COMPLETE------------

LABEL BASE	A HEX	C BIN	D OCT	E DEC
+20	2853	000	112	1
+21	2853	000	112	1
+22	2854	000	052	1
+23	2854	000	052	1
+24	2855	000	372	1
+25	2851	000	010	1
+26	2852	000	010	1
+27	2852	000	010	1
+28	2853	000	112	1
+29	2853	000	112	1
+30	2854	000	052	1
+31	2854	000	052	1
+32	2855	000	372	1
+33	2856	000	356	1
+34	2857	000	000	1
+35	28EC	000	050	1
+36	28ED	000	276	1
+37	2858	000	156	1
+38	2859	000	000	1
+39	28BE	000	226	1

Fig. 3–40. Trace list (called from the graph of Fig. 3–39) showing the program completing a loop

-----------TRACE COMPLETE-----------COMPARED TRACE-COMPLETE-----------

LABEL BASE	A HEX	C BIN	D BIN	E DEC	COMPARED TRACE MODE
START	0000	000	00000000	0	STOP
+01	0000	000	00000000	0	
+02	0000	000	00000000	0	
+03	0000	000	00000000	0	
+04	0000	000	00000000	0	
+05	0000	000	00000000	0	
+06	0000	000	00000110	0	
+07	0000	000	00000000	0	
+08	0000	000	00000000	0	
+09	0000	000	00000000	0	
+10	0000	000	00000000	0	
+11	0000	000	00000000	0	
+12	0000	000	00000000	0	
+13	0000	000	00000000	0	
+14	0000	000	00000000	0	
+15	0000	000	00000000	0	
+16	0000	000	00000000	0	
+17	0000	000	00000000	0	
+18	0000	000	00000000	0	
+19	0000	000	00000000	0	

Fig. 3–41. Trace compare showing analyzer stopping data acquisition when the active data are not equal to the stored data at state +06

03 is equivalent to binary 000 011, which means that the least significant bits are different in the two measurements. A compared trace mode is also available that directs the analyzer to continuously rerun a measurement until the current and stored measurements are either equal or not equal. This makes it much easier to capture intermittent problems.

3–9.4 Self-test

A built-in self-test capability provides assurance that the analyzer is operating properly. The self-test checks the ROM/RAM, display, keyboard, probes, interrupt, and printer functions. The self-test is initiated with a rear panel push button that calls the test program, which is displayed on-screen and directs the operator through the test procedure. Figure 3–42 shows the keyboard self-test called with instructions on how to perform the test.

3–9.5 Trigger Outputs

Once a fault is found, another type of analysis instrument, usually an oscilloscope, is often required to pinpoint the problem. The analyzer's trigger output is stable with respect to the system clock, so an

```
SELECTED TEST KEYBOARD-----------1610 VERIFICATION IN PROCESS

      INSTRUCTIONS-PRESS ALL KEYS ENDING WITH FIELD SELECT


LAST CODE
MISSING CODES ABCDEFHIJKLPQRSTX... #$%&'()
```

Fig. 3-42. Keyboard self-test called with instructions on how to perform the test

oscilloscope can be used for critical timing measurements. The measurement enable output is useful for gating clocks or interrupting the device under test for for added clock-stopper circuits in other parts of the system.

3-10. HEWLETT PACKARD MODEL 1602A LOGIC STATE ANALYZER

Figure 3-43 shows the HP1602A logic state analyzer. The instrument is a portable, keyboard-controlled analyzer for use in design and troubleshooting a variety of digital systems, including microcomputers.

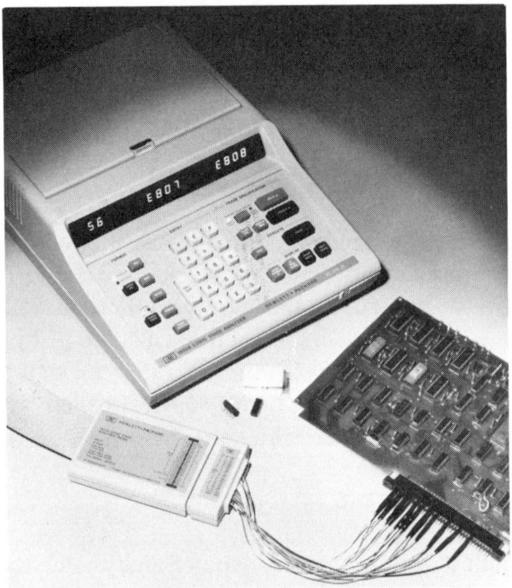

Fig. 3-43. Hewlett Packard 1602A logic state analyzer with probe

A 16-bit-wide and 64-word-deep memory operates at clock speeds to 10MHz, allowing the instrument to capture virtually any 64-word sequence in a system. The data may be registered with versatile pattern recognition trigger and digital delay. Measurements of system activity are displayed on the analyzer's LED readout in hex, decimal, octal, or binary format, which eliminates the need for base conversions by the operator. Keyboard entry of the desired trigger is in the same base as selected for the display.

The keyboard is basically self-teaching. Entry of triggering and display conditions is a series of self-explanatory keystrokes with all entries displayed as they are entered, enabling you to check their accuracy every step of the way.

3–10.1 Data Probe

The probe (Fig. 3–43) is a single pod containing all 16 data lines, clock, qualifier, and ground. At the front of the pod is a standard edge connector that allows you to quickly move the test connection from an address bus to the data bus, control lines, or I/O structures. You need only incorporate a few simple mating printed-circuit-board connectors to your system.

3–10.2 Tracing Data Flow

Capturing data flow of a microcomputer program requires only a logical sequence of key strokes. The following paragraphs give some typical examples.

The first item to define is the *logic polarity* of your system by pressing the logic polarity key. The panel LEDs indicate your selection, positive for high–true and negative for low–true.

Next, select the *clock edge* (leading or trailing) on which you want to gather data. This is also on panel LEDs.

Now select the *display format* that you want to use for the test. If you are running tests on an address or data bus of the microcomputer, you would most likely select either hex or octal display format. However, if the test is on an I/O bus with numerical data, decimal may be preferred. For activity on control lines (microprocessor halt, reset, etc.), binary is a meaningful base. In all cases the LED display indicates the selected format with a base notation. For example, if hex is selected, the letter b (for base) and the numerals 16 appear at the right side of the LED display.

When power is turned on, the instrument is initialized with a *word width* of 16, which may be displayed by pressing the word-width key.

Many times all the input lines are not used, and if you want to blank the more significant bits, you press the word-width key and enter the number of bits to be displayed from 2 to 16.

The desired *data window* is entered from a *trace specification* section of a keyboard. If you want to view data after the desired trigger point, you press a *trigger plus delay starts trace,* which directs the analyzer to start collecting data as soon as the trace specification is satisfied. If you are more interested in data preceding the trigger point, select *trigger plus delay ends trace*. For either mode, start or end, an LED indicates the selected mode.

To define a trigger point, you press the *trigger=* key and enter the desired trigger point in the same format previously selected for the display. The selected trigger word is displayed for verification.

To enter a delay that will position the start of data collection a specific number of clock pulses from the trigger word, press the *delay=* key and enter the number of desired clock pulses. The delay count is entered and displayed in decimal format.

Delays of up to 65,535 clock pulses before or after the trigger point may be entered. When delay is used in conjunction with the *ends trace* mode, it is possible to observe the sequence of transactions leading up to the trigger point, as well as following the trigger point. The trace specification is now complete and the analyzer is ready to capture data. Pressing the trace key instructs the analyzer to start looking for the trigger word. Once the trigger word is recognized, the analyzer captures and stores 64 words in memory as defined by the preset trace specifications. Two words are normally displayed in the viewing window. The number at the far left is the memory location of the word. The number at the far right is the next higher location of the analyzer memory.

The data in the analyzer's memory may be viewed on the display using the four keys in the display block. The *prior word* any *next word* keys permit you to view the memory contents one word at a time, or if you hold a key, the memory contents will sequence rapidly through the display (a form of single stepping). The *word number=* key allows you to quickly address any memory location, and the *at trigger word* key automatically restores the display to the trigger point.

3–10.3 Measurement Techniques

The analyzer has the power to capture more than basic data. For example, if you suspect that a data line is struck in one state, a *trace continuous* mode permits the suspected line to be monitored for activity. The mode is entered by pressing *trace* followed by C, and may be used with any number base.

To capture data on the *n*th *pass of a loop,* a *delay by events* mode is available. Delay by events is entered by pressing in sequence Delay, E, and then entering in decimal format the desired number of events to 65,535. The LED display then shows that the analyzer is set to delay by events with an E, and also shows the selected number of events. When trace is pressed, the analyzer will count the selected number of events (trigger points) before capturing data.

For viewing consecutive occurrences at specific points, such as data being sent to a peripheral, a *trace events mode* is provided. This mode is entered by pressing trace, followed by E, which directs the analyzer to capture only the data that is described by the trigger word plus delay.

When additional qualification is needed for data collection, such as restricting the data to only reads, writes, or outputs, the rear-panel trigger and clock qualifiers are available. These inputs are compatible with the HP10250A TTL trigger probe, allowing expansion to four qualifier inputs.

Once a functional fault is located in execution of the program, another form of analysis instrument, usually an oscilloscope, is frequently required to pinpoint the problem. The analyzer's trigger output is stable with the system clock, which allows an oscilloscope to be used for critical timing measurements.

A *trace point output* is available for generating interrupt signals or for added clock-stopper circuits in other parts of the system under test. The rear-panel outputs can also be used to cascade analyzers.

For those microcomputer troubleshooting situations where the data being gathered are a mixture of information from buses and control lines, a mixed mode of binary and either hex, decimal, or octal bases can be easily entered with a few keystrokes. The resulting trace then displays the captured data in the format most convenient for analysis.

The analyzer also interacts with message codes that assist the operator in gathering and sorting data. The definitions of these message codes are included inside the top cover for easy reference.

For increased confidence of the analyzer's operation, it performs a self-test during turn-on and indicates the results on the display. In addition, there is a multi-level diagnostic software that allows the analyzer to identify virtually any internal fault.

3–11. TEKTRONIX 7D01 LOGIC ANALYZER AND DF1 DISPLAY FORMATTER

Figure 3–44 shows both the 7DO1 and the DF1 units in a 7000-series main frame, together with a 7603 oscilloscope. This combination

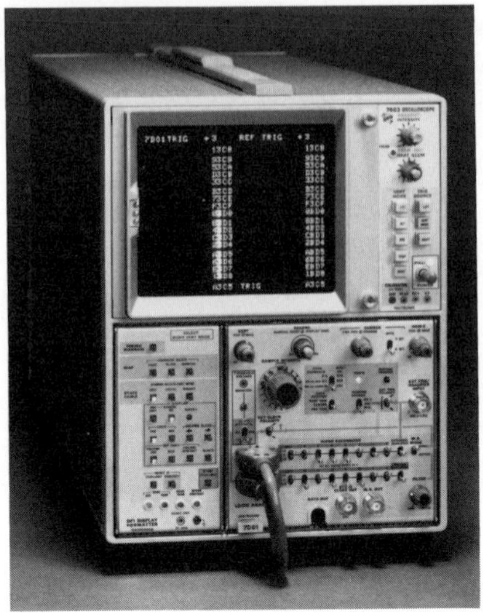

Fig. 3–44. Tektronix\7D01 logic analyzer and DF1 display formatter in a 7000-series main frame

provides complete analyzer functions suitable for troubleshooting a microcomputer system.

3–11.1 7D01 Logic Analyzer

The 7DO1 will store and display up to 16 channels of digital data when installed in a 7000-series main frame. The cursor function provides an intensified zone on the data display, and a corresponding numerical readout display shows the logic state (1 or 0) for each displayed channel of data. The position of the cursor, relative to the trigger, is also displayed on the CRT readout. Cursor readout is displayed in either 3- or 4-bit bytes.

Digital data can be stored in three formats: 4 channels at 1016 bits/channel, 8 channels at 508 bits/channel, or 16 channels at 254 bits/channel. The sample rate is selectable from 10 ns to 5 ms/sample (in a 5–2–1 sequence) when using the internal time base, or can be used with an external clock signal (up to 50 MHz).

The 7DO1 can be triggered from four sources: channel 0 data, an external signal, a built-in 16-channel *word recognizer,* or manually. The triggered data can be produced following the trigger (POST TRIG), centered around the trigger (CENTER), or preceding the trigger (PRE TRIG). The input threshold can be varied from −12 to +12 V, or set to +1.4 V for TTL logic levels.

The word recognizer produces an output when the logic stages of the 16 input data channels match the states of the corresponding word-recognizer switches. Two qualifier inputs are also provided to enable the word-recognizer output. The word recognizer operates in either the synchronous or asynchronous mode. A variable filter (to at least 300 ns) allows rejection of brief false-trigger signals.

3–11.2 DF1 Display Formatter

The DF1 provides data-domain display modes in addition to the existing time-domain display of the 7DO1 logic analyzer. The DF1 adds *state table displays* with a *comparison mode* and a *map display.* The DF1 attaches to the left side of the 7DO1, forming a three-wide plug-in assembly. This assembly operates in a 7000-series oscilloscope main frame to comprise a complete 16-channel logic timing-state analyzer system.

A microprocessor-controlled memory system, contained in the DF1, is capable of recording two 7DO1 information records. Portions of both information records may be displayed concurrently in a state table presentation.

State tables are displayed in terms of either hex, octal, or binary formats. These data bytes may be displayed in up to two tables of 17 lines of 16-bit words each. The left table displays data currently stored in the 7DO1 memory (7DO1 display). The right table displays data that have been transferred from previous 7DO1 displays to the DF1 memory (reference display). The DF1 compares the two tables and resets the 7DO1 when the 7DO1 data equal the reference data.

The *map function* plots a dot display of the 16 data channels in *XY* coordinate points. Each dot location represents one possible combination of up to 16 inputs to the 7DO1 (as discussed in Sec. 3–7.6).

3-11.3 Basic 7DO1 Applications

The 7DO1 with its built-in word recognizer is a versatile measurement tool for detailed logic analysis. A choice of configurations is available to meet a variety of logic analysis and microcomputer troubleshooting requirements. The following paragraphs include some specific application procedures and examples of applications for the 7DO1.

3–11.4 Fault Identification

The following procedure describes a method for finding a fault, determining its location on a data train, and examining it on a real-time

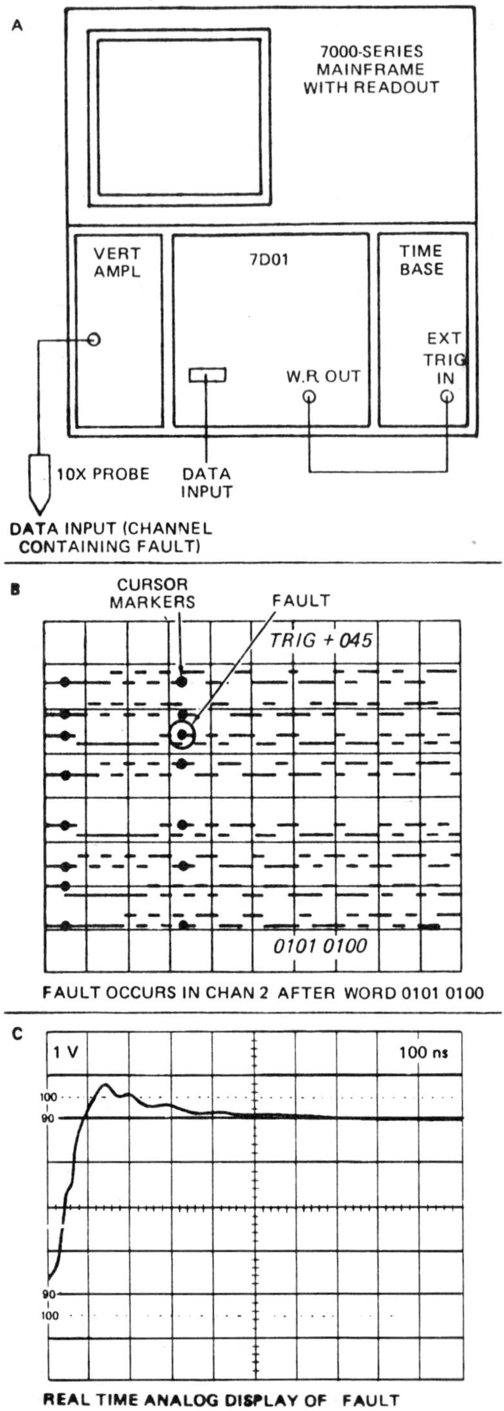

Fig. 3–45. Equipment set-up and displays for finding a data fault and examining it on an analog display

analog display. This method assumes that the fault occurs at a unique word in the microcomputer program. For this application, the 7DO1 is used with a companion vertical amplifier and time-base plug-in unit in a four-compartment main frame with readout.

1. Connect test equipment as shown in Fig. 3–45.

2. Set the 7DO1 W.R. MODE switch to ASYNC and the TRIGGER SOURCE switch to W.R.

3. Set the main frame to display the right vertical and A horizontal compartments.

4. Obtain the desired data display (as shown in Fig. 3–45b).

5. Set the CURSOR controls to position the intensified cursor markers to the leading edge of the displayed fault.

6. Note the binary word readout (bottom-right side of graticule).

7. Set the word recognizer for the binary word code noted in step 6 (0101 0100, as shown in Fig. 3–45).

8. Connect a 10× probe from the vertical amplifier plug-in unit to the data channel that contains the fault as determined in step 5 (channel 2 in the case of Fig. 3–45).

9. Set the main frame to display the left vertical and B horizontal compartments.

10. Set the vertical amplifier deflection factor and time-base plug-in unit sweep rate and triggering for a stable analog display of the data channel selected in step 8 (as shown in Fig. 3–45c).

Note: The 7DO1 FILTER control can be used to provide some horizontal positioning of the display.

3–11.5 Delay by Words

The following describes a method for preselecting a binary word and positioning the data display window anywhere from the first to the ten-millionth time that the binary word occurs. For this application, the 7DO1 is used with a companion digital events delay plug-in unit (Tektronix 7DO1 digital events delay) in a main frame with readout.

1. Connect the test equipment as shown in Fig. 3–46.

2. Set the digital events delay plug-in unit for independent B sweep delay mode and external ac-coupled +slope triggering.

3. Set the 7DO1 W.R. MODE switch to ASYNC and the TRIGGER SOURCE switch to W.R.

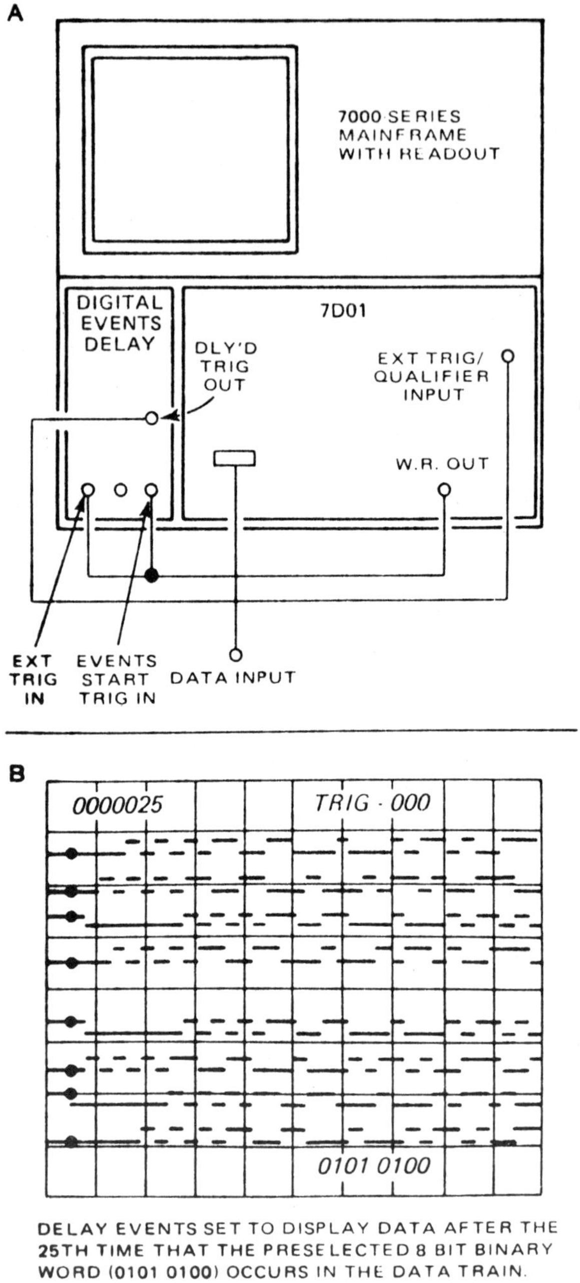

Fig. 3–46. Equipment setup and data display window that has been positioned after a preselected word has occurred 25 times

4. Set the WORD RECOGNIZER channel switches for the desired binary word code.

5. Set the main frame to display the right vertical compartment.

6. Set the digital events delay plug-in unit for a stable display triggered on the +slope of the events-start trigger input.

7. Set the digital events delay plug-in unit to indicate on the events count readout the desired number of times that the preselected binary word is to occur before a data display is initiated. For example, if the digital events delay plug-in is set for an events count readout of 0000025, the word recognizer will initiate a display of the data before, after, or on both sides of the twenty-fifth time that the preselected binary word occurs (as shown in Fig. 3–46b).

3–11.6 Delay by Events

The following procedure describes a method for positioning the data display window to virtually anywhere along a data train. For this application, the 7DO1 is used with a companion digital events delay plug-in unit (Tektronix 7DO1 digital events delay) in a main frame with readout.

1. Connect the test equipment as shown in Fig. 3–47.

2. Set the digital events delay plug-in unit for external ac coupled +slope triggering.

3. Set the 7DO1 TRIGGER SOURCE switch to EXT and trigger from the external trigger input.

4. Set the main frame to display the right vertical compartment.

5. Set the digital events dealy plug-in unit for a stable display triggered on the +slope of the events-start trigger input.

6. Set the digital events delay plug-in unit to indicate the desired number of clock pulses, on the events count readout, that the 7DO1 bit-storage window is to be shifted down the data train. For example, if the digital events delay plug-in unit is set for an events count readout of 0010500, the 7DO1 will initiate a display of the data before, after, or on both sides of the 10,500th clock pulse (as shown in Fig. 3–47b).

3–11.7 State Table and Mapping Displays

The 7DO1 in combination with the DF1 display formatter adds state table and mapping displays to the timing diagram display normally

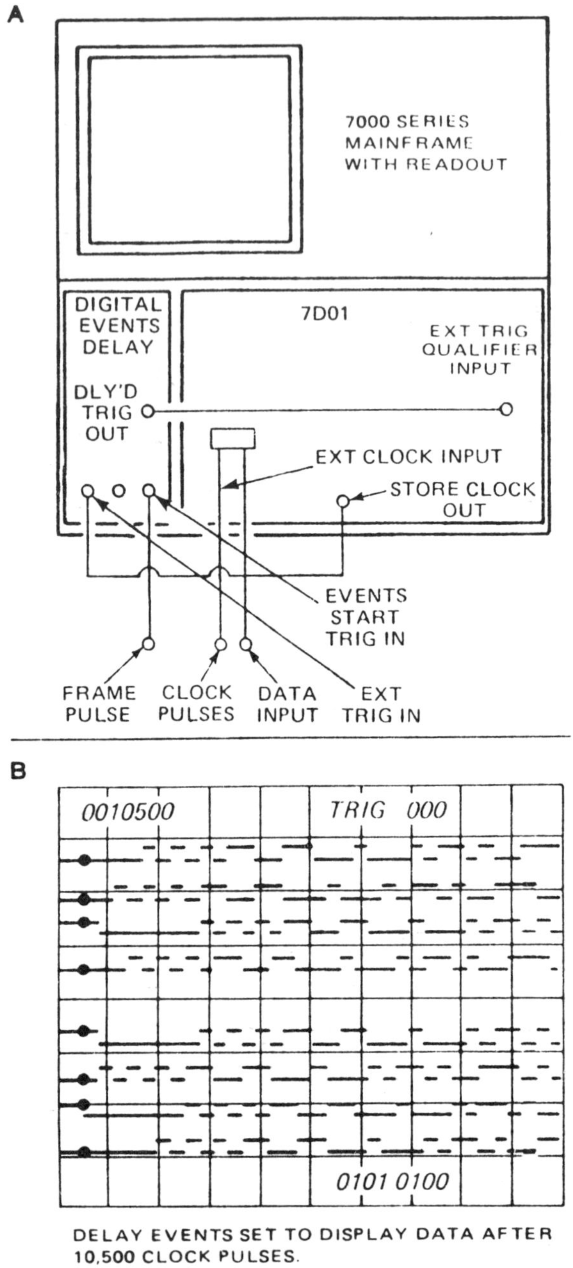

Fig. 3–47. Equipment setup and display window that has been positioned after 10,500 clock pulses have occurred

available with the 7DO1 alone. The basic procedures are described in Sec. 3–11.9 through 3–11.13.

The *state table mode* enables the data stored in the 7DO1 memory to be displayed in tabular format. The DF1 display formatter generates the cursor readout in the timing diagram mode, and the state table mode then generates a state display of 17 samples, starting at the cursor, in hex, octal, or binary.

By using the EXCLUSIVE OR mode (featured with the DF1) the state table from the 7DO1 and a reference state table can be displayed simultaneously, and faulty bits can be quickly identified. For example, data from the 7DO1 memory can be transferred to the DF1 memory for a reference, and then incoming data stored in the 7DO1 data can be compared to the reference data. Any differences in the 7DO1 data can be identified (each bit that does not agree with the reference data is intensified by the DF1) and the problem located by using the timing diagram display.

The map display is useful for fast overall checks of digital system program flow. First, determine the pattern (or map) for a particular set of digital inputs (say the address lines of a microcomputer); then check for a change in the displayed pattern that might indicate abnormal operation.

The mapping and state table modes are particularly useful for checking faulty address lines. For example, evaluate program flow by examining a map display. If a problem word is located, switch to hex state-table display in the EXCLUSIVE OR mode for more precise identification of the problem. Then switch to the binary state-table display to locate the incorrect address line. Further examination of the address line on a timing diagram display reveals a setup and hold problem between the clock and the address line. If desired, use the word-recognizer output to tirgger an analog display of the 7DO1 data output for an even closer examination (as discussed in Sec. 3–11.4).

3–11.8 Basic Microcomputer Analysis with 7D01 Alone

The following is an example of a technique for troubleshooting a malfunctioning microcomputer using the 7DO1 alone (without the DF1).

A malfunctioning microcomputer is shown in Fig. 3–48. Software had previously worked properly, but was still not free of suspicion. Data bits were stored in the RAM. The system program was resident in the PROM. Restart vectors pointed to the address of the first instruction in the restart routine.

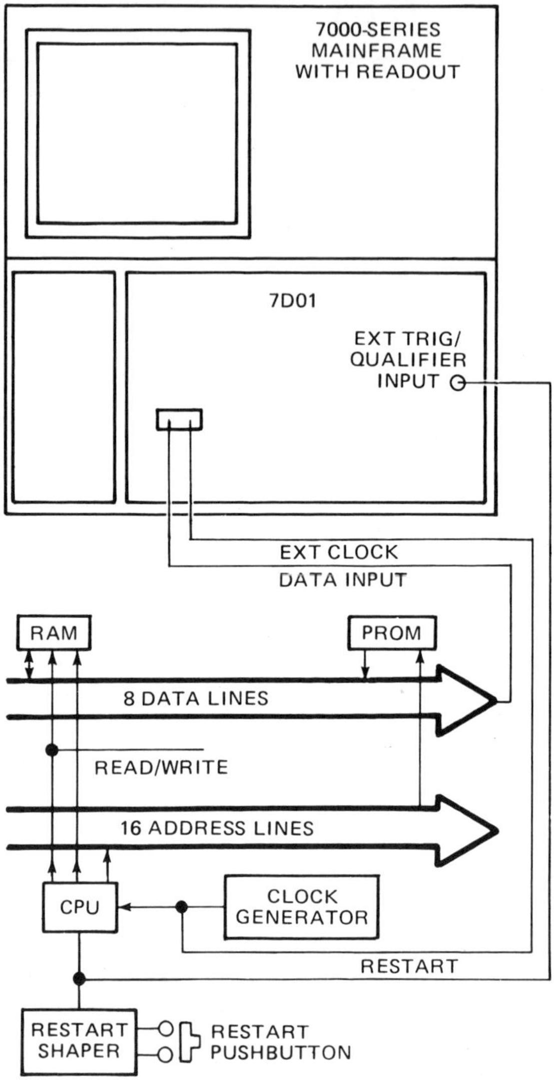

Fig. 3–48. Typical setup for troubleshooting a microprocessor system

When the restart hardware was exercised, the microprocessor should have performed certain initialization routines and then gone to the "wait for interrupt" mode. The terminal would then call up another operating software in the PROM. The failure consisted of a very erratic operation after restart.

The 7DO1 was connected to the system as shown in Fig. 3–48 to store and display a large data block from the eight data lines. The display was obtained by triggering the 7DO1 on the beginning of the restart cycle and using the system clock as an external data-sampling strobe.

Analysis of the data display showed the problem to be a dropped bit in the portion of the PROM that provides the restart routine. Thus, the microprocessor fetched an invalid restart instruction or vector, causing data from the RAM to be executed as instructions.

3–11.9 Basic DF1 Applications

The DF1, when used with the 7DO1 and main frame CRT, displays digital data in three display modes: timing diagram, map, and state table. Figure 3–49 shows the controls required to activate typical DF1 displays. The following paragraphs include some examples of how these displays can be used in microcomputer troubleshooting.

3–11.10 Power on Mode

When power is applied to the main frame, the DF1 reference memory and the memory that acquires data from the 7DO1 are checked for proper operation of the RAM IC. Then the 7DO1 is reset, and the DF1 reference memory and the 7DO1 memory are cleared. The display mode is automatically set to timing diagrams (Sec. 3–11.11), the LOGIC is set to POS, and the cursor location (trigger-to-cursor readout) is set to +0. All other DF1 push-button selections are canceled.

3–11.11 Timing Diagram Displays

The DF1 front panel (Fig. 3–49) TIMING DIAGRAM push button selects the timing diagram display (4, 8, or 16 channels) from the companion 7DO1 logic analyzer. The cursor function of the 7DO1 provides an intensified zone on the data display, and a corresponding numerical readout display shows the logic state for each displayed channel of data. The position of the cursor, relative to the trigger, is also displayed on the CRT readout.

The source of the display readout can be from the oscilloscope main frame readout system or the DF1. When the timing diagram display mode is selected, after either the HEX, OCTAL, or BINARY state table function has been displayed, the cursor word readout is displayed in the same base-number system as displayed previously in the state table display mode. Then the cursor word readout changes

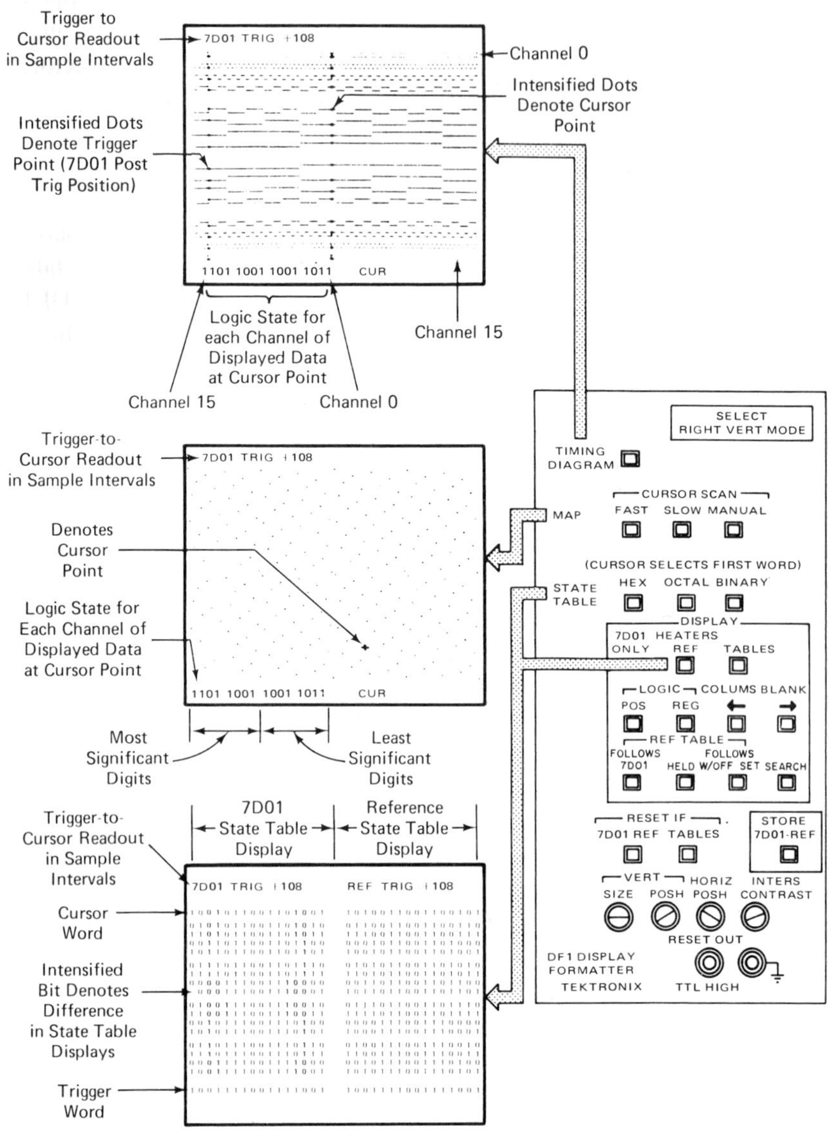

Fig. 3–49. Typical DF1 display modes

between binary and the base-number system in the previously selected state table display mode with every other push of the TIMING DIAGRAM push button. However, if the controls are set for main frame readout, the cursor word readout is displayed only in the binary system.

3–11.12 Map Display

The map function provides a view of the 7DO1 memory displayed as *XY* coordinate dots on the CRT. Figure 3–50 illustrates a map display pattern from 16 signal inputs, and shows that the map display pattern changes when input signals are removed. The vertical axis represents the most significant half of the data word, and the horizontal axis represents the least significant half.

The map display can be formatted from 4, 8, or 16 channels of input data. Thus, 4- and 8-channel map displays are plotted over the entire CRT display area in the same manner as a 16-channel display. A 16-channel display is capable of 64,000 coordinate points, an 8-channel display is capable of 256 coordinate points, and a 4-channel display is capable of 16 coordinate points.

The map display is particularly useful for a fast overall check of microcomputers. First, the map display pattern for a particular set of digital inputs must be known. Then, if there is a change in any one of the input signals, the map display pattern will change. A different map display pattern indicates that the circuits are not operating in the normal manner.

A map cursor, indicated by a plus symbol (+), sequences automatically through the data locations in the order in which the data were loaded into memory. The cursor scans in a FAST or SLOW rate, as determined by the CURSOR scan push buttons. When either the FAST or SLOW push button is held in, the cursor scan is stopped near a desired location on the display, and can be positioned to the exact location with the 7DO1 cursor position controls. Also, when the MANUAL CURSOR SCAN push button is pressed, the 7DO1 cursor position controls are used to manually position the cursor to the exact position desired. The readout display shows the logic state of the cursor word (at the bottom of the CRT), and the position of the cursor point, relative to the trigger point, is displayed at the top of the CRT.

3–11.13 State Table Displays

The state table function enables the data, recorded in the 7DO1, to be displayed in a tabular format. Figure 3–51 illustrates a typical state table display showing offset between the 7DO1 and the reference

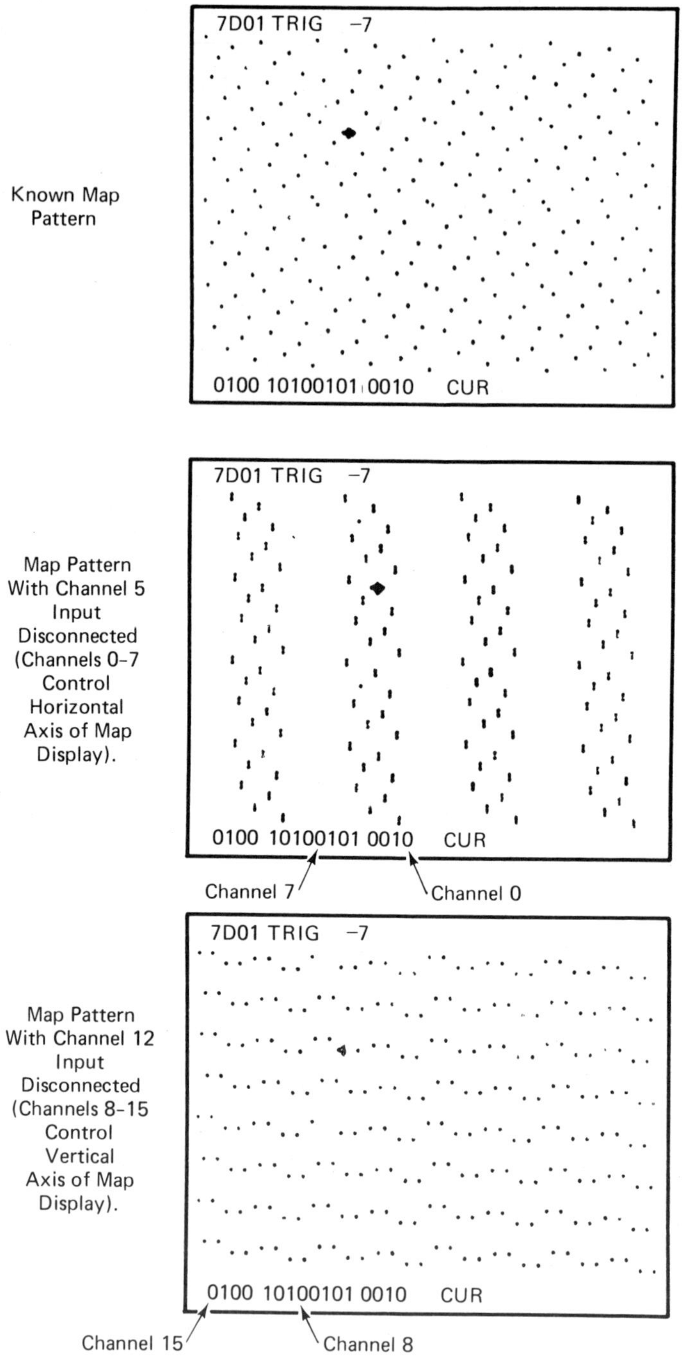

Fig. 3–50. Map display pattern from 16 signal inputs

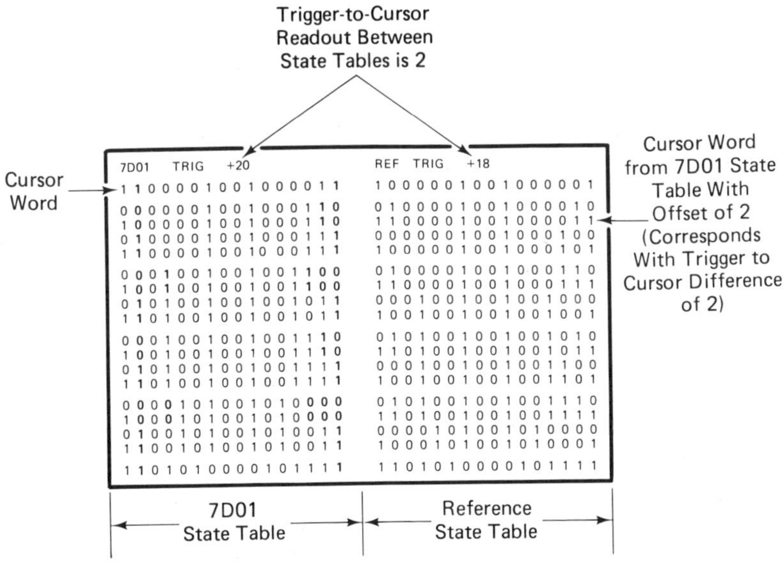

Fig. 3–51. Typical state table display showing offset between the 7D01 and the reference state tables

state tables. The cursor word, the 16 words that follow, and the trigger word are displayed. If the trigger word is displayed in the first 17 words of the state table, it is indicated by a blinking condition. The position of the cursor, relative to the trigger, is also displayed on the CRT readout. Each time the 7DO1 cursor position is changed or the 7DO1 is reset, the display is updated. If the data end before 17 words are displayed, the remainder of the display is filled with an asterisk (*) character. Any "old data" from the 7DO1 memory are indicated by an × character.

Chapter 4

TYPICAL MICROCOMPUTER CIRCUITS AND CIRCUIT TROUBLESHOOTING

This chapter describes the theory of operation for a cross section of present-day microcomputer circuits. These include a basic microcomputer system, CRT video terminal, memory expansion module, parallel interface, serial interface, and a peripheral (a paper tape reader/punch). By studying these circuits thoroughly, you should have no difficulty in understanding the schematics and block diagrams of any microcomputer. This understanding is essential for logical troubleshooting.

A consistent format is used throughout the chapter for each circuit. First, typical circuit diagrams and/or block diagrams are given along with the basic theory of operation. (These diagrams and descriptions are obtained from actual microcomputer service literature.) Next the recommended troubleshooting approach for that particular type of circuit is discussed briefly. Then a group of typical troubles is described along with the most likely cause of such troubles.

Chapter 5 describes the universal or overall troubleshooting approaches to supplement or amplify the descriptions found in this chapter. With this in mind, the first step in troubleshooting any microcomputer is to study the circuits of the microcomputer (using the service manuals). Then compare the circuits with the descriptions covered here. Once you understand the differences and similarities, you can then proceed with the overall procedures discussed in Chapter 5. Again, it is assumed that the reader is familiar with troubleshooting basics, at a level found in the author's *Handbook of Basic Electronic Troubleshooting* (1977, Prentice-Hall, Inc., Englewood Cliffs, New Jersey). If not, you are not ready for microcomputer troubleshooting.

Note that no attempt has been made to duplicate the full schematics for all circuits. Such schematics are found in the service literature for the particular microcomputer. Instead of a full schematic, the circuit descriptions are supplemented with partial schematics and/or blocks that show such important areas as signal flow paths, input/output, adjustment controls, test points, and power source connections. These are the areas most important in troubleshooting. By reducing the schematics to these areas, you will find the circuit easier to understand, and you will be able to relate circuit operation to the corresponding circuit of the microcomputer that you are troubleshooting.

We shall make no detailed discussion of the computer instruction set or programming techniques here owing to the space limitations of this book. Such data are described in boring detail throughout the microcomputer manuals. The instructions and programming are discussed here only as needed to understand circuit operation. Thus, as one of the first steps in troubleshooting, it is assumed that the reader will make a thorough study of the instructions and programming for the microcomputer that he or she is troubleshooting. It is further assumed that troubleshooting will generally take place on microcomputer systems that once worked properly.

4–1. HEATHKIT MODEL H11 COMPUTER SYSTEM

This section describes the Heathkit model H11 digital computer system shown in Fig. 4–1. The H11 is the basic building block for a

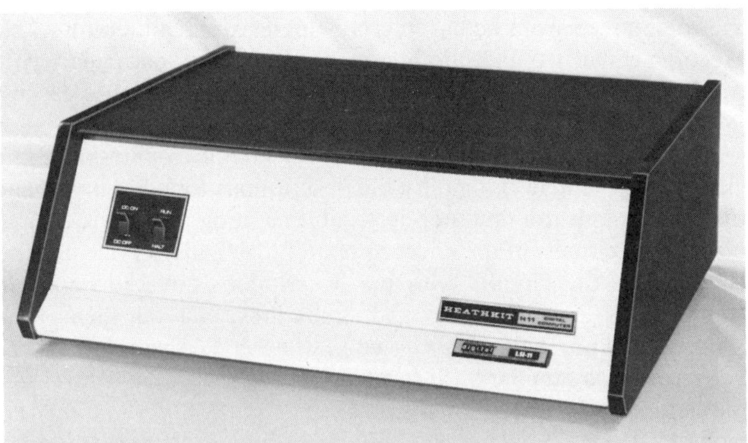

Fig. 4–1. Heathkit model H11 digital computer

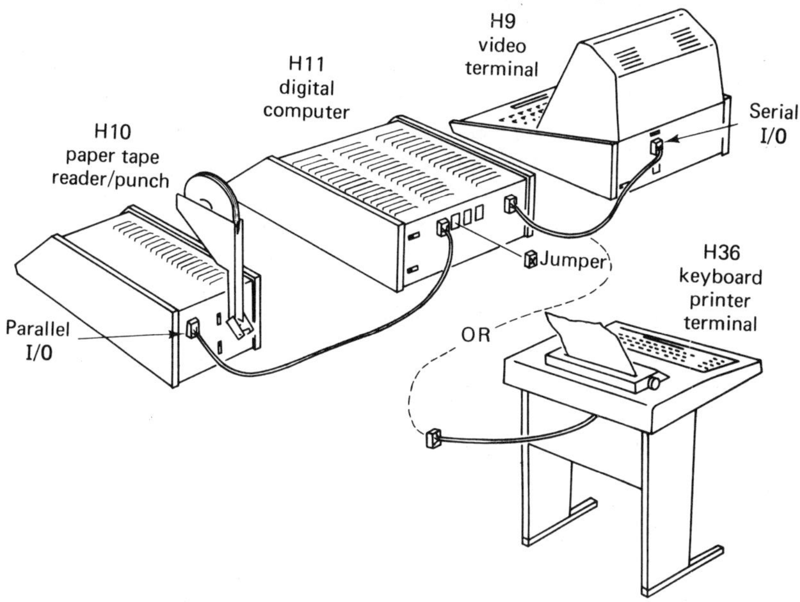

Fig. 4–2. Typical microcomputer system arrangement

complete, sophisticated computer system. There are several Heathkit peripherals available to make the system complete. Figure 4–2 shows a typical system arrangement. The model H9 video terminal, described in Sec. 4–5, is available to communicate with the basic H11. An alternative Heathkit model H36 typewriter (which is essentially an LA36 Digital Equipment Corporation writer II) is available as a hard-copy terminal. The Heathkit model H10 paper tape reader/punch, described in Sec. 4–6, is available to store and load programs for the system. Tape cassette and diskette (floppy disk) units are also available.

In addition to the basic computer and peripherals, there are two interface modules (the H11–5 serial interface module described in Sec. 4–4, and the H11–2 parallel interface module described in Sec. 4–3), as well as an H11–1 4K memory expansion module, described in Sec. 4–2. The H11–5 serial interface is required for either the H9 video terminal or the H36 DEC writer II. The H11–2 parallel interface is required for the H10 tape reader/punch. The H11–1 memory expansion can be used with any system configuration. These modules are mounted within the H11 main frame.

4–1.1 I/O Bus Concept

The H11 I/O bus provides an interface between the H11 microcomputer, memory, and peripheral interface modules. The bus has 17 control lines and a 16-line data/address bus. All modules connected to this bus receive the same interface signals. Address/data and control lines are open-collector lines that are asserted low. The microcomputer module is capable of driving six device locations along the bus. Peripheral interface or memory modules can be installed in any location along this bus.

Both address and data words (or bytes) are time multiplexed over 15 bus lines. For example, during a programmed data transfer, the H11 microcomputer first asserts an address on the bus for a fixed time. After the address time has been completed, the processor performs either and input or output data transfer. The actual data transfer is asynchronous and requires a response from the addressed device. Bus synchronization and control signals provide this function.

Control signal lines include two daisy-chained grant signals that provide a priority-structured I/O system. The highest-priority device is the module electrically closest to the KD11–F module (described in later paragraphs of this section). Higher-priority devices pass a grant signal to lower-priority devices only when not requesting service. (Memory options or devices that do not use these signals must connect the chain.)

The KD11–F module contains a memory address register and 4K bank address decoder for its resident memory, which can be assigned to bank 0 or bank 1. Bank 7 is also decoded when addresses ranging from 160000 to 177777 are placed on the bus. These addresses are normally used for addressing nonmemory devices, thus eliminating the need for bank address decoding on peripheral device interface modules.

The bus provides a vectored interrupt capability for any interface device. Thus, device polling is not required in interrupt processing routines. As discussed in Chapter 1, this results in a considerable savings of processing time when many devices requiring interrupt service are interfaced along the bus. When a device receives an interrupt grant (or an acknowledge), the KD11–F inputs the device's interrupt vector. The vector points to two addresses that contain a new processor status word and the starting address of the interrupt service routine for the device.

One bus signal line functions as an external event interrupt to the KD11–F module. This signal can be connected to a frequency source, such as a line frequency (typically 60 Hz) and used as a line time clock (LTC) interrupt. A jumper on the KD11–F module enables or inhibits this function. When enabled, the device connected to this line has the highest interrupt priority external to the processor. Interrupt vector 100_8 is reserved for this function, and an interrupt request through the BEVNT line causes new PC and PS words to be loaded from locations 100_8 and 102_8.

Memory refresh of dynamic MOS read/write memory is accomplished by bus signals. Refresh operation is controlled by either the processor module microcode or a direct memory access (DMA).

DMA operation is controlled by three bus signals. Logic on the processor module, which is normally bus master, arbitrates DMA requests and grants bus mastership to the highest-priority device requesting the bus. Priority is position-dependent through the use of a daisy-chained DMA grant signal.

4–1.2 Memory Options

Memory options are available for expanding memory to 28K. The basic microcomputer is supplied with read/write memory. The KD11–F memory consists of a 4K dynamic MOS array that is physically located on the processor module. The optional H11–1 (Sec. 4–2) is a 4K by 16 static MOS read/write memory on an 8.5- by 5 in. module. The H11–1 requires one device location on the I/O bus.

4–1.3 Peripheral Interface Options

Two basic interface module options are available for use in the H11 systems. All options can be configured with unique device and vector addresses.

The H11–5 (Sec. 4–4) serial interface is on an 8.5- by 5-inch module, and requires one device location on the bus. Jumpers on the module select crystal-controlled baud rates (50 to 9600 baud) and serial word format, including the number of stop bits, number of data bits, and even, odd, or no parity bit.

The H11–2 (Sec. 4–3) general-purpose parallel interface is on an 8.5- by 5-in. module, and requires one device location on the bus. Two 40-pin connectors are included on the module for user interface application. One connector is the low-byte input/output and the other is the high-byte input/output.

4–1.4 Choosing an I/O Transfer Type

Before interfacing the processor with any peripheral device, the designer or user must determine the type of I/O transfer that would be best suited for the application. There are three choices of transfer types: programmed I/O transfers, DMA, or interrupt-driven transfers.

Programmed I/O transfers are executed by single- or double-operand instructions. The instructions can be used to input or output a 16-bit data word or an 8-bit byte. By including the device address as the effective source or destination address, the user selects the input or output operation. In many instances, the programmer inputs a byte from the device control status register (CSR) to determine that the device has input data ready or that it is ready to accept the processor output data.

DMA *transfers* are the fastest method of transferring data between memory and a peripheral device. DMA transfers can occur between processor bus cycles and do not alter processor status in any way. Addressing, controlling the size of the data block (number of words or byte transfers in the operation), and type of transfer are under the control of the requesting device. The processor does not modify data being moved in the DMA mode. Thus, blocks of data can be moved at memory speeds through the DMA transfer mode. The processor sets up these conditions before the DMA transfer is executed.

Interrupts allow the processor to continue a programmed operation (sometimes called a *background operation*) without waiting for a device to become ready to transfer data. When the device does become ready, it interrupts the processor background program execution and causes execution of a device interrupt service routine. After the device service routine has been executed, the background program is restored, and program execution resumes at the point where it was interrupted.

4–1.5 KD11–F Microcomputer Module

The KD11–F microcomputer (Fig. 4–3) is contained on a 8.5- by 10-in. printed-circuit board. The module includes all basic microcomputer functions and a resident 4K by 16-bit semiconductor read/write memory.

Microprocessor Chip Set. The main function contained on the processor module is the microprocessor chip set. This chip set includes a control chip, a data chip, and two microinstruction ROM chips (microms), as shown in Fig. 4–3. In addition, an optional H11–6 microm that contains an EIS/FIS microcode can be installed on the module. Microprocessor chips communicate with each other over a special 22-bit microinstruction bus, designated WMIB 0–21 L. All address and data communication between the microprocessor chips and other processor module functional blocks is through the data chip and the 16-bit data/address lines, designated WDAL 0–15 H (from the data chip).

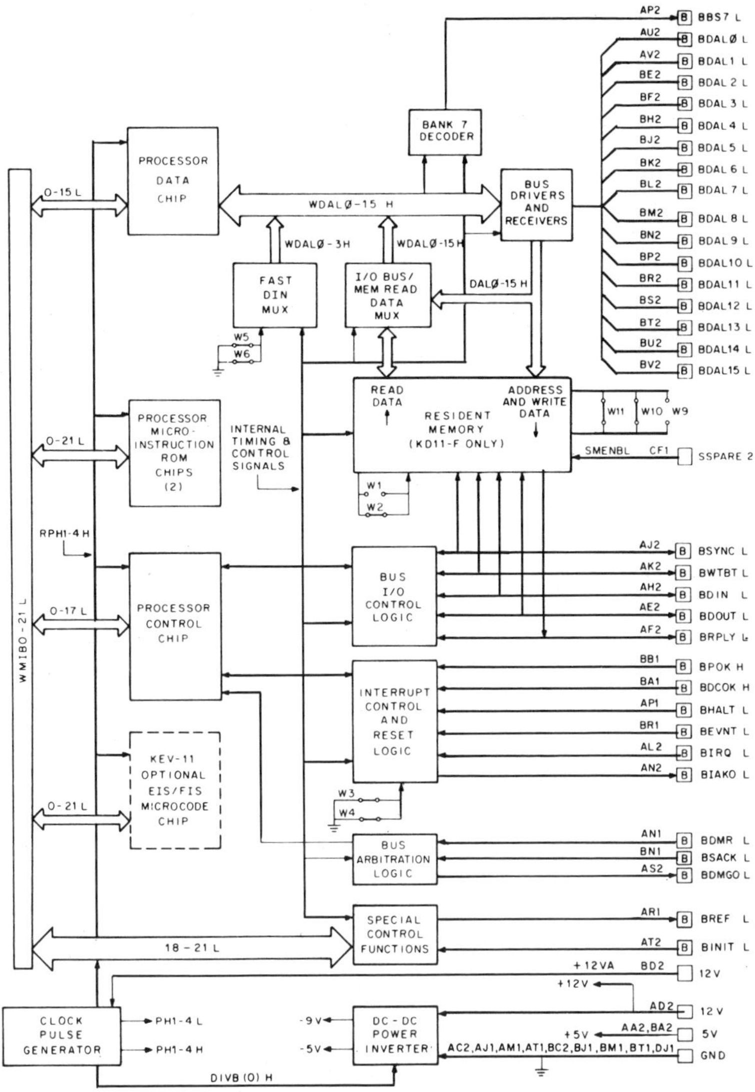

Fig. 4–3. KD11-F microcomputer block diagram

Processor module control signals interface with the microprocessor chips via the control chip. Eight input and five output microprocessor control signals provide this function. Timing and synchronization of all microprocessor chips (and all processor module functions) are controlled by four nonoverlapping clock pulses. Typical operating speed is 400 ns (100 ns each phase), based on a 10-MHz oscillator signal.

The control chip generates a sequence of microinstruction addresses that access the microinstruction microm chips. The addressed microinstruction is then transferred to the data and control chips. Most of the microinstructions are executed by the data chip. However, various jumps, branches, and I/O operations are executed in the control chip.

The data chip contains the data paths, logic, arithmetic logic unit (ALU), processor status bits, and registers. Registers include the eight general registers (R0 to R7) and an instruction register. The user's program has access to all general registers and processor status (PS) bits. All H11 instructions enter this chip through the WDAL bus. Data and addresses to and from the microprocessor are also transferred to and from the processor over this 16-bit bus.

Clock Pulse Generator. The clock pulse generator, shown in Fig. 4–4, produces four nonoverlapping clock signals for processor timing and synchronization. A voltage-controlled oscillator generates a basic 10-MHz CK H signal. Maintenance clock gates receive and distribute the basic CK H signal to a two-stage counter and an RC filter circuit. The two-stage counter outputs are decoded by the four-state decoder, producing the basic four nonoverlapping clock phases. The pulse produced on the leading edge of each basic clock inhibits the decoder for 10 ns, preventing the overlap of each phase. Each of the four phase signals (RPH1 through RPH4) is a positive-going, MOS-compatible, 100-ns (nominal) pulse that is bused to each of the microcomputer chips through resistors. PH1 L through PH4 L and PH1 H through PH4 H

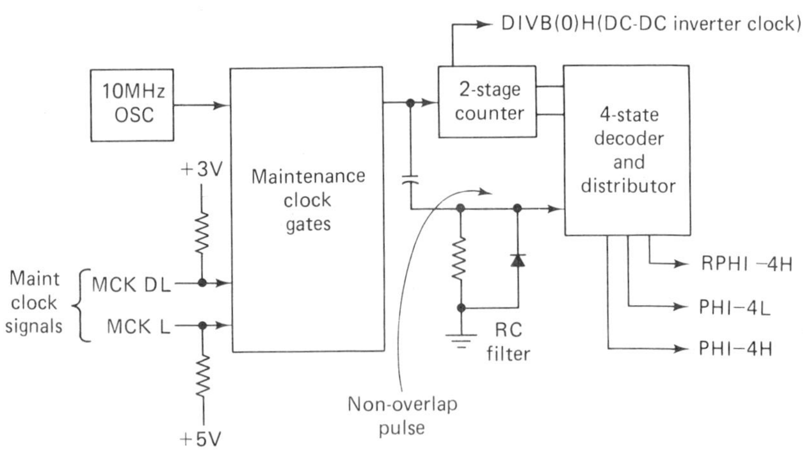

Fig. 4–4. Clock pulse generator

are similarly timed. However, they are TTL compatible for distribution elsewhere on the module.

Bus Interface and Data/Address Distribution. All KD11–F processor module communication to and from external I/O devices and memories is accomplished using the H11 bus 16-bit data/address lines (BDAL 0–15 L) and bus control signals. The processor module interfaces to the bus, using bus driver/receiver chips, as shown in Fig. 4–5. Each DEC 8641 chip contains four open-collector drivers and four high-impedance receivers. Each driver output is common to a receiver input. Therefore, either processor output data (from the driver outputs) or input data (from the bus) can stimulate bus receiver inputs.

Note that all four drivers in a chip are enabled or disabled by a pair of DRIVER ENABLE L inputs. A high input will inhibit all four drivers. When both enable inputs are low, the drivers are enabled and output data are gated onto the bus. Signals that control bus drivers include EDAL L, INIT(1) H, and DMGCY H. False states enable certain control signals, which are described later.

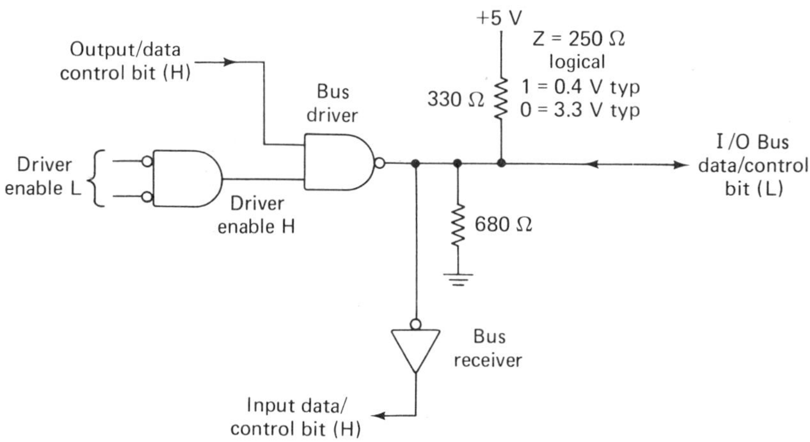

Fig. 4–5. KD11-F bus loading and driver/receiver interface

EDAL L is a control signal that enables the 16-bit data/address bus drivers. When in the active stage, EDAL L gates WDAL 0–15 H onto the BDAL 0–15 L bus. EDAL L is generated by the logic shown in Fig. 4–6. During a processor-controlled address/data output bus cycle, or during the addressing portion of a processor-controlled input bus cycle, SACK L and DMG(1) L are passive (high). The passive signals are gated, producing a low (passive) DMGCY H signal. This

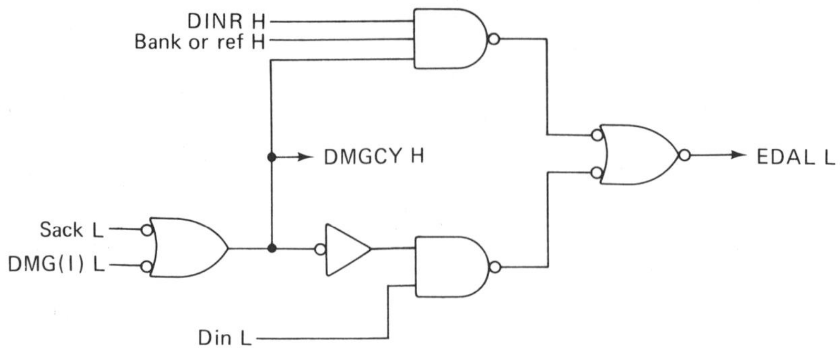

Fig. 4–6. EDAL L logic circuits

signal is inverted and gated with the passive DIN L signal, producing the active EDAL L signal. During a DMA cycle in which data in the processor module's resident 4K memory are to be read by a DMA device, BANK OR REF H goes high. This signal is gated with DINR H and DMG CYCLE H to produce the active EDAL L signal.

DMGCY H and INIT (1) H are processor module logic control signals that inhibit certain bus drivers during an initialize or DMA operation. Bus drivers are enabled when these signals are in the false(low) state. Bus termination resistors are contained on the processor module. Each bus driver output is terminated by a pair of resistors, as shown in Fig. 4–5, establishing the nominal 250-Ω bus impedance and the 3.4-V nominal voltage level. No additional terminations are required for bus-compatible devices.

Address and data information are distributed on the processor module through the WDAL 0–15 H and DAL 0–15 H 16-bit buses. WDAL 0–15 H interface directly with the microprocessor's data chip, the DEC 8641 bus drivers, and the I/O bus/memory read data multiplexer. All processor input data from the I/O bus are through the bus receiver, the DAL 0–15 H bus, the data multiplexer, the WDAL 0–15 H bus, and the microprocessor's data chip. Resident memory data input is discussed later.

Bus I/O Control Signal Logic. Bus I/O control signals include BSYNC L, BWTBT L, BDIN L, BDOUT L, and BRPLY L. In addition, BIAKO L can be considered a bus I/O control signal. However, since it is only used during the interrupt sequence, it is discussed under Interrupt Control and Reset Logic. Logic circuits that produce and/or distribute these signals are shown in Fig. 4–7. Each signal is generated or received as described in the following paragraphs.

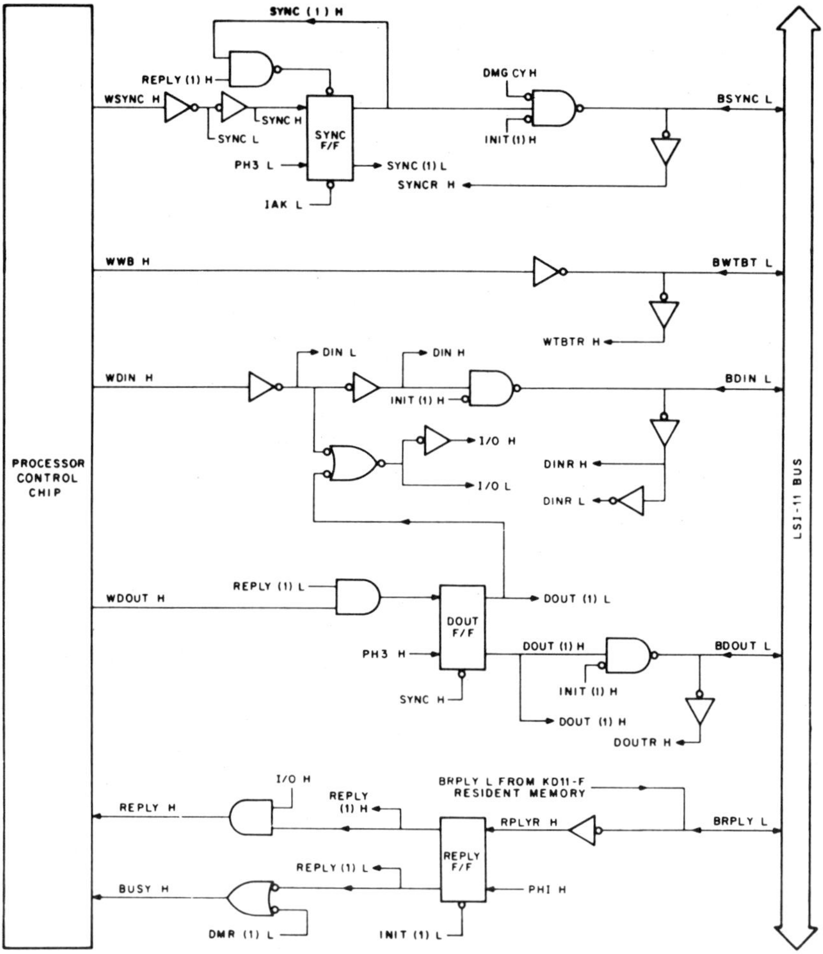

Fig. 4–7. Bus I/O control signal logic

The control chip initiates BSYNC L signal sequence by raising WSYNC H during PH2. Inverters apply the high SYNC H signal to the sync flip-flop D input. On the trailing edge of PH3 L, the synch flip-flop sets, producing an active (high) SYNC (1) H input to the BSYNC L bus driver. SYNC (1) H is gated with REPLY (1) H (when active) to produce a direct preset input to the sync flip-flop. This ensures that BSYNC L will remain active until after the bus slave device terminates its BRPLY L signal, and the reply flip-flop is reset [REPLY (1) H is low]. The sync flip-flop then clocks to the reset (BSYNC L passive) state on the trailing edge of PH3 L.

BWTBT L is the buffered/inverted control chip WWB H output signal. This signal asserts during PH1 of the addressing portion of a bus cycle to indicate that a write (output) operation follows. It remains active during the output data transfer if a DATOB bus cycle is to be executed.

BDIN L is the inverted, buffered control chip's WDIN H signal. This signal goes active during PH2 following an active RPLY H signal.

The control chip initiates the BDOUT L signal sequence by raising WDOUT H during PH2. This signal is gated with the passive REPLY (1) L (high) signal to produce an active low D input to the DOUT flip-flop. The flip-flop sets on the leading edge of PH3 H, producing an active BDOUT L signal. It clocks to the reset state on PH3 following the REPLY (1) L active (low) signal.

BRPLY L is a required response from a bus slave device during input or output operations. DIN L and DOUT (1) are OR'ed to produce and active I/O L signal whenever a programmed transfer occurs. I/O L enables the time-out counter in the bus error detection portion of the interrupt logic. I/O L is inverted to produce I/O H, which enables the reply gate REPLY H signal input to the control chip.

BRPLY L is received either from the H11 bus or resident memory and inverted to produce a high input to the reply flip-flop. PH1 clocks the flip-flop to set state, producing active REPLY (1) H and REPLY (1) L signals. REPLY (1) L is ORed with DMR (1) L to produce an active BUSY H signal. The processor's control chip responds by entering a wait state, inhibiting completion of the processor-generated bus transfer for the duration of REPLY (1) L. The REPLY (1) H is gated with I/O H to produce an active REPLY H signal, informing the processor that the output data have been taken or that input data are available on the bus. REPLY H goes passive when I/O H goes passive. The bus slave device will then terminate the BRPLY L signal, indicating that it has completed its portion of the data transfer. On the next PH1 clock pulse, the replay flip-flop resets and REPLY (1) H and L and BUSY H go passive.

Bank 7 Decoder. The bank 7 decode circuit is shown in Fig. 4–8. Buffers receive WDAL 0–15 H bits and distribute them to the bank 7 decoder and BDAL bus drivers. Bank 7 is decoded during the addressing portion of the bus cycle. If a peripheral device address is referenced, an address in bank 7 (28–32K address space) is used, and WDAL13, 14, and 15 H are all active (high). This address is decoded and BBS7 L is asserted. When active, BBS7 L enables addressing of nonmemory devices along the bus. During interrupt vector bus transactions, IAK L becomes asserted. IAK L inhibits WDAL15 H, preventing BBS7 L signal generation, which could result in an invalid input data transfer.

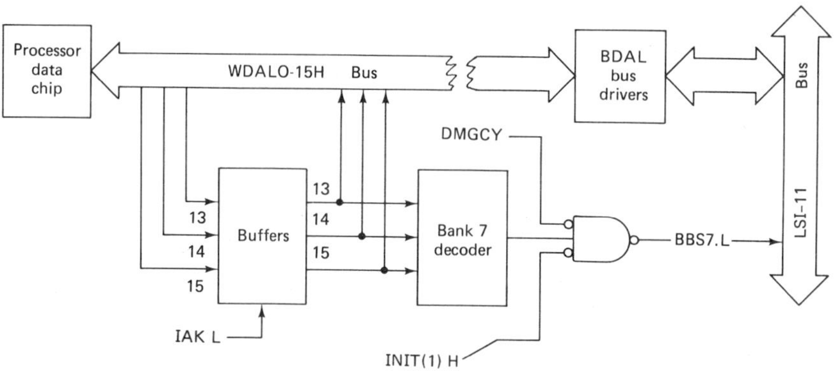

Fig. 4–8. Bank 7 decoder circuits

Interrupt Control and Reset Logic. Interrupt control and reset logic functions are shown in Fig. 4–9. Reset junctions include bus error and powerfail (BDCOK H negated). Interrupt functions include powerfail (impending), halt mode (console microcode control), refresh interrupt, even (or line time clock) interrupt, and external BIRQ interrupts. The various functions are described in the following paragraphs.

Upon entry to this microcode routine, the processor requests a fast DIN cycle. This request is decoded as ROM CODE 15 L, presetting the fast DIN flip-flop. FDIN (0) H goes low, enabling the fast DIN multiplexer to place start-up microcode option jumper data, the passive time-out error [TERR (1) H] signal, and the active PFAIL H signal on WDAL 0–3 H. The processor receives the fast DIN information through the data chip. An active PFAIL H signal informs the processor that a power-fail condition is in progress, rather than the fault condition.

If the power failure continues, BDCOK H goes passive (low) and produces an active DC LO L signal, clearing the power-fail flip-flop and the power-fail/halt and reset latches, and initializing the processor and all devices. The active RESET L signal then initializes the processor, causing it to abort (halt) or power-fail microcode execution and enter a "no operation" state. The processor remains in this condition until BDCOK H returns to the active state.

The power-up restart condition occurs when DC LO L goes false. RESET L goes passive (high) on the next PH2 clock pulse. The processor responds by executing a fast DIN cycle to determine the start-up microcode option jumper configuration. Once the fast DIN cycle has been completed, the processor executes the power-up option selected, and normal operation resumes when BPOK is asserted.

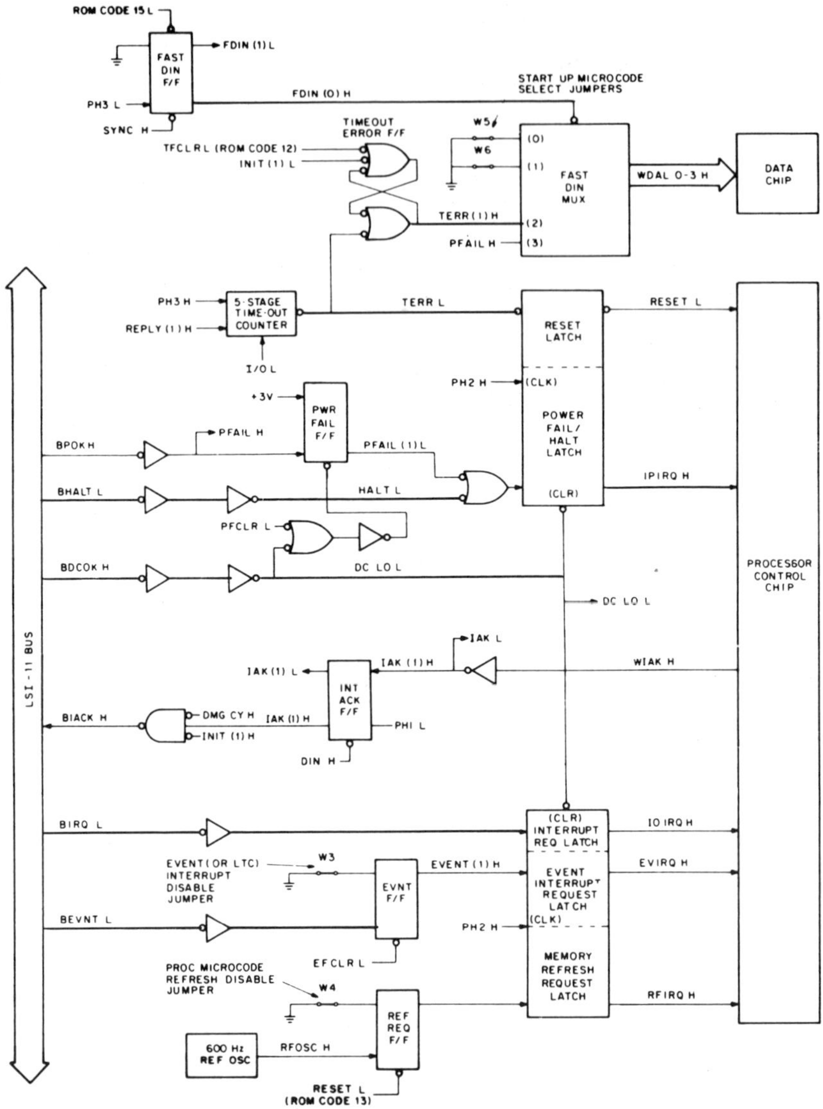

Fig. 4–9. Interrupt control and reset logic

The halt mode is entered by executing the HALT instruction by a device asserting the BHALT L signal, by a double bus error condition, or by a bus error (time out) during an interrupt. The processor halts program execution and enters microcode execution as described for a power-fail operation. However, when the processor executes the fast

DIN cycle, the PFAIL H bit (WDAL3HH) is not active, and console microcode (not a power-fail sequence) is executed. Negation of BHALT L will allow the processor to resume H11 program execution. On the next PH2 clock pulse, IPIRQ H goes false (low) and the processor run mode is enabled.

A bus error results in aborting program execution and entry into a trap service routine through vector location 004. A bus error occurs when a device fails to respond to the processor's BDIN L or BDOUT L signal by not returning a BRPLY L signal within 10 μs (approximately). An active I/O signal inhibits the reset input of the five-state time-out counter, enabling counter operation. [When not in a processor-controlled bus I/O cycle, I/O L is passive (high), clearing the counter.] The counter proceeds with counting PH3 H clock pulse signals. Normally BRPLY L would be asserted, producing an active REPLY (1) H signal, which inhibits the counter. The count would remain stable until cleared by a passive I/O signal. However, if BRPLY L is not received within 10 μs, the full count (32_{10}) is attained. This is the error condition. TERR L goes low and TERR (1) H goes high. The next PH2 H clock pulse clocks the reset latch to the reset (active) state, producing an active RESET L signal. The processor responds by executing the reset microcode. After entering the microcode, the processor executes a fast DIN cycle and determines that a time-out (bus) error TERR (1) H, rather than a power-fail condition, has occurred. The processor then responds by executing the bus error trap service routine. TFCLR L (ROM code 2) is generated by the processor to clear the TERR latch.

Normal I/O interrupts are those interrupt requests that are generated by external devices using bus interrupt request BIRQ L. The request is initiated by asserting BIRQ L. This signal is inverted to produce a high signal, which is stored in the interrupt request latch on the next PH2 H pulse. The stored request produces IOIRQ H, which informs the processor of the request. If processor status word priority is O, the processor responds by producing an active WIAK H (interrupt acknowledge) and WDIN H signals. WDIN H is buffered onto the BDIN L signal line to signal devices to stabalize their priority arbitration. WIAK H is inverted, producing IAK L, setting the interrupt acknowledge flip-flop on the trailing edge of PH1 L one cycle after BDIN L is asserted. The active (high) interrupt acknowledge signal is enabled onto the BIAKO L signal line by passive (low) DMGCY H and INIT (1) H signals. The highest-priority device requesting interrupt service responds to the processor's BDIN L and BIAK L signals by placing its vector on the BDAL bus and asserting BRPLY L, inputting its vector to the processor. Note that BSYNC L is not asserted during this operation and that no device addressing occurs. The device also clears its BIRQ L signal. The processor responds to BRPLY L by terminating BDIN L and BIAK L.

Memory refresh is initiated by a 600-Hz refresh oscillator. This function is enabled when jumper W4 is not installed. The leading edge of RFOSC H clocks the refresh request flip-flop to the set state. On the next PH2 H clock pulse, the memory refresh request latch stores the request and applies an active RFIRQ H signal to the processor's control chip. The processor responds by producing an active RF SET L signal and executing the refresh microcode. RF SET L sets the refresh flip-flop, producing the BREF L signal and clearing the refresh request flip-flop, which terminates the request. TFCLR L resets the refresh flip-flop when the refresh operation is completed. Note that BREF is not asserted if DMGCY H or INIT (1) H is asserted.

The event line interrupt junction can be used as a line time clock interrupt or as desired by the user. This interrupt differs from the normal I/O interrupt request by being the highest-priority external interrupt, and does not input a vector in order to enter its service routine. The interrupt is initiated by the external device by asserting BEVNT L. This section is inverted to produce a high(active) signal, which clocks the event flip-flop to the set state. (Note that when jumper W3 is installed the flip-flop remains reset and the event function is disabled). On the next PH2 H clock pulse, the event interrupt request latch stores the active EVENT (1) signal. An active EVIRQ H signal is then applied to the control chip. If processor status word priority is O, the interrupt will be serviced. Service is gained through vector 100_8, which is dedicated to the event interrupt. Therefore, a bus DIN operation does not occur when obtaining the vector. The request is cleared by the microcode-generated EFCLR L signal.

Special Control Functions. Special control functions include microcode-generated bus initialize and memory refresh operations and five special control signals that are internal to the processor module. Special control function logic circuits are shown in Fig. 4–10. Microinstruction bus lines WMIB18–21 L are buffered to produce the four SROM 0–3 H signals. The actual codes for the special functions are contained on SROM 0–2 H. The SROM 3 H is always active when a special function is to be decoded, enabling the 1-of-8 decoder during PH3 H. The resulting decoded functions are described next.

ROM code 10 is not used.

ROM code 11 (IFCLR and SRUN L): this code is produced by the processor to clear the initialize flip-flop and to assert the SRUN L signal for a RUN indicator in H11 systems (Sec. 4–1.7).

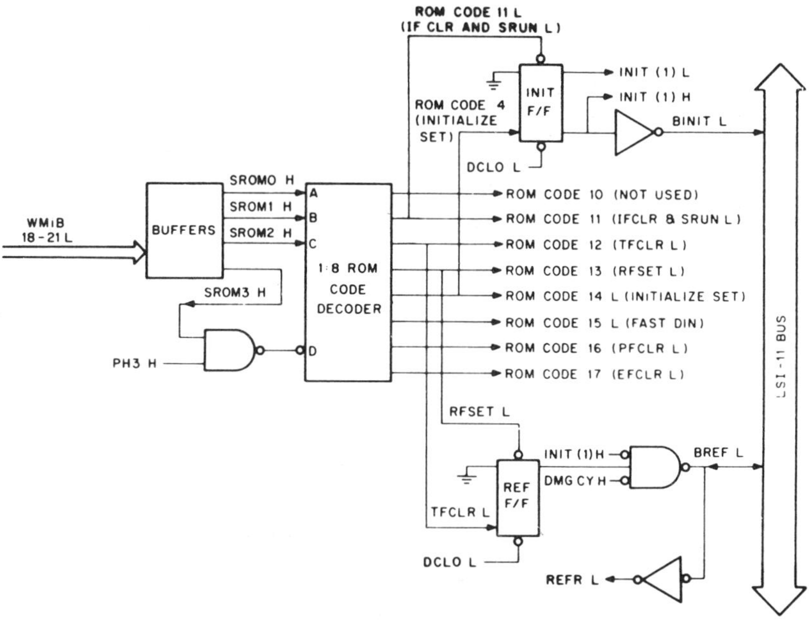

Fig. 4–10. Special control functions

ROM code 12 (TFCLR L): this code is a trap function clear signal, which clears the refresh request and time-out error flip-flops.

ROM code 13 (RESET L): this code is used to set the refresh flip-flop. The active (high) flip-flop is gated with passive (low) INIT (1) H and DMG (1) H signals to produce the active BREF L signal. The flip-flop normally resets by the microcode-generated TFCLR L signal after completing the refresh operation, or whenever a power failure occurs. (DC LO L goes active and clears the flip-flop.)

ROM code 14 (programmed initialize): a programmed H11 bus initialize operation can be performed by executing the RESET instruction. The processor responds by generating ROM code 14 L (decoded). On the positive-going trailing edge of this signal, the initialize flip-flop clocks to the reset (active) state, producing the active initialize signal. Approximately 10 μs later, the processor produces a TFCLR L signal, clearing the initialize signal.

During a power failure, the active DC LO L signal is distributed to the initialize flip-flop clear input. When cleared, the flip-flop is in the active state, and INIT (1) H, INIT (1) L, and BINIT L initialize signals are used to clear (or initialize) all H11 system logic functions. When normal power resumes, the processor microcode terminates the initialize cycle by generating TFCLR L, presetting the initialize flip-flop. This is the passive (noninitialize) or normal flip-flop state, and all initialize signals return to their passive states.

ROM code 15 (fast DIN cycle): the processor generates this code when a fast DIN cycle is required. The fast DIN cycle allows the processor to read (input) the selected startup mode, time-out error, and power-fail signal status.

ROM code 16 (PFCLR L): this code clears the power-fail flip-flop.

ROM code 17 (EFCLR L): this code clears the event flip-flop (or line time clock interrupt request.)

Bus Arbitration Logic. Bus arbitration logic (Fig. 4–11) enables the H11 bus to be used by DMA devices or the processor. This device (or processor) controlling the bus is called the *bus master*. When no DMA requests are pending, the processor is bus master and all data transfers are programmed. When a DMA device is bus master, processor operation is suspended until the DMA operation is finished.

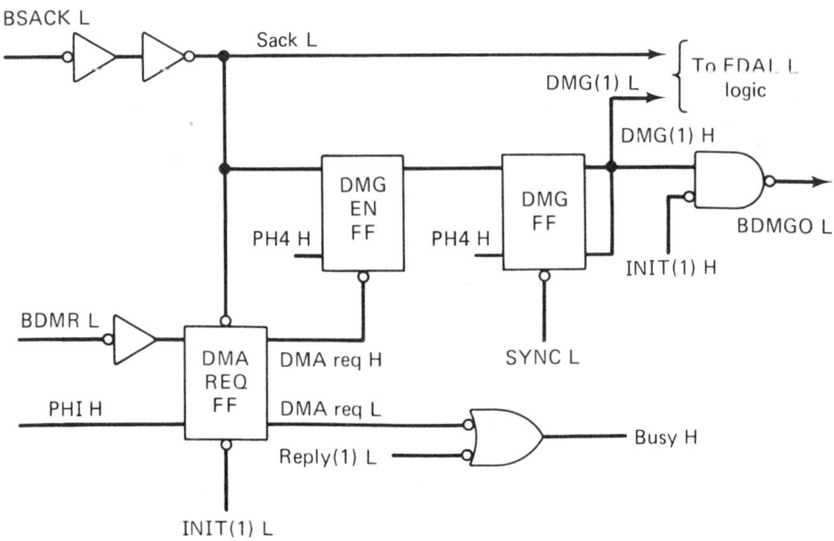

Fig. 4–11. Bus arbitration logic circuits

Prior to a DMA request, the DMA request flip-flop is reset. (The DMA grant sequence is shown in Fig. 4–12.) The DMA REQ H signal is passive (low), clearing the DMG enable flip-flop. A device initiates a DMA request by asserting BDMR L. The request is inverted to produce a high signal, which is clocked into the DMA request flip-flop on the next PH1 H clock pulse, producing active DMA REQ H and L signals.

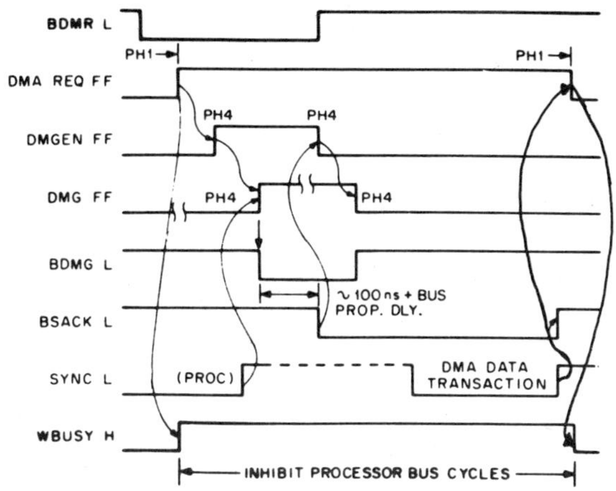

Fig. 4–12. DMA grant sequence

DMA REQ L is OR'ed with REPLY (1) L, producing BUSY H and causing the processor to "wait" after completing its present bus cycle. On the leading edge of PH4 H, the stored DMA request sets the DMG enable flip-flop. The processor is finished with its present bus cycle and releases the bus when SYNC L goes passive (high).

On the first PH4 H clock pulse following the passive state of SYNC L, the DMG flip-flop clocks to the set state, the DMG (1) H and DMG (1) L go to their active states. DMG (1) H produces the active BDMG grant (BDMGO L) signal. DMG (1) L enables EDAL L signal generation when the DMA operation involves KD11–F resident memory. The DMA device responds to the BDMG signal by negating BDMR L and asserting BSACK L, enabling EDAL L signal generation and keeping the DMA request flip-flop in the set state.

On the first PH4 H clock phase following the active state of BSACK L, the DMG enable flip-flop clocks to the reset state and DMG EN H goes low. The following PH4 H clock pulse clocks the DMG flip-flop to the reset state, and BDMGO L goes passive (high), terminating the DMA request/grant sequence. BSACK L remains asserted for the duration of the DMA operation, preventing new DMA requests from being arbitrated.

The DMA device releases the bus by terminating BSACK L. The following PH1 H clock pulse clocks the DMA request flip-flop to the passive state. BUSY H then goes passive, enabling a processor-initiated bus cycle. Once the processor-initiated cycle is entered, SYNC L inhibits (clears) the DMG flip-flop for the duration of the processor's present bus cycle.

KD11–F Resident Memory. The 4K by 16-bit dynamic MOS read/write memory is included on the KD11–F processor module. Resident memory can reside in either the first or second 4K address bank. One of two jumpers can be installed on the module to select the desired bank (bank 0 or 1).

The basic functions involving the resident memory are shown in Fig. 4–13. Resident memory consists of sixteen 4K by 1 bit memory chips, addressing, and control logic. The memory chips, which are 16-pin devices, require an address multiplexer to address the chips with two 6-bit bytes. Ten complete addressing, write, and read operations are described below.

Addressing is initiated by a master device (either the KD11–F processor or a DMA device) by placing the 16-bit address on BDAL 0–15 L and asserting BSYNC L, latching the address in the 16-bit address register. Note that the resident memory address will appear on the BDAL bus even when the processor is bus master. The resident memory functions exactly as a memory located elsewhere along the H11 bus. Address bits are routed through BDAL bus receivers onto the processor module's DAL 0–15 H bus to the address register input. Stored address bits A13H through A15H are then decoded by the bank

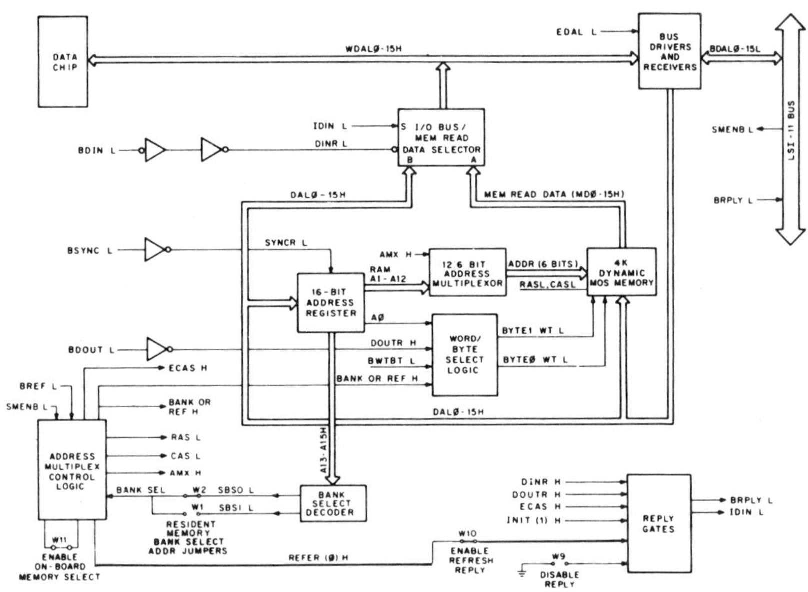

Fig. 4–13. KD11-F resident memory functions

select decoder. SBS0 L (bank 0) and SBS1 L (bank 1) will go active (low) only when their respective bank addresses are decoded.

W1 or W2 and W11 then applies the selected address to the address multiplex control logic, enabling the resident memory response. Address multiplex logic immediately generates an active row address strobe (RAS), which remains active for the duration of the BSYNC L signal. Address multiplex control (AMX) is initially high, multiplexing the stored row address (bits A7–A12 H) through the 12- to 6-bit address multiplexer and into all memory chips. After 150 ns, address multiplex control logic generates an active column address strobe (CAS) and a low AMX signal. The multiplexer output bits (A1–A6) are then strobes into all memory chips, completing the addressing portion of the memory operation.

Resident memory bank selection can be accomplished by an external signal. W11 is removed to disable the on-board memory bank selection SMENB L is then asserted low by the external circuit to select the resident memory.

When in a memory read operation, each of the 16 memory chips places an addressed bit on the memory read data bus. These data are multiplexed through port A of the I/O bus/memory read data selector only when in a resident memory read (or refresh) operation. The select input of the data selectors is asserted low for this data selection. The read data are then placed on WADL 0–15 H, where they can be read by the microprocessor data chip or gated onto the BDAL bus via bus drivers for input to a DMA device.

When in a memory write operation, the addressing portion of the operation is similar to the read cycle addressing, except BWTBT L may be asserted by the master device to indicate that a write operation is to follow. After the addressing portion of the cycle has been completed, BWTBT L either goes passive (high) if a DATO (word) write cycle is to be performed, or remains asserted (BWTBT L remains low) if a DATOB (byte) write cycle is to be performed. Word 1 byte select logic responds to the DATO cycle by asserting both BYTE 1 WT L and BYTE 0 WT L for the duration of the cycle, enabling DAL 0–15 H data bits into the addressed location in all memory chips. However, when in a DATOB cycle, only one active signal is produced, depending upon the state of the stored byte pointer (address bit A0). If A0 is low (even byte), only BYTE 0 WT L goes active, enabling only DAL 0–7 H bits to be written into the addressed location in the appropriate eight memory chips. Similarly, if A1 is high (odd byte), only BYTE 1 WT L goes active, enabling only DAL 8–15 H bits to be written into the addressed location in the appropriate eight memory chips.

Resident memory, as well as any H11 bus device, must respond to any data transaction by generating an active BRPLY L signal. Reply gates provide this function. Approximately 150 ns after CAS L goes true (as previously described), the reply gates are enabled. The gates will respond to either an active BDIN L or BDOUT L signal by asserting BRPLY L. Reply gates are inhibited during an initialize operation.

Reply gates can be disabled by installing W9. When installed, the resident memory will not assert BRPLY L. W10 can be installed to inhibit the reply during memory refresh operations only. REFR (0) H normally enables the refresh reply.

Resident memory requires a refresh operation once every 1.6 ms. This operation is entirely under the control of either processor microcode or an external DMA device, as selected by the user. Resident memory responds to BREF L, generated by the refresh-controlling device, by simulating a "bank selected" operation. (All memory banks are simultaneously refreshed.) Refresh is then accomplished by executing 64 successive BSYNC L/BDIN L operations while incrementing BDAL 1–6 L by one location on each bus transaction. Refresh is simply a series of forced memory read operations where only the row addresses are significant. Each of the 64 rows in all dynamic MOS memory chips in an H11 system are simultaneously refreshed in this manner.

Troubleshooting the KD11–F Module. We shall not discuss the details of this module since the manufacturer recommends that the entire module be replaced as a unit. Individual components or parts on the modules are not available for replacement in the field, only at Heathkit Electronic Centers. This same condition is true for many modules found in a variety of microcomputer systems.

4–1.6 H11 Power Supply and Front-Panel Circuits

The power supply provides dc operating power to all backplane slots (module and bus interconnections) in the H11 microcomputer system. Depending upon the configuration used, the primary power input is 120 or 240 Vac at 50 or 60 Hz. Figure 4–14 is a functional block diagram of the power supply, as well as the logic signal generation and front-panel control circuitry (discussed in Sec. 4–1.7).

Two indicators and two switches are located on the H11 front panel (Fig. 4–1). The RUN indicator turns on when the KD11–F processor is in the run state, and the DC ON indicator turns on when normal dc operating voltages are applied to the backplane. The RUN/HALT switch enables the user to manually assert the BHALT L bus signal. This signal causes the microcomputer to enter the console

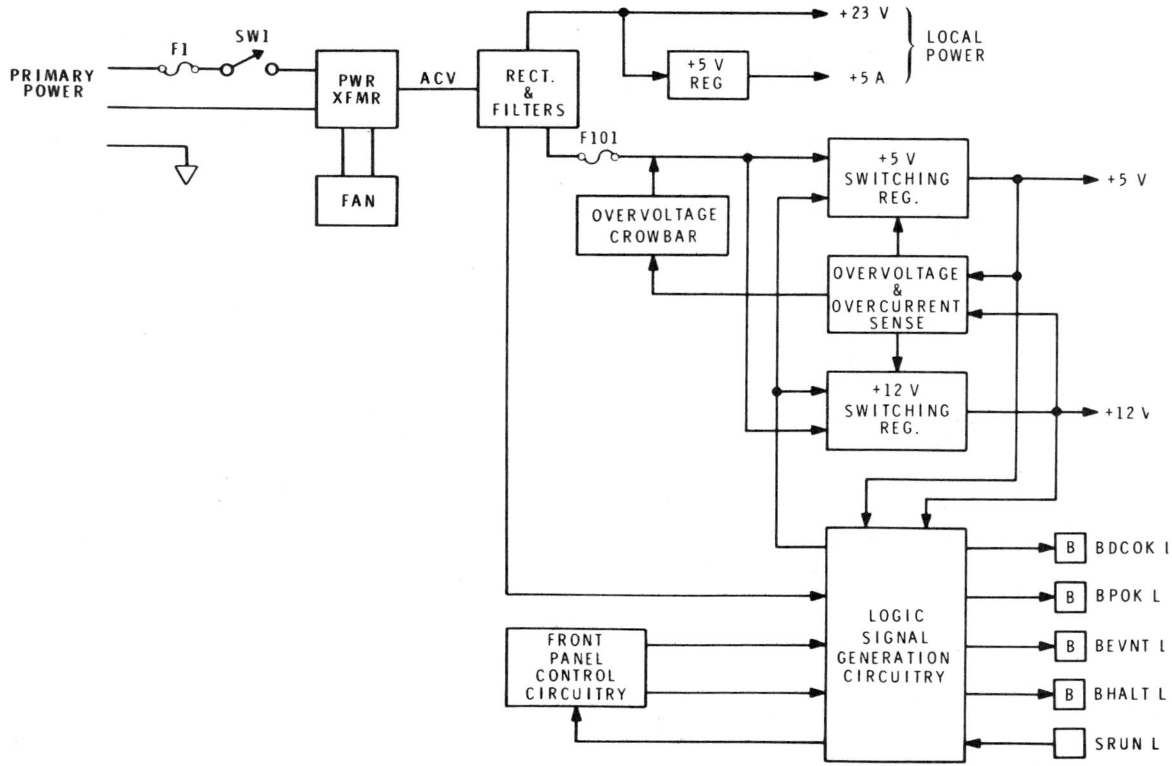

Fig. 4–14. H11 power supply block diagram

microcode and execute a halt function. The DC ON/OFF switch allows the user to turn off the dc output voltages without turning off the system's primary power. This feature allows safe module installation and removal without dc power supplied to the backplane. A normal power-up/power-down sequence is produced when the DC ON/OFF switch is used.

Unregulated Voltage and Local Power Circuits. These circuits, shown in Fig. 4–15, provide operating power for the power supply logic and control circuits, front-panel control circuits, and dc power for the +5- and +12-V switching regulators. Switch S101, mounted on the rear panel of the H11, applies power to the power supply. Normally, this switch remains in the ON position, allowing ac power to be controlled by the power distribution and control circuits in which the H11 is installed. Fuse F1 mounted on the rear panel provides primary circuit overload protection. The cooling fan operates directly from the primary power when switch SW2 is in the 120-Vac position. However, the fan uses the transformer primary windings as an autotransformer for 240-Vac operation.

A single center-tapped secondary winding supplies ac power for the rectifier, filter, and logic signal generation circuitry. Conventional full-wave rectifier D101 and capacitor C101 rectify and filter the ac power to provide dc power for the +5- and +12-V switching regulators. Diode D102 acts as a disconnect diode between C101 and C102. When ac power is lost and C101 begins to discharge, D102 is reverse biased. Thus, C102 continues to supply dc power to the power supply control circuitry after C101 has discharged. The unregulated +23-V local power is obtained directly from C101, while a standard three-terminal regulator IC101 furnishes the regulated +5-V local power.

Alternating-current voltage from one side of the transformer secondary is dc restored around ground by C109 and half-wave rectified by D105. This signal provide 60-Hz timing signals for the line time clock (LTC) in the logic signal generation circuits (Sec. 4–1.7). Capacitor C108 dc restores the other half of the transformer secondary to ground, while D103 and D104 full-wave rectify both halves to provide a 120–Hz ac dropout signal to the logic signal generation circuits.

Basic Regulator Circuits. These circuits, shown in Fig. 4–16, receive a +24-V unregulated input from D101 through F101. Both the +5- and +12-V regulator circuits are similar, except for component values. Thus, only the +5-V regulator is described in detail.

The basic regulator is a switching regulator that operates at approximately 33 kHz. The main controlling element is an adjustable, low-power, linear voltage regulator IC106. Transistors Q104 and Q105

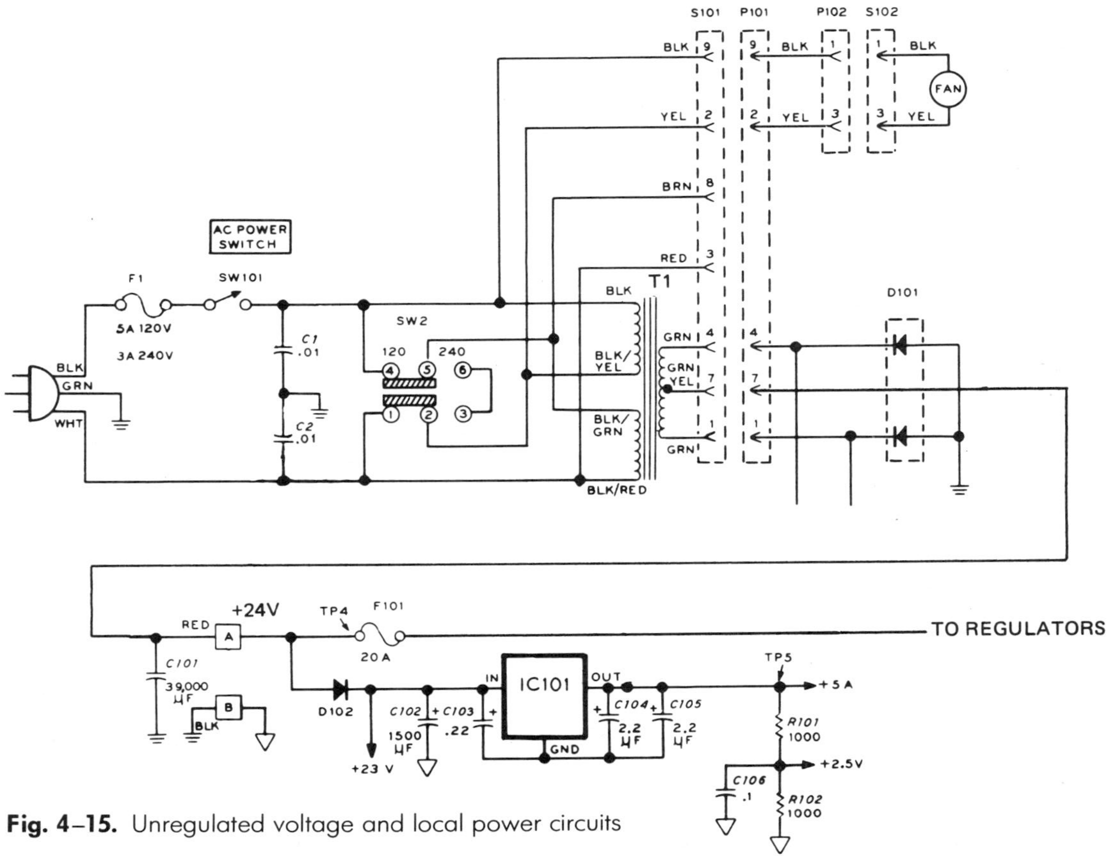

Fig. 4–15. Unregulated voltage and local power circuits

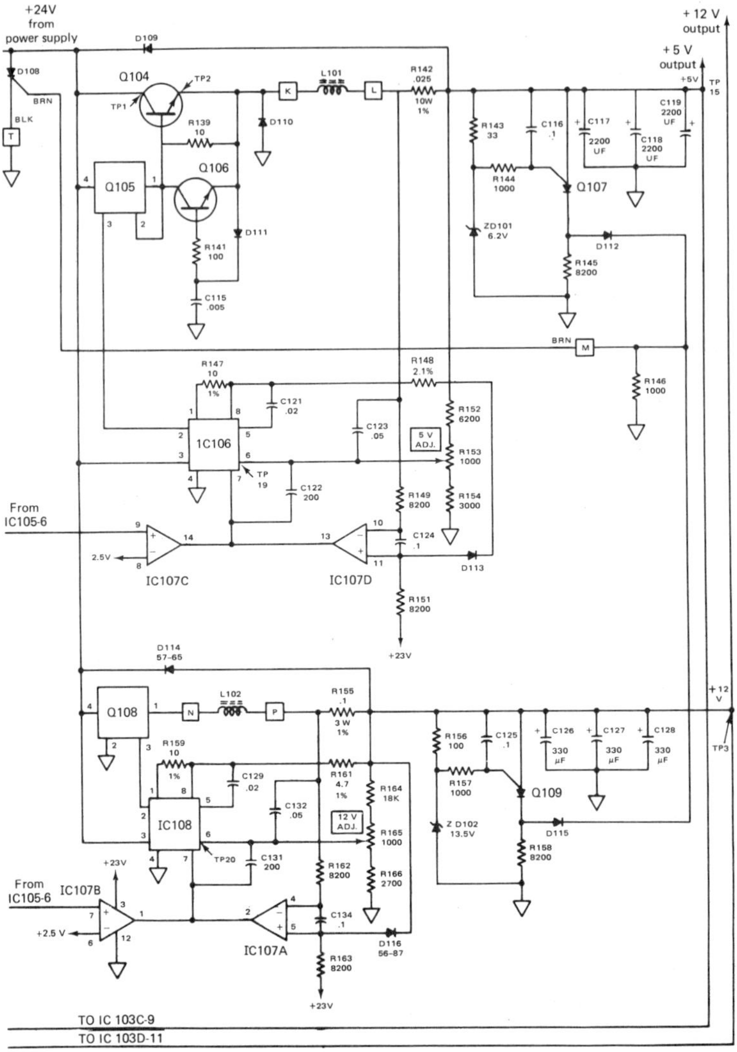

Fig. 4–16. Basic regulator circuits

are configured as a complementary Darlington pair to increase the current capabilities of IC106. The +5-V output voltage is fed back to IC106 through voltage divider network R152 through R154. IC106 compares this voltage at pin 6 with its internal reference voltage at pin 5. The result of this comparison turns on Q104 if the output voltage is too low and turns off Q104 if the voltage is too high. Resistor R147, by virtue of the internal current limiting circuitry of IC106, limits the drive current to Q105. This protects Q105 and, therefore, Q104 from power-consuming overdrive conditions.

Thus far, circuit operation has been no different than that of a linear regulator. The addition of C121 and C123 causes IC106 to turn on and off at an ultrasonic rate in the following manner. Assume that IC106 and Q104 are turned on. The current flowing through R147 also flows through R148, causing the reference voltage at IC106 pin 5 to increase by approximately 60 mV owing to the coupling of C121. During this time, direct current is flowing through L101 and R142 to supply the load requirement at the +5-V output. There is also an alternating current flowing through L101 and R142, which causes a rising voltage across R142. This voltage is coupled through C123 to IC106 comparator input (pin 6). As soon as the voltage at pin 6 rises above the reference, plus the 60-mV offset at pin 5, IC106 and Q104 turn off, which removes the 60-mV offset from pin 5 of IC106.

During the time Q104 is on, L101 is storing energy. When Q104 turns off, L101 begins releasing its stored energy through D110 to the load. As this energy is used by the load, the ac component begins decreasing. This causes a decreasing voltage across R140, which is coupled to pin 6 of IC106 through C123. When the voltage at pin 6 decreases below the reference voltage at pin 5, the circuit again turns on and the cycle is repeated.

The +5-V circuitry includes a speed-up circuit to assist Q104 during turnoff. When Q104 is on, diode D111 charges C115. When Q104 begins to turn off, its emitter voltage decreases, reverse biasing D111 and turning on Q106 due to the base drive supplied by C115. Q106 shorts the base–emitter junction of Q104, ensuring its complete turnoff.

The +12-V regulator requires no turn-off circuitry, nor is a catch diode (D110 in the +5-V regulator) required since it is part of Q108 between pins 1 and 2.

Overvoltage and Overcurrent Sensing Circuits and Crowbar Circuit. These circuits are shown in Fig. 4–16. Except for component values, both regulators use a similar circuitry.

The dc component of the current through L101 is determined by the output load on the +5-V regulator. This component causes a dc voltage across R142, which is applied to pin 10 of IC107. Diode D113 applies an initial offset of one diode drop to pin 11 of IC107. As soon as the voltage across R142 rises above the offset furnished by D113, IC107 turns on and therefore IC106 turns off. As long as dc voltage remains across R142, IC106 remians off. When this voltage, and thus the load current, is reduced to a safe level, IC106 is allowed to turn on again.

R149 and C124 perform two functions. First, they prohibit the ac component across R142 from reaching pin 10 of IC107. Second, they cause a time delay in the turn on of IC106 after the overload condition is removed. The first function ensures that the switching action of the regulator will be independent of the current-limiting circuitry. The second function ensures that there is sufficient time for the components to thermally recover from the overload condition before normal operation is resumed.

The overvoltage circuitry uses a zener diode ZD101 as the detector. When the output of the +5-V regulator exceeds 6.2 V, ZD101 begins to conduct and current flows through R143. This causes a voltage differential to develop between the gate and anode of Q107. Thus, Q107 turns on, forward biasing D112 and firing the SCR D108. This places a short across the +24-V line, which opens fuse F101. Resistor R144 limits the gate current of Q107, and capacitor C116 prevents Q107 from conducting as a result of voltage spikes during normal regulator switching.

4–1.7 Logic Signal Generation and Front-Panel Control

The logic signal generation circuits produce the H11 bus signals for power normal/power fail and line time clock (LTC) interrupt functions. The front-panel control circuits provide the switches for the processor run/halt mode and dc power ON/OFF, and the indicators for a DCOK signal and a processor run signal.

The RUN indicator (Fig. 4–17) monitors the SRUN L line, a nonbussed signal that is a series of pulses occurring at 3- 5-μs intervals whenever the processor is in the run mode. Transistor Q101 is an emitter follower that isolates a 200-ms one-shot IC102A from the SRUN L line. Since this signal is occurring at a rate faster than the one-shot timing, the one-shot remains triggered and lamp PL202 is turned on. When the processor is in the HALT mode, the SRUN L pulses cease. After a 200-ms delay, the one-shot resets, turning off PL202.

The RUN/HALT switch SW202 (Fig. 4–18) allows the operator to manually assert the BHALT L signal low, causing the processor to

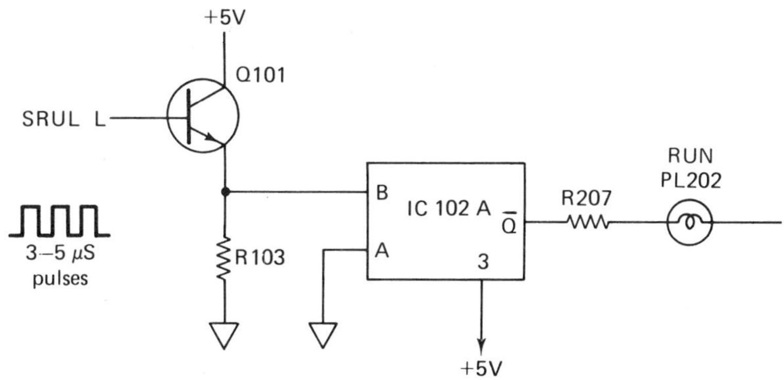

Fig. 4–17. RUN indicator/monitor circuit

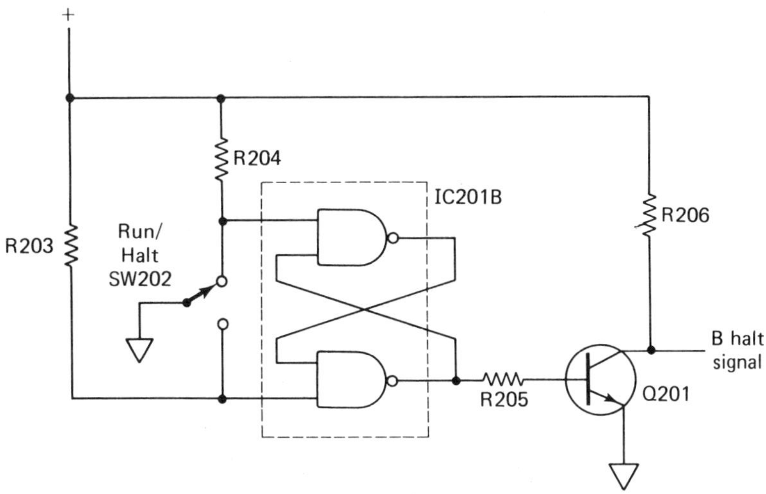

Fig. 4–18. RUN/HALT switch control circuit

execute the console microcode. When in the RUN position, BHALT L is not asserted, and the run mode is enabled. Cross-coupled gates IC201B provide switch debouncing.

The line time clock (LTC) function (Fig. 4–19) is implemented by detecting and squaring the 60-Hz signal from the unregulated voltage and power circuits (Sec. 4–1.6). IC103B acts as a squaring amplifier. The resulting pulses, after inversion by Q102, are the BEVNT L signal. If this function is not desired, jumper J is installed. This effectively shorts the base–emitter junction of Q102, turning Q102 off. The BEVNT L line now remains passive high. D106 functions as a disconnect diode to permit a full 5-V signal swing at pin 1 of IC103B. This results in a

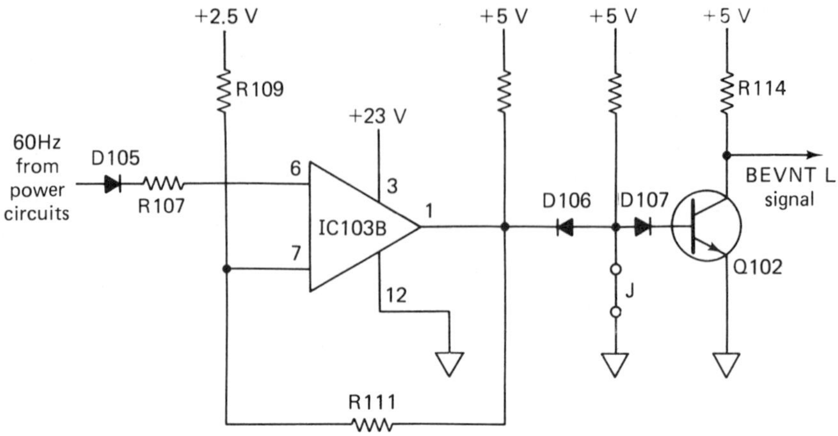

Fig. 4–19. Line time clock (LTC) circuits

2.5-V hysteresis at pin 6, and virtually eliminates false triggering due to noise spikes on the primary power lines.

The power-fail circuit (Fig. 4–20) receives 120-Hz signals from D103/D104. Schmitt trigger IC103A detects and squares the 120-Hz signal, and delivers an 11 ms trigger pulse to one-shot IC102B. As long as normal primary line voltages are present, IC102B remains triggered. Approximately 11 ms after the primary power goes abnormally low (or is removed), IC102B resets. This forces pin 11 of IC105 high and turns on Q103 through IC104A. Line BPOK H goes active low and initiates a power-fail processor interrupt. At the same time, pin 12 of IC104C goes passive, allowing C112 to charge through R122. If normal power is restored before C112 charges (approximately 4 ms), pin 11 of IC105D goes low and pin 1 of IC104A goes passive. C114 now begins to charge through R134. After 70 ms (minimum), Q103 is turned off. BPOKH goes passive high, and the power-fail interrupt is terminated. If normal power is not restored before C112 charges, pin 2 of IC105A goes low, forcing pin 13 of IC104D high. The DC ON lamp PL201 is turned off, and BDCOK H is forced active low. Pin 6 of IC105B then goes low and turns off the +5- and +12-V switching regulators (Fig. 4–16). Normal output voltages from the switching regulators are available for 50 μs minimum (depending upon the dc loading of the regulator outputs) after BDCOK H goes low. This is due to the charges on C117, C118, C119, C126, C127, and C128 in the switching regulators.

The DC ON/OFF switch (Fig. 4–20) simulates an ac power fail by holding IC102B reset when swtich SW201 is off. Cross-coupled gates

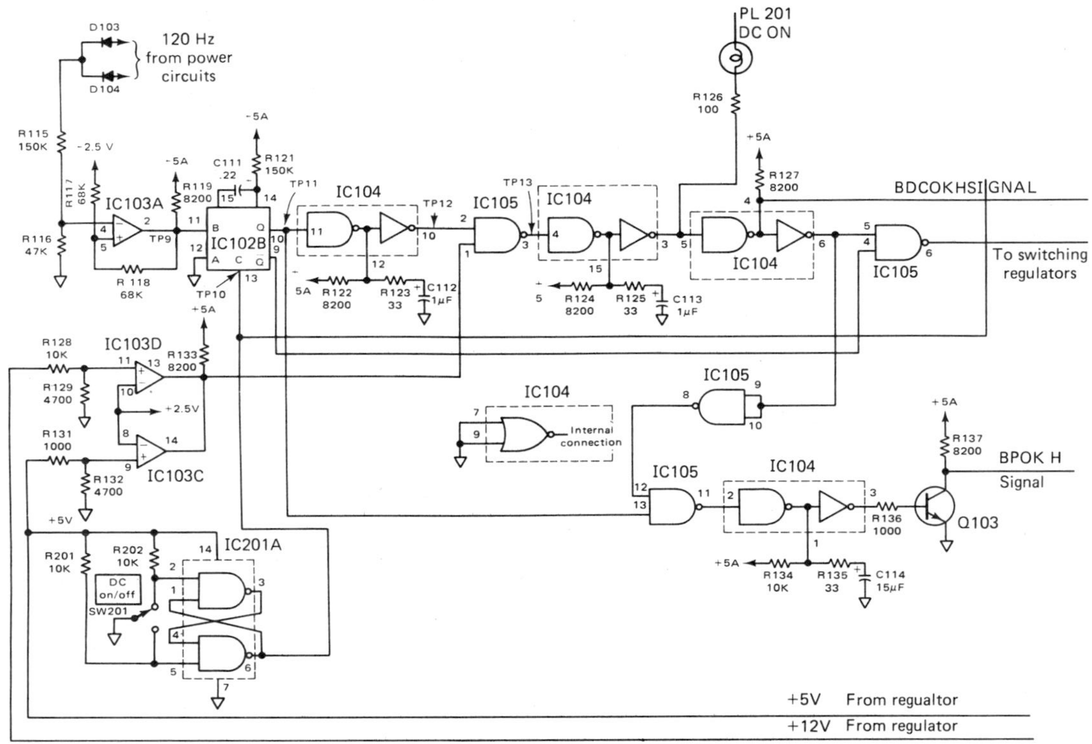

Fig. 4–20. Power control logic circuits

IC201A provide switch debouncing. When SW201 is turned on, IC102B is allowed to trigger (pin 10 goes high and pin 9 goes low). This places a low at pin 4 of IC105B (assuming normal ac power conditions), which forces pin 6 high and turns on the +5- and +12-V regulators (Fig. 4–16). With pin 10 of IC102B high, pin 12 of IC104C goes active low, discharging C112 and forcing pin 2 of IC105A high. When proper dc voltages are present on the bus, pin 1 of IC105A goes high. Pin 14 of IC104D now goes low, which allows C113 to charge through R124. After a minimum of 4 ms, pin 13 of IC104D goes low, turning on the DC ON lamp. The BDCOK H line goes passive high, and a low is presented to pin 2 of IC104A. This removes the short across R135 and C114, allowing C114 to charge through R134. A 70-ms (minimum) delay occurs while C114 is charging, and then BPOK H goes passive high.

The dc voltage monitor circuits (Fig. 4–20) respond to both the +5- and +12-V outputs. As these outputs rise, the voltages at pins 9 and 11 of IC103C and D rise. When these voltages exceed +2.5 V, the output (pins 13 and 14) of the respective comparator goes passive. As soon as both outputs are passive, pin 1 of IC105A goes high. This indicates that proper dc voltages are present on the bus.

If either or both of the regulator outputs go low (approximately 3 V for the +5-V regulator, and 7.8 V or the +12-V regulator), pin 1 of IC105A goes low. The DC ON lamp immediately goes off, and BDCOK H goes active low, indicating that a power-fail condition exists.

4–1.8 Troubleshooting H11 Circuits

Figure 4–21 shows the basic system troubleshooting approach for the H11 computer system. You follow the YES arrow when you obtain the proper result or condition. You follow the NO arrow when you do not obtain the proper result or condition. The information in Fig. 4–21 is based on the assumption that there is total failure of the system, or no response. The general approach is to remove all the modules and check the power supply. If there is an indication of power supply failure, you then check power supply components as described in Sec. 4–1.9. If the power supply is normal with all modules removed, you replace each of the modules, one at a time, starting with the KD11-F (Sec. 4–1.5). If there is an indication of module failure, you then check components of that module as described in Sec. 4–2 through 4–4. Note that the KD11-F module components are not to be checked on an individual basis. Instead, you replace the entire module, as discussed in Sec. 4–1.5.

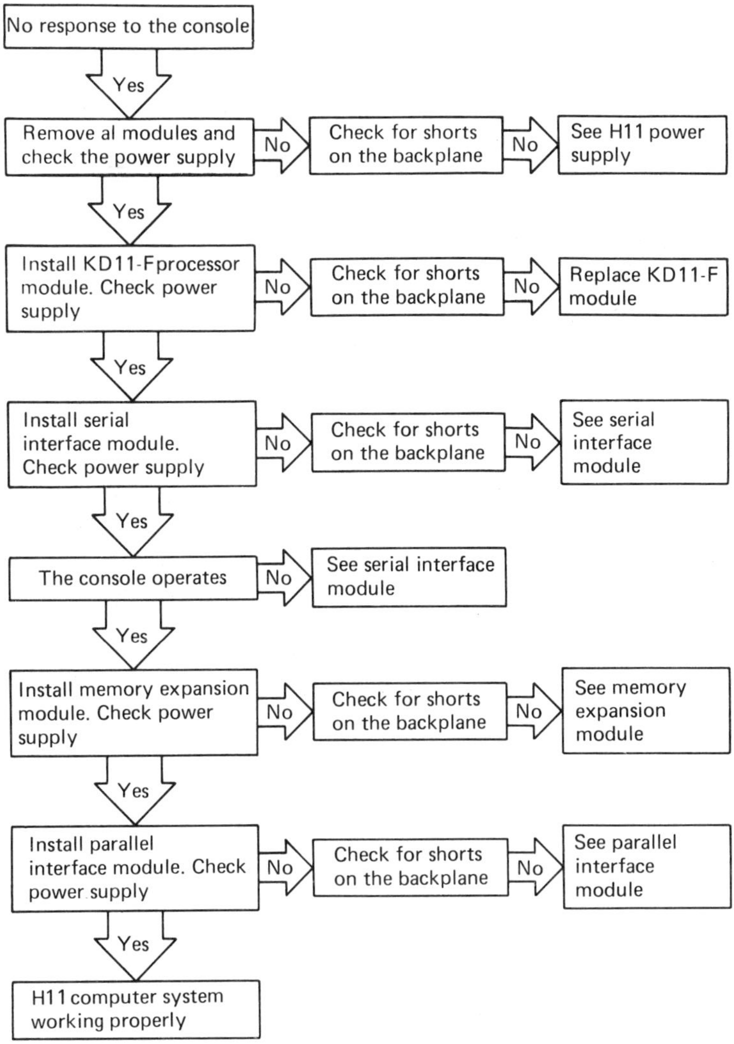

Fig. 4–21. Basic system troubleshooting approach

4–1.9 Troubleshooting the H11 Power Supply Circuits

Figure 4–22 shows the troubleshooting approach for the H11 power supply circuits, as well as the logic signal generation and front-panel control circuits. Figure 4–22 also lists a group of typical troubles, along with the most likely cause of such troubles. Note that Fig. 4–22

Condition	Possible cause
Fuse F1 opens	C1, C2, T1, D101, C101 or the cooling fan (Fig. 4-15)
Fuse F101 opens	D101 (Fig. 4-15)
Fuse F101 does not open	Check the +5 V and +12 V outputs
Both outputs (+5 V and +12 V) are correct	Check the voltages across R145 and R158 (Fig. 4-16)
Voltages across R145 and R158 are more than 0.3 V	ZD101, ZD102, Q107 or Q109 (Fig. 4-16)
+5 V output is too high	Check for a rectangular waveform with a period between 20 μS and 50 μS at K (Fig. 4-16)
No rectangular waveform at K	Q104, Q105, D109 or D110 (Fig. 4-16)
Rectangular waveform present at K	IC106, R152, R153 or R154 (Fig. 4-16)
Period of the rectangular waveform at K is less than 20 μS	L101 shorted (Fig. 4-16)
+5 V output is too low	IC106, IC107, Q106, D113, C117, C118 or C119, adjustment of R153 (Fig. 4-16)
No +5 V output	Logic signal generation circuitry (Fig. 4-20)
+12 V output is too high	Check for a rectangular waveform with a period between 20 μS 50 μS at N (Fig. 4-16)
No rectangular waveform at N	Q108 or D114 (Fig. 4-16)
Rectangular waveform present at N	IC108, R164, R165, or R166 (Fig. 4-16)
Period of the rectangular waveform at N is less than 20 μS	L102, shorted (Fig. 4-16)
+12 V output is too low	IC107, IC108, D116, C126, C127 or C128, adjustment of R165 (Fig. 4-16)
No + 12 V output	Logic signal generation circuitry (Fig. 4-20)
No DC On lamp Indication	PL201 (Fig. 4-20)
No RUN lamp indication	IC102, Q101 or PL202 (Fig. 4-17)
No local +23 V	D102 (Fig. 4-15)
No local +5 V	IC101 (Fig. 4-15)

Fig. 4–22. Troubleshooting approach for H11 power supply circuits

shows the order in which circuits are to be tested. For example, the first steps are to check fuses F1 and F101. If these fuses are good (not open), the next step is to check the +5- V and +12-V outputs. Also note that the "possible cause" column of Fig. 4–22 lists the illustrations on which the components and circuits are shown. For example, ZD101, ZD102, Q107, and Q109 are found on Fig. 4–16.

4–2. HEATHKIT H11–1 4K MEMORY EXPANSION MODULE

This section describes the Heathkit H11–1 memory expansion module shown in Fig. 4–23. The H11–1 uses static memories organized as 1024 words by 4 bits wide. Figure 4–24 shows the H11–1 block

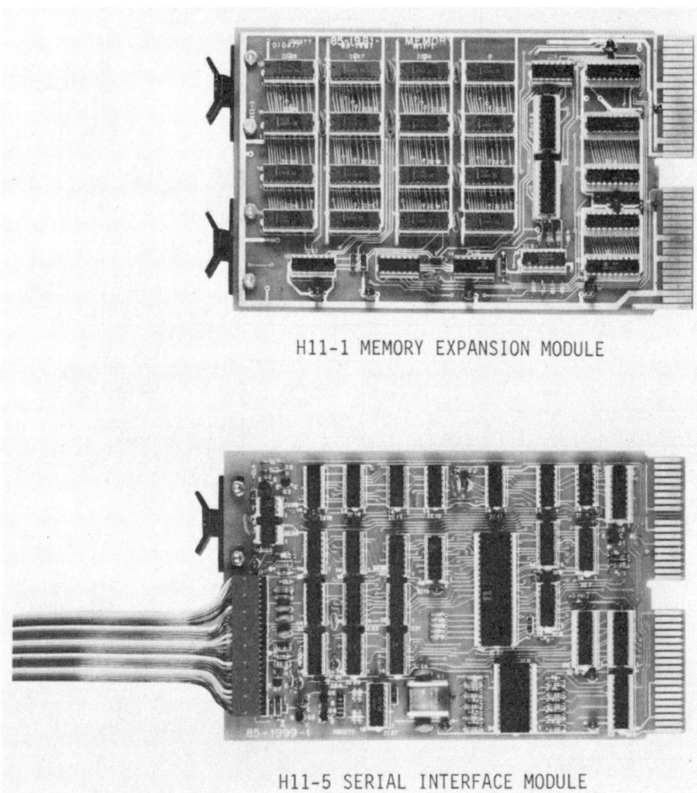

Fig. 4–23. Heathkit H11-1 memory expansion module and H11-5 serial interface module

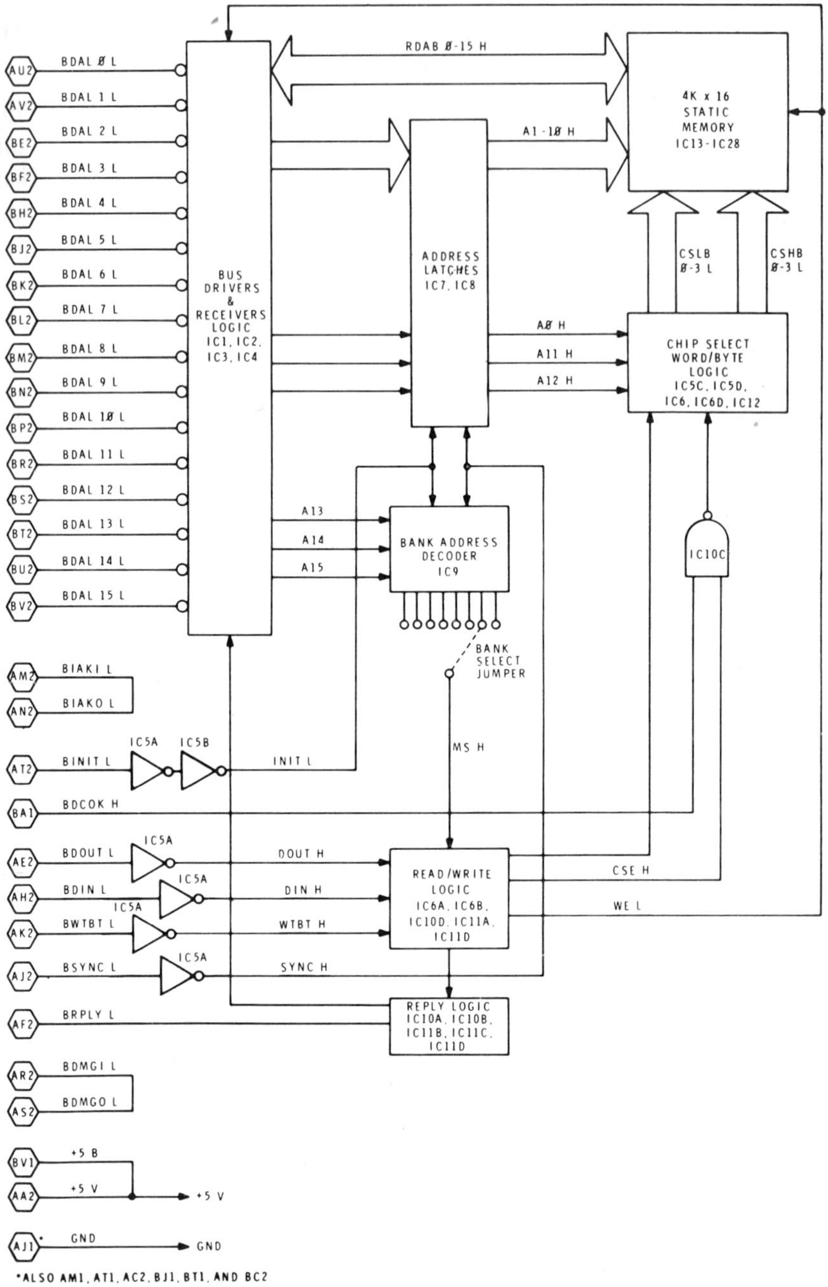

Fig. 4–24. Memory expansion module block diagram

diagram. A complete 4096-word by 16-bit wide memory bank is contained on a single circuit board. A single wire jumper locates the memory board in any one of eight available 4096-word increments throughout the memory area. The H11–1 is completely compatible with the H11 backplane.

4–2.1 Addressing

In this mode, line BSYNC L is quiescent high, which causes bus receivers IC1 and IC3 to become active through gate IC11B. At the same time, IC10A causes bus drivers IC2 and IC4 to be inactive (high impedance output). When the bus controlling device (the processor or a peripheral DMA device) places an address on the bus through the BDAL 0 through BDAL 15 L lines, BSYNC L is asserted low 150 ns (minimum) later. This pulse edge, which is translated to SYNC H by IC5A, latches the address information in ICs 7 through 9.

Address line A0 H, when asserted, selects the high byte of the word that is addressed by lines A1 H through A10 H. Address lines A11 H and A12 H are decoded by IC12 to determine which 1K segment of the 4K bank is to be addressed. IC9 latches and decodes lines BDAL 13 L through BDAL 15 L to determine the bank position within the total memory area for which each expansion module will respond.

4–2.2 Write Cycle

One hundred nanoseconds (minimum) after BSYNC L is asserted low, the bus controlling device places the data to be written into the memory on the BDAL 0 L through BDAL 15 L lines. After another 100 ns (minimum), the BDOUT L line is asserted low. This information is converted to DOUT H by IC5A and is used in conjunction with the memory-select signals (MS H) to generate the WE L signal. The WE L signal enables the bus receivers (IC1 and IC3) and forces the bus drivers (IC2 and IC4) to remain inactive. At this time, the data to be written into the memory are present at memory ICs 13 through 28. The WE L signal inhibits the output buffers of the memory ICs and, in conjunction with the chip-select lines, enables the input buffers of the memory ICs.

In the write mode, the following operations can occur: write high byte, write low byte, and write word. Lines A H and WTBT H determine which of these operations occurs by selecting only the required memory ICs. IC12 decodes this information and also determines which 1K segment of the 4K bank is enabled.

4–2.3 Read Cycle

One hundred nanoseconds (minimum) after BSYNC L is asserted low, the bus controlling device (processor or peripheral) removes the address information from the BDAL 0 through BDAL 15 L lines. At the same time, BDIN L is asserted low and is converted to DIN H by IC5A. Since both SYNC H and WE H are high, IC11B disables bus receivers IC1 and IC3. The RPLY H line enables the bus drivers, IC2 and IC4 through IC10A, as is discussed in Sec. 4–2.4.

In the read mode, only the read word operation can occur. IC6 (which is a NAND circuit) combines DIN H and MS H to produce a low (RE L) at IC11A pin 2. This is the same as if WTBT H were low.

4–2.4 General

As soon as either DOUT H or DIN H occurs, IC12 is enabled by IC10C and D. However, BRPLY L and RPLY H do not occur until after a delay of approximately 150 ns. This ensures that the memory ICs have fully responded before the bus controlling device terminates either the read or write cycle.

If BDCOK H goes low (indicates a dc power failure), IC12 is immediately disabled through IC10C. Therefore, none of the memory ICs can be selected, and no false data can be written into memory.

BINIT L occurs whenever a reset operation is performed, and also during the power-up sequence. IC5A and IC5B convert this signal to INIT L, which, when asserted, clears IC7 and IC8.

4–2.5 Troubleshooting the H11–1 Module

Since the H11–1 is a plug-in module, the first step in troubleshooting is to replace the module. If this corrects the malfunction, individual components and circuits of the module can be tested and replaced as necessary. The user literature describes elaborate test procedures for module circuits, as well as troubleshooting charts. These will not be duplicated hered here, owing to space limitations, and because the circuits are unique to the H11 computer system (unlike the circuits of the H9 video terminal of Sec. 4–5, and the H10 paper-tape reader/punch of Sec. 4–6).

4–3. HEATHKIT H11–2 PARALLEL INTERFACE MODULE

This section describes the Heathkit H11–2 parallel interface module. Figure 4–25 shows the H11–2 block diagram. The H11–2 parallel interface module (or PIM) interfaces an I/0 device (such as the paper-tape reader/punch of Sec. 4–6) to the H11 computer bus. The PIM contains the necessary logic to control the I/0 device and interrupt the processor.

4–3.1 Addressing

Each PIM has a unique address that the processor treats as a memory location. Jumpers A3 through A12 program the address decoding circuitry to select the desired address of the PIM. The address decoder circuitry performs an EXCLUSIVE-OR operation between these jumpers and the address on the bus, and asserts AD H when they are equal. BBS 7 L (bank select 7) is asserted by the processor when it addresses any location between 28K and 32K. AD H is logically ANDed with BS 7 H and is latched by the assertion of BSYNC L and produces ME H.

Address-selection jumpers A3 through A12 represent 10 bits of the 16-bit address word. BBS 7 L is decoded by the processor from BDAL 3 through BDAL 15. The remaining three bits (BDAL 0 through BDAL 2) are decoded by the *function decoding and control circuitry*.

4–3.2 Function Decoding and Control

Input signals WTBT H, DIN H, DOUT H, and RDAB 0 H are decoded by this circuitry to select the function desired. BRPLY L is generated by this circuitry in response to DIN X MEL or VEC 1 L.

4–3.3 Data Selection

The data-selection circuitry gates the appropriate signals to the bus drivers in response to the function decoding and control output signals.

Data inputs to the data selectors are RCSR status signals, XCSR status signals, vector address, and low-byte received data.

RCSR status signals are applied to the low-byte bus drivers by the data selector when both DAL 2 H and DAL 1 L are not asserted. The low-byte bus drivers (in ICs) are then enabled by the assertion of DIN X ME.

The data selector applies the XCSR signals to the low-byte bus drivers if DAL 2 H is asserted and DAL 1 L is not asserted. The low-byte bus drivers are then enabled by the assertion of DIN X MEL. If VEC 1 L is asserted by the interrupt logic, the data selector applies the vector address to the low-byte bus drivers. The bus drivers are enabled by assertion of VEC 1 L. The vector address is determined by jumpers V3 through V7 and VEC 2 H.

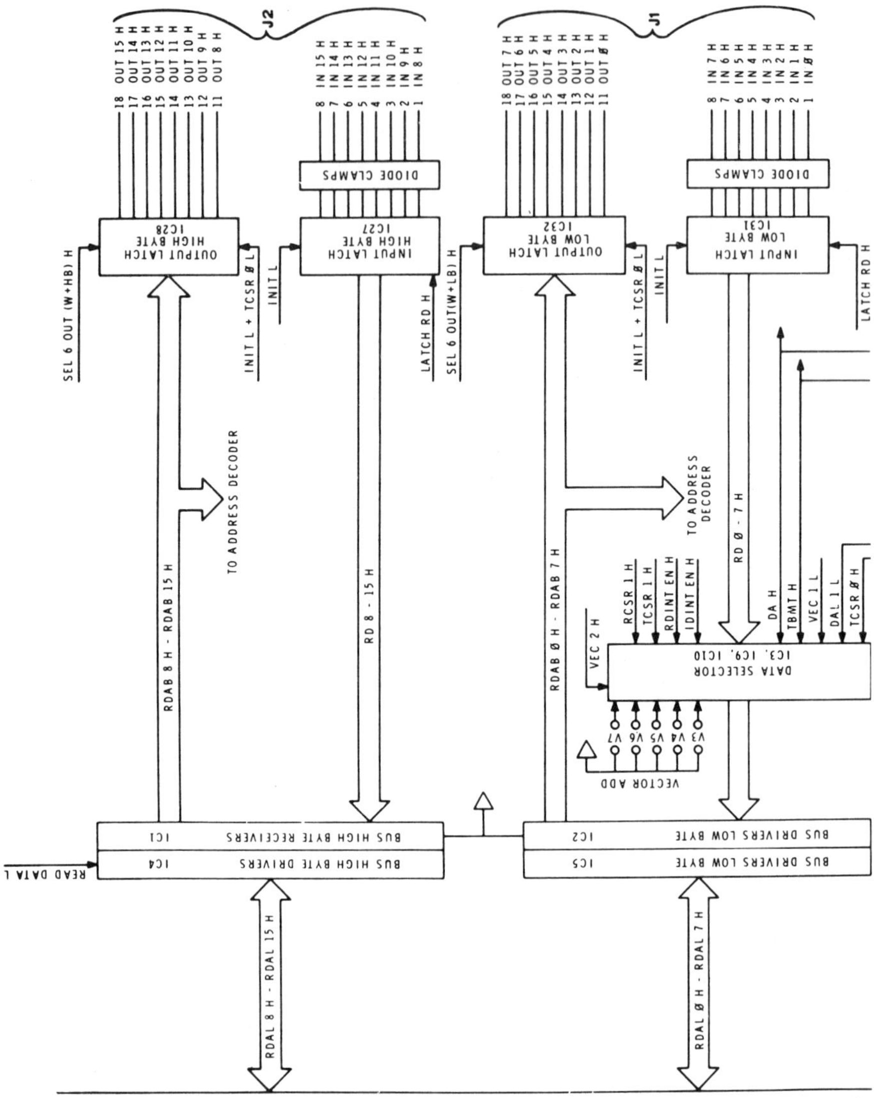
J2
J1
OUT 15 H
OUT 14 H
OUT 13 H
OUT 12 H
OUT 11 H
OUT 10 H
OUT 9 H
OUT 8 H
IN 15 H
IN 14 H
IN 13 H
IN 12 H
IN 11 H
IN 10 H
IN 9 H
IN 8 H
OUT 7 H
OUT 6 H
OUT 5 H
OUT 4 H
OUT 3 H
OUT 2 H
OUT 1 H
OUT Ø H
IN 7 H
IN 6 H
IN 5 H
IN 4 H
IN 3 H
IN 2 H
IN 1 H
IN Ø H
DIODE CLAMPS
DIODE CLAMPS
OUTPUT LATCH HIGH BYTE IC28
INPUT LATCH HIGH BYTE IC27
OUTPUT LATCH LOW BYTE IC32
INPUT LATCH LOW BYTE IC31
SEL 6 OUT (W+HB) H
INIT L + TCSR Ø L
INIT L
LATCH RD H
SEL 6 OUT(W+LB) H
INIT L + TCSR Ø L
INIT L
LATCH RD H
TO ADDRESS DECODER
TO ADDRESS DECODER
RDAB 8 H - RDAB 15 H
RD 8 - 15 H
RDAB Ø H - RDAB 7 H
RD Ø - 7 H
VEC 2 H
RCSR 1 H
TCSR 1 H
RDINT EN H
IDINT EN H
DA H
TBMT H
VEC 1 L
DA 1 L
TCSR Ø H
DATA SELECTOR IC3, IC9, IC10
V7 V6 V5 V4 V3
VECTOR ADD
BUS HIGH BYTE RECEIVERS IC1
BUS HIGH BYTE DRIVERS IC4
BUS DRIVERS LOW BYTE IC2
BUS DRIVERS LOW BYTE IC5
READ DATA L
RDAL 8 H - RDAL 15 H
RDAL Ø H - RDAL 7 H

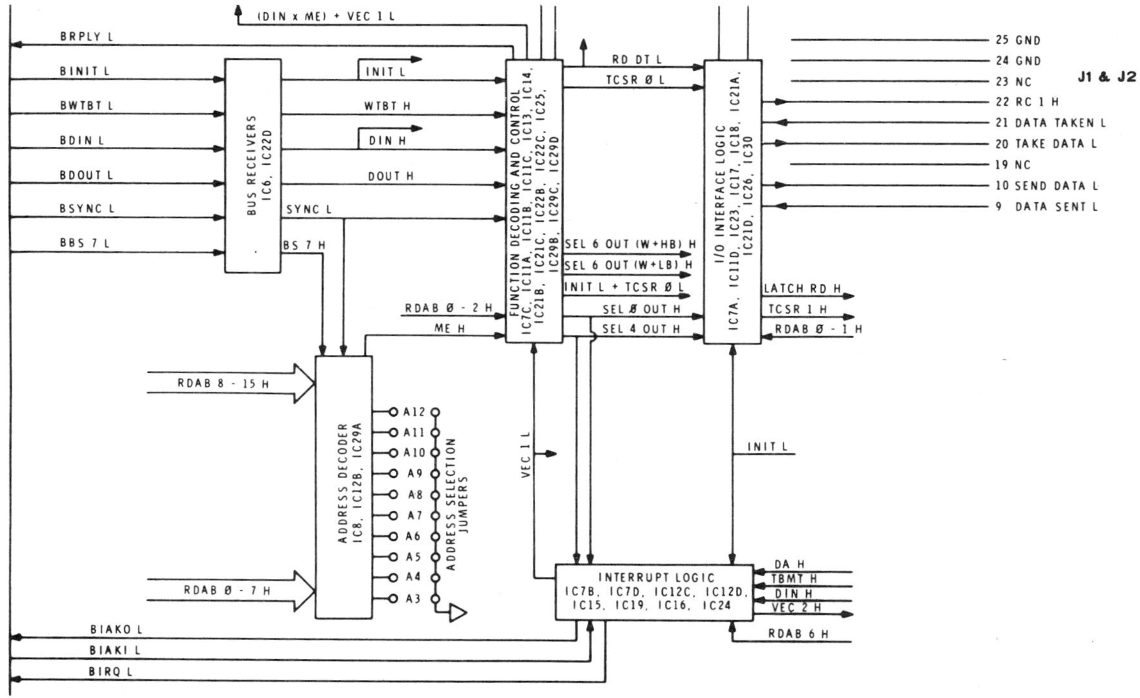

Fig. 4–25. Parallel interface module block diagram

If PAL 1 L is asserted, low-byte data RD 0–7 H is applied to the low-byte bus drivers. These drivers are then enabled by the assertion of DIN X MEL. The assertion of read data L by the function decoding and control circuitry (Sec. 4–3.2) enables the high-byte bus drivers, which applies high-byte data (RD 8 H through RD 15 H) to the bus.

4–3.4 I/O Interface Logic

This circuitry is responsible for controlling and monitoring the I/O device connected to the PIM.

The paper-tape reader/punch (Sec. 4–6) is enabled by setting bit 00 in the RCSR RDAB 0 H is applied to the D input of the reader flip-flop (IC30B) and is clocked by SEL 0 OUT H. When the reader is enabled, data valid L is negated and clears the reader enable flip-flop (IC30B). This causes reader enable L to be negated. Data valid low is asserted when the reader is ready to output data. Four hundred nanoseconds after the assertion of data valid low, the clear is removed from the reader enable flip-flop (IC30B), and the data status flip-flop (IC18A) is toggled to produce DA H. DA H is cleared by read data low.

If bit 01 is set in the RCSR, the reader is enabled and runs continuously. The RC flip-flop (IC30A) is set by RDAB 1 H and SEL 0 OUT H. The Q output of the RC flip-flop IC30A presets the reader flip-flop IC30B, asserting reader enable L, and also clears the data status flip-flop IC18A. This holds DA H false. DA H will remain false until the RC flip-flop IC30A is reset or cleared. A low-to-high transition on data valid L will cause reader enable L to go high. A high-to-low transition on data valid L will cause reader enable L to go low after a 400-ns time delay (determined by R1 and C1). These transitions do not affect DA H, which remains low.

If bit 00 in the XCSR is set, continuous 0s will be punched. IC17A is set by RDAB 0 H and SEL 4 OUT H, thus generating TSCR 0 L. This presets IC17B and clears the output latches.

New data valid L is asserted 150 ns after IC17B is preset. New data valid L remains asserted until IC17A is reset or cleared. TBMT H remains low. If bit 01 is set in the XCSR, the punch is inhibited from punching. IC18 is set by RDAB 1 H and SEL 4 OUT H. This forces new data valid L to a high level until IC18 is set by RDAB 1 H and SEL 4 OUT H. This forces new data valid L to a high level until C18 is reset or cleared.

If SEL 6 OUT H is asserted (output data), IC17B is set; 150 ns later TAKE DATA L is asserted. When IC17B is set, TBMT H goes low. When DATA TAKEN L goes high, IC17B is cleared and forces

TAKE DATA L to a high level. When punch ready L goes low, TBMT H goes high and indicates that the punch is ready for another character.

4–3.5 Input/Output Latches

The input and output latches are TTL, positive edge-triggered, D-type flip-flops. Input data are clamped to a +5.6 V maximum by the diode clamps before they are applied to the input latches. The input data are latched by latch RD H 400 ns after data valid L is asserted by the I/0 device.

SEL 6 OUT (W + LB) H and SEL 6 OUT (W + HB) H are generated by the function decoding and control circuitry (Sec. 4–3.2) in response to input signals. Assertion of SEL 6 OUT (W + LB) H latches the data present at the low-byte bus receiver's outputs to the low-byte output latch. Assertion of SEL 6 OUT (W + HB) H latches the data present at the output of the high-byte bus receivers into the high-byte output latch.

4–3.6 Interrupt Logic

The interrupt logic circuitry allows the PIM to interrupt the processor. Interrupts may be either receiver generated or transmitter generated. The receiver-generated interrupt however, has the highest priority.

A receiver-generated interrupt occurs if bit 6 in the RCSR is set (interrupts enabled) and DA H is asserted. Bit 6 is set under program control and is latched by IC24A. This asserts RD INT EN H. DA H is asserted by the I/O interface logic when it has received data from the I/O device. The combination of DA H and RD INT EN H causes the interrupt logic to assert BIRQ L. The processor then responds (if program status word, bit 7, is not set) by asserting BDIN L. Approximately 150 ns later, BIAKO L causes the interrupt logic to clear IC16A, which negates BIRQ L if the transmitter is not also requesting an interrupt. BIAKI L also causes the interrupt logic to assert VEC 1 L, which enables the data selector to gate the vector jumper address to the low-byte bus drivers. The PIM asserts BRPLY approximately 150 ns after the assertion of VEC 1 L. When the processor receives BRPLY L and the vector address, it negates BDIN L and BIAKO L. The PIM responds by negating VEC 1 L and BRPLY L.

A transmitter-generated interrupt operates similarly to a receiver-generated interrupt. A transmitter-generated interrupt occurs if bit 6 in the XCSR is set. TBMTH is asserted, and a receiver interrupt is not present. Bit 6 is set under program control and is latched by IC16B.

This asserts TD INT EN H. TBMT H is asserted by the I/O interface logic when it is ready to accept another character for transmission to the parallel I/O device (such as the paper-tape reader/punch of Sec. 4–6). When a transmitter interrupt is initiated, the same sequence of signals occurs as in a receiver-generated interrupt, except that VEC 2 H is asserted by the interrupt logic when the processor asserts BDIN L. VEC 2 H is gated through the data selector to the bus drivers when VEC 1 L is asserted. This causes the least-significant octal digit of the vector address to be 4_8.

The interrupt logic will pass the BIAKO L signal out to the system bus if the PIM is not requesting an interrupt. If the PIM is requesting an interrupt, it will not pass the BIAKO L. The module *electrically nearest to the processor* will be serviced first if more than one module is requesting an interrupt. This feature allows the user to select interrupt priority by physical placement of the modules in the H11 backplane.

4–3.7 Troubleshooting the H11–2 Module

Since the H11–2 is a plug-in module, the first step in troubleshooting is to replace the module. If this corrects the malfunction, individual components can be tested and replaced as described in the user literature. Refer to Sec. 4–2.5.

4–4. HEATHKIT H11–5 SERIAL INTERFACE MODULE

This section describes the Heathkit H11–5 serial interface module shown in Fig. 4–23. Figure 4–26 shows the H11–5 block diagram. The H11–5 interfaces and I/O device (such as the video terminal of Sec. 4–5) to the H11 computer bus, and contains the necessary logic to both control the I/O device and to interrupt the processor.

4–41. Addressing

The H11–5 has a unique address that is treated as a memory location by the processor. This address is user programmable by jumpers A3 through A13. When an address appears on the system bus, it is coupled through bus receivers to IC5, where an EXCLUSIVE-OR operation occurs between the jumpers and the address on the bus. If the address on the bus and the programmed address are equal, AD H is asserted. BBS 7 L (bank select 7) is asserted by the processor when it addresses any location between 28K and 32K. BBS 7 L and AD H are then logically ANDed and latched when BSYNC L is asserted, producing ME H. This remains asserted until BSYNC L is negated.

Address-selection jumpers A3 through A12 represent 10 bits of the 16-bit address word. BBS 7 L is decoded by the processor from BDAL 13 through BDAL 15. The remaining three bits, BDAL 0 through BDAL 2 are decoded by the function decoding and control circuitry of Sec. 4–4.2.

4–4.2 Function Decoding and Control Circuitry

RDAB 1 H and RDAB 2 H are decoded by this circuitry to select one of four registers. The register is determined by the least-significant octal digit of the device address. For example, the console device address is 177560. This address can be 177560 to 177566, depending on which register is selected. RDAB 1 H and RDAB 2 H are latched at address time when SYNC L is asserted. After SYNC L is asserted, a DIN (data into the processor) or a DOUT (data out of the processor) occurs, which causes BRPLY L to be asserted after an approximate 150-ns delay. If a DIN occurs, the bus drivers are enabled and the data selector receives the function select signals, which determine the registers that will be gated to the bus drivers. If a DOUT occurs, the bus drivers remain off; and again the function select signals determine which of the registers will be written into. The registers are various flip-flop and logic circuits on the serial module.

4–4.3 UART

The UART (universal asynchronous receiver transmitter) performs the parallel-to-serial and serial-to-parallel conversions necessary to interface a serial I/O device to the parallel system bus. The UART can be divided into two basic sections: receiver and transmitter. The receiver converts serial start, data, parity, and stop bits (Sec. 2–2, Fig. 2–3) into parallel data, and verifies proper code transmissions, parity, and stop bits. The data word length can be 5, 6, 7, or 8 bits. Parity may be odd or even, and parity checking and generation can be inhibited. The stop bits may be one or two, or one and one-half when transmitting a 5-bit code.

The UART receives data by TTL SDIN H. The serial data are converted to parallel data and sent out RD 0–7 H to the data selector. Parallel data enter the UART by the bus receivers and appear on RDAB 0–7 H. The UART stores these data in its own buffer, converts them to serial data, and outputs them at SO L.

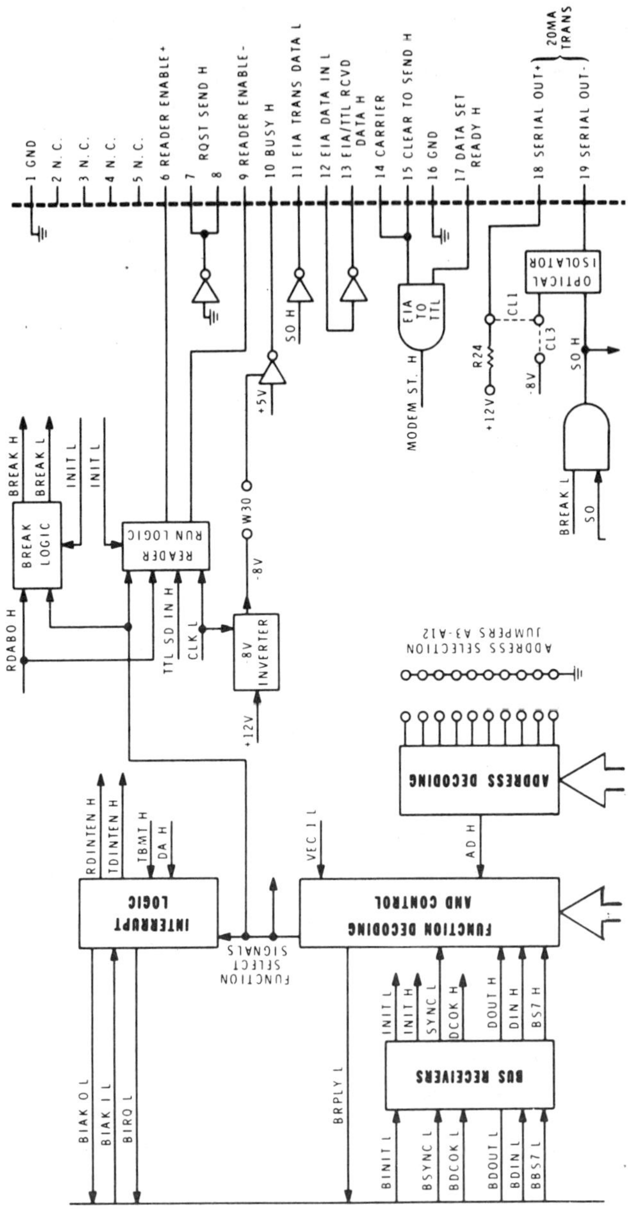
1 GND
2 N.C.
3 N.C.
4 N.C.
5 N.C.
6 READER ENABLE+
7
RQST SEND H
8
9 READER ENABLE-
10 BUSY H
11 EIA TRANS DATA L
12 EIA DATA IN L
13 EIA/TTL RCVD DATA H
14 CARRIER
15 CLEAR TO SEND H
16 GND
17 DATA SET READY H
18 SERIAL OUT+
19 SERIAL OUT-
20MA TRANS
OPTICAL ISOLATOR
CL1
CL3
R24
+12V
-8V
SO H
EIA TO TTL
MODEM ST. H
BREAK L
SO
BREAK H
BREAK L
INIT L
INIT L
BREAK LOGIC
READER RUN LOGIC
RDABO H
TTL SD IN H
CLK L
-8V INVERTER
+12V
-8V
W30
+5V
ADDRESS SELECTION JUMPERS A3-A12
ADDRESS DECODING
AD H
RDINTEN H
TDINTEN H
TBMT H
DA H
INTERRUPT LOGIC
VEC 1 L
FUNCTION DECODING AND CONTROL
FUNCTION SELECT SIGNALS
INIT L
INIT H
SYNC L
DCOK H
DOUT H
DIN H
BS7 H
BUS RECEIVERS
BIAK O L
BIAK I L
BIRQ L
BRPLY L
BINIT L
BSYNC L
BDCOK L
BDOUT L
BDIN L
BBS7 L

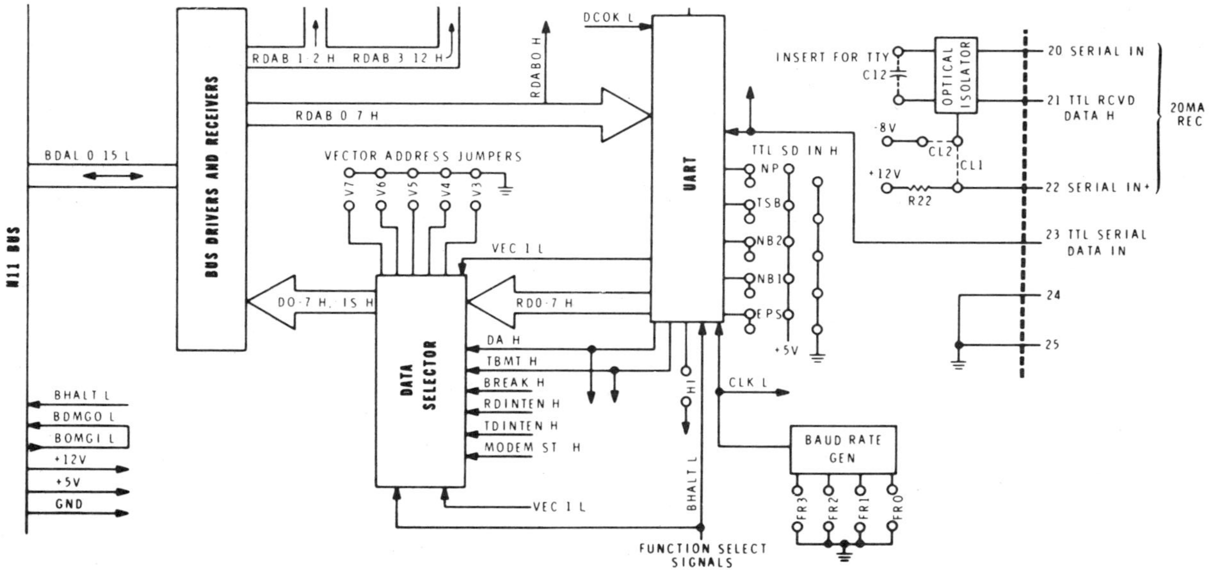

Fig. 4–26. Serial interface module block diagram

The UART status is specified by DA H, TBMT H, and FE H. DA H is bit 7 in the RCSR, which is asserted when an entire character has been received and is ready for input to the processor. TBMT H is bit 7 in the XCSR, which is asserted when XBUF is empty and can accept another character for transmission. FE H is connected to BHALT L through an inverter and jumper H1. FE H asserted indicates that the first stop bit was invalid.

4–4.4 Data Selector

The data-selector circuitry gates the appropriate signals to the bus drivers in response to function-select signals and VEC 1 L. Normally, VEC 1 L is not asserted. If the RCSR (receiver control status register) is addressed, the data selector gates the receiver status signals to the bus drivers. If a DIN occurs, the bus drivers are enabled, and the information is presented to the bus.

If RBUF (receiver buffer register) is addressed, the data selector gates RD 0–7 H from the UART to the bus drivers. If a DIN occurs, the bus drivers are enabled.

If XCSR (transmitter control status register) is addressed, the data selector gates the transmitter status signals to the bus drivers, and the assertion of DIN enables the bus drivers.

If XBUF (transmitter buffer register) is addressed, the data selector is turned off because XBUF is a "write only" register.

If a DOUT occurs during the addressing of any of the above registers, the bus drivers will remain off. The function-decoding circuit decodes DOUT and gates the signals from the bus receivers to the register selected. RBUF is the only "read only" register and therefore cannot be written into.

If an interrupt occurs and VEC 1 L is asserted, the data selector gates the vector jumper information to the bus drivers.

4–4.5 Interrupt Logic

The interrupt logic allows the serial module to interrupt the processor. Interrupts may be either receiver or transmitter generated, with receiver-generated interrupts having the highest priority.

A receiver-generated interrupt occurs if bit 6 in the RCSR is set (interrupt enabled) and DA H is asserted. Bit 6 in the RCSR is set under program control and latched by IC13A, asserting RD INT EN H. DA H is asserted by the UART when it has received data from the serial I/O device. The combination of DA H and RD INT EN H causes the interrupt logic to assert BIRQ L. The processor responds (if the program status word, bit 7, is not set) by asserting BDIN L. Approximately 150 ns later, BIAKO L is asserted. BIAKO L is received by the serial module from the system bus as BIAKI L. BIAKI L clears IC15A, which negates BIRQ L and enables the data selector to gate the vector jumper address to the bus drivers. BRPL Y L is asserted approximately 150 ns after the assertion of VEC 1 L When the processor receives BRPL Y L and the vector address, it negates BDIN L and BIAKO L. The serial module responds by negating VEC 1 L and BRPL Y L.

Transmitter-generated interrupts operate similarly to receiver-generated interrupts. A transmitter-generated interrupt occurs if bit 6 in the XCSR is set (interrupt enabled), TBMT H is asserted, and a receiver interrupt is not present. Bit 6 in the XCSR is set under program control and latched by IC13B, asserting TD INT EN H. TBMT H is asserted by the UART when it is ready to accept another character for transmission to the serial I/O device. When a transmitter-generated interrupt is initiated, VEC 2 H is asserted by the interrupt logic when the processor asserts BDIN L. Otherwise, the same sequence of signals occurs as when a receiver interrupt is initiated. VEC 2 H is gated through the data selector to the bus drivers when VEC 1 L is asserted. This causes the least-significant octal digit of the vector address to be 4_8.

The interrupt logic will pass BIAKO L to the system bus if the serial module is not requesting an interrupt. BIAKO L will not pass if the serial module is requesting an interrupt.

The module electrically nearest to the processor will be processed first if more than one module requests an interrupt. This feature allows you to select interrupt priority by physical placement of the modules in the backplane.

4–4.6 Baud-Rate Generator

The baud-rate generator (which sets the rate of serial bit transmissin) is composed of a 2.4576-MHz crystal oscillator and a jumper programmable divider circuit. The jumpers select the divide ratio to produce the desired baud rate. The CLK L output from the baud-rate generator is used by the UART as a clock to determine the proper receive and transit baud rate. The baud rates available are 50, 75, 110, 134.5, 150, 200, 300, 600, 1200, 1800, 2400, 4800, and 9600.

4–4.7 Troubleshooting the H11-5 Module

Since the H11-5 is a plug-in module, the first step in troubleshooting is to replace the module. If this corrects the malfunction, individual components can be tested and replaced as described in the user literature. Refer to Sec. 4–2.5.

4–5. HEATHKIT MODEL H9 VIDEO TERMINAL

This section describes the Heathkit H9 video terminal shown in Fig. 4–27. An overall block diagram of the H9 is shown in Fig. 4–28. The H9 can display information coming from a digital computer (such as, but not limited to, the H11) or information typed in from the keyboard. This information is displayed on a 12-in. (diagonal) cathode ray tube (CRT) that is capable of displaying 960 characters at one time (12 rows with 80 characters per row).

A 67-key ASCII keyboard, which permits you to compose and edit directly on the CRT, has a capability of 64 different characters and 24 different functions. This message or program can be transmitted through a standard serial I/O interface (Sec. 4–4) to a digital computer or through the parallel I/O interface (Sec. 4–3) to a paper-type reader/ punch (Sec. 4–6).

Fig. 4–27. Heathkit H9 video terminal

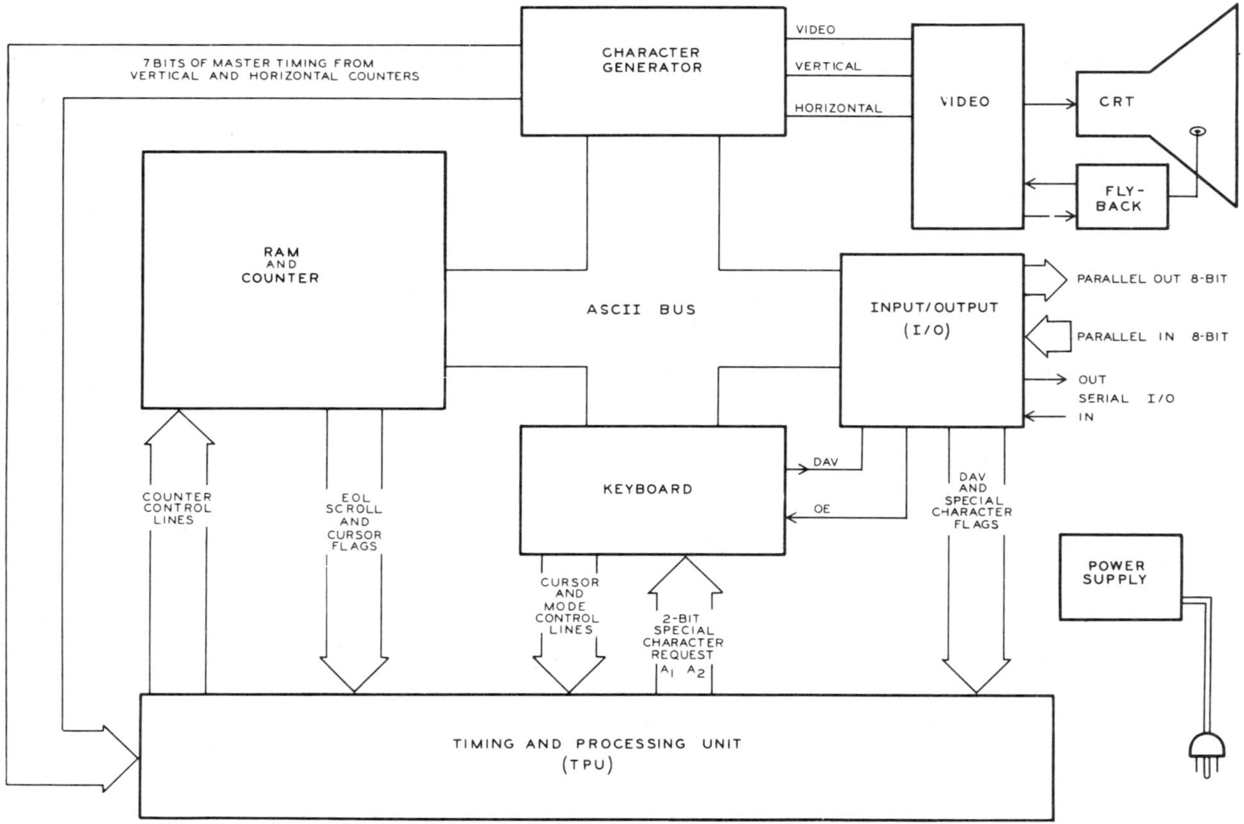

Fig. 4–28. Video terminal block diagram

The H9 video terminal can be used with any digital computer in a dedicated format, in a stand-alone application, or in a time-sharing system. The H9 lets you communicate with a digital computer in higher-level language (Basic, assembler, etc.) rather than just using toggle switches. The H9 is also much faster (up to 9600 baud) than the standard electromechanical teletypewriter systems. You can select any data rate between 110 and 9600 baud.

4–5.1 Basic Overview of the H9

The block diagram of Fig. 4–28 shows how the H9 can be divided into a series of functional blocks that coordinate the movement of data on an 8-bit ASCII bus. These blocks, which include the character generator, the RAM and counter, the keyboard, and the I/0, are interconnected directly to the ASCII bus. Data bits are transferred from one block to another and to the external devices over the ASCII bus under control of the timing and processing unit (TPU). Other functional blocks include the video circuits, a line-operated power supply, and a high-voltage power supply, or flyback system, which is operated from the video circuits.

The character generator has a master oscillator and dividers that generate the timing signals for all the functional modules within the H9. Basically, the character generator takes data from the RAM and converts them from 8-bit parallel ASCII information to *serial dot* information. The serial dot information is then used to modulate the raster scan on the CRT screen.

The video module contains a video amplifier that converts the TTL dot data from the character generator into voltage levels that drive the cathode of the CRT. The video circuits also have a vertical oscillator and amplifier that generate the vertical sweep and drive the vertical portion of the CRT yoke. The video circuits contain the horizontal oscillator and driver that drive the horizontal flyback and sweep systems. The vertical and horizontal oscillators are synchronized by sync pulses generated by the character generator.

The RAM and counter board contain the memory that stores the information to be displayed on the screen. Everything that appears on the face of the CRT is stored in the RAM. The RAM and counter circuit board also contain the RAM address counter, a cursor latch, which remembers where the cursor is supposed to appear on the screen, and scroll counters that remember the start of a page, or scroll information.

The keyboard contains a standard ASCII keyboard and a series of other special-function keys that control operation of the H9. The keyboard includes five cursor control keys, a number of keys that control operation of the serial I/O, erase keys, and screen display mode keys. The keyboard also includes a special character generator that puts selected ASCII information on the bus whenever it is required.

The I/O board contains latches and buffers to control parallel data transfers between the H9 and any external device. The I/O board also contains the UART that controls serial data transfers between the H9 and any external devices. The I/O board has a special character detector that monitors the bus and looks for special characters such as carriage returns, bells, control characters, and the like.

The timing and processing unit (TPU) controls all the other functional blocks. The TPU is the decision-making module within the H9. Data bits are moved, written, or transmitted under control of the TPU as a function of the front panel switches and the data themselves. The TPU also controls cursor movements, scrolling operations, erasing, and the RAM counter configurations.

4–5.2 Operation of Video Terminal Keys

Before going into the H9 circuit descriptions and circuit troubleshooting, we shall discuss the functions of the terminal keys shown in Fig. 4–27. It is essential that you understand the key functions in order to follow the circuit descriptions given in later paragraphs.

The H9 generates and displays 64 ASCII coded characters in response to operation of the keys. The characters include the alphabet (uppercase only), numbers, punctuation, and many symbols. Thirty-two standard control characters and twenty-four special functions can also be generated.

Local Function Keys. The local function keys do not transmit ASCII characters. Instead, they alter or otherwise affect the screen display.

The *cursor control keys* (at the far right of the keyboard) are labeled with arrows: UP CURSOR (↑), DOWN CURSOR (↓), RIGHT CURSOR (→), and LEFT CURSOR (←).

These keys move the cursor one character position or one character line as indicated by the arrow.

HOME key. This key moves the cursor to the first character location on the first line.

ERASE EOL (end of line) key. This key erases the text from the current cursor location to the end of that line.

ERASE PAGE key. This key erases all text and fills the page

(screen) with spaces. The ERASE PAGE key also places the cursor in the home position.

AUTO CARRY key. When this key is pushed in, the cursor automatically goes to the beginning of the next line after a full line of text is typed. At the end of the bottom line of text, the cursor will start over at the beginning of the first line (home position), providing the H9 is not in scroll mode (SCROLL key released). Also, refer to the HOLD SCREEN mode of operation.

SHORT FORM key. When this key is pushed in, the display format is changed from 12 lines of 80 characters (key released) to four columns, with each column consisting of 12 lines of 20 characters. Short form is useful for writing programs in machine language where entries are short.

SCROLL key. When this key is pushed in, and after the first 12 lines of text are typed the first line is erased (scrolled upward) and lost. Each remaining character line moves up one line position, and the cursor moves to the bottom line. In short form, the left column of 240 characters (12 lines of 20 characters) is erased and lost. The remaining three columns move to the left one column position, and the cursor moves to the right column. When the SCROLL key is released (in the nonscroll position), and after the first 12 lines of text are typed, the cursor returns to and flashes at the start of page position. Further typed entries will write over the existing text on the first line. Also, refer to the HOLD SCREEN mode of operation.

Special-Function Keys

RETURN (carriage return) key. This key moves the cursor to the first character position of the line it is currently in and transmits the return ASCII code (control M). Return can be written into a RAM location only if that location contains a space. That is, a carriage return will not write over any other character. Return is a nondisplayable character, except in the plot mode.

LINE FEED key. This key moves the cursor down one line, and it transmits the line feed ASCII code (control J). Line feed does not write into RAM and it is not a displayable character, except in the PLOT mode.

RUB OUT key. This key transmits an ASCII rub out code (delete). Rub out does not write into RAM and it is a nondisplayable character, except in the PLOT mode.

ESC (escape) key. This key transmits an ASCII escape code.

Escape does not write into RAM and it is a nondisplayable character, except in the PLOT mode.

REPT (repeat). When this key is held in, along with another key, it will repeat the function of the other key at a preset rate as long as both keys are held down. The presettable repeat rates are 3.7, 7.5, 15, or 30 characters per second. If the baud rate that has been selected is less than the repeat rate, the repeat function will operate at the slower rate.

PLOT key. When this key is pushed in, the text is blanked except for the first line of the page. This first line, however, is displayed on each of the four bottom lines of the screen. The screen area above the bottom four lines is divided into 128 scan lines, as shown in Fig. 4–29. A dash, one character wide, will appear above each of the characters displayed in the bottom four lines. The position of the dash above the bottom line (line 0) is proportional to the binary value of the 7-bit ASCII code for that character. For example, a CTRL/SHIFT P, or ASCII null, is all zeros, its binary value is zero, and it appears at the bottom of the 128-line space directly above the ASCII null. A RUB OUT (delete) or all ASCII 1's has a binary value of 127, so the dash appears at the top line (line 128) in the space above the rub out character. In the PLOT mode, all characters are written into RAM, but

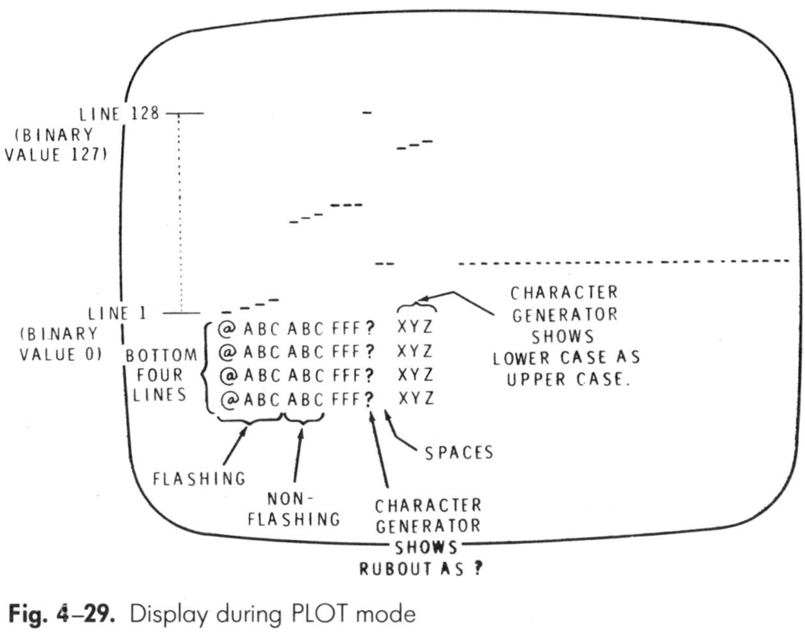

Fig. 4–29. Display during PLOT mode

their special cursor movements are not implemented. That is, a RETURN (carriage return) is written into RAM, but the cursor does not move. Any control character that appears in the text will flash. Even though the lowercase alphabetic characters cannot be generated from the keyboard, they can be entered into RAM from the digital computer. Like all other characters, the binary value of the lowercase characters is stored in RAM and the dash is displayed on the appropriate line in the 128-line space. Lowercase letters stored in RAM are displayed as the characters represented by the ASCII words 010 0000 through 011 1111.

BAUD RATE key. When this key is released (out), the H9 will operate at 110 baud. When this key is pushed in, the rate is set by a BAUD RATE switch on the rear panel. This rear panel switch selects either 300 baud or the preset baud. The preset baud is determined by a jumper wire on the I/O circuit board (as discussed in Sec. 4–5.9).

OFF LINE key. When this key is pushed in, the H9 is inhibited from transmitting or receiving data from the serial I/O, but it does not interrupt transmission or reception through the parallel I/O port. This lets you punch or read tape on the paper-tape reader/punch (Sec. 4–6) while the H9 is off line from the digital computer.

BREAK key. When this key is pushed in, it generates a continuous space at the serial output. BREAK is generally used to tell the computer that you wish to interrupt execution. Do not confuse this space with an ASCII space. It is defined as a zero current in a 20mA current loop (which is the circuit used in many serial data-transmission systems to pass serial data), an EIA positive voltage, or a TTL logic 0. The BREAK key can be pressed any time you want to terminate the transmit page function.

FULL DUPLEX key. When this key is released (out), the H9 operates in the *half-duplex* mode. That is, data from the keyboard or parallel input are written directly into RAM and, at the same time, ASCII characters are sent out the serial and parallel outputs. When the FULL DUPLEX key is pushed in, the H9 operates in the *full duplex* mode; data from the parallel input or the keyboard are sent to the computer and echoed back to the H9 before they are written into RAM and displayed on the screen.

XMIT PAGE (transmit page) key. When you momentarily press this key, data bits are transmitted from the RAM (screen), starting from the current cursor location and proceeding to the end of the page. When it has completed the page, the cursor returns home and the transmit page mode stops. The data bits are transmitted simultaneously out both the parallel and serial ports at a rate determined by the slower of the two ports. Press the BREAK key to interrupt the transmit page function.

CTRL (control) key. When this key is used in conjunction with some of the other keys, it changes those keys to special-function keys. For example, CRTL M is equivalent to a return (carriage return).

SHIFT key. When this key is used in conjunction with another key, the character printed on the upper portion of that key will be displayed. Since the H9 does not generate lowercase alphabetic characters, it is not necessary to push the SHIFT key to generate uppercase characters (they are shifted automatically in the keyboard encoder).

CTRL/SHIFT keys. These two keys are used in conjunction with other keys to provide additional special-function keys. For example, CTRL/SHIFT P (which means, press the CTRL, the SHIFT, and the P keys at the same time) puts an ASCII null (all zeros) on the bus.

Control Characters. The H9 generates all 32 ASCII control characters from the keyboard. Normally, these characters do not write into RAM, nor are they displayed on the screen. Exceptions are outlined in the description of the PLOT mode. The H9 recognizes only four of the control characters and will recognize them from the keyboard or from the parallel or serial input ports. The four characters are the following:

Line feed (LF or CTRL J): this character duplicates the LINE FEED key.

Carriage return (CR or CTRL M): this character duplicates the RETURN key.

Back space (BS or CTRL H): this character moves the cursor to the left one character position without disturbing the character being displaced.

Bel (Bel or CTRL G): this character causes the H9 to sound a short audible tone through an internal speaker.

Hold Screen. If the screen has been filled and a scroll function should occur, but cannot because the SCROLL key is not pushed in, the H9 goes into the hold screen mode. The cursor returns to the start of page location and blinks. All external inputs are disabled when this occurs. Data can only be transmitted out of the H9 by the keyboard. The H9 stays in the hold screen mode until the SCROLL key is pushed in or until the ERASE PAGE key is pressed.

The hold screen feature can be used in conjunction with the paper-tape reader/punch for reviewing program tapes. The reader/punch can read the tape at its maximum speed to fill up the screen quickly; then after the last line has been written, the hold screen mode disables the handshake signal coming from the H9. This stops the tape from running.

You can then review the contents of the screen. When you are finished, just press the ERASE PAGE key and receive another screen full of program information automatically.

4–5.3 Power Supply Circuits

The power supply circuits are shown in Fig. 4–30. The primary of the power supply consists of slow-blow fuse F1, ON/OFF switch SW1, and the dual primary windings of transformer T1. The dual primary windings may be connected in series for 240-V operation or in parallel for 120-V operation.

The red secondary winding of T1 supplies 9-Vac to the diode bridge rectifier D101 through D104. The rectified output of the bridge rectifier is filtered by C1. Integrated circuits IC101 and IC102 provide two regulated 5-V supplies. The ICs are internally protected against short circuits, overloads, and high temperature. Capacitors C101 and C102 stablize the regulators.

The orange secondary winding supplies 28 Vac to diode bridge rectifier D105 through D108. The 36-V output of the bridge rectifier is filtered by C2. This 36-V supply is one of the outputs of the power supply. IC103 is a 20-V regulator, but its output is programmed by resistors R103 and R104 to supply 26 V. IC103 draws its input current from the base of transistor Q101, which, in turn, provides the larger current required by the video circuits (Sec. 4–5.4) and regulates the output at 26 V. Transistor Q102 and resistor R102 limit the short-circuit current to about 2 A. Capacitor C103 provides stability for IC103. IC104 is a 12-V regulator. The input to IC104 comes from the 26-V supply. Capacitor C104 provides stability for IC104.

The green secondary winding supplies 15 Vac to diode bridge rectifier D109 through D112. The d+c output voltage is filtered by C105. IC105 is a negative, adjustable voltage regulator that is programmed to −12 V by resistors R105 and R106. Capacitor C106 provides stability for IC105, while C107 lowers the high-frequency output impedance. Resistor R107 reduces the 15 Vac from the green secondary winding to provide 11 Vac to power the CRT filaments.

Troubleshooting the Power Supply Circuits. The following steps apply to the circuits shown in Fig. 4–30. The first step in troubleshooting any power supply circuit it to plug in the equipment and turn it on. Make certain that the primary line cord is good and that there is power. If nothing happens at turn on, check fuse F1, switch SW1, and the T1 primary wiring. Check for 120 (or 240) V across the T1 primary.

Now assume that the fuse blows, then SW1 is turned ON. Unless the fuse is of the incorrect value, or there is an internal short in T1 (neither of which is likely in practical situations) a blown fuse is a result of shorts (either intermittent or permanent). Check for shorts on the power supply circuit board, across the T1 secondary windings, at the outputs of bridge rectifiers C1, C2, and C105, between the collector of Q101 and the heat sink, and at the regulator outputs P101-1 through 101-6. Use an ohmmeter and/or the current probe described in Sec. 3–4. Also check for shorted rectifier diodes D101 through D112 and regulators IC101 through IC103.

If the fuse does not blow, and there is no obvious arcing, burning, smoke, or flame, the next step is to check each of the power supply output voltages (+5, +12, −12, +26 and +36 V).

If there is no +5-V output, or if the +5-V supply is incorrect (too high or too low) check the obvious components D101 through D104, T1 red winding (for 9 V), IC101, IC102, and C1. Also check the not-so-obvious connection at the +5-V reference P101–6. If this point is not grounded properly, the +5-V supply will "float" and appear at some higher voltage when measured with reference to ground.

If there is no +12-V output, or if it measures too high or low, check the +26-V supply. If the +26-V supply is below +15V, the +12-V supply will also be low. If the +26V supply is correct, check IC104 and the +12-V reference ground (P101–6).

If there is no −12-V output, or if it measures too high or low, check IC105, R105, R106, D109, D112, T1 green winding (for 15 V) and C107. Also check for proper ground at P101–6.

If there is no +26-V output, or if it measures too high or low, check IC103, R103, R104, Q101, Q102, D105 through D108, and the T1 orange winding (for 28 V). Also check for proper ground at the +26-V reference (P101–11).

If there is no +36-V output, or if it measures too high or low, check D105 through D108 and C2. (If there is no +36-V output, there will be no +26- and +12-V outputs.)

4–5.4 Video Circuits

Video circuits are shown in Fig. 4–31. The video circuits include the vertical sweep circuits, horizontal sweep circuits, high voltage circuits, and video amplifier.

Vertical Sweep Circuits. At the beginning of each vertical scan cycle, the vertical sync pulse (from the character generator, Sec. 4–5.5) turns on transistor Q301. This discharges the voltage across C303. At the end of the sync pulse Q301 turns off. Transistor Q302, a current source, charges capacitor C303 with a constant current. Note that the

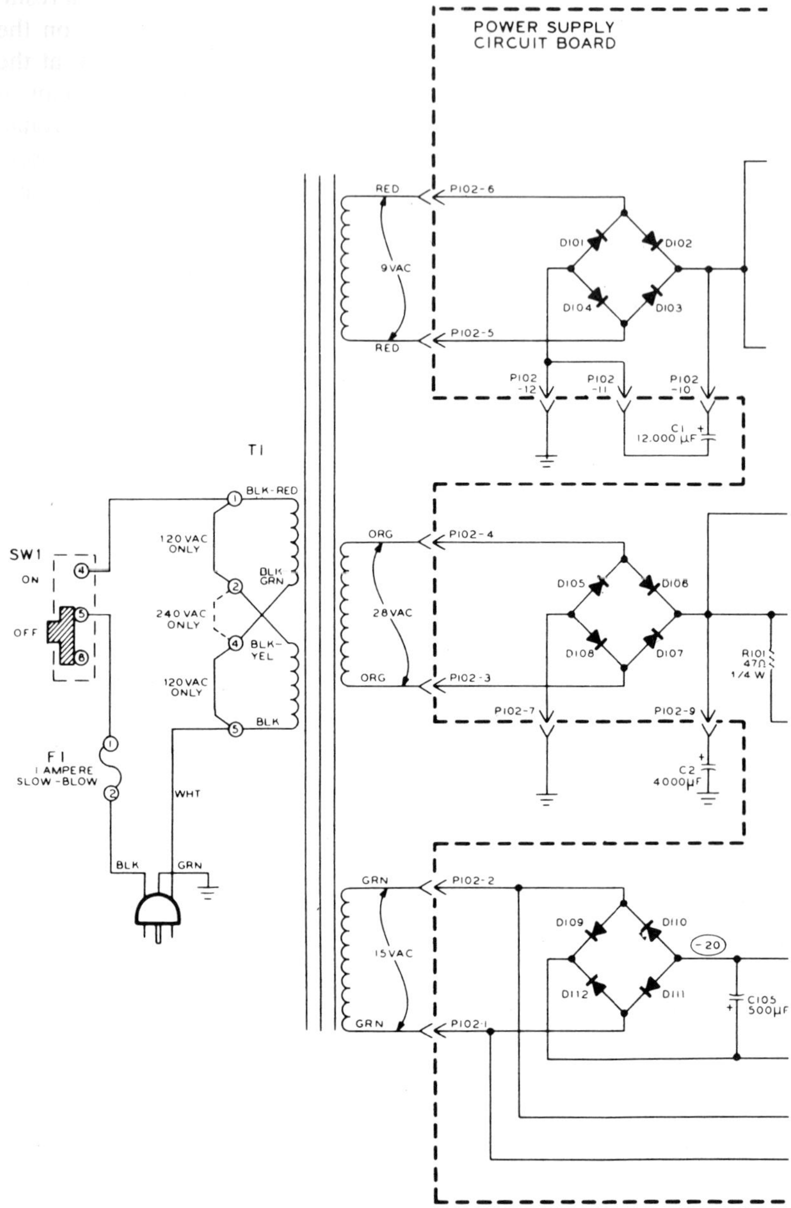

Fig. 4–30. Power supply circuits

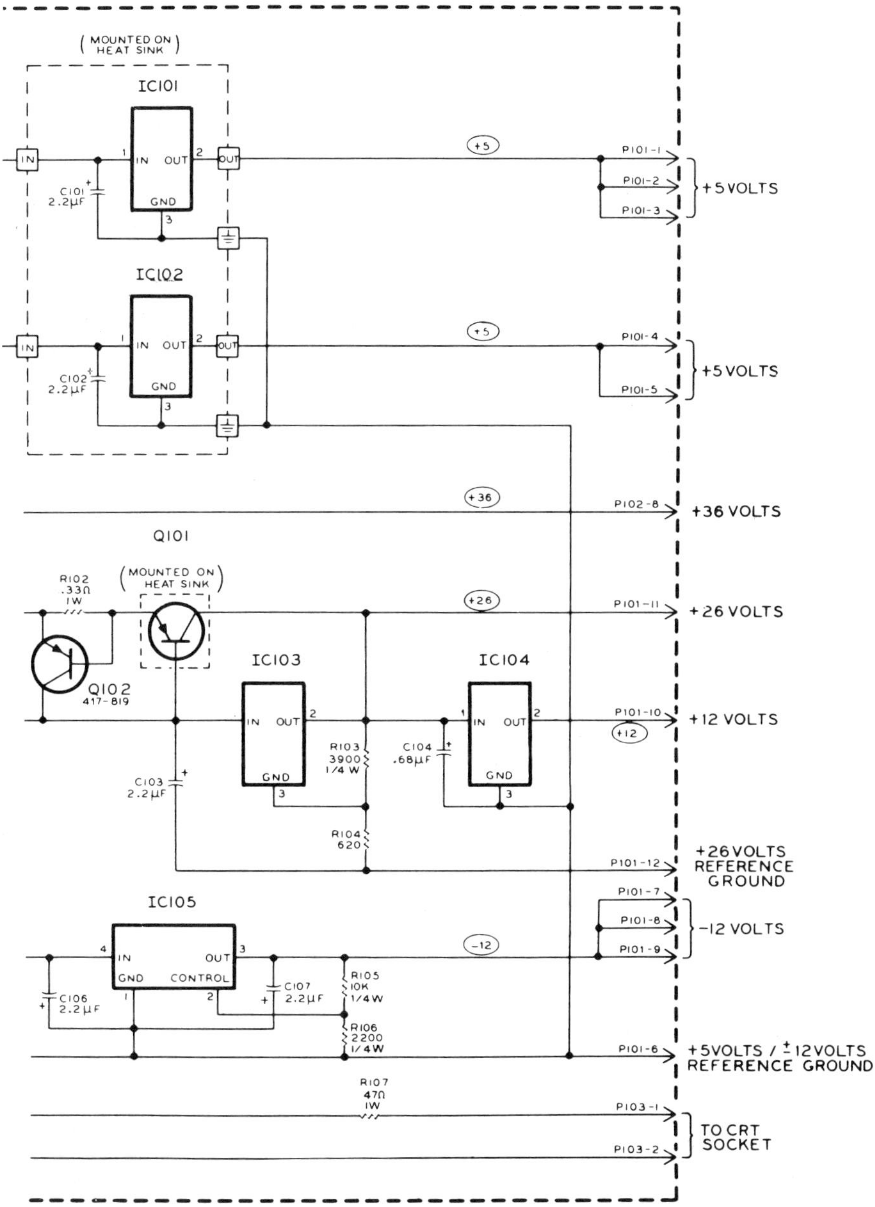
(MOUNTED ON HEAT SINK)
IC101
IN
OUT
GND
C101 2.2µF
IC102
C102 2.2µF
+5
P101-1
P101-2
P101-3
+5 VOLTS
P101-4
P101-5
+5 VOLTS
+36
P102-8
+36 VOLTS
Q101
R102 .33Ω 1W
(MOUNTED ON HEAT SINK)
+26
P101-11
+26 VOLTS
Q102 417-819
IC103
IC104
R103 3900 1/4 W
C104 .68µF
C103 2.2µF
P101-10
+12
+12 VOLTS
R104 620
P101-12
+26 VOLTS REFERENCE GROUND
IC105
CONTROL
C106 2.2µF
C107 2.2µF
R105 10K 1/4 W
R106 2200 1/4 W
-12
P101-7
P101-8
P101-9
-12 VOLTS
P101-6
+5 VOLTS / ± 12 VOLTS REFERENCE GROUND
R107 47Ω 1W
P103-1
P103-2
TO CRT SOCKET

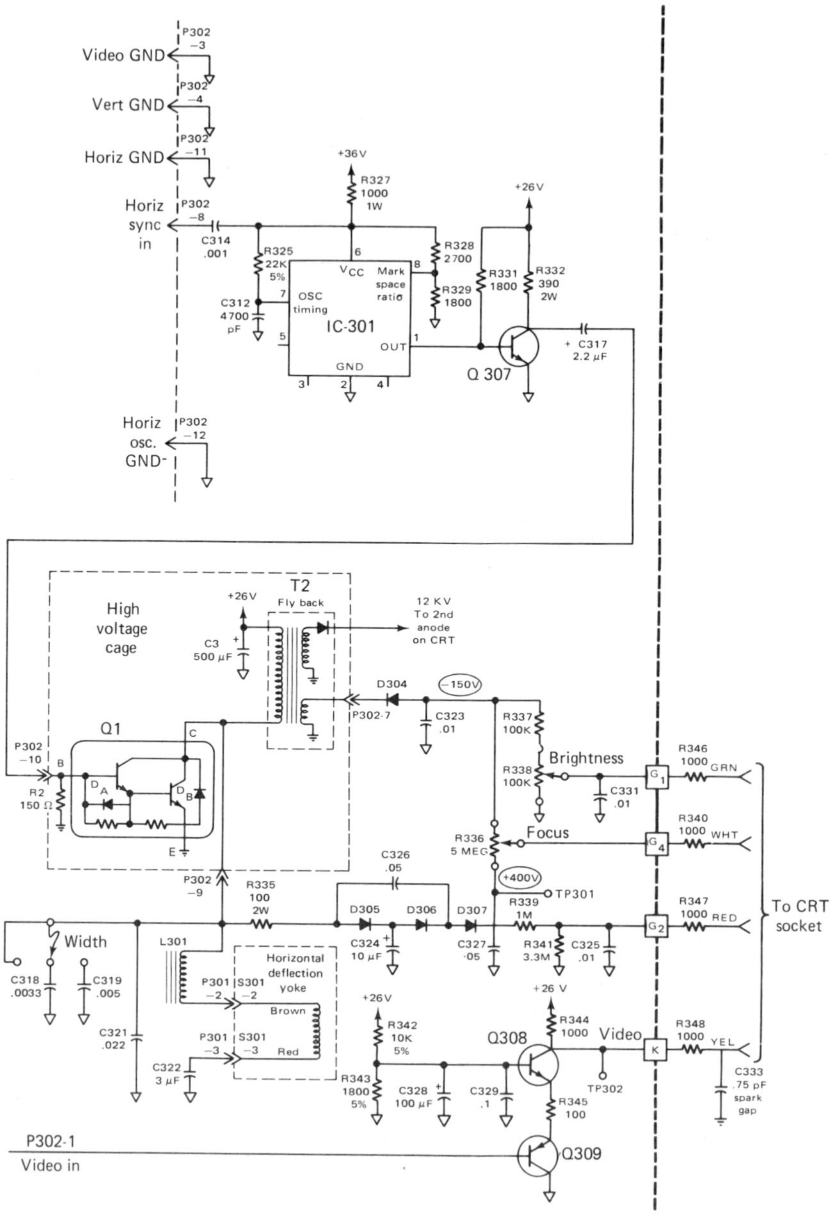

Fig. 4–31. (a) Video circuits (horizontal).

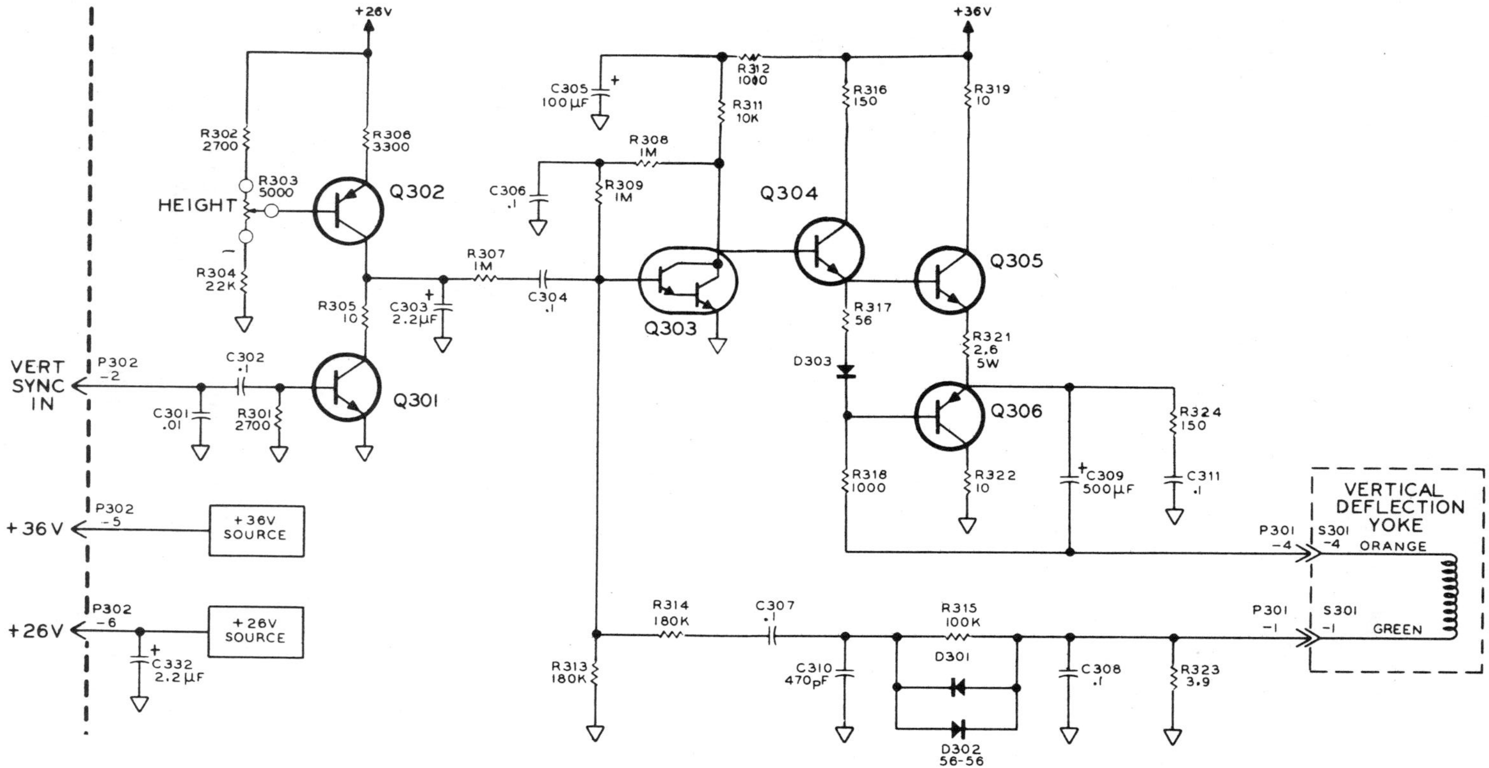

Fig. 4–31. (b) video circuits (vertical)

amount of current produced by Q302, and thus the amount of vertical drive (and the height of the vertical display), is set by HEIGHT control R303. The charging of C303 generates a linear ramp that is coupled through R307 and C304 to Q303.

Transistors Q303 through Q306 form a conventional class B amplifier that amplifies the ramp to drive the vertical deflection yoke of the CRT. Resistor R323 samples the current through the yoke and provides a feedback voltage through divider R313, R314, and R315 to the base of Q303. Diodes D301 and D302 increase the amount of feedback applied at the extremes of the scan. This, in effect, keeps the scan linear from the top to the bottom of the screen. The vertical scan rate is 60.5 Hz.

Horizontal Sweep Circuits. The horizontal sweep system is controlled by triggered oscillator IC301. The free-running frequency of IC301, which is set by R325 and C312, is slightly less than the 15,494-Hz horizontal sweep rate. Horizontal sync pulses (from the character generator, Sec. 4–5.5) are coupled through C314 to the +VCC input (pin 6) of IC301. The sync pulse changes an internal reference voltage that causes the oscillator to reset prematurely and oscillate at the desired horizontal rate.

The output (pin 1) of IC301 drives Q307, which, in turn, drives the horizontal output transistor Q1. The duty cycle (the on-to-off ratio) of Q1 is determined by R328 and R329. The collector of Q1 drives the primary of the horizontal output transformer T2. The high-voltage secondary is rectified internally to provide 12 kV for the anode of the CRT.

When the horizontal oscillator causes Q1 to turn off, the rapid collapse of the flux in transformer T2 generates a 200-V pulse across the primary winding. Capacitor C321 charges immediately to the maximum of this pulse. C321 then discharges quickly through linearity coil L301, the horizontal deflection yoke, and capacitor C322 until the yoke current is maximum. The current through the yoke at this point is considered negative (flowing from C321 down through the linearity coil, the yoke, and C322). This negative current causes the magnetic field of the yoke to quickly pull the electron beam to the extreme left side of the CRT screen (retrace). The yoke field begins to collapse as it tries to keep the current flowing in the same direction.

Diode D_B, which is part of Q1, now conducts and effectively removes C321 (shorts it out) from the circuit. As the yoke continues to collapse, the charge on C322 continues to increase. This action produces a near linear change (decrease) in current, which causes a linear change in the yoke field. As the yoke field decreases, the electron beam moves from the left toward the center of the CRT screen. Before the yoke current reaches zero at the center of the screen, transistor Q1 is turned on by the horizontal oscillator. Transistor Q1 also keeps C321 out of the circuit. Current will cease to flow when the yoke field collapses completely. At this point, the electron beam will be at the center of the CRT screen.

The charge stored in C322 now begins to discharge through the horizontal deflection yoke, linearity coil L301, and Q1 in a positive direction. The current through the yoke is considered positive (flowing from C352 up through the yoke, the linearity coil, and Q1). Diode D_B is now reverse biased and out of the circuit. The change in polarity of the yoke field, as the yoke current increases in a positive direction, moves the electron beam from the center toward the right side of the CRT screen. Capacitor C322 continues to discharge until the beam is at the right side of the screen and Q1 turns off again. This process repeats for each horizontal scan line.

High-Voltage Supply. During retrace, the 200-V pulse across the primary of T2 is coupled through R335 to voltage doubler D305, D306, D307, C324, C326, and C327. This provides a 300-V supply for grid 2 (red) of the CRT. The voltage from the blanking winding of T2 is rectified by diode D304 to produce a −150-V supply for the CRT focus control circuit (grid 4, white, of the CRT, and the FOCUS control R336). Diode D304 also provides −150 V for the CRT brightness circuit (grid 1, green, of the CRT, and the BRIGHTNESS control R338).

Video Amplifier. The video information (VIDEO IN, P302-1) that comes from the character generator is a string of 1s and 0s. These data are coupled to the base of Q309, which drives the emitter of video output transistor Q308. The collector of Q308 drives the cathode of the CRT.

Video Circuit Adjustments. Figure 4–32 shows the physical location of the video circuit adjustment controls. The following steps describe the procedures for setting these controls. Keep in mind that the procedures and locations apply specifically to the H9, but most video terminals have similar controls and procedures.

Brightness is adjusted to suit your own needs. A dim display is easier on your eyes when you look at the screen for long periods of time. Whenever you change the brightness, it is also a good idea to readjust focus. To adjust the brightness,

1. Remove the cabinet shell and set it aside.
2. Fill the screen with characters.

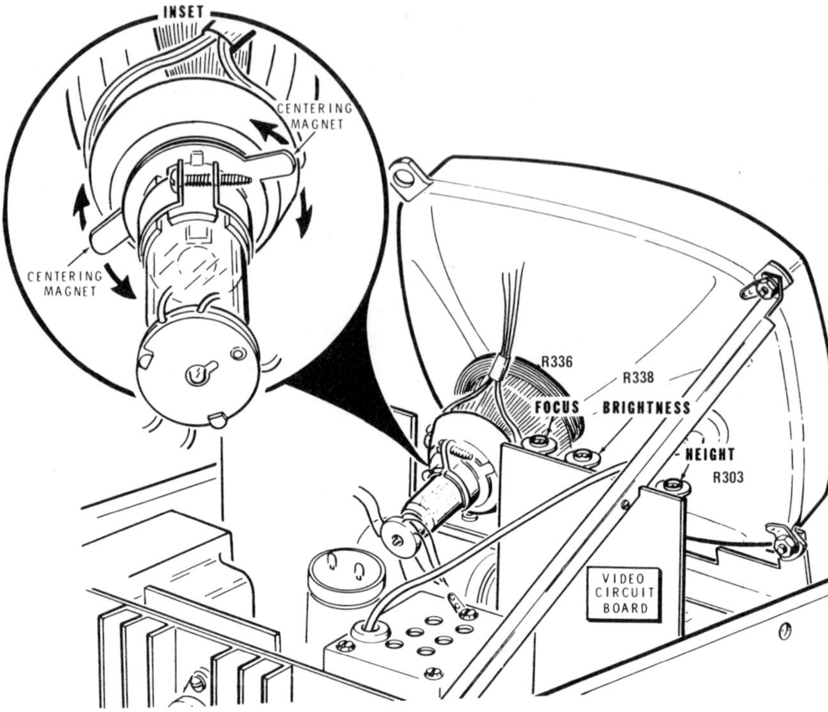

Fig. 4–32. Physical location of the video circuit adjustment controls

3. Adjust the BRIGHTNESS control R338 to obtain a desirable character brightness.

4. Reinstall the cabinet shell.

Focus adjustment, which should be made whenever brightness is readjusted, assures distinct characters on the screen. To adjust the focus,

1. Remove the cabinet shell and set it aside.

2. Fill the screen with characters.

3. Adjust the FOCUS control R336 to obtain the best focus. Look at the characters at the *edges and corners of the screen* as you make this adjustment.

4. Reinstall the cabinet shell.

Center the display on the screen when the screen is full of characters (not with just a few lines).

To adjust the centering,

1. Remove the cabinet shell and set it aside.
2. Fill the screen with characters.

Note: Use an insulated screwdriver and be careful you do not touch the video circuit board or the anode lead of the CRT when you make the following adjustments.

3. Rotate the centering magnets, first one, then the other, to center the display on the screen. Because the centering magnets will affect the vertical and horizontal linearity of the display, use the minimum amount of correction (magnet tabs spread as far apart as possible) that is necessary. Sometimes you will have to compromise between perfect centering and perfect linearity.
4. Reinstall the cabinet shell.

Height of the display is not critical. However, the dots that form the character become more apparent on a large display. A small display provides sharper, more distinct characters. To adjust the height of the display,

1. Remove the cabinet shall and set it aside.
2. Fill the screen with characters.
3. Turn the HEIGHT control R303 through its range while you watch the display. Leave the control at the postion that provides the most appealing display. If you prefer a large display, make sure that all 12 character lines appear on the screen.
4. Reinstall the cabinet shell.

Width is adjusted by a width *jumper wire* on the video circuit board (Fig. 4–31), which selects one of three display widths: normal, wide, and extra wide. The width of the display should normally be about 0.5 to 1 in. from the right and left sides of the screen. In most cases, the normal setting will provide adequate width. The wide and extra wide settings are usually required only in low line voltage areas.

Warning: There is high voltage present on the video circuit board. *Do not* attempt to change the width jumper when the power is turned on.

Troubleshooting the Video Circuits. The following steps apply to the circuits shown in Fig. 4–31. The first step in video circuit troubleshooting is to check the screen after the power is turned on. If the screen is blank (no video), try turning the BRIGHTNESS control R338 up. Then check the CRT voltages. The CRT second anode voltage is approximately 12 kV, and *must be checked with a high-voltage probe and/or meter,* as discussed in Chapter 3. The remaining CRT voltages

(−150 V and +400 V) can be checked with a conventional meter and probe (but be careful).

If there are no voltages for the CRT, check for a horizontal sync pulse at P302-8. If there is no horizontal sync pulse from the character generator, there will be no CRT voltages (except the heater) and no horizontal sweep.

If the horizontal sweep is present, check IC301, Q307, Q1, T2, and L301. Check for shorts in these components and circuits. If the service literature shows waveforms for these circuits, duplicate the waveforms with an oscilloscope. Make certain that the width jumper is not shorted to ground.

If the −150 V is absent or abnormal, check D304 and C323. If the +400 V is absent or abnormal (it can be monitored conveniently at test point TP301), check R335, D305 through D307, and C324 through C327.

If all the CRT voltages are present and correct, and the BRIGHTNESS control is turned up, but there is no video (blank screen), check for a drive signal at the CRT cathode (yellow lead of the CRT socket). Then check for a video signal at P302-1. If the video input is present, but there is no drive to the CRT cathode, check Q308 and Q309. If there is no video input at P302-1, the problem is in the character generator board (Sec. 4-5.5).

If the screen is all white (similar to a TV raster) and you cannot see any characters, check that BRIGHTNESS control R338 is not turned up too far. Then check for a drive signal at the CRT cathode, Q308, C309, as in the case of a "no video (blank screen)" symptom. Also check the CRT grid voltages.

If these is insufficient brightness or contrast at any setting of the BRIGHTNESS control, check Q308, Q309, R342, R343, C328, and C329. Also check the CRT grid voltages.

Keep in mind that all the symptoms discussed thus far (for the video circuits) could be the result of a defective CRT. If you have not thought to do so already, check that the CRT filaments (heater elements) are lit.

If a single, bright horizontal line appears on the screen, the problem is in the vertical circuits. Check for a vertical sync in signal at P302-2. If this sync signal is absent, the problem is on the character generator. If the vertical sync is present and normal, check the vertical amplifiers Q301 through Q306 and the vertical deflection yoke. Also check the setting of the HEIGHT control R303. However, in most cases, there will be some vertical display (more than a horizontal line) even with the HEIGHT control turned all the way down.

If the height of the display cannot be brought within reasonable limits by adjustment of the HEIGHT control, look for problems in the Q301 and Q302 circuits. For example, the value of C303 may have changed or (more likely) C303 may be leaking.

If the width of the display cannot be brought within reasonable limits by selection of the width jumper connections, look for a defective horizontal deflection yoke or a defective L301. Of course, it is possible that T2 is defective and not delivering the required voltage. However, this will show up with other symptoms described thus far. Also check that C321 is not leaking, open, shorted, or has changed value drastically.

If the display is present, but there is no horizontal sync, check for a good horizontal sync pulse at P302-6. If such a pulse is present, but without horizontal sync, IC301 is the most likely cause of trouble. Also check R325 and C312.

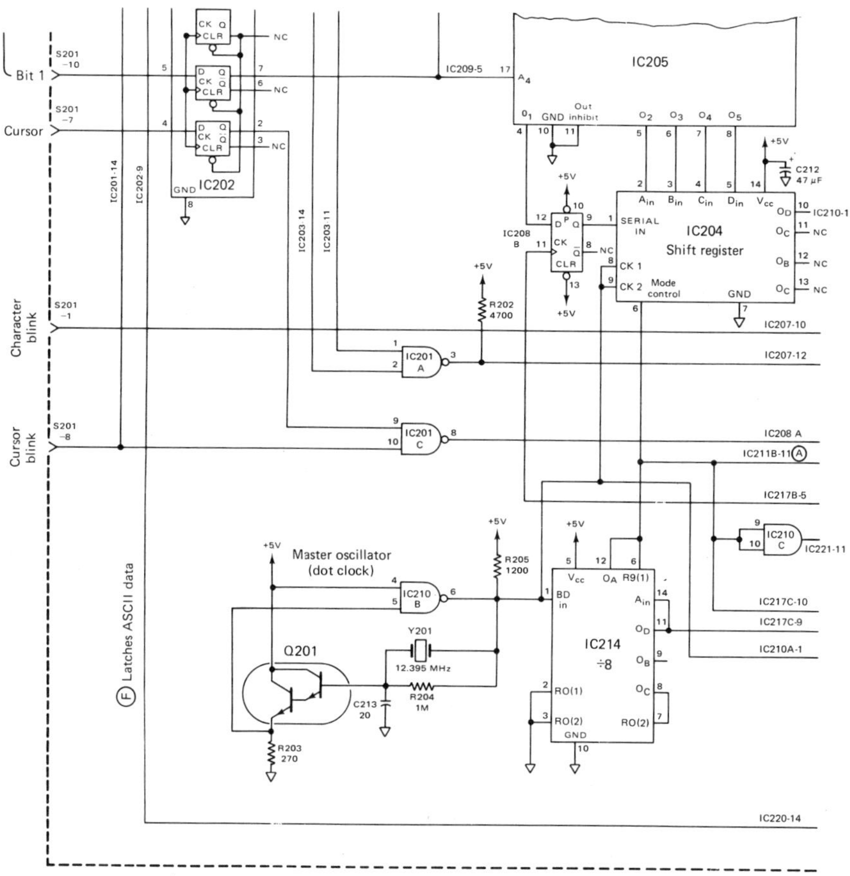

Fig. 4–33. (a) Character generator circuits

If the display is present, but there is no vertical sync, check for a good vertical sync pulse at P302-2. If such a pulse is present, but without vertical sync, Q301 and Q302 (and their associated circuit parts) are the most likely causes of trouble.

4–5.5 Character Generator Circuits

The character generator circuits are shown in Fig. 4–33. As discussed in Sec. 4–5, the CRT screen is divided into 12 lines, each having 80 character locations, for a total of 960 character locations. This is shown in Fig. 4–34. Each location corresponds to a specific memory address in RAM. For instance, the character location at the upper-left corner of the screen might correspond to RAM address 000000000. A location somewhere in the middle of the screen might

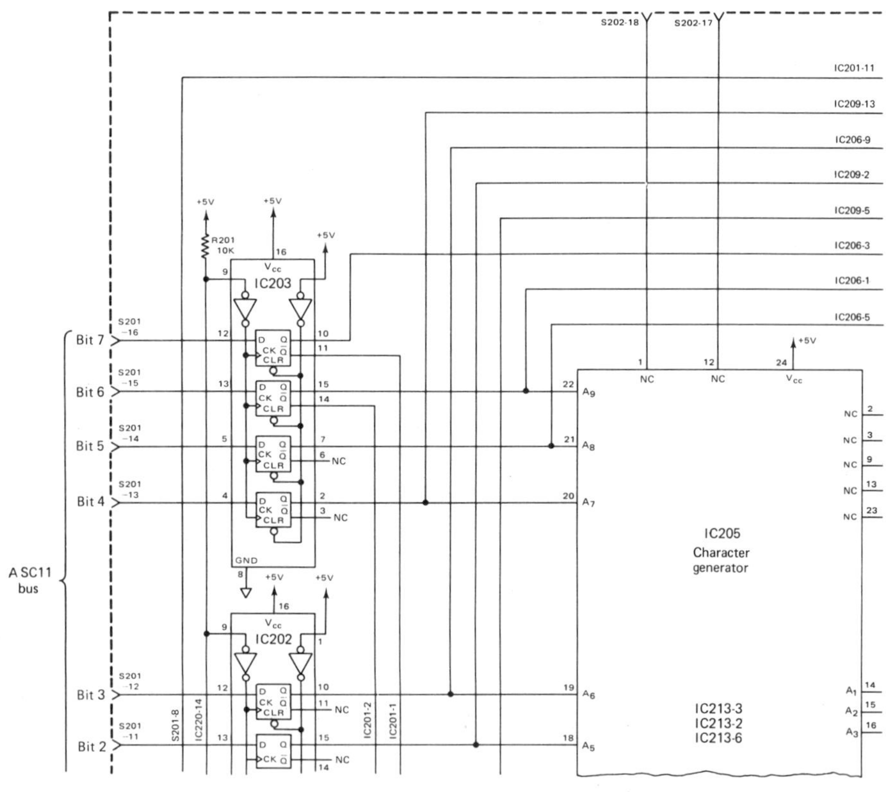

Fig. 4–33. (b) Character generator circuits

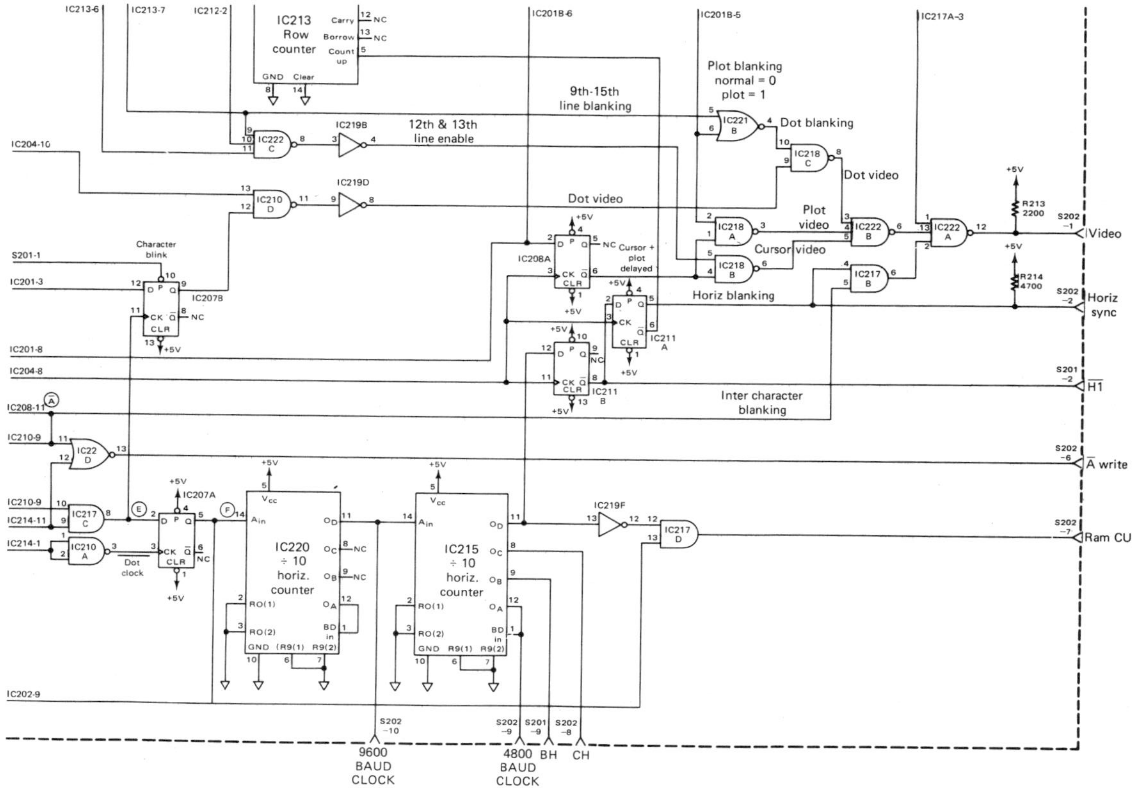

Fig. 4–33. (c) Character generator circuits

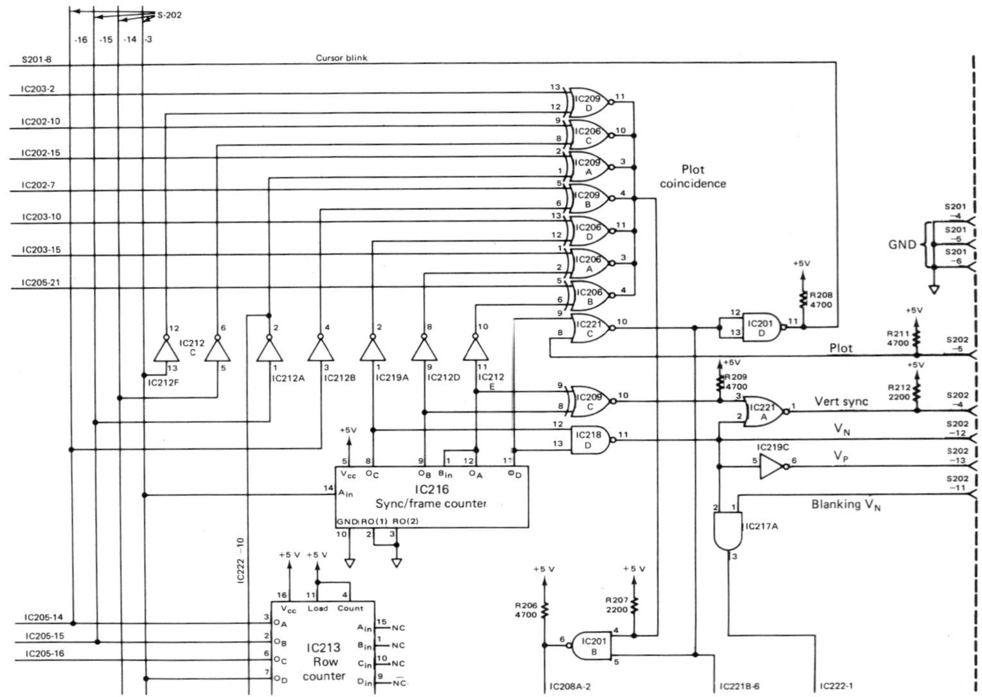

Fig. 4–33. (d) Character generator circuits

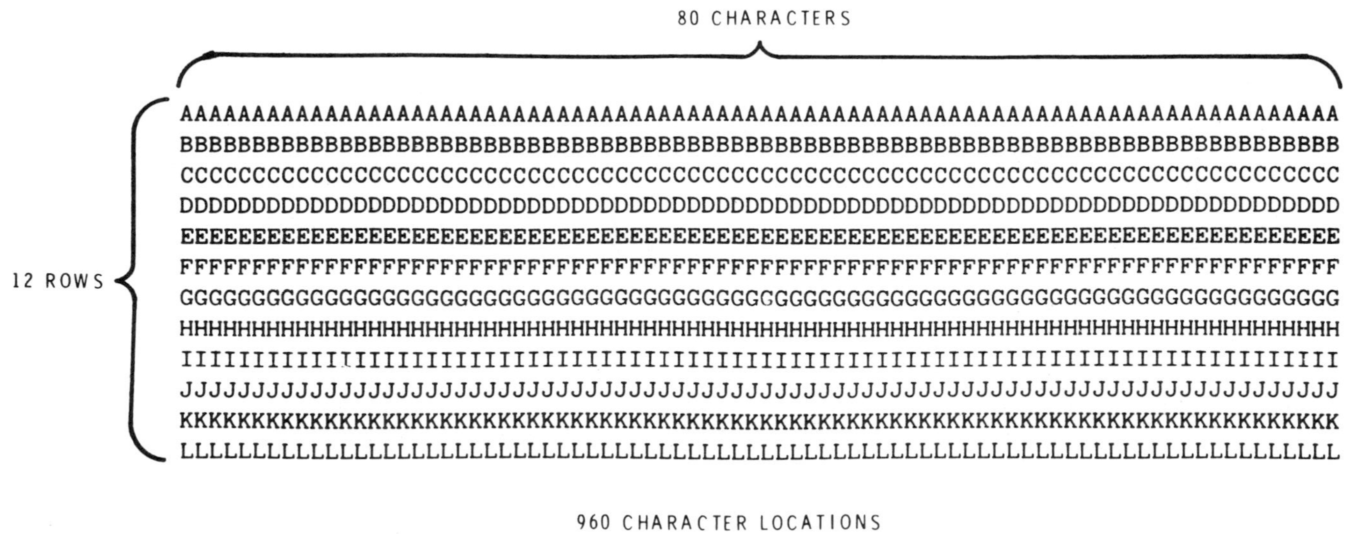

Fig. 4–34. Nine hundred and sixty character locations on the CRT screen

correspond to address 0111101011. Each character location on the screen is in a 128-space matrix arranged in 16 horizontal lines and 8 vertical rows, as shown in Fig. 4–35.

Figure 4–36 shows the block diagram of the character generator circuits. At the end of a vertical retrace, the RAM address counter is initialized to the address for the upper-left corner of the screen. The address counter addresses one of the 960 RAM locations. Each memory location contains the ASCII code for the character to be displayed. The ASCII code is applied through a latch to the character generator. However, only the six least significant bits of the 7-bit ASCII word are used to address the character generator. Sixty-four characters are stored in the character generator ROM, each at its own address, as shown in Fig. 4–37. For instance, the 6-bit ASCII word 001000 addresses the character H.

Since the electron beam in the CRT scans only one line at a time, the dots that make up the characters must be shifted out serially, one row at a time. To do this, the character generator puts out up to five dots in a row for each character. Figure 4–38 shows the row output for

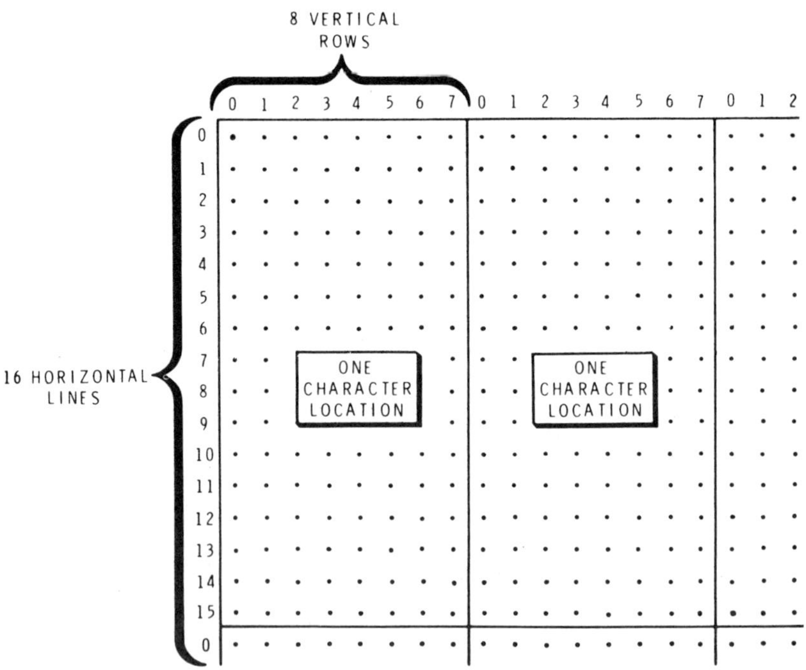

Fig. 4–35. One hundred and twenty-eight space matrix for each character location

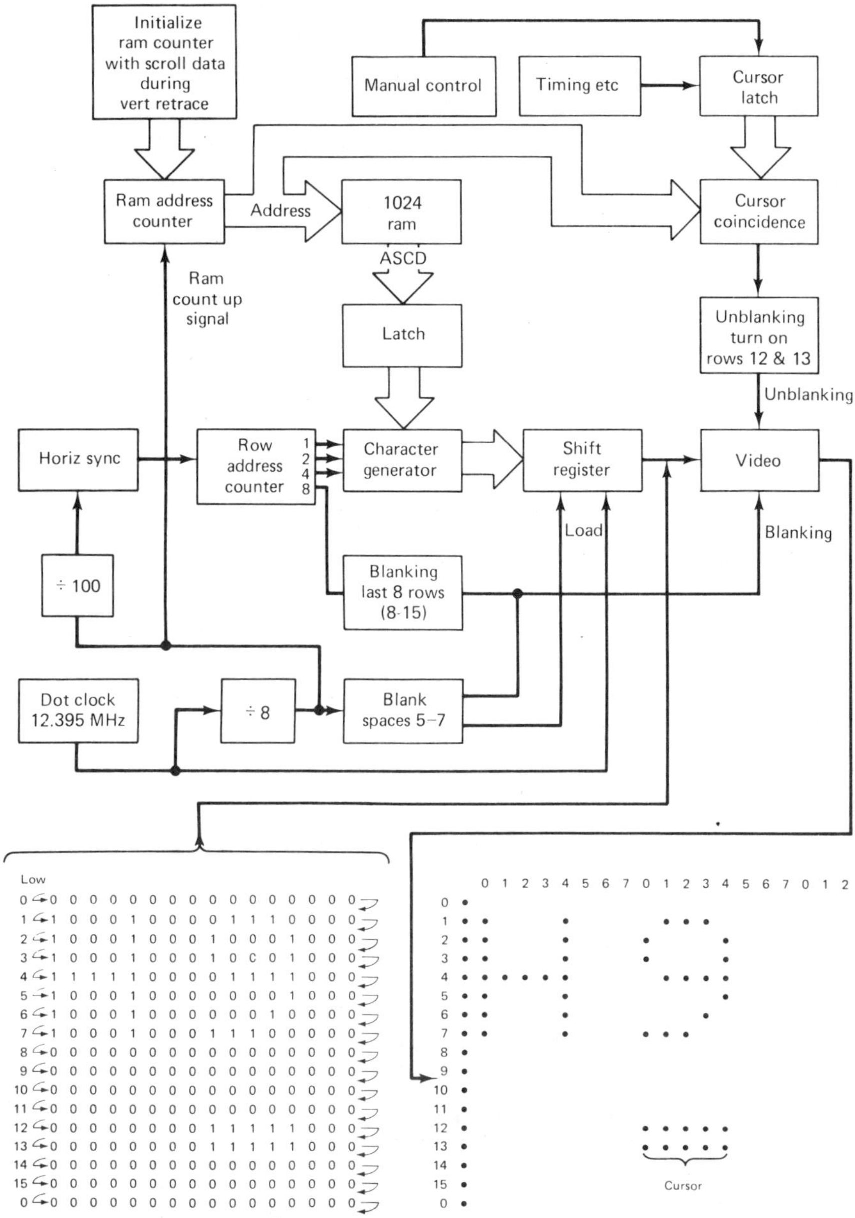

Fig. 4–36. Character generator circuits block diagram

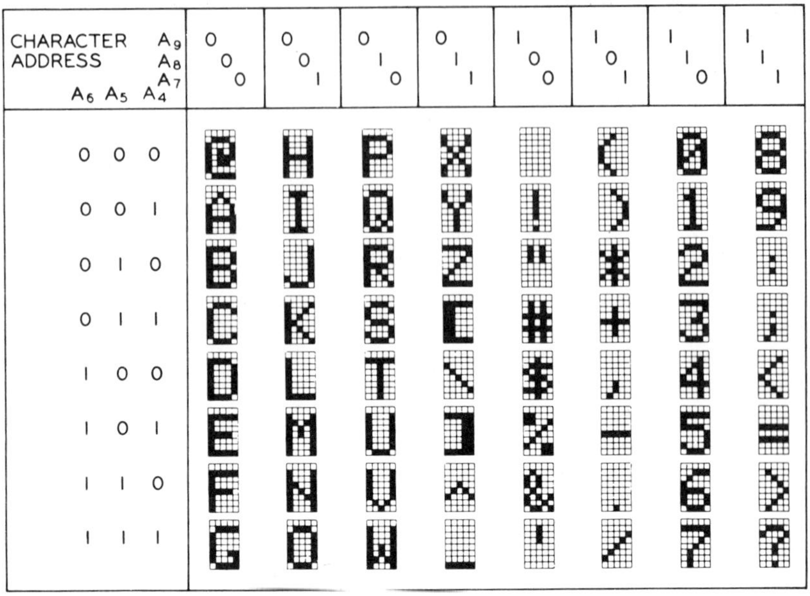

Character H

ASCII BIT	6	5	4	3	2	1
CHARACTER GENERATOR INPUT	A_9	A_8	A_7	A_6	A_5	A_4
6-BIT ASCII WORD	0	0	1	0	0	0

Fig. 4–37. Sixty-four character stored in the character generator ROM

ROW ADDRESS	O_5	O_4	O_3	O_2	O_1	OUTPUTS
000	0	0	0	0	0	ROW 0 IS ALWAYS BLANK
001	1	0	0	0	1	
010	1	0	0	0	1	
011	1	0	0	0	1	
100	1	1	1	1	1	
101	1	0	0	0	1	
110	1	0	0	0	1	
111	1	0	0	0	1	

Fig. 4–38. Row output for the character H

the character H. The 5-bit dot data are always followed by three spaces (the absence of dots) before the dots for the next character are shifted out.

Since the CRT scanning process requires the dot data to be applied to the video circuits in a serial format, the 5-bit dot data are loaded into a shift register and shifted eight times. This shifts out the five bits of the dot data followed by three spaces. The three spaces are formed when a blanking signal is applied to the video circuits during the fifth through seventh shift sequence. The spaces are also necessary because the character location on the screen has been defined as being eight rows wide. The spaces provide space between characters.

During the fifth through the seventh shift sequence, the shift register is loaded with new dot data for the next character. The RAM address counter is also incremented to its next address. This process of addressing succeeding RAM locations and outputting dot data continues until a horizontal sync pulse is generated at the end of a scan line. The horizontal sync pulse increments the row counter, and causes the electron beam to begin a new scan line. The character generator now outputs dot data for the next row in the dot matrix. This process continues until all seven rows of dot data have been outputted. Horizontal scan lines 8 through 15 are normally blanked. The cursor will appear on lines 12 and 13. A new character line (16 scan lines) begins after scan line 15 is completed.

The cursor is displayed on scan lines 12 and 13 when an unblanking signal is applied to the video circuits. This happens when the cursor location, which is stored in the cursor latch, is coincident with the address coming from the RAM address counter.

Master Clock. The master clock of the entire H9 terminal is located on the character generator circuit board. The clock is composed of IC201B, crystal Y201, and transistor Q201, as shown in Fig. 4–33. Clock frequency is 12.395 MHz. The true and complemented outputs are provided for the dot clock and other system timing. IC214, IC210C, IC221D, IC217C, and IC207A generate timing signals A, E, and F from the master clock signal. (These timing signals are shown on very elaborate timing diagrams in the H9 service literature.) An important point to remember in all H9 timing sequences is that the trailing edge (the negative transition) of the clock pulse always preceeds any logic level transition of the other ICs by approximately 30 ns.

Character Generation Cycle. At the start of the character generation cycle, the RAM counter (on the RAM and counter circuit board) is told by the trailing edge of waveform F to count up. After 565 ns, the RAM data are latched into IC202 and IC203, and then transferred to the input of the character generator by the next leading edge of waveform F. Eighty nanoseconds later, the trailing edge of waveform F tells the RAM to count up again. In the meantime, the character generator is starting to access its internal dot information and, after approximately 450 ns, the five bits of dot data appear at the output of the character generator.

Waveform A is used as a load pulse for shift register IC204. The dots are latched into the shift register by the trailing edge of the dot clock before the load pulse goes back to zero. Actually, the shift register is loaded three times (at time 6, time 7, and time 0), but only the load at t0 is used. The next five cycles of the dot clock shift the dots out serially as video information, which, in turn, is applied to the CRT. At the end of the fifth pulse, waveform A is used as a blanking signal to provide intercharacter blanking. Besides latching RAM data for the character generator, waveform F is used to increment the character counter, which is composed of IC215 and IC220. After 80 characters have been accessed and shifted out, the D output of IC215 provides a retrace blanking signal. This signal blanks the video during the retrace time, and it also inhibits further RAM count-ups.

The D output of IC215 does not turn on the blanking directly. Instead, the D output is delayed by two character times in IC211 to allow for the last character accessed to be shifted out. The outputs of the IC211A generate blanking and sync pulses and count up to IC213, the row counter, which tells the character generator to access the next row of dot information. When the retrace blanking period is over, the process is repeated until all eight scan lines of information for the same 80 characters have been shifted out, and a complete row of characters is displayed on the screen. During the next eight scan lines, the entire process is repeated and the same 80 characters are shifted out once again, but the video is blanked to provide spacing between character lines. IC222C decodes the row counter output of IC213 so that the cursor information can only appear in scan rows 12 and 13 of the character row cycle.

At the end of the sixteenth scan line, the D output of IC213 (the row counter) is used to count up the ÷ 12 (divide-by-12) counter in the RAM to access the next row of 80 characters. The D output is also used to increment the sync or frame counter IC216, which keeps track of the number of rows of characters that are displayed on the screen. At the end of the sixteenth scan line of the twelfth character row, the C and D outputs of IC216 generate the vertical blanking signal. IC209 and IC221A, in conjunction with the vertical blanking signal, generate the vertical sync pulse to start vertical retrace.

Cursor information from the RAM and TPU is latched into IC202 along with the ASCII data by waveform F. This cursor signal is delayed by IC208A for the duration of the character generator access time, and it appears as video information at inputs 1 and 4 of IC218 in the video chain.

If the ASCII character latched in IC202 and IC203 is a control character, bits 6 and 7 will be 0, and the $\overline{Q}$ outputs of the latches will both be high, causing the output of IC201A to go to a logic 0. This logic 0 is delayed by IC207B for the duration of the character generator access time, and it is used to blank the dot information for that control character. The preset input of IC207B is driven by a 4-Hz clock pulse that will unblank the control character dots four times a second, causing them to appear to blink on the screen.

Plot Mode. In the plot mode, the first 128 scan lines are used to display information that corresponds to the binary value of a 7-bit ASCII word. In this mode, the first row of characters that would normally be seen on the screen is repeated four times, starting with the 129th scan line (in the ninth, tenth, eleventh, and twelfth character lines). In the space directly above each character, the beam is turned on to display a lighted dash in the scan line that corresponds to the binary value of that character.

The 128 scan lines are arranged so that the 128th line (line 127) is at the top of the screen, and the first line (line 0) is at the bottom of the eighth character line (128 lines from the top). For example, if the character is a rub out, which is all 1s, the dash will appear at the very top of the screen. If the character is a K (binary 1001011), its value will be 75 and it will appear on plot line 75 (see Fig. 4–29).

The four outputs of IC213 and the A, B, and C outputs of IC216 count the scan lines from 0 at the top to 127 at the end of the eighth character row. The seven outputs are inverted by IC212 and IC219A so that the count will be 127 at the top and 0 on the 127th row. The outputs of the inverters are applied to the inputs of exclusive NOR gates (IC206 and IC209A, B, and D). The other inputs to the NOR gates are connected to corresponding bits from the outputs of latches IC202 and IC203. When the seven data bits at the latches are exactly coincident with the outputs of the inverters, a logic 1 will appear at the outputs of IC206 and IC209. If the plot function has been selected by the PLOT button on the keyboard, this coincidence signal will appear at the output of IC208A. After a delay of one character time, the plot coincidence signal will appear at the output of IC208A as a plot video signal that will then be displayed on the screen as a short dash. During the plot time, the cursor information is blanked by the output of IC201D, and the ASCII dot information is blanked by the output of IC221B.

Video Blanking. The video and blanking channels can be broken down into three video channels and two basic blanking channels. The dot information video channel consists of IC210D, IC219D, and IC218C. If there is no dot blanking signal present, the dots that shift out of IC204 will appear directly at pin 8 of IC218C. The dot video will be blanked by the output of IC207B if the dots represent a control character by the 9-to-15 line blanking signal from the D output of IC213, or by the plot blanking signal from pin 10 of IC221C, which blanks the first 128 scan lines.

The cursor video channel consists of IC201C, IC208A, and IC218B. In the absence of cursor blanking signals, the cursor video signal from pin 2 of IC202 will appear (after the proper delay) at pin 6 of IC218B. The cursor can be blanked by a cursor blanking signal from the TPU or by a plot signal, both of which appear at pin 10 of IC201C. The cursor is also normally blanked by the output of IC219B, except during the twelfth and thirteenth scan rows. This blanking signal appears at pin 5 of IC218B.

The plot video channel consists of IC201B, IC208A, and IC218A. The plot video signal that appears at the outputs of IC206 and IC209 will appear after the proper delay at the output of IC218A. This video signal can be blanked by the plot blanking signal that comes from the output of IC221C.

The dot, cursor, and plot video signals are logic 1s in the absence of any video information and drive the inputs of a three-input NAND gate IC222B. Any video information (logic 0s) will appear at the output of IC222B at logic 1s. This is the composite video output.

The vertical blanking information appears as a negative logic signal at pin 3 of IC217A. The blanking signal will be developed for the vertical retrace period and for the duration of a refresh interrupt signal from the TPU circuit board.

Horizontal blanking information appears as a negative logic signal at the output of IC217B. This signal is developed during the horizontal retrace time and during the three dot spaces between characters.

The vertical and horizontal blanking and the video signals drive the inputs of NAND gate IC222A. The output appears as negative logic video information. That is, a logic 0 will turn on the electron beam in the CRT.

The A write pulse, which is used in the screen erase cycle, is generated by IC221D from the A and D outputs of the master clock divider IC214.

Troubleshooting the Character Generator Circuits. Troubleshooting for these circuits is discussed simultaneously with the keyboard circuits (Sec. 4–5.6) since the circuits are closely interrelated.

4–5.6 Keyboard Circuits

Keyboard circuits are shown in Fig. 4–39. The keyboard contains a 52-key ASCII keyboard and encoder, a special ASCII character generator, four cursor control latches, and 12 mode control switches. The keyboard controls are discussed further in Sec. 4–5.2.

The ASCII keyboard is a matrix of single-pole, normally open switches that are scanned by IC402, the keyboard encoder. The X2 through X9 outputs are scanned with a series of pulses. When a key is pressed, one of these pulses appears at one of the eight Y inputs. After an appropriate debounce period, the encoder recognizes the pulse as a valid key depression, decodes the X and Y pulse data into the appropriate 7-bit ASCII word, latches the word in buffer IC403, and puts a logic 1 on the data strobe output to indicate that there is valid data present in the buffer. The negative true logic output of the keyboard encoder IC402 is inverted (to positive true logic) by inverter/buffer IC403 to provide positive true logic for the bus. When the output enable line (OE) is brought to a logic 0, the three-state buffers are turned on and the ASCII data are put on the bus. A logic 0 on the output enable lines also resets the data strobe output of the IC402 to indicate that the data in the buffer have been read.

IC401 is a divide-by-16 counter that generates four repeat rates from the 60.5-Hz vertical frequency. The frequencies set the rate of the repeat (REPT) function. A special character generator composed of IC404, IC405, and IC406 is also connected to the ASCII bus. IC406 decodes inputs A1 and A2 into four states: (1) a three-state OFF, (2) an ASCII carriage return, (3) an ASCII feed line, and (4) an ASCII space. When both inputs are low, the three-state outputs of IC404 and IC405 are turned off. When A1 is high, a carriage return is put on the bus. When A2 is high, a space is put on the bus. When both A1 and A2 are high, a line feed is put on the bus. These characters are used in the transmit page mode and during the erase cycle (Sec. 4–5.2).

IC407 and IC408 are latches that are set by the four cursor control keys. During the vertical scan cycle, Q401 is turned on, enabling the cursor controls. When any of the cursor keys is pressed, the corresponding latch is set so that the data can be remembered until the next TPU cycle. During the TPU cycle (vertical retrace time), Q401 turns off so that the data in the latches cannot change and confuse the TPU circuits.

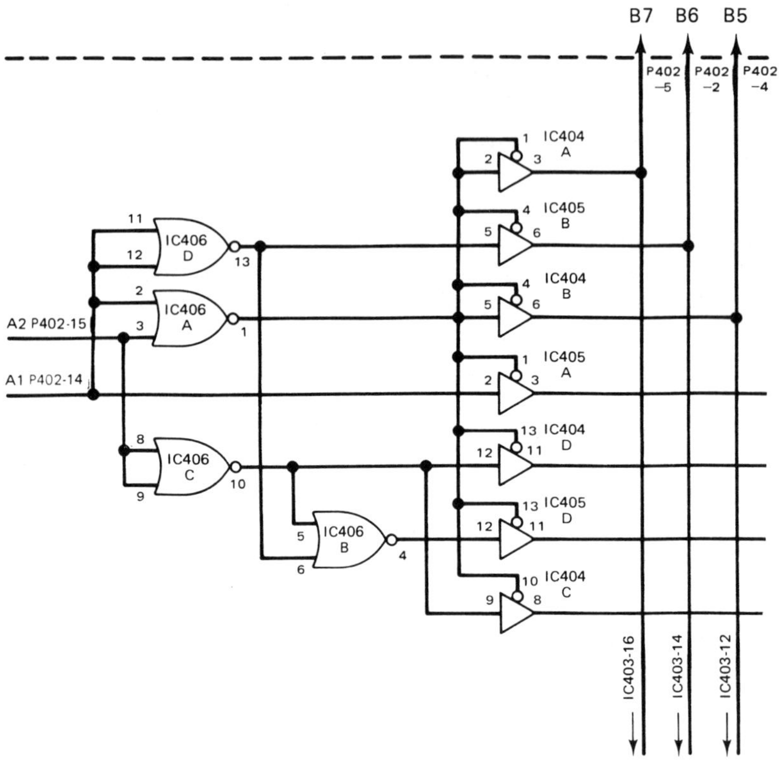

Fig. 4–39. (a) and (b) Keyboard circuits

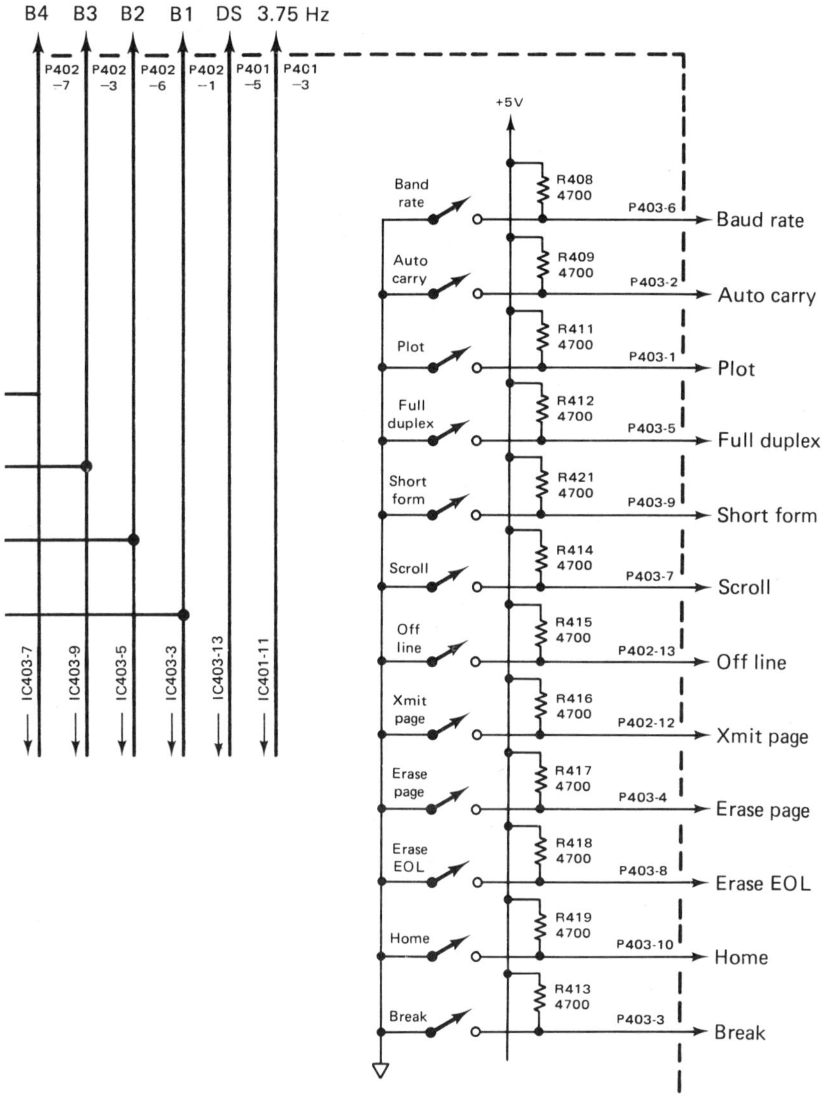
B4 B3 B2 B1 DS 3.75 Hz
P402 -7
P402 -3
P402 -6
P402 -1
P401 -5
P401 -3
IC403-7
IC403-9
IC403-5
IC403-3
IC403-13
IC401-11
+5V
Band rate
Auto carry
Plot
Full duplex
Short form
Scroll
Off line
Xmit page
Erase page
Erase EOL
Home
Break
R408 4700
R409 4700
R411 4700
R412 4700
R421 4700
R414 4700
R415 4700
R416 4700
R417 4700
R418 4700
R419 4700
R413 4700
P403-6
P403-2
P403-1
P403-5
P403-9
P403-7
P402-13
P402-12
P403-4
P403-8
P403-10
P403-3
Baud rate
Auto carry
Plot
Full duplex
Short form
Scroll
Off line
Xmit page
Erase page
Erase EOL
Home
Break

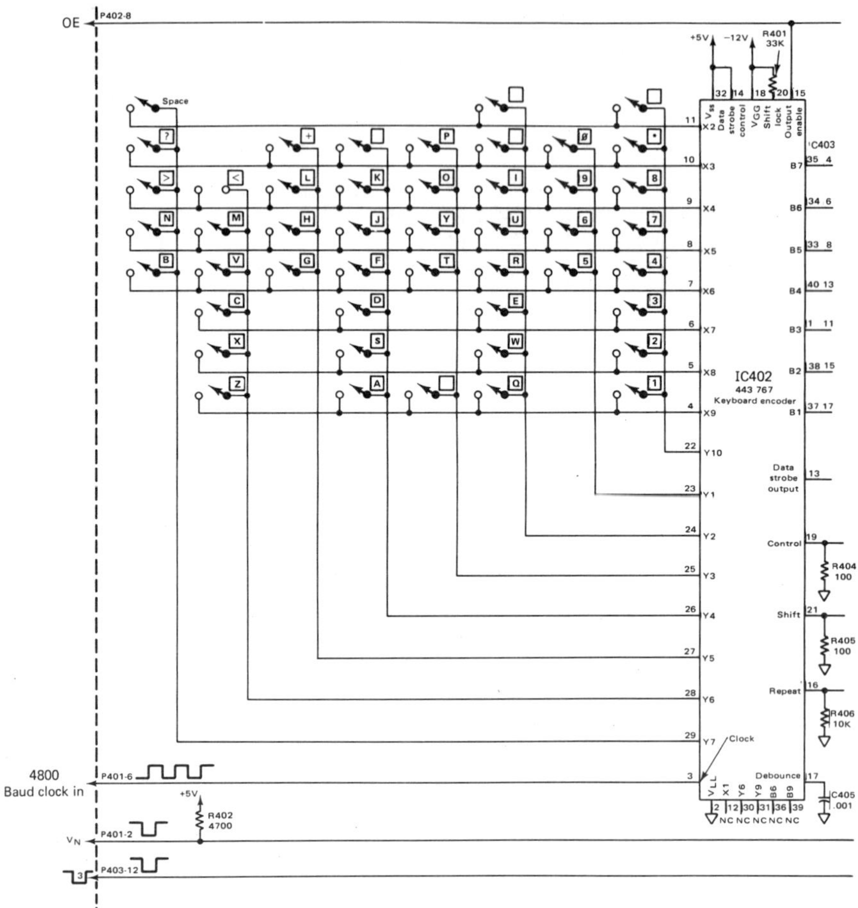
OE
P402-8
+5V
−12V
R401
33K
Space
IC402
443 767
Keyboard encoder
IC403
Data
strobe
output
Control
R404
100
Shift
R405
100
Repeat
R406
10K
Clock
Debounce
C405
.001
4800
Baud clock in
P401-6
R402
4700
V_N
P401-2
P403-12

Fig. 4–39. (b)

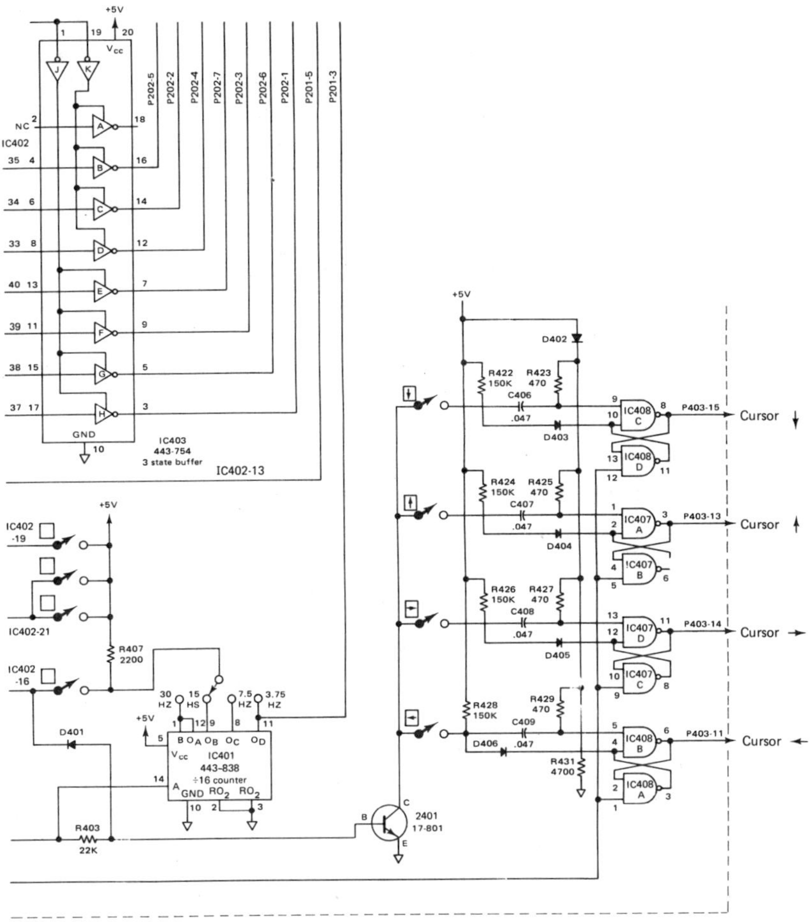
+5V
Vcc
IC402
NC
P202-5
P202-2
P202-4
P202-7
P202-3
P202-6
P202-1
P201-5
P201-3
GND
IC403
443-754
3 state buffer
IC402-13
IC402
-19
IC402-21
IC402
-16
R407
2200
D401
R403
22K
30
HZ
15
HS
7.5
HZ
3.75
HZ
IC401
443-838
÷16 counter
2401
17-801
D402
R422
150K
R423
470
C406
.047
D403
IC408
C
D
P403-15
Cursor ↓
R424
150K
R425
470
C407
.047
D404
IC407
A
B
P403-13
Cursor ↑
R426
150K
R427
470
C408
.047
D405
IC407
D
C
P403-14
Cursor →
R428
150K
R429
470
C409
.047
D406
R431
4700
IC408
B
A
P403-11
Cursor ←

The 12 function keys are single-pole, single-throw, normally open switches with pull-up resistors. These switches generate logic 1s and 0s to convey the proper operator mode to the TPU circuits.

Troubleshooting the Keyboard and Character Generator Circuits. The following steps apply to the circuits shown in Figs. 4–33 and 4–39. The 200-series and 400-series parts are shown in Figs. 4–33 and 4–39, respectively.

If characters do not write on the screen, check that the DUPLEX switch is not in FULL when it should be in HALF. Then check if the special character generator IC404, IC405, and IC406 is latched on (A1 or A2 high).

If the wrong characters write on the screen, check the keyboard encoder IC402 and the keyboard IC403. It is also possible that the baud rate is set wrong, or that the bus wires are shorted to ground or to plus.

If the screen is filled with the same character, the RAM counters are not counting. Check IC219F and IC217D and the associated RAM counters on the RAM and TPU circuit boards.

If the same line is repeated 12 times, the divide-by-12 counter is not counting up. The divide-by-12 circuits are found mostly on the RAM board.

If blocks of characters are repeated left to right, the divide-by-4 counter is not counting. These circuits are found mostly in the RAM board.

If two characters are written, the DUPLEX KEY is set for half-duplex (released) instead of full duplex (pushed in).

If characters write erratically, check the baud rate. The same is true if the terminal misses characters coming from the computer. At 110 baud, the computer may not be programmed for two stop bits.

If the terminal writes the wrong character from the keyboard, check for shorts between the X and Y scan and address lines of the keyboard encoder IC402. Also check IC402 and IC403.

If the terminal cannot write any character from the keyboard, but does write from the computer, check the cabling at P402. If the cabling is good, check that the output enable (OE) pulse from the I/O is available to IC403.

If control characters do not blink in the PLOT mode, check for a 3.75-Hz signal from IC401. Also check the control character video/decoder circuits IC201A, IC207B, IC210D, and IC219D.

If there is no cursor whatsoever, check the character generator cursor chain IC202, IC201C, IC208A, and IC218B. Also check the cursor coincidence gate on the RAM board and the TPU cursor gates.

If none of the cursor controls moves the cursor, check the cursor movement latches on the keyboard (IC407, IC408, and Q401). Also check the cursor circuits on the TPU.

If the cursor moves continuously, the cursor movement latches IC407 and IC408 are not being reset. Check that the TPU pulse at P403-12 resets all four latches simultaneously.

If there are multiple cursor movements, again check the movement latches.

If the cursor does not blink for the hold screen mode, check IC401 for a 3.75-MHz signal. Also check the cursor chain on the character generator circuit board IC202, IC201C, IC298A, and IC218B.

If there are additional cursor problems, such as wrong cursor movements from cursor controls, wrong cursor from ASCII data, cursor will not home, cursor moves on control characters, or rub outs when the terminal is not in the PLOT mode, or there is no cursor movement on line feed, carriage return, or back space, check the RAM and TPU boards (where most of the cursor circuits are located).

4–5.7 RAM and Counter Circuits

The RAM and counter circuit board contains a 1K by 8 static RAM, an address decoder, and a RAM address counter. Twelve character lines can be displayed on the screen. Each line is composed of four blocks of 20 characters. We shall not discuss these circuits here owing to space limitations and because the circuits are unique to the H9 terminal.

4–5.8 Timing and Processing Unit (TPU) Circuits

The timing and processing unit is the central controller for all terminal functions. The TPU manages the reading, writing, and all data transfers, scrolling, and erasing. The TPU also generates an end-of-line bell signal, generates a power up reset routine, handles cursor movements, and implements the transmit page function. We shall not discuss these circuits here owing to space limitations and because the circuits are unique to the H9 terminal.

4–5.9 Input/Output (I/O) Circuits

The I/O circuit board handles all data transfers between the H9 and all external devices, such as a reader/punch or a digital computer.

The I/O circuits are shown in block diagram form on Fig. 4–40. These circuits contain separate 8-bit parallel input and output ports and a 4-bit parallel handshake. The circuits also include a serial input, serial output, and a UART that interfaces the 8-bit parallel system bus with the serial I/O ports. A special character detector, a baud rate generator, a data priority latch, and a reader start/stop control are also located on the I/O circuit board.

The parallel input connects to the master ASCII bus through IC620, an octal tristate buffer that is normally turned off. An external device can signal to the H9 that there are parallel data available at the parallel input by setting the $\overline{DAV_i}$ input to zero. This causes a logic 1

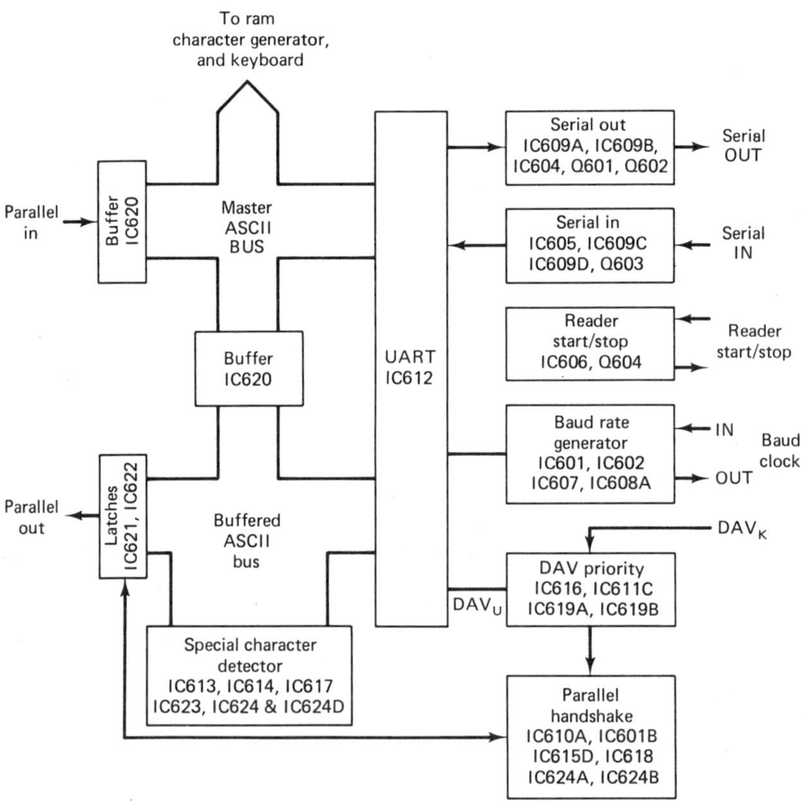

Fig. 4–40. I/O circuits block diagram

to appear at the data input of IC616, the data priority latch. At the start of the TPU cycle, the logic 1 is clocked through the latch and into a priority encoder, IC611C, IC619A, and IC619B. The priority encoder permits only one data-available signal (DAV) to be transmitted to the TPU at a given time. The UART data-available signal (DAV_u) has the highest priority, the parallel data available (DAV_p) is next, and the keyboard data-available signal (DAV_K) has the lowest priority. The TPU reacts to the parallel DAV signal by turning on the outputs of the tristate buffers IC620. This puts the parallel input data on the master bus, which allows it to be written into the RAM at the cursor location.

When the H9 is finished writing the parallel input data into the RAM, it tells the external device that it is finished by transmitting a negative-going pulse on the ($RDAV_i$) output. If the H9 has data to transmit to an external device, the H9 will first load that data from the bus into parallel output latches IC621 and IC622. The H9 then transmits a (DAV_0) signal to the external device by setting flip-flop IC618B. When the external device has finished reading the data, a negative-going pulse is transmitted to the ($RDAV_0$) input.

Serial Input/Output. The serial input and output can be jumper-wired for standard TTL, EIA (Electronic Industries Association), or TTY (also known as *20-mA current loop*) input and output signals. (These are the three most commonly used serial I/O configurations found on terminals and peripherals of all types.) The two logic states of a serial input or output are called a *mark* and a *space*. (Refer to Chapter 2 for a discussion of serial data transmission.) A mark is defined as a TTL logic 1, an EIA minus voltage, or 20 mA flowing in the current loop between the peripheral and the I/O board. A space is defined as a TTL zero, an EIA positive voltage, or zero current flowing in the 20-mA current loop. The idle state of both the input and output is defined as a mark.

EIA input/output circuit connections are shown in Figure 4–41. In the idle state, the EIA input is a negative voltage that keeps transistor Q603 biased off. Since the collector voltage of Q603 is 5 V, a logic 1 is placed at the input (pin 20) of the UART. When the EIA input voltage goes high, Q603 turns on and its collector voltage goes low. This places a space (logic 0) at the input of the UART. The serial output from the UART (pin 25) drives IC609A, which, in turn, drives IC609B. The output of Q609B drives optoisolator IC604. When the output is a mark, the photo transistor in IC604 turns off, and Q602 (a constant-current source) turns Q601 on. The current flows from the +12-V supply through R631 and Q601 to the −12-V supply. This makes the EIA output approximately −10 to −12 V. As the output of IC609B goes

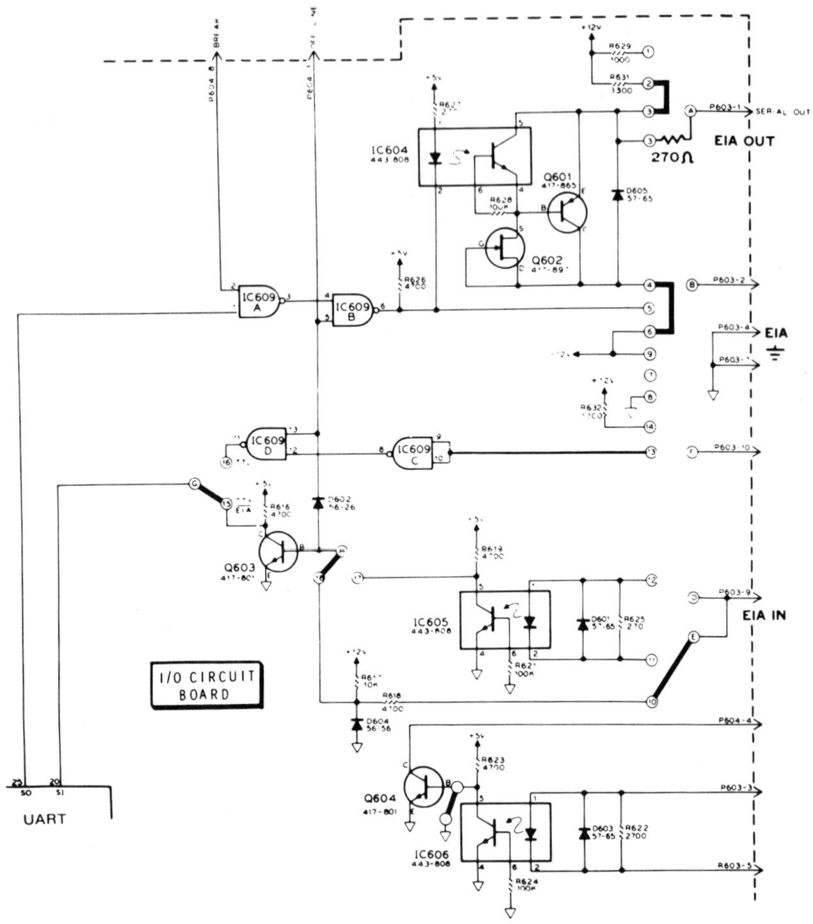

Fig. 4–41. EIA input/output circuit connections

low, the LED in the optocoupler turns on the photo transistor, which turns Q601 off. This causes the EIA output to go to approximately +12 V.

Figure 4–42 shows the *20-mA current loop input/output connections*. When a mark is applied, a loop current passes through diode D601 and optoisolator IC605, which turns Q603 off. A logic 1 then appears at the serial input to the UART. The reader start/stop circuitry, composed of optoisolator IC606 and transistor Q604, works in exactly the same manner. As long as there is mark current flowing in the loop, the collector of Q604 is high. This tells the TPU that the external device wishes to see another character.

Figure 4–43 shows the *TTL input/output connections*. A TTL input signal is coupled to pins 9 and 10 of IC609C. The output of IC609C drives IC609D, which, in turn drives the serial input of the UART. The TTL output signal comes directly from the output of IC609B.

Break Circuit. The input labeled *break* at pin 2 of IC609A generates a continuous space at the serial output as long as the break key on the keyboard is pressed. The *off line* input at pin 5 of IC609B causes a continuous mark to be generated at both the serial output and the serial input. This effectively inhibits the H9 from either transmitting or receiving.

Baud Rate (Fig. 4–40). IC602 successively divides the 4800-baud-rate clock by 2 to produce the 2400-, 1200-, 600-, and 300-baud-rate clocks. IC601, in conjunction with IC607A and IC608A, divides the 1200-baud-rate clock by 11 to generate the 110-baud-rate clock. One of the baud rate clocks (600 to 9600) can be jumper connected to the "preset baud out" from the I/O circuit board. This output and the 300-baud-rate output are connected to the baud rate switch SW2 on the back panel of the terminal. Switch SW2 selects either 300 baud or the preset baud rate. IC607B, IC607C, and IC607D, in conjunction with the keyboard baud rate key, drive the clock pulse inputs of the UART with either 110 baud or the baud rate selected by the baud rate switch.

Special Character Detector (Fig. 4–40). A special character detector, formed by IC613, IC614, IC617, IC623, and IC624, monitors the ASCII bus to detect the presence of certain special characters. IC613 and IC617A detect a rub out and a control character, respectively. The remaining ICs detect a back space, line feed, bell, space, and carriage return. These outputs are used by the TPU for cursor movements and special writing operations.

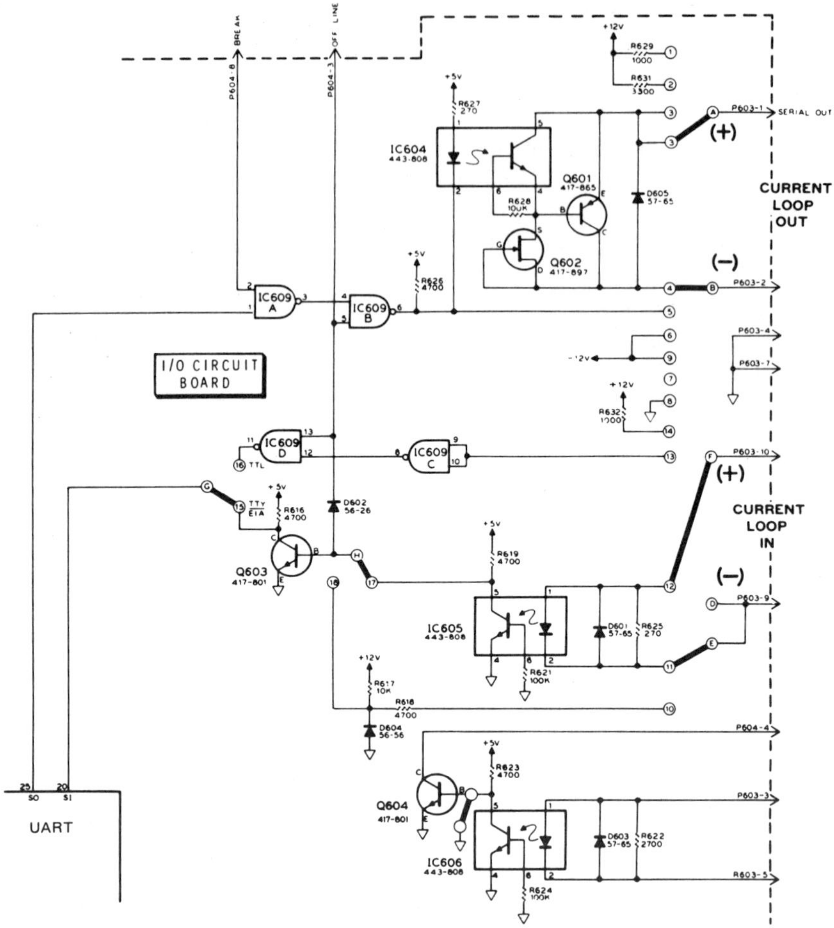

Fig. 4–42. Twenty-milliampere current loop input/output circuit connections

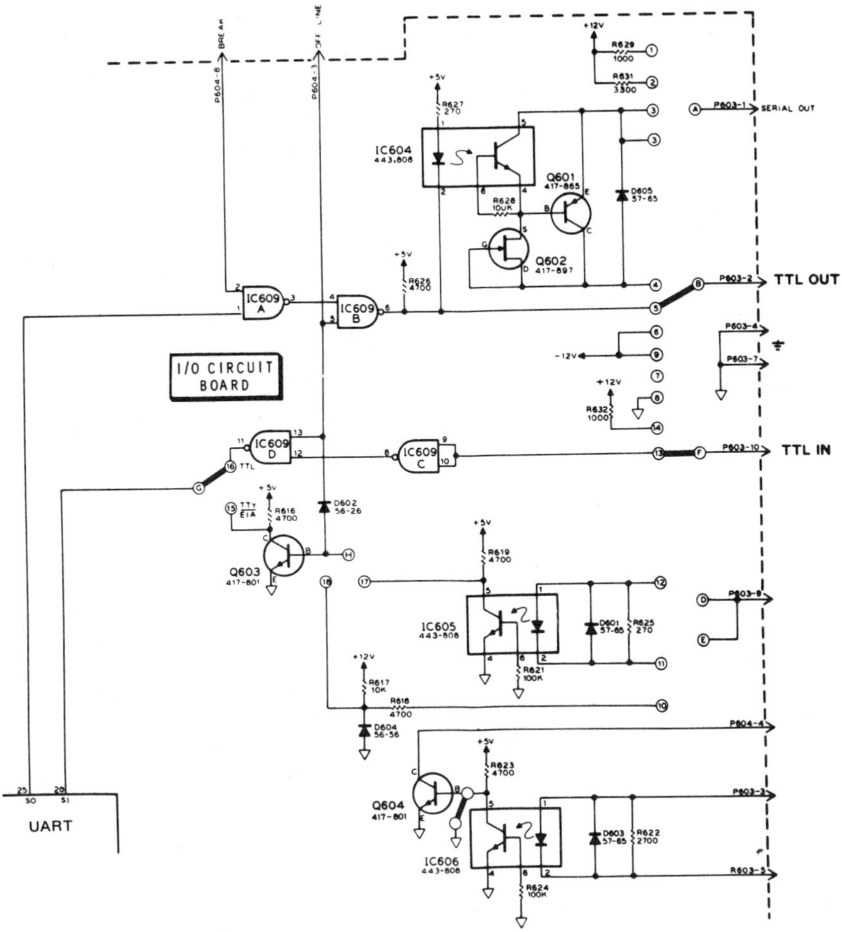

Fig. 4–43. TTL input/output circuit connections

Troubleshooting the I/O Circuits. The following steps apply to the circuits shown in Figs. 4–40 through 4–43.

If there is no serial EIA input or TTY input, check D603, D602, and Q603. If there is no TTL input, check IC609C and IC609D.

If there is no EIA output or TTY output, check that the OFF LINE or BREAK keys are not pushed in. Then check IC609A, IC609B, IC604, Q601, Q602, and D605.

If there is no TTL output, check IC609A and IC609B.

If the terminal stays off line or will not go off line, check the OFF LINE switch. Then check Q603, IC609B, IC609D, and D602.

4–6. HEATHKIT MODEL H10 PAPER-TAPE READER/ PUNCH

This section describes the Heathkit H10 Paper-Tape Reader/Punch shown in Fig. 4–44 (along with an H8 computer system and an H9 terminal). Figures 4–45 and 4–46 show some of the mechanical details for the H10. The reader/punch reads and punches standard eight-level, 1-in. (10-in. maximum diameter roll or fan-fold), oiled or unoiled paper tape. The reader and punch may be operated simultaneously, and yet controlled independently. The H10 has a standard TTL parallel interface, has a pushbutton feed switch to generate leader tape, uses a photo-electric tape reader (Chapter 2), and has a stepper motor for the tape reader transport. Reading speed is 50 characters per second maximum. Punching speed is 10 characters per second.

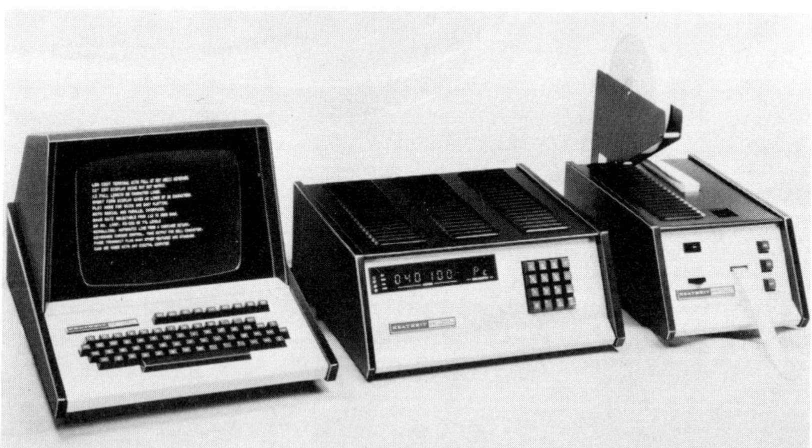

Fig. 4–44. Heathkit H10 paper-tape reader/punch (shown with H8 computer and H9 video terminal)

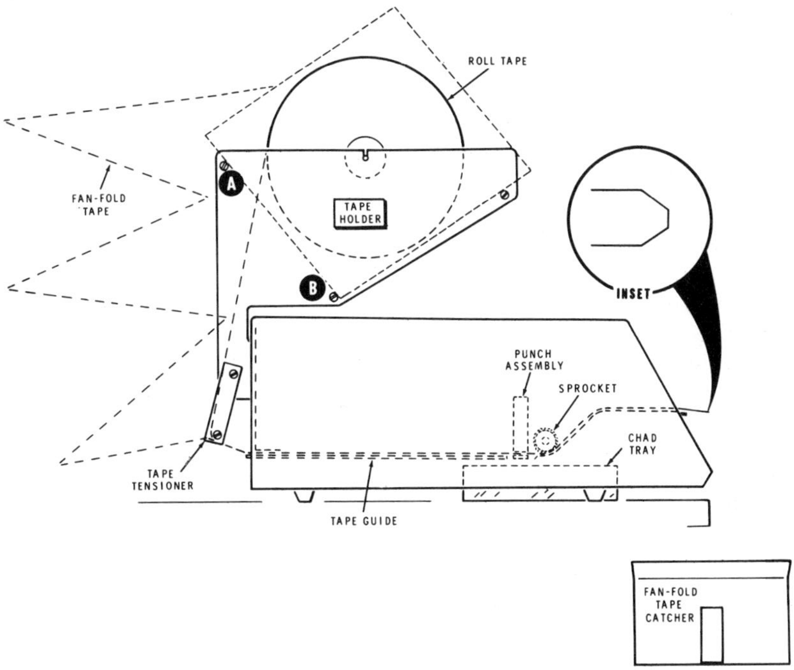

Fig. 4–45. Mechanical details of tape punch

WARNING: Some types of paper tape contain toxic chemicals. Therefore, be careful not to use the tape such that it can contact a person's mouth or be inhaled. Be especially careful of the chad, or holes punched from the tape, since these tiny bits can be picked up on the fingers. This warning applies to all types of paper-tape reader/punches.

4–6.1 Tape Reader Circuits

There are eight tape reader circuits, one for each of the eight channels on the paper tape. All eight reader circuits operate in the same manner. Therefore, only one circuit, shown in Fig. 4–47, is discussed.

As a hole in the paper tape is positioned between the lamp (Fig. 4–46) and photo-Darlington transistor Q101 (Fig. 4–47), the light causes Q101 to turn on for the time that the tape hole is between the lamp and Q101. This causes the output of comparator IC2B to go high. In turn, this causes buffer IC4F to go high. The signal is then applied to the data output connectors and switch SW4.

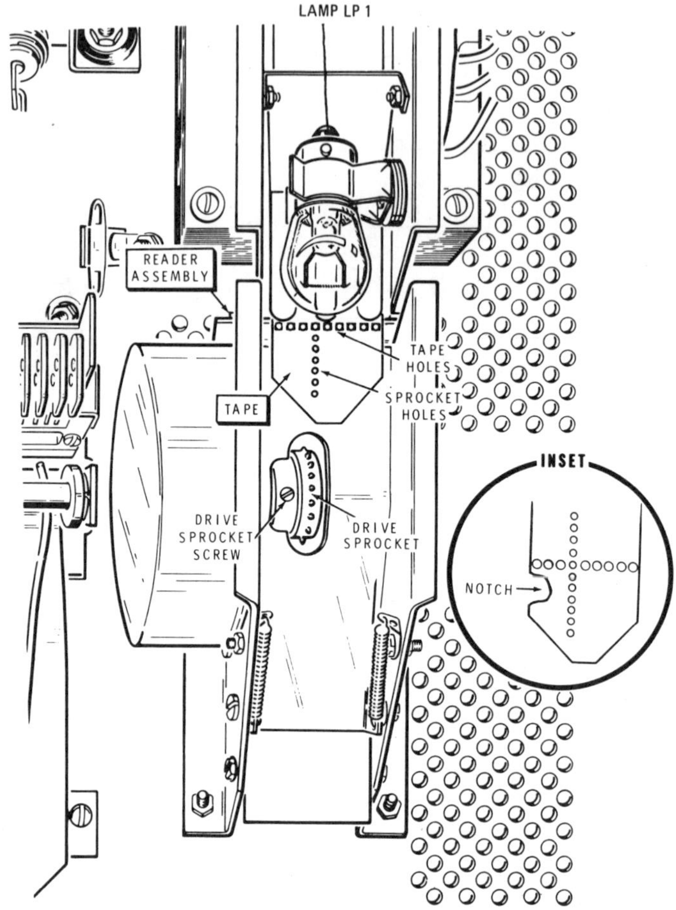

Fig. 4–46. Mechanical details of tape reader

Resistor R42 and control R1 set the sensitivity of photo-Darlington transistor Q101. Resistors R43 and R44 set the reference trigger level of comparator IC2B. R47 is an output pull-up resistor. Resistors R45 through R47 provide positive feedback for IC2B to eliminate false triggering.

4–6.2 Tape Motor Timing

Timing for the stepper motor drive circuitry is generated by one-shot multivibrator IC14, shown in Fig. 4–48. When READ switch SW7 is pushed ON, pin 12 of IC13D goes low. This causes pin 11 to go high

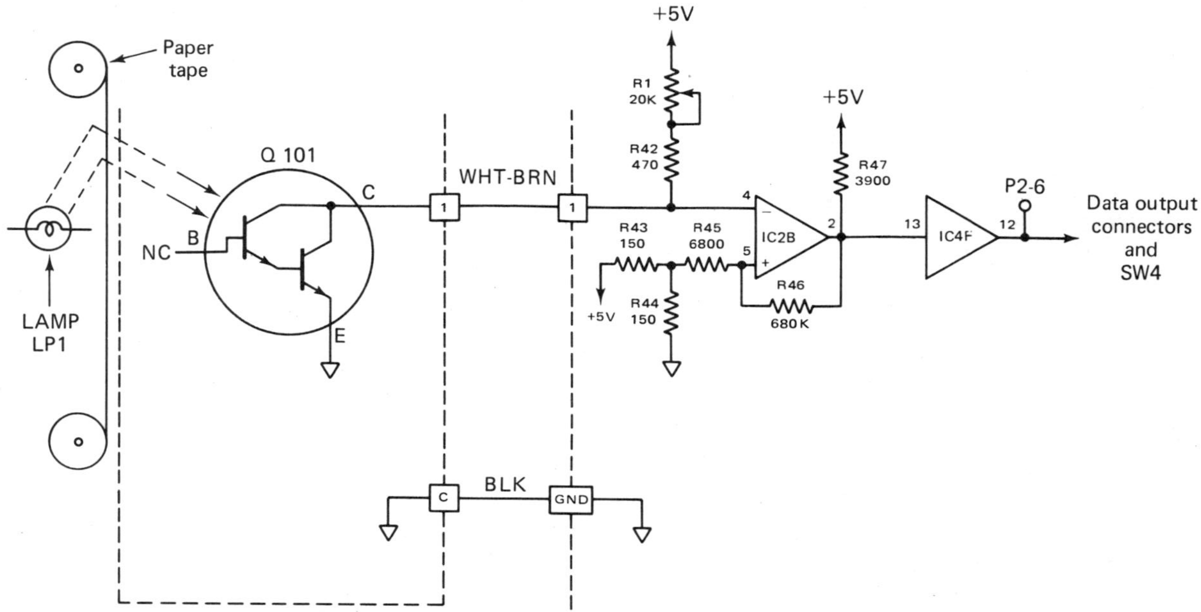

Fig. 4–47. Tape reader circuit (typical)

and trigger IC14, if the (reader start) line is low, Pin 6 is then driven low, and this low is applied to IC15, pin 12 of the motor drive circuitry (Sec. 4–6.3) and pin 9 of (reader ready) gate IC13C.

At this time, IC13C pin 8 goes high, and drives IC7D, which indicates that the reader is busy. After IC14 times out, Q (pin 6) goes high again and waits for another 1-to-0 transition from the reader start line (IC14, pin 1). When READ switch SW7 is ON, a 1-to-0 on IC14 pin 1 will advance the tape one character.

4–6.3 Motor Drive

IC15 divides (Fig. 4–48) the timing signal at pin 12 (either from the reader timing circuits, Sec. 4–6.2, or punch timing, Sec. 4–6.6) by 2 and produces two output signals (at pins 8 and 6) that are 180° out-of-

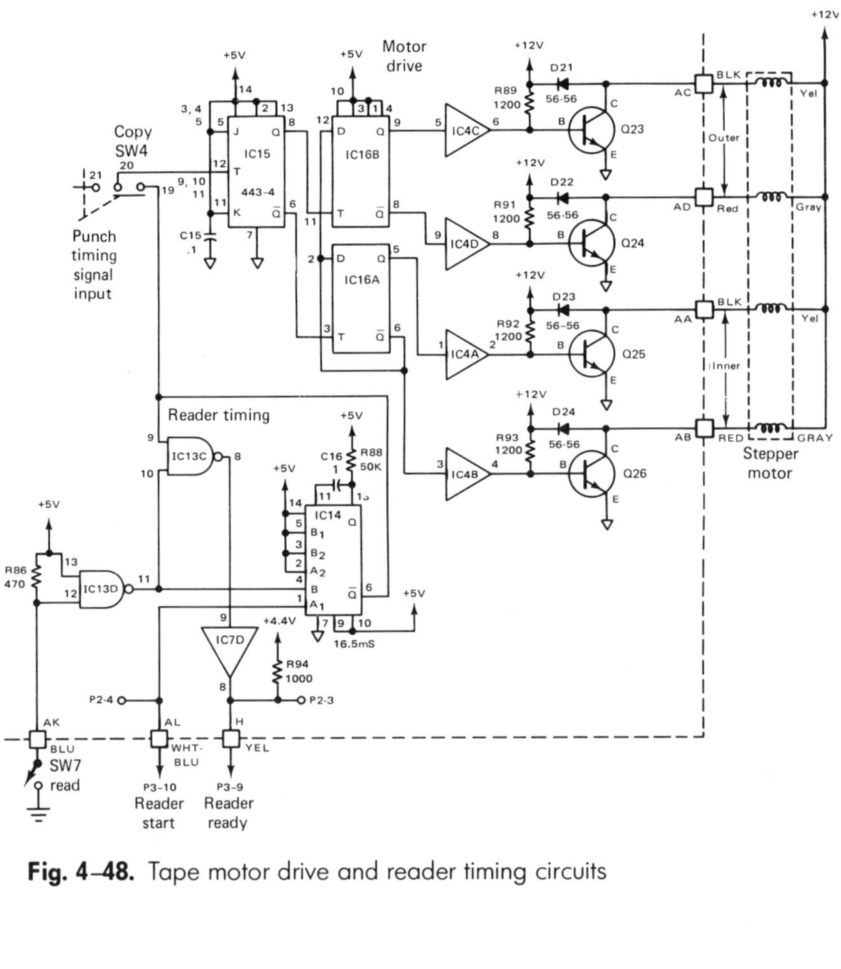

Fig. 4–48. Tape motor drive and reader timing circuits

phase with each other. The remaining circuitry produces a four-phase signal to drive the stepper motor.

When power is applied, assume that IC15 $\overline{Q}$, IC16B Q, and IC16A $\overline{Q}$ are high. Then, because the D inputs of IC16 Q are tied to IC16A, IC16A $\overline{Q}$ is driven high and the timing sequence shown in Fig. 4–49 begins.

With the first pulse to IC15T (pin 12), IC15 Q goes high and $\overline{Q}$ goes low. Because of the high on the D inputs of IC16, IC16B goes high, and $\overline{Q}$ goes low. IC16A remains unaffected by the transition. The next time, IC15 changes state, IC16B remains unaffected, and IC16A changes. As the input pulses continue, a four-phase signal is produced that is applied through buffers A, B, C, and D of IC4 to drive stepper motor transistors Q23 through Q26. Diodes D21 through D24 suppress the inductive kickback from the motor windings.

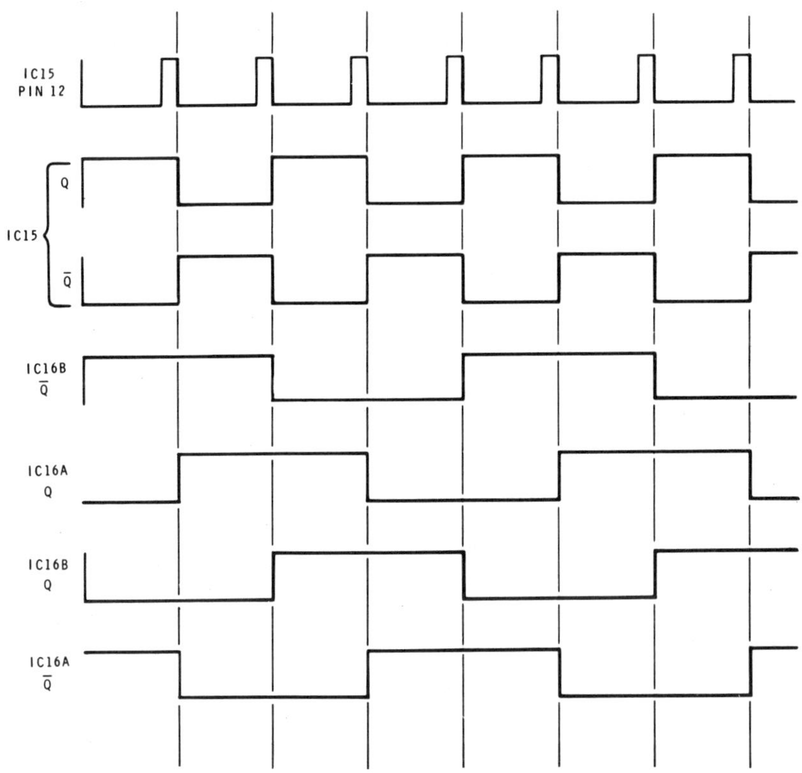

Fig. 4–49. Tape motor timing diagram

4–6.4 Tape Punch

Because the tape punch circuits are so similar, only channel 1 (shown in Fig. 4–50) is described. Tape punch signals (from either the tape reader circuits, Sec. 4–6.2, or the data input connector) are coupled through switch SW4 to AND gate IC6A. When the signal at pin 2 is high, and the timing signal (explained in Sec. 4–6.6) at pin 1 is high, pin 3 goes high and turns on Darlington transistor pair Q17 and Q18. This allows current to flow through solenoid L1, and a hole is punched in the paper tape. Diodes D10 and D19 suppress the inductive kick of L1. Diode D10 also causes L1 to release energy quicker than normal by waiting until the inductive kickback reaches approximately 20 V above the supply before zener action occurs and suppression begins.

4–6.5 Power Supplies

The power supply circuits are shown in Fig. 4–51.

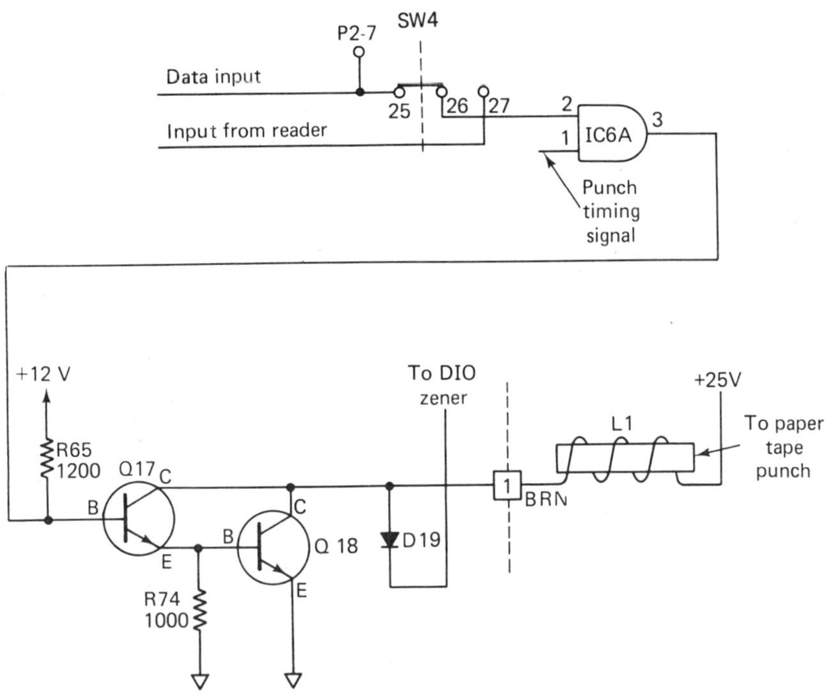

Fig. 4–50. Tape punch circuit (typical)

+25-, +12-, and +9V supplies: ac voltage from the secondary winding of transformer T1 is rectified by diodes D2 and D7, and filtered by capacitor C3 to produce +25 V. The +12- and +9-V supplies operate in a similar manner.

+5- and +.4-V supplies: IC17 is a voltage regulator that changes +9 V to +5 V. Capacitors C7 and C8 provide noise suppression. Diode D25 keeps externally connected equipment from supplying power to the +5-V supply and turning on some of the output buffers when the reader/punch is off.

Lamp supply: the constant zener voltage of diode D1 is applied to the base of transist Q1 and holds the Q1 emitter constant (as the emitter follows the base voltage). This, in turn, holds the base and emitter of transistor Q2 constant, and the lamp receives a constant voltage independent of variations in the +9-V supply.

4–6.6 Punch Timing

As shown in Fig. 4–52, three one-shot multivibrators control the punch timing. IC9 controls the duration of the punching operation, IC12 provides the time for the punches to return to their normal positions, and IC11 times the paper-advance solenoid. The multivibrators are interconnected so they will perform their timing functions in the proper sequence.

Gate IC10B is for circuit protection. Without IC10B, when the unit is turned on, the Q output of IC8A could be high, and possibly turn on all the solenoids continuously. This could blow the fuse or damage the solenoids.

When the FEED switch SW6 is pushed, the pulse is debounced by Q27 and Q28, and the output of gate IC10C goes low and starts the timing of IC9 (the Q output of IC9 goes high). This operates solenoid L9 (through IC7F, Q19, and Q20), and transfers the low at the D input of IC8A to the Q output. With a low and a high at the inputs of IC10B, solenoids L1 through L8 remain off.

When the Q output of IC9 goes high, the $\overline{Q}$ output goes low. After IC9 times out, the $\overline{Q}$ output goes high again and starts IC12, driving the $\overline{Q}$ of IC12 low. This does not affect IC11 at this time, but it does clear IC8A and turns off the punch drivers.

When IC12 times out, its $\overline{Q}$ output goes high and starts IC11, driving the Q output of IC11 high. This drives IC7A and transistors Q21 and Q22, to drive the tape advance solenoid L10. When IC11 times out, its $\overline{Q}$ output goes high and forces a high at the Q output of IC8B, which

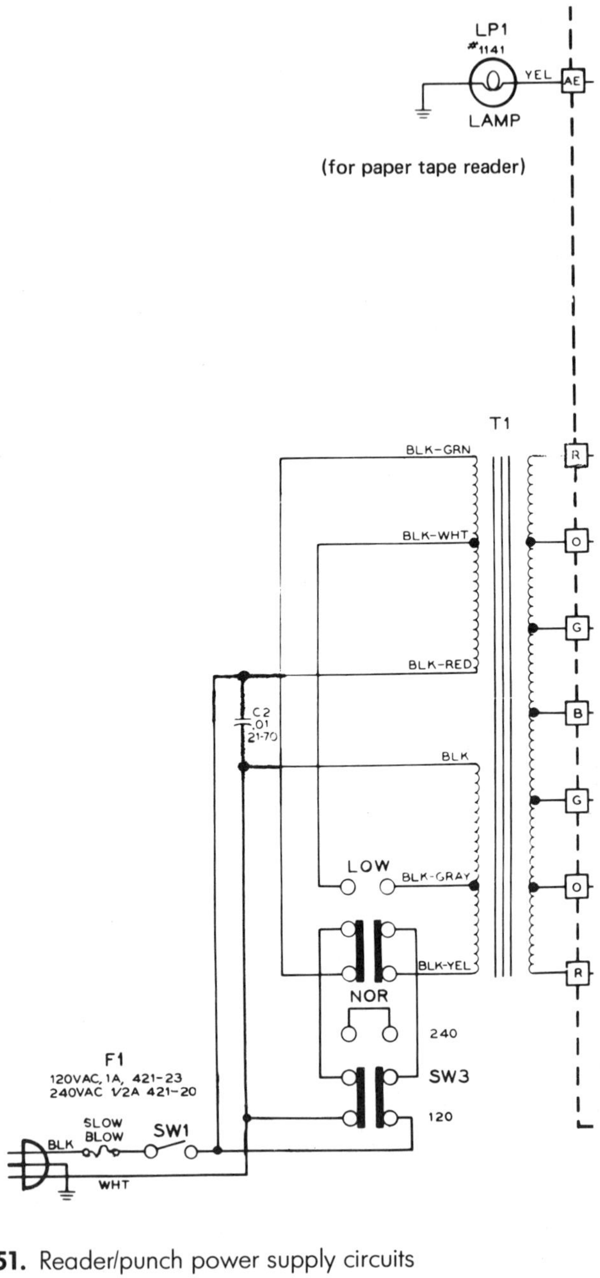

Fig. 4–51. Reader/punch power supply circuits

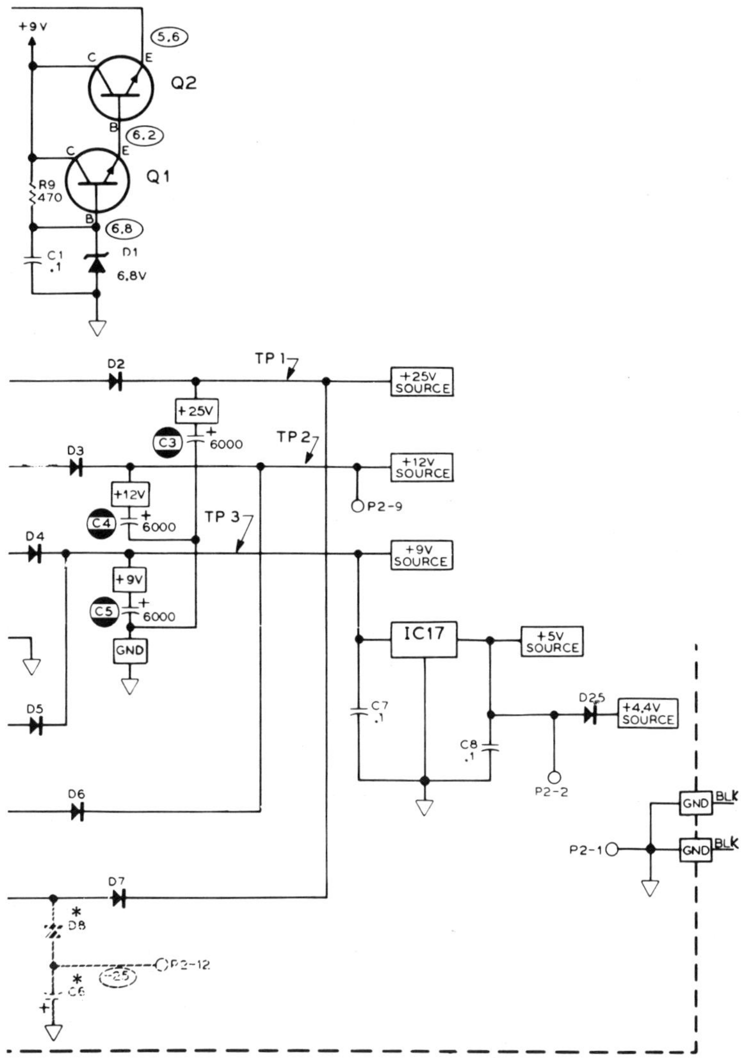
+9V
5.6
Q2
6.2
Q1
R9
470
6.8
C1
.1
D1
6.8V
D2
TP 1
+25V SOURCE
+25V
C3
6000
TP 2
D3
+12V SOURCE
P2-9
+12V
C4
6000
TP 3
D4
+9V SOURCE
+9V
C5
6000
GND
IC17
+5V SOURCE
D5
C7
.1
D25
+4.4V SOURCE
C8
.1
P2-2
D6
GND
BLK
P2-1
GND
BLK
D7
D8
P2-12
-25
C6

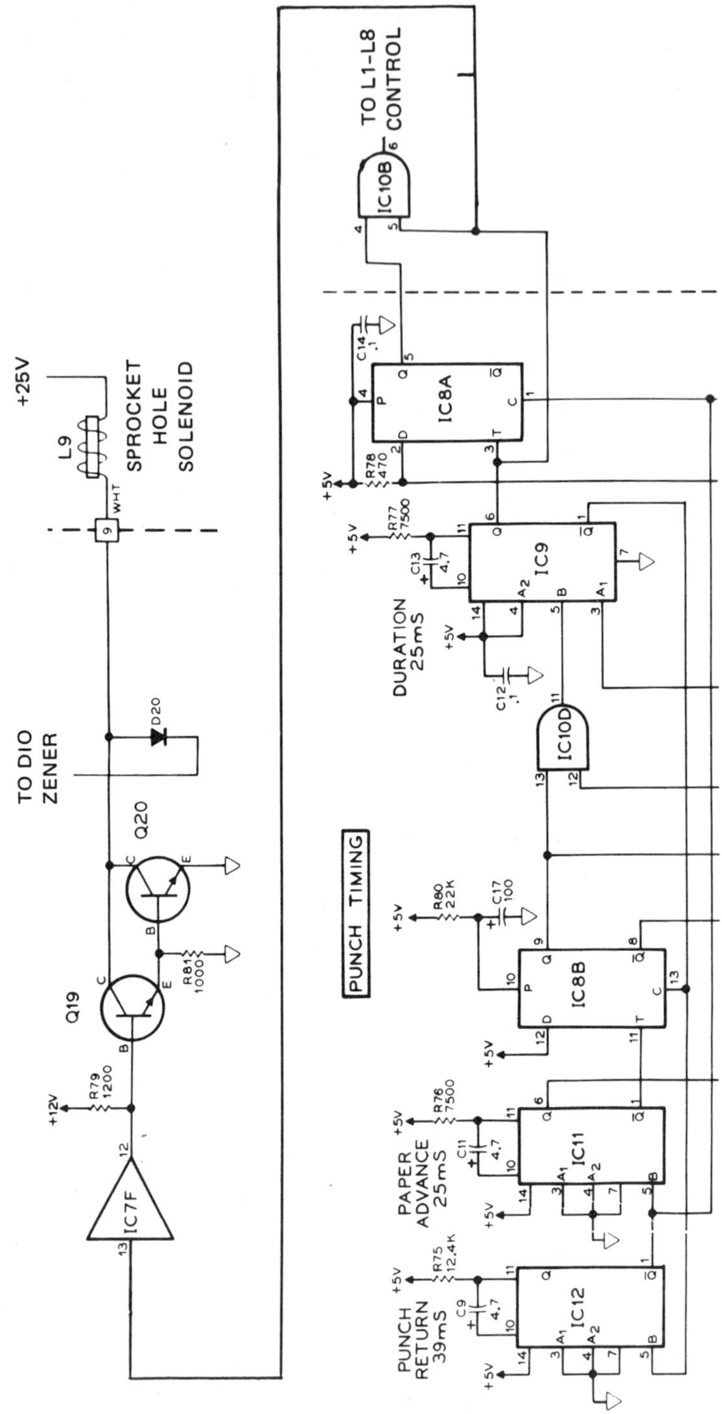

TO L1-L8 CONTROL
IC10B
+25V
L9
SPROCKET HOLE SOLENOID
WHT
IC8A
C14 .1
R78 470
R77 7500
IC9
C13 4.7
DURATION 25mS
C12 .1
D20
TO DIO ZENER
IC10D
Q20
PUNCH TIMING
R80 22K
C17 100
IC8B
Q19
R81 1000
R79 1200
+12V
IC7F
R76 7500
C11 4.7
IC11
PAPER ADVANCE 25mS
R75 12.4K
C9 4.7
IC12
PUNCH RETURN 39mS

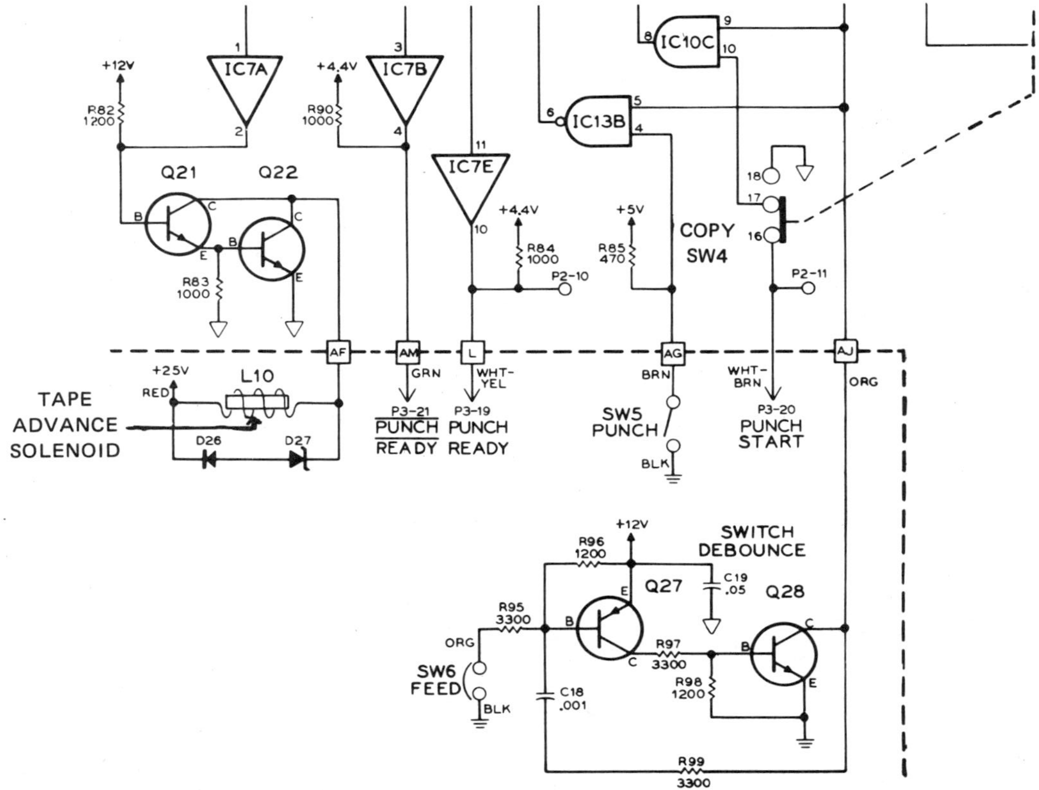

Fig. 4–52. Punch timing circuits

has been cleared when IC9 started timing out. This is transferred to the punch ready output (P3–21) by IC7E. This high at pin 13 of IC10D now allows the PUNCH and FEED switches (SW5 and SW6), or a *punch start* signal at P3-19, to control the punching.

In normal operation, a transition from high to low on the punch start line (P3–19) will be coupled through IC10C to trigger IC9.

4–6.7 Troubleshooting the Reader/Punch Circuits

If only one solenoid punch does not operate, with other solenoid punches normal, check the corresponding tape punch circuit (Fig. 4–50).

If all punch solenoids are continuously activated, but the paper drive solenoid is not operating, check IC9 (Fig. 4–52).

If all punch solenoids (except sprocket hole solenoid L9, Fig. 4–52) are continuously activated, but the paper drive solenoid operates normally, check IC10B (Fig. 4–52).

If all punch solenoids (except sprocket hole solenoid L9, Fig. 4–52) fail to energize, but the paper drive solenoid operates normally, check IC8A.

If all punches are inoperative, check the +25-V supply (Fig. 4–51). Then check IC8B, IC9, IC10C, IC10D, and IC13B.

If the punches and motor M1 (Fig. 4–48) are inoperative, check the +12-V supply (Fig. 4–51).

If all solenoids are energized, the tape reader is inoperative, the reader lamp lights, but the fuse F1 (Fig. 4–51) blows in a short time, check IC17 and the +5-V supply.

If the punch solenoids energize for only one character after power is applied, check IC11 and IC12 (Fig. 4–52).

If the sprocket teeth tear the punched tape, check for binding in the solenoid linkage, for tape that is not properly threaded, for a drive sprocket that is incorrectly aligned, and for tape tensioner binding. Also check IC12 (Fig. 4–52).

If the chad is not completely removed from the tape, check for punch solenoids incorrectly adjusted, unsuitable tape, and worn die block assembly. Also check for low line voltage and a defective IC9 (Fig. 4–52).

If the tape does not advance or is erratic, but the tape advance solenoid L10 actuates normally, check that the detent or solenoid is properly adjusted. Also check if one or more punches are not returning to their released positions.

If the tape advance solenoid L10 (Fig. 4–52) does not operate, but the punches operate normally, check L10, IC7A, Q21, Q22, and IC11. Also check for binding in the ratchet mechanism.

If the tape reader lamp LP1 does not light, but the tape advances normally, check for a burned-out lamp LP1 or for defective transistors Q1 and Q2 (Fig. 4–51).

If only one data line does not change state at a tape hole, with other data lines normal, check the corresponding tape reader circuit (Fig. 4–47). Also check for dirt in the light passage to Q101 and for proper adjustment of R1.

If motor M1 (Fig. 4–48) is inoperative or erratic in both READ and COPY modes, but the punch operates normally, check M1, Q23 through Q26, IC4, IC15, and LC16. (If motor M1 runs backward, check that the red and black leads are not interchanged.)

If motor M1 is inoperative in the READ mode, but operates normally in the COPY mode, check IC13D and IC14 (Fig. 4–48).

If all outputs remain low with no tape in the reader, and adjustments R1 through R8 (Fig. 4–47) have no effect, check R43. Also check the position of the lamp.

If all outputs remain high with blank tape in the reader, and adjustments of R1 through R8 have no effect, check R44. (It is also possible that the tape is too transparent.)

If there are consistent reading errors, check for marginal adjustments of R1 through R8 (Fig. 4–47), marginal adjustment of tape to photocell housing, incorrect tape hole spacing, tape holding spring too high, excessive drag on unread tape supply, damaged tape, dirt in photocell housing, or tape too transparent. It is also possible that IC14 (Fig. 4–48) in the reader timing circuit is defective, but a mechanical defect is more likely. (It has been the author's experience that technicians have more difficulty in locating and correcting mechanical defects, such as occur in tape reader/punches, floppy disks, and cassettes than defects in the electronic circuits.)

Chapter 5

OVERALL MICROCOMPUTER TROUBLESHOOTING APPROACHES

This chapter describes the overall approaches to microcomputer troubleshooting, or how the basics of Chapters 1 and 2 are combined with the practical use of test equipment discussed in Chapter 3, together with a knowledge of typical circuits and circuit troubleshooting in Chapter 4, in order to locate specific faults in various types of microprocessor-based systems. Considerable emphasis is placed on "universal" tests, service, and troubleshooting procedures that apply to all microcomputers. The chapter also concentrates on the relationship between software and troubleshooting.

There are several different problem areas involved in microcomputer troubleshooting. These include basic digital IC troubleshooting techniques, troubleshooting in the development stage, analyzing microcomputer program flow, using logic analyzers, and serial pattern recognition problems. Each problem area requires a somewhat different approach, and each approach is discussed fully.

5–1. BASIC DIGITAL IC TROUBLESHOOTING TECHNIQUES

The circuits of a typical microcomputer are mostly digital (rather than analog or linear), and are mostly IC (rather than discrete). Troubleshooting in discrete linear or analog circuits (even in most discrete digital circuits) can be done with traditional tools such as the volt-ohmmeter (VOM), diode checker, oscilloscope, and pulse or signal generator. These same basic troubleshooting techniques have been used for many years, as described in the author's various troubleshooting and service handbooks. Such procedures will not be described here. Instead, we shall concentrate on the specific problems of digital IC troubleshooting.

As in the case of a linear IC, you do not have access to the internal circuits of a digital IC. Thus, you must determine if the IC is performing its function, or failing, without actually getting into the circuits. (From a practical standpoint, it is very helpful if you can make this decision *before* you pull the IC from the printed-circuit board.) Unfortunately, the traditional tools for discrete digital troubleshooting often provide little or no help in making these decisions in the case of digital ICs. Let us consider two classic examples of digital troubleshooting techniques, the comparison of timing functions, and point-to-point signal pulse tracing.

5–1.1 Timing in Digital IC Troubleshooting

An often-used method for troubleshooting of discrete digital circuits is to introduce a pulse train at the circuit input while monitoring various points throughout the circuit with an oscilloscope. If any of the pulses are absent or abnormal (such as very low amplitude pulses or pulses that occur at the wrong time), this means a failure or degrading of the components between the pulse source (pulse generator) and monitor (oscilloscope). For example, a degraded diode or transistor can introduce an abnormally long delay and cause an output pulse to occur too late to open a buffer. A leaking capacitor can appear as "pulse jitter" on the oscilloscope. However, when a digital IC fails, there is total failure. Digital IC timing parameters rarely degrade or become marginal. Thus, critical timing measurements are usually not too important in troubleshooting.

This does not mean that timing measurements are to be omitted from microcomputer troubleshooting. Timing measurements are often critical *during the design and development* stage of microcomputer systems. Generally, it is a case where some IC (or group of ICs) does not operate fast enough to perform each program step, as initially programmed. Such problems are solved by debugging (changing the program sequence), rather than by troubleshooting. As a general rule, once a program has been debugged and the microcomputer performs properly, timing will remain good (or will fail completely).

There is an exception to this general rule. Digital ICs tend to speed up when power supply voltages are high and slow down with low power supply voltages. Thus, if program timing is on the borderline and there is a drastic change in power supply voltage (particularly if the voltage is low), system timing can result in improper timing.

5–1.2 Point-to-Point Pulse Tracing

Point-to-point pulse tracing is used in microcomputer troubleshooting. A pulse is introduced on a line or at some point in the circuit (with a pulse generator or logic pulser, Sec. 3–3), and then monitored at another point on the line (with an oscilloscope or logic probe, Sec. 3–2). Unfortunately, there are certain cases where this does not work too well with digital ICs.

Consider the circuit of Fig. 5–1, which is part of the output buffer (connected to one line of the data bus) in a microcomputer RAM. (The circuit is sometimes referred to as a "transistor totem pole.") In either the high or low (1 or 0) state, the circuit is a low impedance. In the low

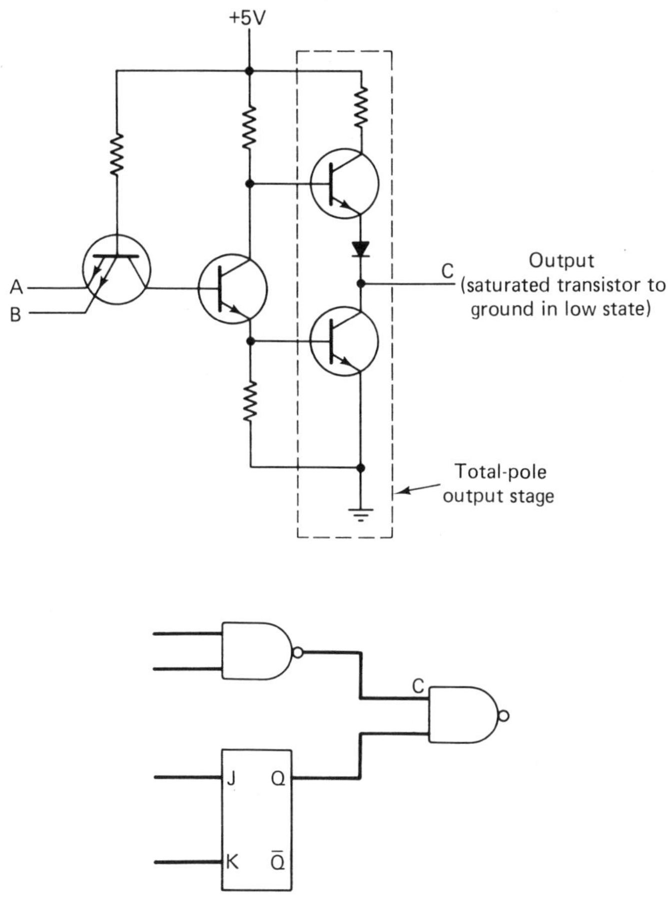

Fig. 5–1. Point-to-point pulse tracing problems

state, the circuit output is a saturated transistor to ground, and appears as about 5 or 10Ω to ground. This presents a problem in pulse tracing. A signal source used to inject a pulse at a point that is driven by this output (such as trying to inject a pulse on that line of the data bus) must have sufficient power to override the low impedance output state.

A typical pulse generator (even a logic pulser) may not have this capability. Instead, it is necessary to either cut printed circuit traces (or lines) or pull IC leads in order to inject the pulse. Both of these practices are time consuming and lead to unreliable repairs. However, there are basic digital IC troubleshooting techniques, using logic probes and pulsers, as well as current tracers (Sec. 3–4), that will resolve such problems. These techniques are discussed in the following paragraphs. But first let us consider the how and why of digital IC failure.

5–1.3 How Digital ICs Fail

It is essential that you understand the types of failure that occur in digital ICs if you are going to troubleshoot a microcomputer efficiently. There are two classes of digital IC failure: (1) those caused by *internal* failure, and (2) those caused by a failure in the microcomputer circuit *external* to the IC.

Four types of failure can occur internally to a digital IC. These are (1) an *open bond* on either an input or output, (2) a *short* between an input or output and V_{CC} or ground, (3) a *short* between two pins (neither of which is V_{CC} or ground), and (4) a failure in the internal circuitry (often called the steering circuitry) of the IC.

Four types of failure can occur in the circuit external to the IC. These are (1) a *short* between a point (or node, as it may be called) and V_{CC} or ground, (2) a short between two nodes (neither of which are V_{CC} or ground), (3) an open signal path, and (4) a failure of an external component.

Effects of an Open Output Bond. When there is an open output bond, as shown in Fig. 5–2, the inputs driven by that output are left to float. In a typical TTL IC, a floating input rises to approximately 1.4 to 1.5 V and usually has the same effect on circuit operation as a high logic level. Thus, an open output bond will cause all inputs driven by that output to float to a bad level, since 1.5 V is less than the high threshold level of 2 V and greater than the low threshold level of 0.4 V. In TTL ICs, a floating input is interpreted as a high level. Thus, the effect will be that these inputs will respond to this bad level as though it were a static high signal.

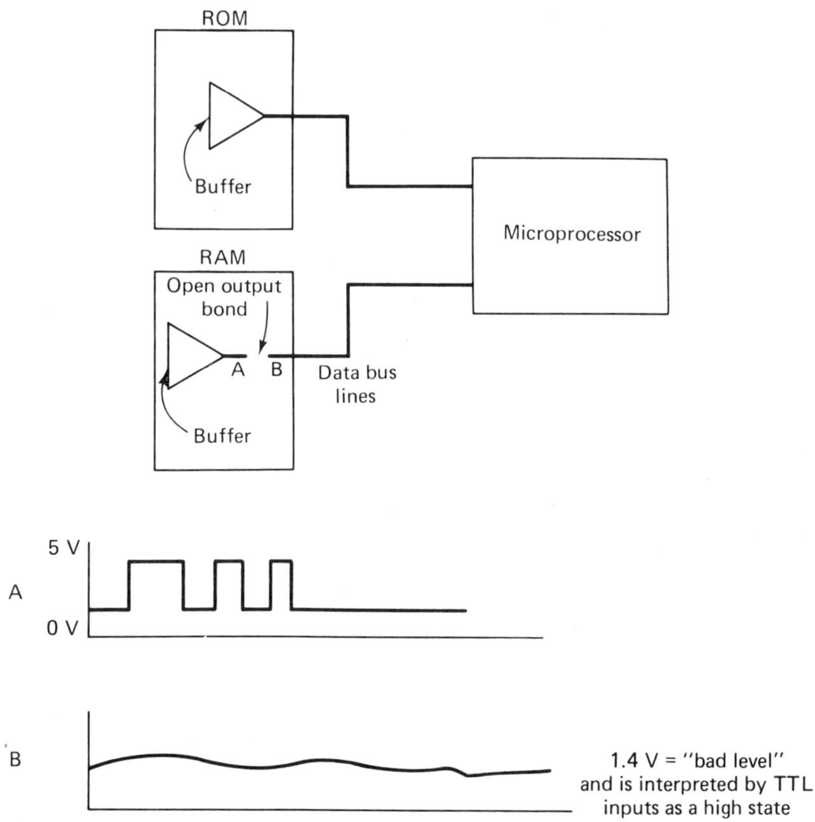

Fig. 5–2. Effect of an open output bond on circuit operation

Effects of an Open Input Bond. When there is an open input bond, as shown in Fig. 5–3, we find that the open circuit blocks the signal driving the input from entering the circuit (the microprocessor data bus buffer, in this case). The input line is thus allowed to float, and will respond as though it were a static high signal. It is important to realize that, since the open occurs on the input inside the IC, the digital signal driving this input will be unaffected by the open. That is, the signal is blocked to the microprocessor buffer inside the IC, but there will be no effect on other ICs. Of course, the microprocessor will respond as if there is a static 1 on that line of the data bus, and will thus not respond properly to those commands or words where a 0 is to appear on that line of the bus.

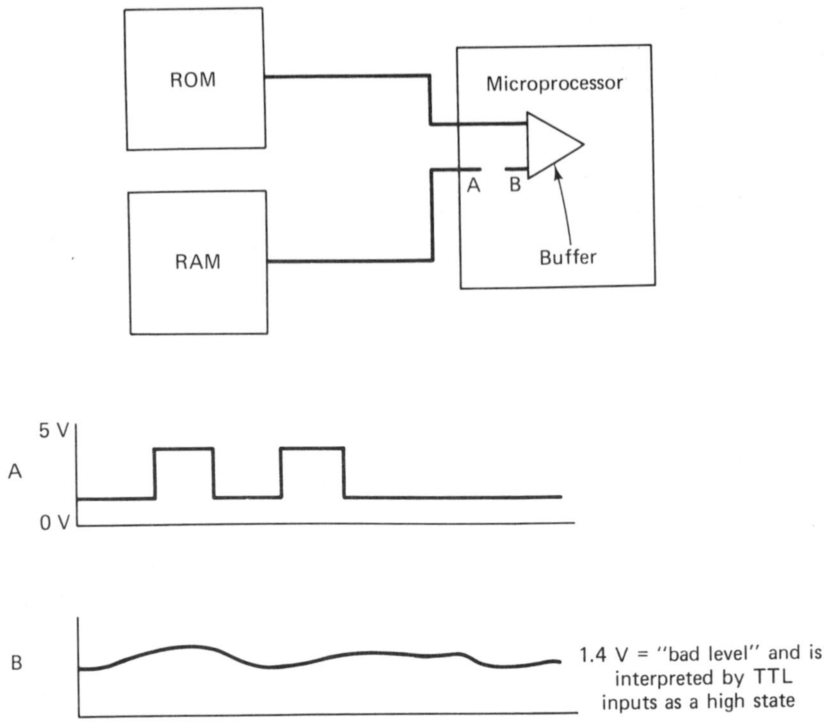

Fig. 5–3. Effect of an open input bond on circuit operation

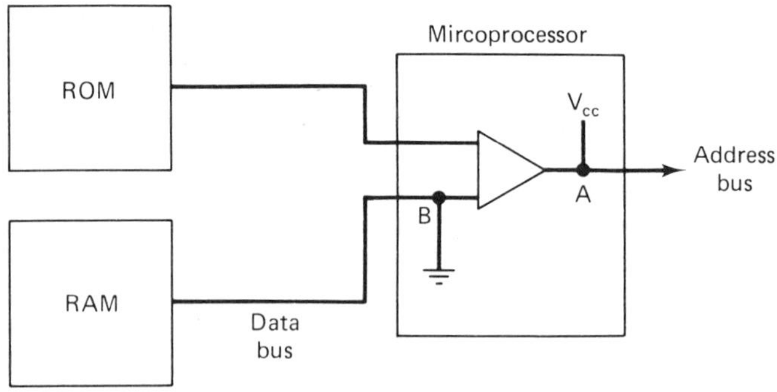

Fig. 5–4. Effect of a short between an input or output and V_{CC} or ground

Short Between an Input or Output and V_{CC} or Ground. A short as shown in Fig. 5–4 has the effect of holding all signal lines connected to that input or output either high (in the case of a short to V_{CC}) or low (if shorted to ground). In the case of Fig. 5–4, the address line connected to point A is held in the high (1) state, and the data line connected to point B is held low (0). In most cases, this will result in total disruption of the program, and is thus one of the easiest types of digital IC failure to locate.

Short Between Two Pins. Shorts such as shown in Fig. 5–5 are not as straightforward to analyze as the short to V_{CC} or ground. When two pins are shorted, the outputs driving those pins (the ROM and RAM in this case) oppose each other when one attempts to pull the pins high while the other attempts to pull them low. In this situation, the output attempting to go high will supply current, while the output attempting to go low will sink this current. The net effect is that the short will be pulled to a low state. Whenever both outputs attempt to go high simultaneously or to go low simultaneously, the shorted pins will respond properly. But whenever one output attempts to go low, the short will be held low.

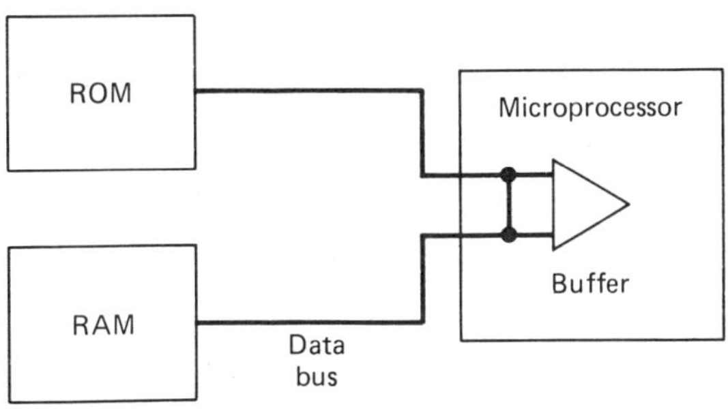

Fig. 5–5. Effect of a short between two pins

Failure of Internal Control Circuitry. The effects of internal failure are difficult to predict. For example, in the case of Fig. 5–6, a failure of the internal circuit has the effect of permanently turning on either the upper transistor of the buffer output totem pole, thus locking the buffer output in the high state, or turning on the lower transistor to lock the buffer output in the low state. Of course, this failure blocks data bus signal flow and has a catastrophic effect on microcomputer operation.

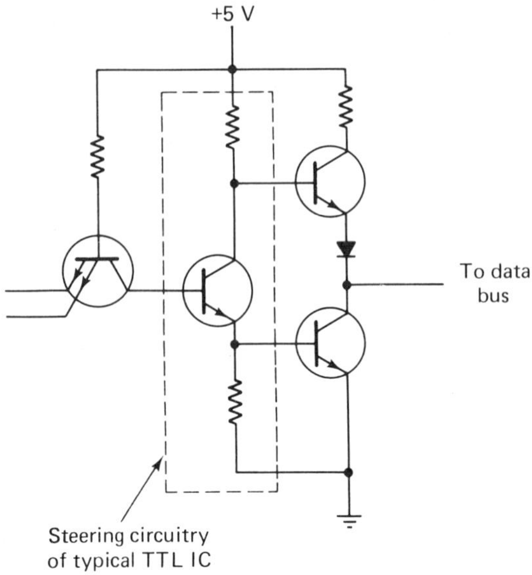

Fig. 5–6. Effect of a failure in the internal steering circuitry of a typical TTL IC

External Shorts. A short between a node and V_{CC} or ground external to the IC cannot be distinguished from a short internal to the IC. Both will cause the signal lines connected to the node to be either always high (for shorts to V_{CC}) or always low (for shorts to ground). When this type of failure is found, only a very close physical examination of the circuit will show if the failure is external to the IC. The current tracer (Sec. 3–4) is an effective tool for locating such shorts.

Open Signal Paths in Circuit. An open signal path in the external circuit has a similar effect as an open output bond driving the node. As shown in Fig. 5–7, the input (microprocessor) to the right of the open will be allowed to float to a bad level and will thus appear as a static high level in circuit operation. Those inputs to the left of the open (data bus) will be unaffected by the open and will thus respond as expected.

5–1.4 Digital Troubleshooting Examples

The first step in any troubleshooting process is to narrow the malfunctioning area as much as possible by examing the observable characteristics of the failure. In the case of a microcomputer, this often involves punching in data at the keyboard and noting the response on the CRT screen. Furthermore, the designers of some microcomputers have developed *diagnostic routines* or short programs that isolate

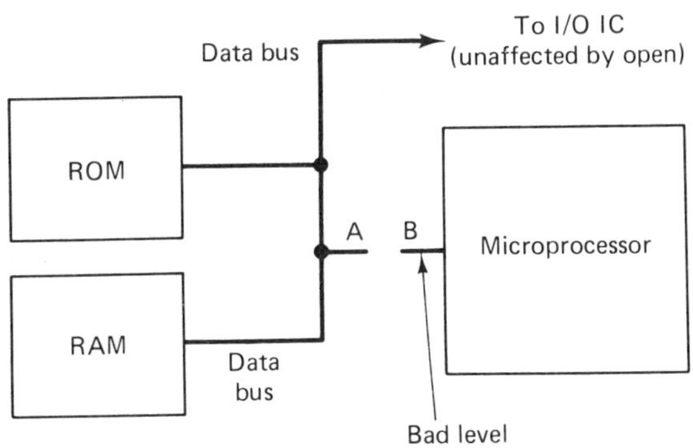

Fig. 5–7. Effect of open signal path in external circuits (data bus)

troubles down to specific ICs or groups of ICs. Such routines should be followed religiously. In the absence of good diagnostic routines, and when CRT responses are meaningless, the logic analyzer described throughout Chapter 3 (and in later sections of this chapter) is the most effective tool for observing characteristics of failure. As discussed, a logic analyzer makes it possible to observe the full transfer of data in a microcomputer for each step of the program. That is, you can see and compare the data word (on the data bus) at each address (on the address bus) for all program steps. This can be done one step at a time, in groups of steps, or you can move quickly through the program steps to an area of the program where trouble is suspected.

Based on observations of the logic analyzer (or CRT/keyboard and diagnostic routines), you can localize the failure to as few ICs or other circuits as possible (hopefully to one circuit or IC). At this point it is necessary to narrow the failure further to one suspected circuit by looking for improper *key signals or pulses* between circuits. The logic probe (Sec. 3–2) is a most effective tool for tracing key signals in microcomputers.

In many cases, a signal will completely disappear (no clock signals, no read/write signals, etc.). By rapidly probing the interconnecting signal paths (clock line, read/write lines, etc.), a missing signal can be readily found, Another important failure is the occurrence of a signal on a line that should not have a signal. The *pulse memory* option found on probes (such as described in Sec. 3–2) allows such signal lines to be monitored for single-shot pulses or pulse activity over extended periods of time. The occurrence of a signal will be stored and indicated on the pulse memory LED.

Isolating a failure to a single circuit requires knowledge of the microcomputer or system and its operating characteristics. In this regard, a well-written service manual is invaluable. Properly prepared manuals will show where key signals are to be observed. The logic probe will then provide a rapid means of observing the presence of these signals.

Once a failure has been isolated to a single circuit or IC, the logic probe, logic pulser, and current tracer (Chapter 3) can be used to observe the effects of the failure on circuit operation and to locate the failure to its cause (either an IC or a fault in the circuit external to the IC). The clip and comparator (Chapter 3) can also be used, if they will accommodate 24 or 40 pints (which is not the case at this writing).

The classic approach at this point is to test the suspected IC (or ICs) using a logic comparator or by substitution. However, the following steps are based on the assumption that neither of these approaches is practical (the comparator will not accommodate the ICs, and the ICs are very difficult to remove).

Checking for Pulse Activity on a Line. The logic probe can be used to observe signal activity on inputs and to view the resulting output signals. From this information, a decision can be made as to the proper operation of the IC. For example, if a clock signal is occurring on the clock line to a RAM or ROM, and the enabling inputs (such as read or write signals, chip enable signals, etc.) are in the enabled state, then there should be signal activity on the data bus lines. Each line should be shifting between high and low (1 or 0) as the program goes through each step. The logic probe will allow the clock and enabling input to be observed and, if pulse activity is indicated on the outputs (each of the data bus lines, in this case), then the ROM or RAM can be considered as operating properly. As discussed, it is usually not necessary to measure actual timing of the signals since ICs generally fail catastrophically. A possible exception is when an output buffer does not open and close at the proper time. However, with few exceptions, the occurrence of pulse activity is usually enough indication of proper operation.

When more detailed study is desired or when input signal activity is missing, the logic pulser can be used to inject input signals and the probe used to monitor the response. The logic pulser is also valuable for replacing the clock, thus allowing the circuit to be single-stepped, while the logic probe is used to observe the changes in the output state (such as changes on the address and data bus lines).

When using this first step to compare inputs and outputs of the ROM, RAM and so on, it is wise to check all the output lines before you try to check the first fault you find. Prematurely studying a single fault can result in overlooking faults that cause multiple failure, such as shorts between two lines in the data or address bus. This often leads to the needless replacement of a good IC and much wasted time. The extra work can be minimized by systematically eliminating the possible failures of digital circuits discussed above.

Testing for Open Bond. The first failure to test for is an open bond in the IC driving the failed node. The logic probe provides a quick and accurate test for this failure. If the output is open, then the node will float to a bad level. By probing the node, the logic probe will quickly indicate a bad level. If a bad level is indicated, the IC driving the node is suspect.

Testing for Short to V_{CC} or Ground. If the node is not at a bad level, then test for short to V_{CC} or ground. This can be done using the logic pulser and probe. (The current tracer described in Sec. 5–1.5 can also be used effectively to locate shorts.) While the logic pulser is powerful enough to override even a low-impedance output, the pulser is not powerful enough to effect a change in state on a V_{CC} or ground bus. Thus, if the logic pulser is used to inject a pulse while the logic probe is used simultaneously on the same node to observe the pulse, a short to V_{CC} or ground can be detected. The occurrence of a pulse indicates that the node is not shorted, and the absence of a pulse indicates that node is shorted to V_{CC} (if it is a high) or ground (if it is a low).

Causes of V_{CC} or Ground Shorts. If the node is shorted to V_{CC} or ground, there are two possible causes. The first is a short in the circuit external to the ICs, and the other is a short internal to one of the ICs attached to the node (as discussed in Sec. 5–1.3). The external short should be detected by an examination of the circuit. If no external short is found, the cause is likely to be any one of the ICs attached to the node. These can be eliminated one at a time. Also check for shorted capacitors and resistors on the line. (Note that resistors do not usually short, but their terminals can be shorted by mechanical vibration.)

Testing for Shorts Between Nodes. If the node is not shorted to V_{CC} or ground, nor is it an open output bond, then look for a short between two nodes. This can be done in one of two ways. First, the logic pulser can be used to pulse the failing node being studied, and the logic probe can be used to observe each of the remaining failing nodes. If a short exits between the node being studied and one of the other failing nodes, the pulser will cause the node being probed to change state (i.e., the pulse will detect a pulse). To ensure that a short exists, the probe and pulser should be reversed and the test made again. If a pulse is again detected, a short is definitely indicated.

Causes of Shorts Between Nodes. If the failure is a short, there are two possible causes. The most likely cause is a problem in the circuit external to the IC. This can be detected by physically examining the circuit and repairing any solder bridges or loose wire shorts found. Only if the two shorted nodes are common to one IC can the failure be internal to that IC. If after examining the circuit no short can be found external to the IC, the IC should be replaced.

Testing for an Open Signal Path. If no nodes are indicated as failing, but there is a definite failure of the circuit, an open signal path can be suspected. From a practical standpoint, it is generally easier to check for open signal paths than to replace ICs. The logic probe provides a rapid means of not only detecting but also *physically locating* an open in a circuit, such as shown in Fig. 5–8. Since an open signal path allows the input to the "right" of the open (point B) to float to a bad level, the logic probe can be used to test the input of each IC for a bad level. Once an input floating at a bad level is detected, the logic probe can be used to follow the circuit back from the input, while looking for the open. This can be done because the circuit to the "left" of the open (point A) will be a good logic level (either high, low, or pulsing), while the circuit to the right (point B) will be a bad level. Probing back along the signal path (from right to left) will indicate a bad level until the open is passed. Thus, the probe will precisely find the physical location of the open.

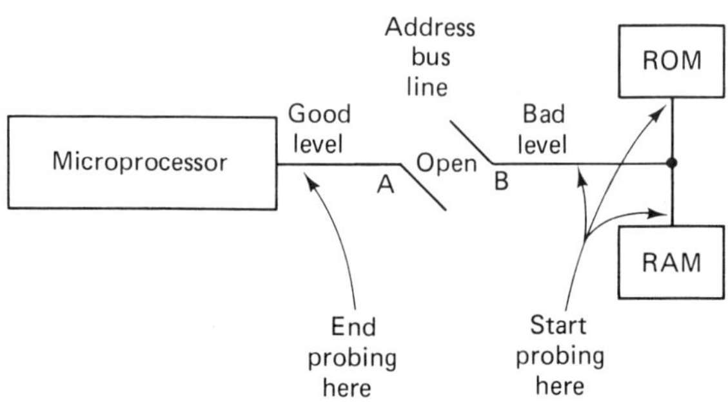

Fig. 5–8. Tracing an open signal path in an address bus line

5–1.4 Using the Current Tracer in Digital Troubleshooting

The basic procedures for using the current tracer are discussed in Sec. 3–4. The following paragraphs describe some additional uses for the current tracer in digital troubleshooting. From a practical standpoint, whenever a low-impedance fault exists, whether on a digital board or not, the shorted node can be stimulated with a logic pulser and the current followed by means of the current tracer.

Ground Planes. Occasionally, defective ground planes can cause problems in microcomputer circuits. It is possible to determine the effectiveness of a ground plane by tracing current distribution through the plane. This is done by injecting pulse current into the plane from a logic pulser (or any pulse generator) and tracing the current flow over the plane. Generally, current flow should be even over the entire plane. However, it is possible that the current will flow only in a few paths, particularly along the edges of the ground plane.

V_{CC}-to-Ground Shorts. The existence of a V_{CC}-to-ground short is generally easy to determine. Generally, there is a drop in power supply voltage or a complete failure of the power supply. However, locating the exact point of the short can be quite difficult. To use the current tracer in this application, disconnect the power supply from the V_{CC} line, and pulse the power supply terminal using the logic pulser, with the supply return connected to the ground lead of the pulser. Even if capacitors are connected between V_{CC} and ground, the current tracer will usually show the path carrying the greatest current.

Stuck Line Caused by Dead Driver. Figure 5–9 shows a frequently occurring troubleshooting symptom: a line (say in the address or data bus) has been identified on which the signal is stuck high or low. The particular line is suspect since it shows no pulse activity (as discussed in Sec. 5–1.4). Is the driver (or signal source) dead, or is something, such as a short, clamping the line to a fixed value (such as to ground or V_{CC})? This question is readily answered by tracing current from the

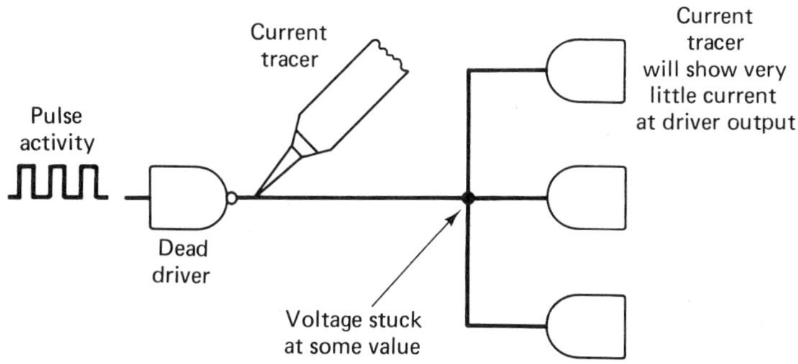

Fig. 5–9. Using the current tracer to determine that a stuck node is caused by a dead driver

driver to other points on that line. If the driver (source) is dead, the only current indicated by the tracer will be that caused by parasitic coupling from any nearby currents, and this will be much smaller than the normal current capability of the driver. On the other hand, if the driver is good, normal short-circuit current will be present and can be traced to the short or element clamping the line.

Stuck Line Caused by Input Short. Figure 5–10 illustrates this situation, which has exactly the same voltage symptoms as the previous case of a stuck line caused by a dead driver. However, the current tracer will now indicate a large current flowing from the driver, and will also make it possible to follow this current to the cause of the problem, the shorted input. The same procedure will also find the fault when the short is on the interconnecting line (for example, a solder bridge to another line).

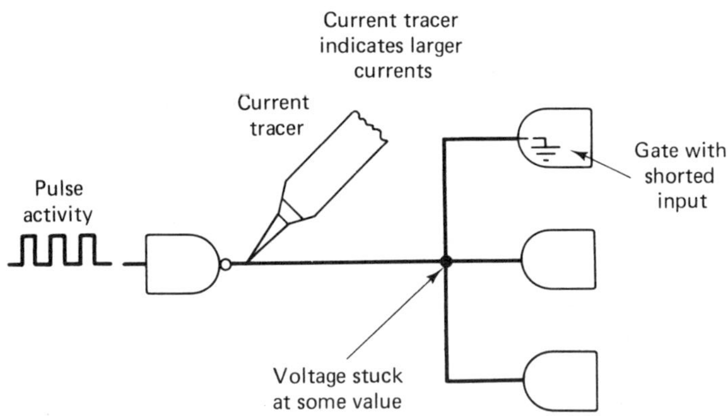

Fig. 5–10. Using the current tracer to show that stuck node is caused by an input short

Stuck Three-State Data or Address Bus. A stuck three-state bus, such as a microprocessor data or address bus, can present a very difficult troubleshooting problem, especially to voltage-sensing measurement tools (such as a logic probe). Because of the many bus terminals (typically 8 or 16), and the fact that several ROMs and RAMs may be connected, it is very difficult to isolate the one element (ROM and RAM) holding the bus in a stuck condition. However, if the current tracer indicates high current at several outputs of a ROM or RAM, it is likely that one (and most likely only one) element is stuck in a low-impedance state. The defective element is located by placing the ROM or RAM control input line to the appropriate level for a high-impedance output state (the "off" condition), and noting whether high current flow persists at the ROM/RAM buffer output. This is repeated for each ROM/RAM until the bad one is located.

If the current tracer indicates high currents at only two elements (say two RAMs), the problem is a *bus fight*. That is, both RAMs are trying to drive the bus at the same time. This is probably caused by improper timing of control signals to the RAMs. (One RAM buffer is opened before the other RAM buffer is closed.)

If the current tracer indicates the absence of abnormally high current activity at all elements, yet the bus signals are known to be incorrect, the problem is an element stuck in the high-impedance state. This can be found by placing a low impedance on the bus, such as a short to ground, and using the current tracer to check for the element that fails to show high-current activity.

Current Tracer Problems. Efficient use of the current tracer usually requires a longer familiarization period than does the operation of voltage-sensing instruments (such as the probe). This is primarily because most electronic technicians are not used to thinking in terms of current and the information that current provides, simply because this information has not been available conveniently. Most troubleshooting techniques involve measurement of voltage and resistance. Without a current tracer, it is necessary to open a line and insert an ammeter. This is not practical for most situations, so current is determined by calculation (based on observed voltage and current).

Use of the current tracer also requires some skill to avoid the *crosstalk* problem. That is, if a small current is being traced in a conductor that is very close to another conductor carrying a much larger current, the sensor at the tip of the current tracer may respond to the current in the nearby line. The sensor of the current tracer has been designed to minimize this effect, but crosstalk can never be entirely eliminated. However, by observing the variation of the current tracer's display as the tracer is moved along the line, the operator can learn to recognize interference or crosstalk from a nearby line.

5–2. TROUBLESHOOTING IN THE DEVELOPMENT STAGE

In this book, we are primarily concerned with troubleshooting rather than debugging. That is, most of the procedures are based on the assumption that the microcomputer or other system was once working properly. However, during the development stage of a microcomputer, the line between troubleshooting and debugging is difficult to distinguish. This is particularly true for the hobbyist and experimenter. Take the classic example of the hobbyist who has assembled an experimental "microcomputer" similar to that shown in Fig. 5–11. The microprocessor, ROM, RAM, I/O, clock, and reset switches are all interconnected, the keyboard/CRT is connected to the I/O, and power is applied. There is no smoke, arcing, or flame, but nothing seems to work!

Several questions can arise in the hobbyist's mind. Are all of the elements (microprocessor, ROM, RAM, I/O, etc.) good? Is the wiring correct? If the answer is "yes" to both of these, then the problem is in software. The program has bugs. But are you sure?

The basic problem in this situation is one of *feedback*. The microcomputer operates in response to data words appearing on the data bus. In turn, the data words depend on the ROM/RAM address selected by the word on the address bus. Furthermore, the address word depends on the address register in the microprocessor (which depends on the word on the data bus)!

To further confuse matters, the microprocessor will probably increment to a new address each time the data word is changed. And, if there are any words or parts of words appearing on the I/Os, these can be applied to the address and data buses. Now imagine if one address line or data line (only one) is open so that it is always at a 0 (or at a 1, depending on design). Or consider what will occur if two data lines are interchanged. With any of these conditions, the microprocessor

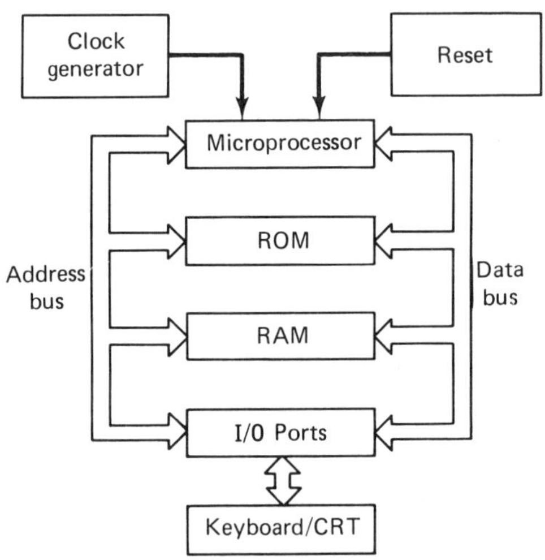

Fig. 5–11. Typical minimum microcomputer system

will deliver an incorrect address to memory (possibly an unused address), and memory will play back an incorrect data byte (possibly a meaningless instruction). Even with a perfect program, the result will be chaos.

The following paragraphs describe a general procedure for resolving these problems. In brief, the procedure involves *breaking the feedback loop into sections*. Then each section is "turned on" independently of all other sections. This is sometimes known as "bringing up the microcomputer." Once a section is proved good, you go on to another section until all sections in the feedback loop are operating properly. If each section in the loop is normal, but the system still fails to work, the problem is one of interconnections (unless of course, the program is simply not practical). In any event, the following procedure will isolate the problem areas. The procedure is not limited to the development stages, but can be applied whenever there is a problem that does not yield to routine troubleshooting approaches.

5–2.1 Clock and Reset Circuits

Once you are sure that power is applied to all the elements in the system, both the clock and reset circuits should be checked before you break into the feedback loop.

The clock line is connected to all the elements (in most systems). Verify this by checking for a stream of good clock pulses at each element, using a logic probe or oscilloscope. The clock pulses must be of correct amplitude (typically about 5 V), width, and frequency. If there are two clocks, the clock pulses must be shifted in phase from each other (typically by 90°).

The reset line is usually connected only to the microprocessor. Generally, the reset line is held at 0 V until the reset button is pressed. This action applies +5 V, and the microcomputer is reset. Reset operation can be verified by monitoring the reset line while pressing reset button. Make sure that the line goes from 0 to +5 V when reset is pressed. However, this does not verify if the microcomputer is responding properly to a reset signal. In most systems, proper reset operation of the microcomputer can be verified by monitoring the address bus with the reset button pressed. The address bus should be at 0000.

5–2.2 Breaking the Microprocessor Loop

The simplest way to isolate the microprocessor is to plug in only the microprocessor, and leave the RAM, ROM, and I/O out of the system. (During the development stage, the ICs are generally mounted in sockets. This is not always true when the system is assembled in final form.) Leave the clock and reset circuit, as well as all the wiring, in the final form.

Next apply a *no-operation* data word or instruction on the data bus. This instruction may be called by many names (NOP, IDLE, WAIT, etc.) in various microprocessors. However, most microprocessors have some form of no-op instruction. The instruction can be applied by connecting each line in the data bus to +5 or 0 V as needed to form the correct binary word, as shown in Fig. 5–12. Note that resistors are used between the supply or ground and the data bus. The resistors (typically 100 kΩ) are included to prevent damage to the microprocessor. Many microprocessors will try to put data onto the bus during an operating cycle. If the data bus is wired directly to the supply or ground, the data output buffer in the microprocessor can be damaged.

An alternative method for setting a no-op word onto the data bus is through three-state gates. Connect the control line for all the gates to the microprocessor read/write line so that the gates are active only when the microprocessor reads data.

With a fixed no-op instruction word on the data line, the program counter in the microprocessor will increment repeatedly. That is, the

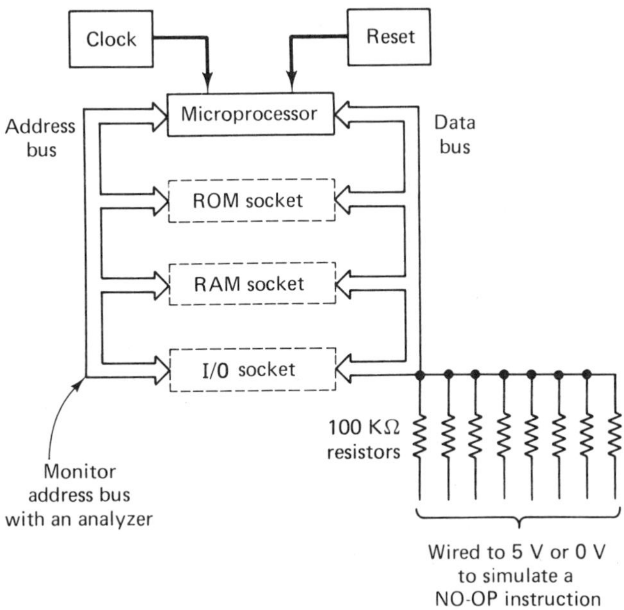

Fig. 5–12. Applying a no-operation instruction to the data bus

microprocessor will execute a no-op, increment the program counter, execute the next no-op, and so on.

5–2.3 Counting Sequence on the Address Line

With the setup shown in Fig. 5–12, the microprocessor should increment continuously through all the addresses. This can be verified by connecting the input probes of an analyzer to all 16 lines of the address bus, and setting the analyzer controls for a count function (most analyzers have some form of count function). Make the connection at the ROM end of the address bus to ensure that correct addresses are being transmitted to the ROM. Start by pressing the reset button and checking for an address or count of 0000. Then release the reset button and check that the count goes through FFFF in sequence. In most systems, the microcomputer will continue to execute no-ops indefinitely with the Fig. 5–12 setup. That is, when FFFF is reached, the address register will continue on to 0000 again, and repeat all addresses.

By using this procedure, you verify that the microprocessor is executing no-ops and that the addresses are correctly transmitted to the ROM. If the addresses do not form a counting sequence, examine the address pattern to determine if address lines are interchanged or are inactive (fixed at 0, 1, or a high-impedance state), or if the microprocessor is executing an unexpected branch instruction.

5–2.4 Checking Waveforms at Each Change

At this point, it is also important to examine the waveforms on all the buses and control lines. This can be done with an oscilloscope and with analyzers that have a timing display. All timing functions should be compared against the timing diagrams shown in the microcomputer service literature. Any incorrect timing, marginal voltage levels, noise, or crosstalk should be eliminated before proceeding. Timing should be checked as each new block or section is added. Although such testing may seem needlessly repetitive, it takes very little time if there is no problem. If there is a problem, a check at this stage can save a great deal of time. Consider the following problems.

The timing of control signals is particularly important. It is obvious that a control signal (such as a read, write, or chip enable signal) must be applied at exactly the right time. For example, if a data bus buffer is held open too long, all or part of another data word will appear on the bus.

Marginal voltage levels can be a problem, particularly on data and address buses. For example, assume that +5 V normally represents a 1, but that a data bus input buffer (say at the microprocessor) will recognize anything above about +3 V as a 1. If the pulses appearing on the data bus drop to something in the order of +2.75 V, they might be recognized as a 0.

Noise and crosstalk can also be a problem on data and address buses, even on control lines. For example, if a line has noise pulses (or crosstalk, which is noise picked up from adjacent lines), and these pulses are near the 2.75-V level, they may appear as 1s. The results are obvious if that particular line is supposed to be at a 0.

5–2.5 Checking the ROM

Once you are satisfied that the microprocessor is functioning normally (executing no-op commands, issuing all control signals such as read/write and chip-select, and incrementing through all addresses in sequence), connect the ROM into the circuit. Make all connections as normal, except for the data bus. As shown in Fig. 5–13, the data output of the ROM should be monitored with an analyzer, but should not be connected to the data bus. Instead, leave the fixed no-op instruction

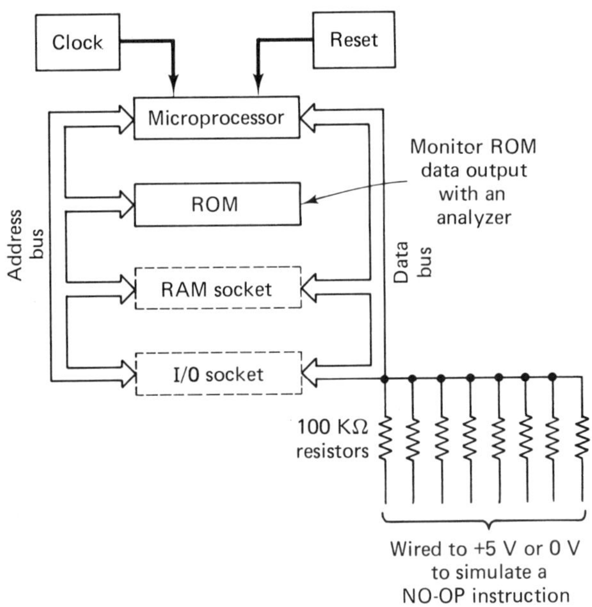

Fig. 5–13. Checking ROM data output

word on the data bus (via the resistors or three-state gates). In this way, the microprocessor will continue to see a no-op instruction, and will continue to increment or count through the addresses as discussed. This time, however, the ROM will cycle through all possible addresses so that you can measure the ROM data outputs with the analyzer. It is assumed that the ROM has some known stored information that you can check on an address-by-address basis. If not, make up a test PROM by programming predetermined words at each address and then inserting the PROM in the ROM socket. It is also assumed that, if there is more than one ROM, each ROM will be checked in turn. If the analyzer has the capacity, continue to monitor all the address lines, as well as the data lines.

Since not all the addresses are ordinarily allocated to ROM, it might be necessary to connect some temporary pull ups to the ROM data outputs. This can be done by connecting the lines to +5 V through 100-kΩ resistors. With such pull ups, an address outside the allocated ROM addresses will generate a known data word (all 1s).

Keep in mind that it is not absolutely necessary to monitor all possible ROM outputs, although such a check can be beneficial. However, if there is more than one ROM, you should check sufficiently to verify that the correct ROM is selected, and that every ROM is addressed correctly (in sequence).

You should also check some addresses outside those of the ROM to verify that the ROMs are off when they are not addressed. This is often overlooked. Remember to check the waveforms (sec. 5–2.4) on the address bus and control lines, particularly on the ROM control lines. It is possible for two ROMs (or a ROM and RAM) to be on at the same time.

5–2.6 Completing the Microprocessor-to-ROM Link

Once satisfied that the ROMs are being addressed in sequence and delivering the correct outputs, connect the ROMs to the data bus and remove the fixed no-op instruction word. In effect, restore the microprocessor-to-ROM link, but do not insert the RAM or I/O at this time.

To make a comprehensive test, install a ROM (or test PROM) with a simple diagnostic routine or program. The test program should contain several unconditional jumps. A flow chart of such a program is shown in Fig. 5–14. Verify operation of the test program by monitoring the address bus with the analyzer.

Note that the program includes RAM access and I/O instructions

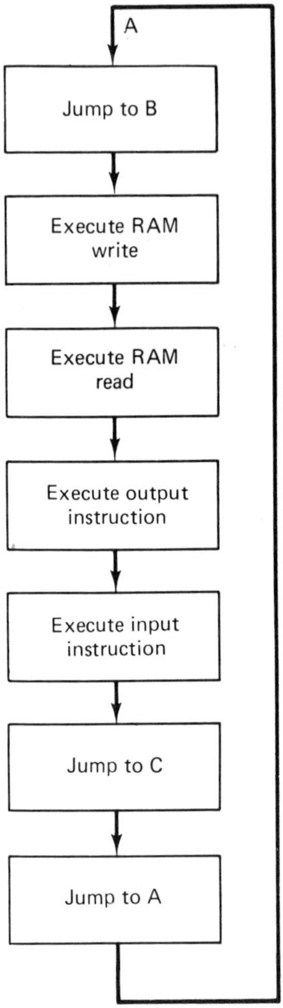

Fig. 5–14. Simple diagnostic routine to verify microprocessor-to-ROM link

so that the RAM and I/O control cycles can be checked before the RAM and I/O devices are installed. RAM and I/O timing should also be checked at this point (as discussed in Sec. 5–2.4). Generally, it is not necessary to monitor the data bus unless there is a problem, because the sequence of program addresses is ample to verify proper execution of the program. That is, if you have put each of the Fig. 5–14 steps in addresses in sequence, and each address appears in that sequence as monitored on the address bus, the correct word must be appearing on the data bus. Although the diagnostic program of Fig. 5–14 appears simple, it is generally adequate to test the microprocessor-to-ROM data link, as well as the RAM and I/O control cycles, of a typical microcomputer. Of course, if another more elaborate program is available in the service literature, use the manufacturer's program. As in the case of other electronic troubleshooting, when all else fails, follow instructions.

In no case should any branches on RAM or I/O instructions be used at this point, as the RAM and I/O blocks have not yet been turned on and debugged. The checkout of the microprocessor-to-ROM data link is by far the most tedious. The reason is that this link must always be a feedback process. That is, each instruction depends on the address, and each address depends on the previous instruction. The RAM and I/O blocks can be turned on much more directly and in any order. If you choose the RAM first, you can connect it to the system in one operation.

5–2.7 Turning on the RAM

With the RAM connected to the system, run the ROM test program (Fig. 5–14) briefly to verify operation. Pay particular attention to the timing of the RAM control signals during the RAM read and write instructions. The usual cause of failure at this point is a shorted address or data line, two lines shorted together, or an unwanted RAM response. With the ROM program verified, now run a RAM test.

A RAM test program should write to every location in memory, and then read each location back and verify the data. With an 8-bit-wide memory, watch out for the following problem.

The 8 bits of memory represent only 256 states. Conventional memories are usually much longer. This means that each possible data pattern must be written several times to fill the memory. If the same data words are written into each block of 256 words, an error in any of the higher-order addresses can be masked.

An extreme example of such masking is the case where all address lines are disconnected. Any slight change in the 256-word pattern, such as shifting the pattern one word location in each block, will reveal the problem. For example, if you count from 0 to 255 in the first block, you should count from 1 to 255, then go back to 0 in the next block. Next, count 2 to 255, and go back to 0 and 1 in the next block, and so on.

Figure 5–15 shows typical connections for testing the RAM functions. Figure 5–16 shows the flow chart of a RAM test program. This test program verifies that the memory system is working correctly, but does not provide a check of each cell at each memory location. However, you can design the program so that all locations are written and then read back. In addition to checking the data words at each address in RAM, check the timing of all RAM functions as discussed in Sec. 5–2.4.

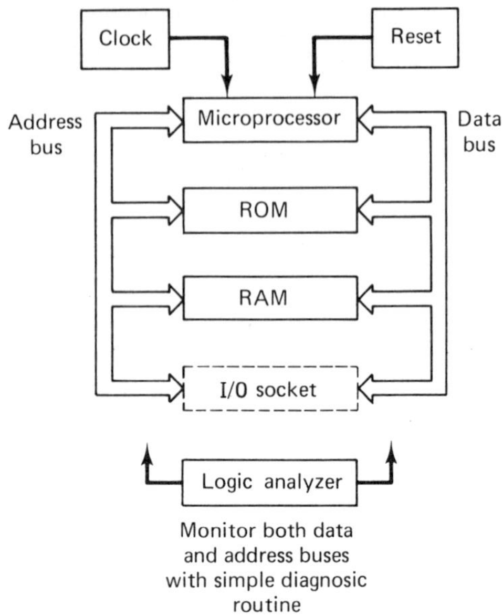

Fig. 5–15. Checking RAM functions with simple diagnostic routine

5–2.8 Turning on the I/O

Although the I/O section is relatively easy to turn on, the discussion here is somewhat general, since I/O structures vary more than other blocks from one system to another. The main point is to test the I/O ports before connection to the peripheral devices, such as keyboards, CRTs, or circuits to be controlled.

The first step is to connect the I/O ports into the circuit and then run the ROM test program (Fig. 5–14). This will verify that the control timing is correct with the I/Os in the system. Once you are satisified that timing is correct, and that input/output instructions can be executed, the next step is to test the I/O functions with diagnostic programs.

You can check the output ports easily with a simple program that first sets all the ports to 0, then sets each port in turn to 1, and finally sets each port back to 0, one at a time. When testing the output ports, connect the analyzer to one block at a time. If the analyzer has suffieient channels, connect these to the address bus, as well as the input/output ports, as shown in Fig. 5–17. The object of this exercise is to see if the output ports are connected in proper order and can be set both high and low.

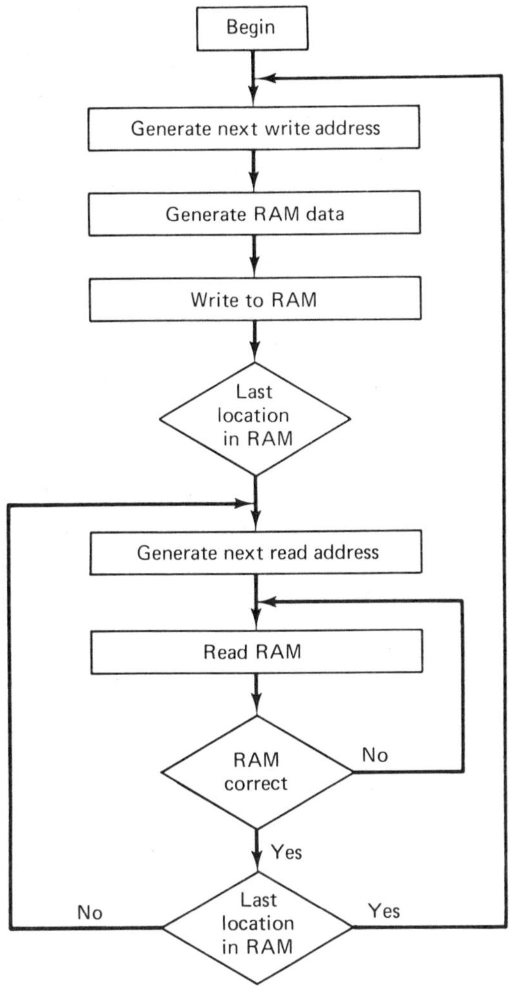

Fig. 5–16. Simple diagnostic routine to test RAM module

The input ports can be tested in a similar fashion. The program should check for each input high, then for each input low. Figure 5–18 shows a typical input port test program. This program loops until the input under test is forced to the desired state, then jumps to another loop. A simple approach is to pull all the inputs, either high or low through a resistor, as shown in Fig. 5–17.

Assume that you select the "high" approach. You then write a program that has two loops (Fig. 5–18). The first loop tests for a specific

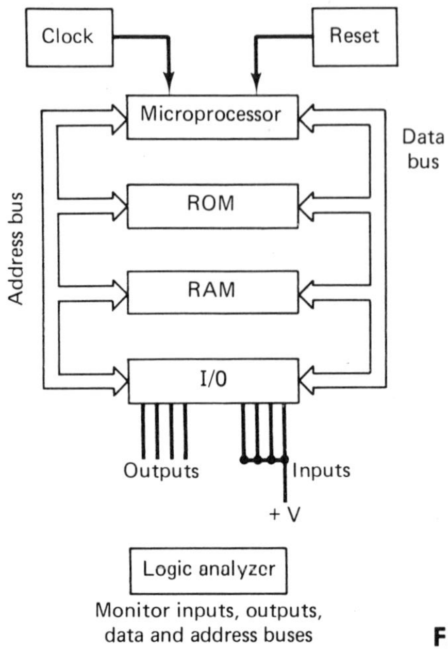

Fig. 5–17. Checking I/O functions

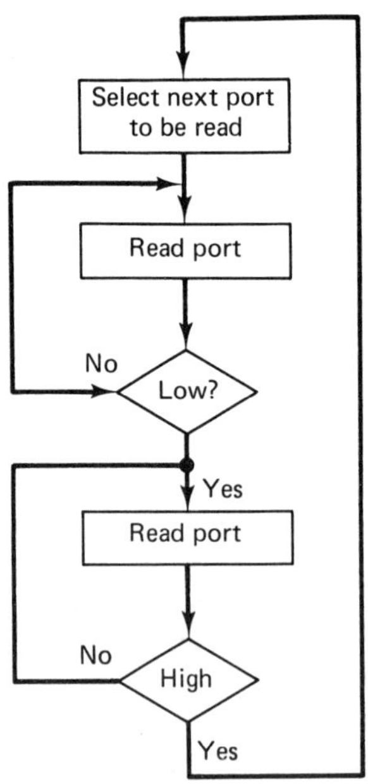

Fig. 5–18. Simple diagnostic routine to test I/O module input port

input low, and the second loop tests for that same input high. While the analyzer monitors the address bus and at least the one input under test (preferably all the inputs, if the analyzer has the capability), force the monitored input low with a grounded wire. Then the analyzer will show which loop the microprocessor is in, exactly when the input goes low, and (in a second pass) when the input goes high.

Although this process may seem tedious, the time required to write the test programs must be spent only once. The programs will then be available at every phase of system development.

5–2.9 Developing Software During Design and Troubleshooting

To be effective, software must be developed in sections, preferably at the same time as when the hardware sections are turned on. In this way, you can develop and test programs in manageable bytes. There are few, if any, wizards who can write a complete program and have it work the very first time. There are three approaches to developing software, just as there are for hardware. These approaches include single-step, simulator, and analyzer.

With any of the approaches, you must write a few steps of program, say to complete one function, and then test that section of program. The obvious drawback to single-stepping is that it is slow and tedious. A not so obvious drawback is that a program may work at the very slow speeds of single-stepping, but not work when the system is operated at normal speeds (1 to 3 MHz). A simulator (either a development system supplied by the microprocessor manufacturer or a large computer or computer time-sharing system) can be a valuable aid in testing complex portions of a program such as mathematical functions. However, it is uslly difficult to simulate I/O functions in software, and it is at the I/O ports that major trouble usually develops. It is generally more practical to write an I/O program, and then check the results using actual hardware wired in final form. This is where an analyzer can be of maximum benefit.

When using an analyzer in developing software, either for diagnostic routines or final program functions, it does not really matter whether the software has been simulated beforehand or not. (Of course, if a simulator is available, it can be a help in developing some parts of the hardware, as discussed above.) The main advantage of the analyzer approach is that the *hardware and software can be debugged at the same time*. Another advantage is that the analyzer can monitor the program flow in single steps, in a group of steps (typically 16 at a time), or can monitor the entire program in a single pass.

In debugging software, you use the analyzer in the same way as when debugging hardware. In fact, most of the hardware debugging techniques described in this section are simply a matter of developing a short program (or taking a section of a larger program), monitoring the flow of the program or section, and then fixing the hardware when the program does not work. (If you are troubleshooting an already developed system, you break the desired program into small sections, and check the flow through the sections.)

In reality, the process of debugging software is really more a problem of identifying the problem, deciding how the software and hardware contribute to the problem, and then doing the fix. The logic analyzer is the ideal tool in pinpointing whether software or hardware is the culprit. Once the hardware is checked out as described in this section (from the clock and reset, through the microprocessor, ROM and RAM, to the I/O), the software can be loaded in small blocks and tried out.

Although you can debug the software in any order, several rules may be helpful. It is usually best to turn on the keyboard or other entry device first, and then turn on any display or output device. That is, check the input/output routines of the program first. Next, turn on the remaining hardware and software together.

5–3. ANALYZING MICROCOMPUTER PROGRAM FLOW DURING TROUBLESHOOTING

This section describes how basic microcomputer program flow is analyzed during a typical troubleshooting sequence. These same procedures can also be used during design and development (or debugging) of a microcomputer system. The section concentrates on *real-time analysis* of program flow using an analyzer. Techniques such as triggering on a specific event and paging of program sections are discussed.

The microprocessor selected for discussion is the M6800 manufactured by Motorola Semiconductor Products, Inc. The M6800, which forms the nucleus of the M6800 microcomputer family, is discussed in Chapter 1. In brief, the M6800 features include a 16-bit three-state address bus (allowing 65K addressable bytes of memory) and a three-state 8-bit bidirectional data bus. The M6800 system, which includes both maskable and nonmaskable interrupts, operates at clock rates up to 1 MHz.

The first step in making the analysis is to connect the analyzer probes to the microcomputer system buses and control lines, and then operate the analyzer controls as necessary to produce the desired displays. The exact procedures for such connections and operating control sequence will depend on the analyzer. The procedures will be found in the analyzer user manuals. Here we shall concentrate on analyzing program flow.

In many cases, it is possible to analyze program flow by monitoring only the address bus. In other cases, it is necessary to monitor both the data and address buses, as well as some of the control lines (such as read/write and interrupt request). Section 5–3.1 illustrates an example of program flow analysis using nothing but the address bus. Section 5–3.2 illustrates how analysis of the same program flow can be expanded by monitoring both buses and certain control lines.

Keep in mind that all analyzers are not capable of monitoring all these functions, and the program format will vary with the type of microprocessor involved. Also, the display format is not the same for all analyzers. However, the same basic procedures will apply to analysis of program flow.

5–3.1 Analyzing Program Flow with Address Bus Display Only

Figure 5–19 illustrates system response to an interrupt, and compares the real-time state analysis (as displayed on an analyzer) to the M6800 cross-assembler program listing. The M6800 microprocessor responds to an interrupt in the following sequence:

First, the microprocessor completes the current instruction. Next the microprocessor stores the contents of its registers on a stack in memory (as discussed in Chapter 1). Next the program counter is loaded with an interrupt service routine vector fetched from memory locations FFF8 (program counter high, PCH) and FFF9 (program counter low, PCL). Finally, the microprocessor begins execution of the interrupt service routine at the vectored location.

Consider the program listing of Fig. 5–19b. Observe the vector routine beginning at location 274C with the instruction LDA B $1A80. This is a three-byte instruction: the first byte (F6) is the operation code, with the second (1A) and third (80) being a double byte operand. In this case the operand is an extended address.

Proper operation of the vector fetch is confirmed by observing that the address *immediately following* the intensified trigger word FFF9 (Fig. 5–19a) is 274C. This means that the microprocessor fetched 27 from FFF8 and 4C from FFF9.

The LDA B $1A80 may be confirmed by observing the second,

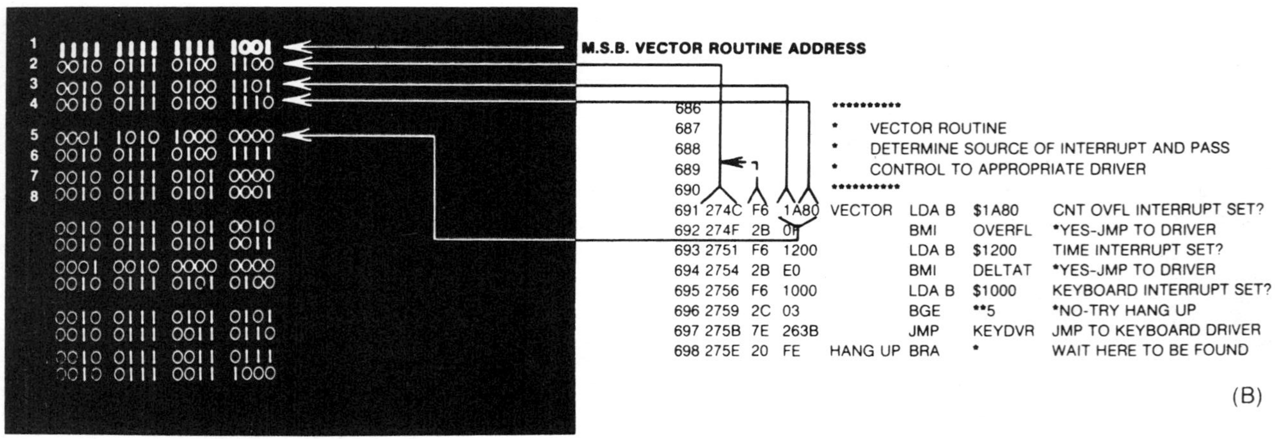

(A) (B)

Fig. 5–19. M6800 system response to an interrupt

third, and fourth lines of the state analysis display (Fig. 5–19a). Line 2, address 274C, is the fetch of the operation code LDA B (F6), and lines 3 and 4 are the fetch of 1A80. Address 274D contains 1A, and address 274E contains 80. The next line (line 5) shows the address to be 1A80, which implies correct execution of the instruction in the routine. In a similar fashion, each instruction may be shown to have been properly executed.

5–3.2 Analyzing Program Flow with Full Display

Figure 5–20 illustrates an amplification of the example described in Sec. 5–3.1 (analysis of an interrupt response) and shown in Fig. 5–19. As shown in Fig. 5–20, when the address and data buses, as well as the control lines (interrupt request IRQ and read/write) are monitored by the analyzer, it is possible to confirm exact system operation with respect to an interrupt response, including the storing of microprocessor registers on the stack.

With reference to lines 0 through 2 of Fig. 5–20a, observe that the IRQ line is low (at 0) for three clock periods. This signals the microprocessor to begin executing an interrupt service operation. Confirmation that the microprocessor completed the current instruction is shown in lines 3 and 4 of Fig. 5–20a.

Similarly, it can be shown that the microprocessor saved the internal registers on the stack by an examination of lines 4 through 11. Line 4 shows the completion of the current instruction at location 2674. Line 5 shows the least significant byte of this address (74) being written into location OFFD, while the read/write line is low (0), or in the "write" mode. Line 6 shows the corresponding operation for the most significant byte or the program counter (26) being written into location OFFC. This process continues until all registers have been stored on the stack as shown in Fig. 5–21. You can see that seven stack locations are required to save the microprocessor status. This may be confirmed by lines 5 through 11 inclusive of Fig. 5–20a.

As discussed in Sec. 5–3.1, the microprocessor then reads memory locations FFF8 and FFF9 to set the interrupt service vector. Observe that the program listing (Fig. 5–20b) defines this to be 274C, which means that memory location FFF8 must contain the data 27, and FFF9 must contain 4C.

These functions are confirmed by lines 12 and 13 of Fig. 5–20a. Also observe that fetch was executed properly, as the next address following FFF9 is 274C (line 14). In addition, the data at location 274C are F6 (Fig. 5–20b), which corresponds with the program listing.

(A)

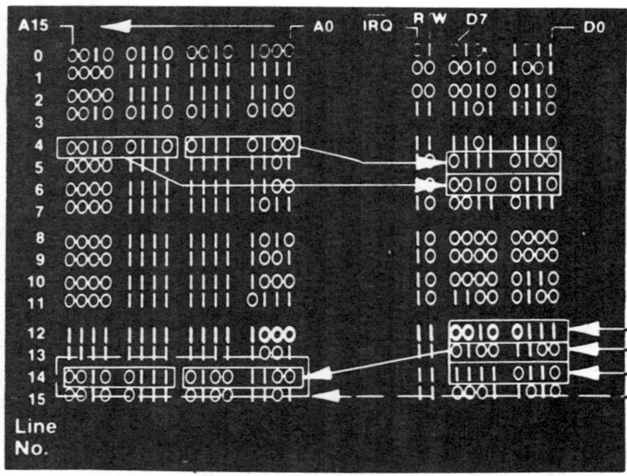

NOTE: The conditions on the $\overline{IRQ}$ line are shown for a system without the PIA chip. With PIA's the $\overline{IRQ}$ line remains low until the PIA with interrupt flag set is found and read.

(B)

```
                        **********
                        *     VECTOR ROUTINE
                        *     DETERMINE SOURCE OF INTERRUPT AND PASS
                        *     CONTROL TO APPROPRIATE DRIVER
                        **********
274C F6  1A80  VECTOR   LDA B  $1A80   CNT OVFL INTERRUPT SET?
274F 2B  0F             BMI    OVERFL  *YES-JMP TO DRIVER
2751 F6  1200           LDA B  $1200   TIME INTERRUPT SET?
2754 2B  E0             BMI    DELTAT  *YES-JMP TO DRIVER
2756 F6  1000           LDA B  $1000   KEYBOARD INTERRUPT SET?
2759 2C  03             BGE    **5     *NO-TRY HANG UP
275B 7E  263B           JMP    KEYDVR  JMP TO KEYBOARD DRIVER
275E 20  FE    HANG UP  BRA    *       WAIT HERE TO BE FOUND
```

Fig. 5–20. M6800 system response to an interrupt on address, data, and control lines

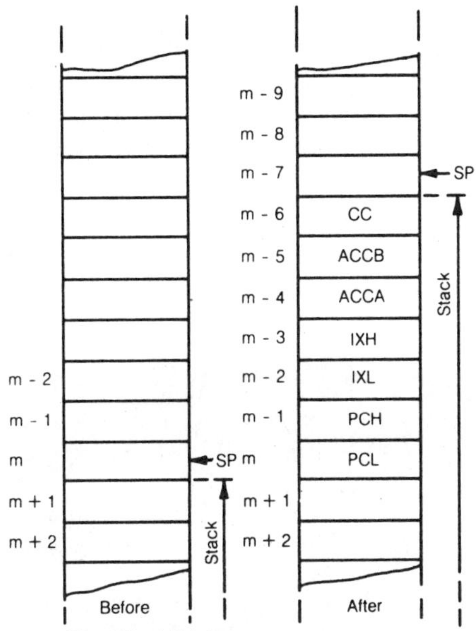

SP = Stack Pointer
CC = Condition Codes (Also called the Processor Status Byte)
ACCB = Accumulator B
ACCA = Accumulator A
IXH = Index Register, Higher Order 8 Bits
IXL = Index Register, Lower Order 8 Bits
PCH = Program Counter, Higher Order 8 Bits
PCL = Program Counter, Lower Order 8 Bits

Fig. 5–21. Saving the status of the microprocessor in the stack

5–4. USING THE HEWLETT PACKARD 1610A LOGIC STATE ANALYZER

This section describes the use of the 1610A logic analyzer for various troubleshooting situations. As discussed in Sec. 3–9, the 1610A is keyboard controlled, provides a tabular display and a graph display (instead of a map function), and offers general-purpose measurements for microcomputers. Although the following paragraphs provide specific information necessary to set up and use the 1610A (use of controls, display functions, etc.), the troubleshooting situations or problems described here are common to many microcomputers. When you understand the problems, you can adapt the features of other analyzers to solve the troubleshooting situations. Of course, all the 1610A features are not always available in other analyzers.

5–4.1 Format Specification (Setting up the Data Inputs)

In this example, the data pod (or probe) and the clock pod are plugged into the read panel ports on the 1610A. When power is applied to the 1610A, the *format specification* menu is automatically displayed, as shown in Fig. 5–22. The test conditions are set to positive clock slope (+), all inputs are labeled F in hex display code, and logic is positive. The 1610A is now ready to acquire data without any other setup required.

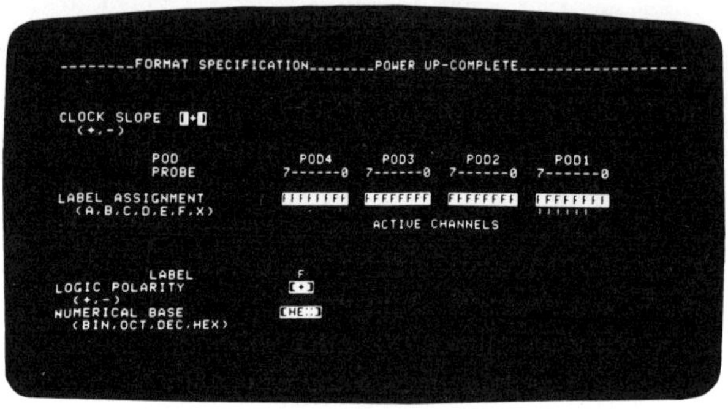

Fig. 5–22. Format specification display

Pressing the *trace* key results in a *trace list* similar to that in Fig. 5–23. Note that this list has data only in the two right-hand columns. In hex, this means activity on all eight channels of pod 1. Now switch back to the format specification menu (Fig. 5–22), and you will see that this activity is also evident as indicated by the exclamation marks. (The two least significant bits of the data pod do not indicate channel activity with the pod connected to the self-test port.)

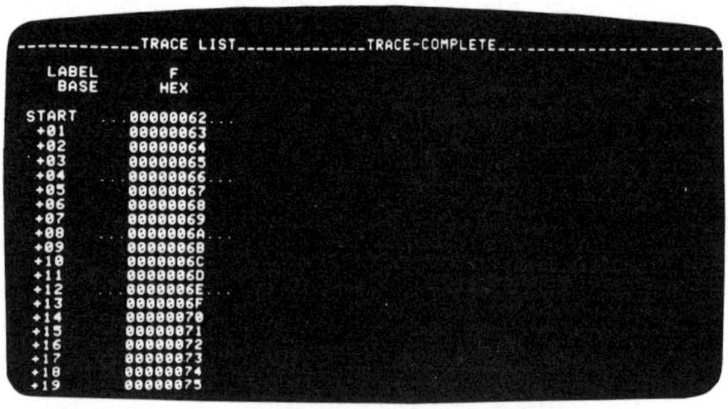

Fig. 5–23. Trace list of the results of the format specification

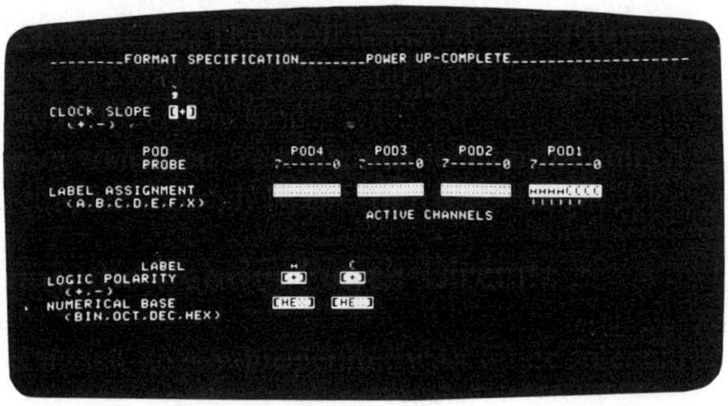

Fig. 5–24. Format specification showing how labels may be assigned to group data for easier interpretation

There are now many ways to set up the input channels in the format specification. For example, all unused inputs could be turned off (so they would not be displayed) by positioning the cursor in the appropriate pod display and entering "don't cares" (as indicated by an ×) in all pods, except pod 1. Since pod 1 is connected to a two-unit hex counter, it might be desirable to display each unit separately by assigning a different label to each counter. In this example, arbitrarily assign label A to the upper unit counter and label C to the lower unit counter, as shown in Fig. 5–24. Pressing the trace key now provides a trace list, as shown in Fig. 5–25, with the display listed by label and in hex format.

If desired, the numerical base for label C could be changed to binary, as shown in Fig. 5–26. The resultant trace list would be as in Fig. 5–27. Any combination of labels or numerical base selection can be

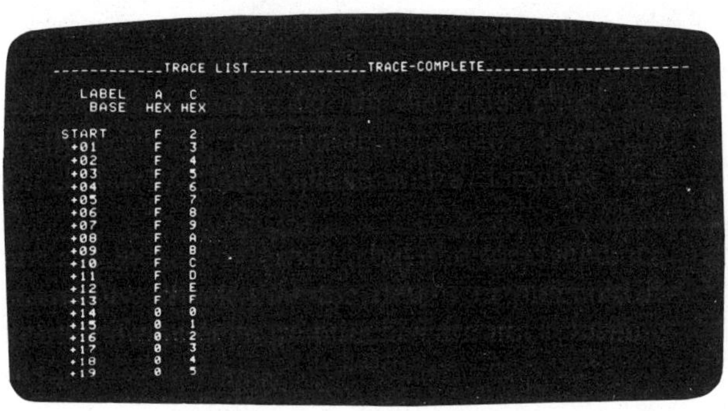

Fig. 5–25. Trace list with display listed by label and in hex format

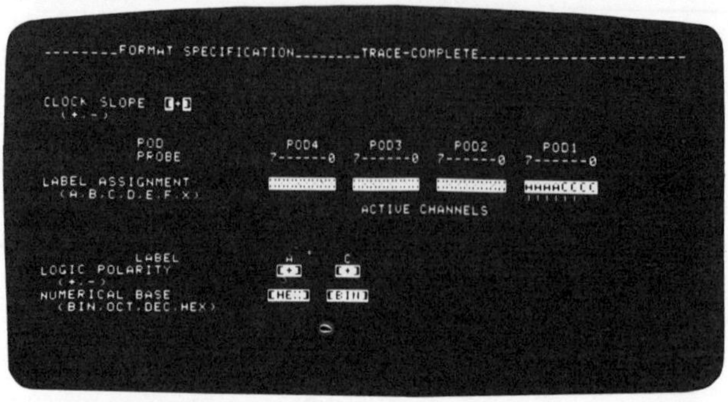

Fig. 5–26. Display showing the base of label C changed to binary

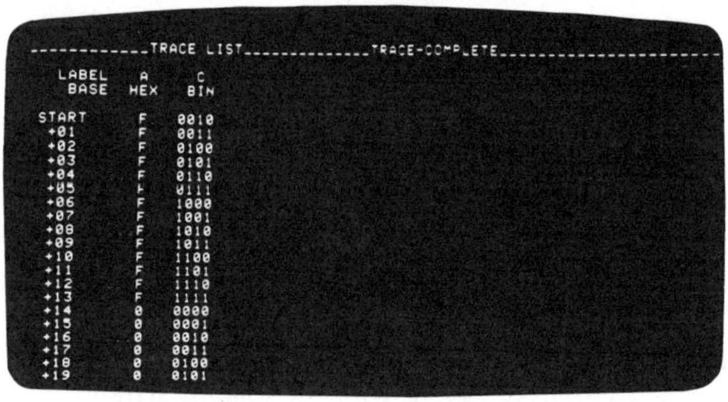

Fig. 5–27. Resulting trace list of format specification in Fig. 5–26 showing label C data displayed in binary

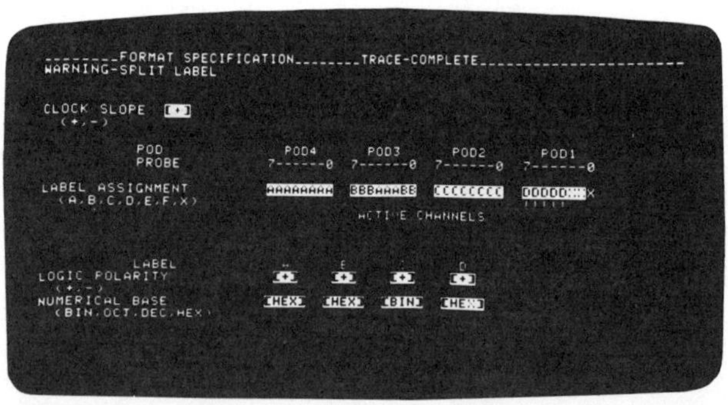

Fig. 5–28. Display showing mixed labels (the 1610A detects the illogical condition and requests an error correction)

assigned to the input channels. However, if labels are not assigned sequentially, but are mixed as shown in Fig. 5–28, an illogical condition results and the 1610A will request a correction of the error (such as the note WARNING-SPLIT LABEL on Fig. 5–28).

5–4.2 Trace Specification

The *trace specification* menu, which is called to the display with the trace specification key, permits the user to define what data will be acquired as well as how they will be acquired. Notice that the label base at the top of the display (Figs. 5–23, 5–25, and 5–27) is as it was defined from the format specification (Figs. 5–22, 5–24, and 5–26).

The next function to enter is the *trigger conditions* for the trace. The conditions are entered by positioning the cursor in the desired label and entering the trigger word. A trigger value may be entered for each field selected in the format specification. The trigger condition may be positioned to start a trace, be in the center of a trace, or end a trace. For even more trace conditioning, the *insert* and *delete* edit keys may be used to specify up to seven levels of sequential triggering. In addition, each level of triggering may be specified to occur a multiple number of times (1 to 65,536) before its sequential condition is satisfied. The following explanations will demonstrate the ability of the 1610A to trace simple as well as very complex program flow.

Trace Sequence. For simple in-line program flow such as shown in Fig. 5–29, the trace specification is set to detect state 2848_{16}, and then trace the program flow until memory is full (63 remaining states).

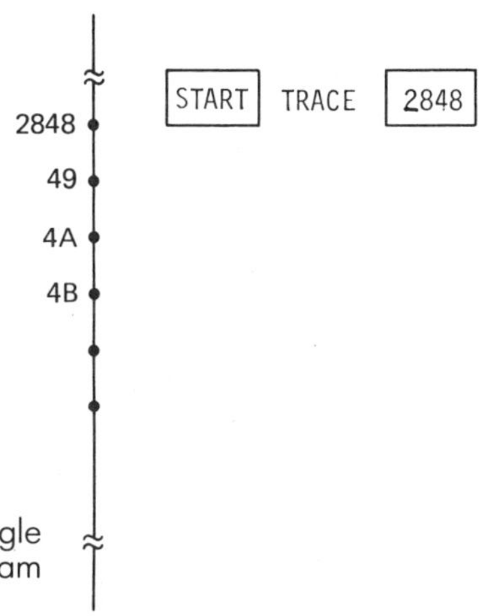

Fig. 5–29. Trace specification with a single state trigger for acquiring in-line program flow

Now, if a branch (Fig. 5–30) is added around the in-line flow of Fig. 5–29, sequential conditions must be added to the trace specification to be able to trace a specific branch. As shown in Fig. 5–30, the 1610A will first have to recognize state 2848_{16}, then $287F_{16}$, and the trace list will start at state $284D_{16}$.

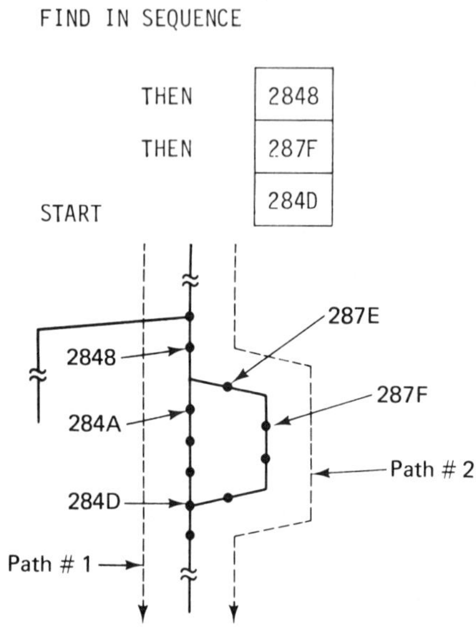

Fig. 5–30. Trace specification for tracing a specific branch of program flow

Unfortunately for the troubleshooter, programs rarely are as simple as those shown in Figs. 5–29 and 5–30. The program in Fig. 5–31 is the level of network branching more commonly found, even in simple microcomputers. Figure 5–31 also shows the trace specification for following a specific path (given as path 2) through the network.

In addition to being able to follow a particular branch of a network, the sequence capability of the 1610A has the ability to acquire parameters (such as data values at specific addresses) that will be used in later subroutines. For example, if it is necessary to evaluate that a multiplication subroutine is operating properly, it is necessary to look at the program flow of the subroutine, as well as the parameters that were used as the multiplier and multiplicand. Normally, the parameter would occur well ahead of the subroutine and be loaded into registers to be recalled later and used in the subroutine. The sequence capability, as shown in Fig. 5–32, allows the data at addresses $286A_{16}$, $286D_{16}$, and 2877_{16} to be acquired. When the trace starts at $29A7_{16}$, the parameters

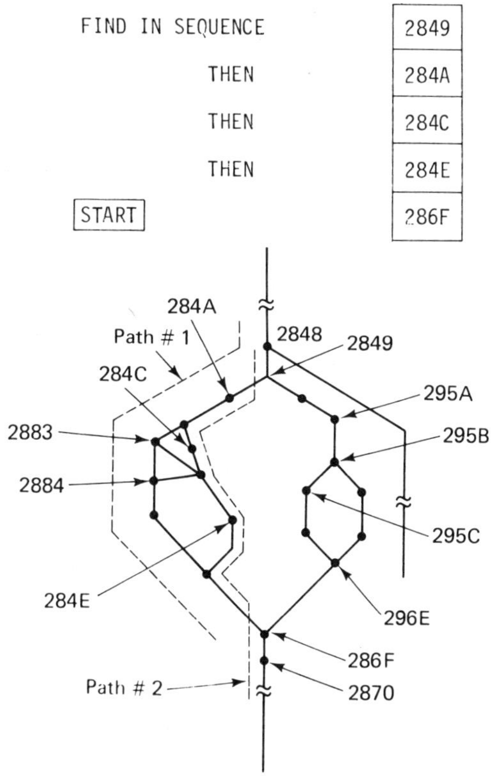

Fig. 5–31. Trace specification for tracing a specific path in a program with a complex (but commonly encountered) branching network

are displayed in the trace list just prior to the trace listing, as shown in Fig. 5–33.

Sequence Restart. In addition to being able to follow a specific path in a complex network, it is often necessary to analyze program flow only if the path was completed in one pass. In some complex networks, such as shown in Fig. 5–34, it is possible to first follow the sequential conditions of path 1 (satisfying states 2849_{16} and $284A_{16}$,) and then exit the network. This means that the 1610A would be looking for the next sequential condition $284C_{16}$. When the program returns to this network and follows path 3, the remaining conditions are satisfied, and the 1610A would capture the data. However, the resultant trace list, beginning at state 286F, would not show the correct activity for a path 2 branch.

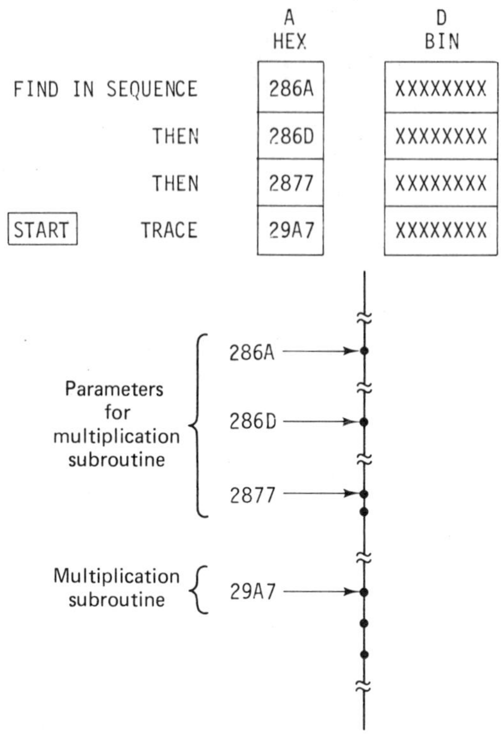

Fig. 5–32. Trace specification demonstrating how the 1610A would be set to acquire the parameters that would be used in a subsequent program subroutine

```
---------TRACE LIST---------TRACE COMPLETE---------

LABEL          A             D
BASE          HEX           BIN

SEQUENCE...  286A.......01101000
SEQUENCE...  286D        10000111
SEQUENCE     2877        11101001
 START       29A7        00000000
  +01        29A8        00011001
  +02        29A9        10011000
  +03        29AA        11100000
  +04          ↓            ↓
  +05
```

Fig. 5–33. Resultant trace list of Fig. 5–32 showing the parameters in the D label that will be used in a subroutine starting at $29A7_{16}$

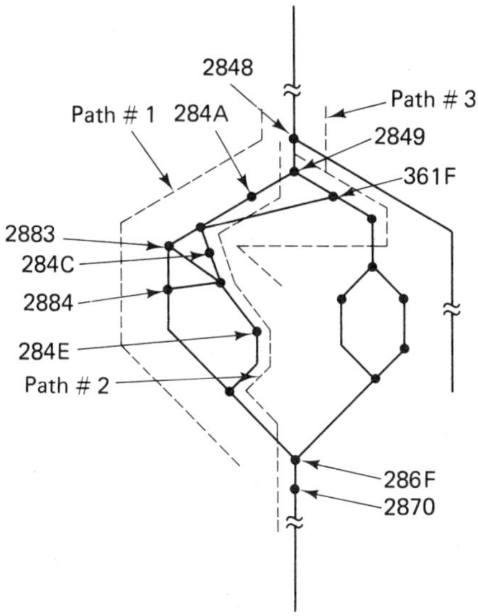

FIND IN SEQUENCE	2849
THEN	284A
THEN	284C
THEN	284E
START	286F
SEQ RESTART ON	2870

Fig. 5–34. Trace specification for tracing a specific path (path 2, Fig. 5–31) in a branching network and using sequence restart on an exit state to guarantee that the specific path is satisified after only one pass through the network

By turning the *sequence restart* function of the analyzer on, and specifying an exit (or entry) state of the network, the 1610A will monitor both the sequential condition and the restart condition. This examination is done simultaneously on each state acquired. If the sequence condition is satisfied, the analyzer will advance to the next state, disregarding whether restart is satisfied or not. If the sequence was not satisfied and the restart was satisfied, then a restart will be executed on the entire sequence.

As an example, if path 1 (Fig. 5–34) was initially followed, states 2849_{16} and $284A_{16}$ would be satisfied. However, path 1 would lead to exit state 2870_{16}, which would recycle to the first sequence state of 2849_{16}. Note that a sequence restart state at the entry of the network at state 2848_{16} would have worked just as well as the exit state for a sequence restart.

Another major difficulty found in tracing program flow is to trace a *direct jump* (sometimes called a *zero path branch*). The three common forms of program paths, *variable, fixed* and *zero length,* are shown in Fig. 5–35. Defining a trace on branch 1 (variable) or branch 3 (fixed) is easy with a sequential state trace specification. However, the zero length (branch 2) cannot be defined reliably by specifying "find in sequence 2849_{16}, start $287C_{16}$," because either branch 1 or branch 3 will also satisfy these conditions.

The solution for capturing a zero length branch is to use a sequence restart with a restart state of don't cares (all ×s). With a don't care restart state, the 1610A will first look to see if a sequence condition is satisfied and, if not, will then examine if the restart condition is satified. Now, if branch 1 or 3 is followed, a state after 2849_{16} other than 287C will be found, the restart condition (don't care) will be satisfied, and the 1610A will return and look for a 2849_{16}. Only when the sequence of 2849_{16}, directly followed by $287C_{16}$, is found will a trace bc captured.

Multiple Occurrences. Another form of program flow is the *nested loop* (Chapter 1) in which a set of states occurs a number of

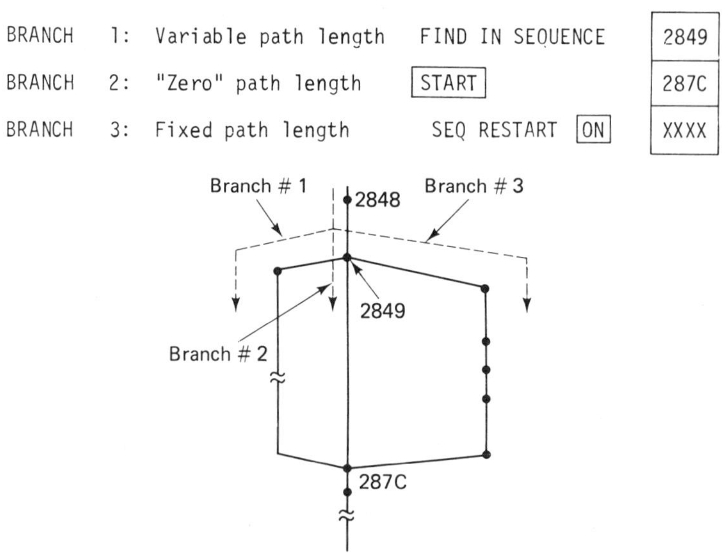

Fig. 5–35. Trace specification for tracing a zero length branch (direct jump) using sequence restart

times prior to advancing the program. These subloops within loops are referred to as *nesting* (Chapter 1). An example of programs requiring nested loops would be a microcomputer that progressively samples many peripherals (a major loop), receives data from each peripheral (a minor loop), and then formats the data from each data transmission (a subminor loop). The need for tracing loops is common where it is necessary to examine program activity only when it is working on the *n*th pass of a subminor loop, such as examining the sixth data format of the fourth data transmission of peripheral 3.

The 1610A is capable of determining the number of occurrences of each state sequence. This allows nested loop routines to be traced. The three-level nested loop in Fig. 5–36 has a major loop (I) that repeats

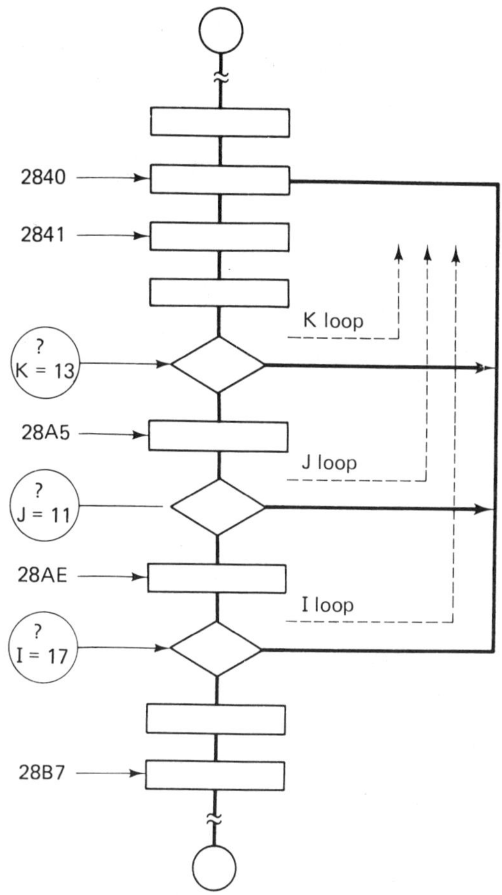

Fig. 5–36. Typical example of a three-level nested loop

(or iterates) 17 times, a minor loop (J) that iterates 11 times for each occurrence of the I loop, and a subminor loop (K) that interates 13 times for each occurrence of the J loop and 143 times for each occurrence of the I loop. The trace specification in Fig. 5–37 will direct the 1610A to acquire data at state 2841_{16} only when the program is in the ninth pass of the I loop, the eighth pass of the J loop, and the seventh pass of the K loop. Note that the occurrence counter for each state is represented as a decimal number for ease of use. The range of each counter is from 1 to 65,535.

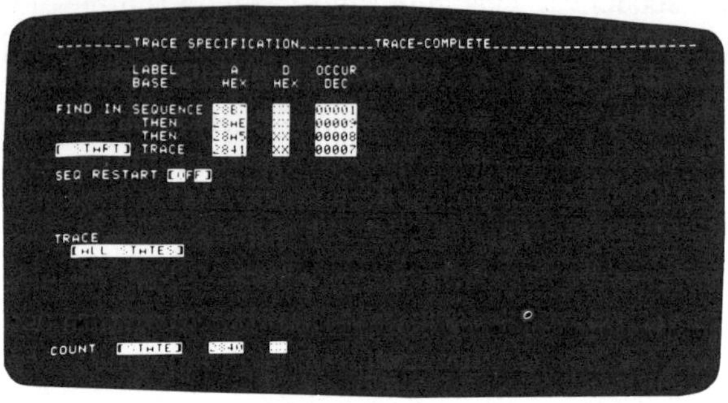

Fig. 5–37. Trace specification that will direct the 1610A to acquire data in a nested loop at specified passes through each loop

5–4.3 Digital Delay

Many logic analyzers provide digital delay for the examination of data at some point that is at a number of clock pulses from a reference state or a trigger point. As shown in Fig. 5–35, the digital delay capability is useful only for a path of fixed length (branch 3 for example). Trying to examine a variable path length using a preset delay will cause variation in acquired data.

However, if proper sequence states are unknown to define a specific path of fixed length, then digital delay is useful. Digital delay, while not specified directly, can be easily implemented on the 1610A by specifying a sequence state of all don't cares and using the occurrence counter to determine the delay. A trace specification for a single state trace point with delay (from 1 to 65,536) is shown in Fig. 5–38. Maximum delay in the 1610A is 393,216, and is implemented with six sequences, also as shown in Fig. 5–38.

Setting up the Data to be Acquired. The next step after defining where information will be traced (the trace sequence) is to decide what information is to be stored in memory. There are two possible modes

```
                                                OCCUR
                                                 DEC
FIND IN SEQUENCE     2848      XX              00001
START                XXXX      XX              00837

                                                OCCUR
                                                 DEC
FIND IN SEQUENCE     2848      XX              00001
            THEN     XXXX      XX              65536
            THEN     XXXX      XX              65536
            THEN     XXXX      XX              65536
            THEN     XXXX      XX              65536
            THEN     XXXX      XX              65536
START      TRACE     XXXX      XX              65536
```

Fig. 5–38. Digital delay is implemented by specifying "don't cares" as a sequence condition and using the occurrence counter for delaying the window; the maximum delay that can be implemented is 393,216 (6 × 65,536)

to select in the 1610A: (1) tracing all states, (2) or tracing only specific states. The *trace all* mode is self-explanatory in that all states occurring after the specified trigger conditions are stored. The *trace only* mode allows the user to selectively edit program flow and acquire information only of interest.

By using the *insert* and *delete* key when the cursor is in the trace only field, additional lines (up to seven) can be added to permit seven choices of qualification, as shown in Fig. 5–39. Note that there can only

```
-------TRACE SPECIFICATION----TRACE COMPLETE-------

                LABEL              A             OCCUR
                BASE              HEX             DEC

START           TRACE             XXXX           00001

TRACE

ONLY STATE                        XXXX           00001
       OR                         XXXX
       OR                         XXXX
       OR                         XXXX
       OR                         XXXX
       OR                         XXXX
       OR                         XXXX
       OR                         XXXX
COUNT        OFF
```

Fig. 5–39. Display showing trace only field, which permits seven choices of qualification for acquiring only information of interest

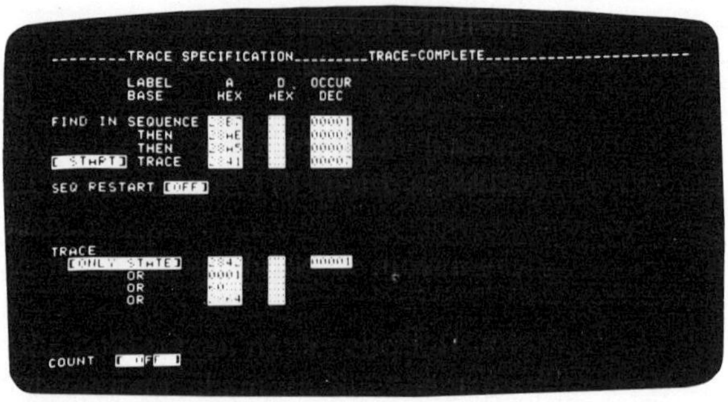

Fig. 5–40. Display showing the trace specification for acquiring the nested loop in Fig. 5–36

be a total of eight specifications for trace sequence and trace only. That is, if three trace sequence conditions are defined, then only five trace only states remain available. Figure 5–40 shows the trace specification for the nested loop of Fig. 5–36. Since there were four trace sequence conditions specified, only four trace only states remain available. These states were selected to be 2842_{16}, 0001_{16}, $60XX_{16}$, and 2864_{16}. When data are acquired,only specific states 2892_{16}, 0001_{16}, 2864_{16}, and anything within the range from 6000_{16} to $60FF_{16}$ are stored in memory. Figure 5–41 is the resultant trace list for this trace specification.

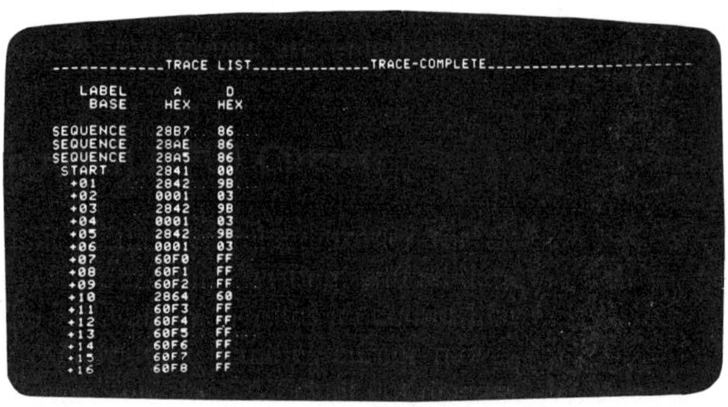

Fig. 5–41. Resulting trace list for the trace specification of Fig. 5–40

To further reduce the acquired information, as well as the need to view data that are not of interest (and thus eliminate the need for a large memory in the analyzer), a *multiple occurrence counter* on trace only is available. The effect of this counter is to permit the periodic acquistion of the specified states only after they have occurred the number of times set in the counter. For example, if it is specified to trace only state 2842_{16}, with an occurrence of eight, then only every eighth occurrence of state 2842_{16} will be stored, thereby increasing the memory capacity by a factor of 8. This capability is also very important when used with the *trace graph* (Sec. 5–4.8) to expand or contract the horizontal time base.

5–4.4 Count measurements

Microcomputers are often compared on the basis of quantitative evaluations, such as (1) the *elapsed time interval* for two different microcomputers to execute the same programs, (2) the time interval for one microcomputer to execute two different programs (to measure program efficiency), or (3) counting events during execution of specific programs (such as the number of byte transfers during a direct memory access, or DMA). These functional measurements give users the insight as to which microcomputer to buy, how to optimize programs by detecting slow, inefficient subroutines, and, in general, where problems exist in systems.

The 1610A has two modes of displaying time interval and state count measurements, the *absolute* and *relative* modes. The difference between the two modes is simply the choice of one reference point. In the absolute mode, the count is between the start (center, or end) of the trace, and the acquired state (Fig. 5–42). In the relative mode, the count is between each state and the previously acquired state (Fig. 5–43). These two modes allow maximum flexibility for making evaluations such as benchmarks (Sec. 5–4.5), or optimizing programs, and detecting errors.

5–4.5 Benchmarks

Peforming a benchmark that represents a valid figure of merit for a microcomputer system is generally quite difficult. Such considerations as word size, functional intent of the architecture, I/O techniques, and so on, all contribute to the total evaluation of a system. The elapsed time interval for the execution of a specific task is one of the important considerations. Figure 5–44 shows a setup for a trace specification to measure the time intervals of the sample program that is composed of four segments.

Quite often, it is important to know not only the total program time, but the time of each segment. The resultant trace list of Fig. 5–45 indicates the total program time of 2.168 s between $617E_{16}$ (the beginning) and $A83C_{16}$ (the end of the program). Since this is the absolute

--------TRACE LIST--------TRACE-COMPLETE-----------------------------

	LABEL BASE	A HEX	D HEX		TIME DEC
SEQUENCE		28B7	86	-	1.183 S
SEQUENCE		28AE	86	-	94.05 MS
SEQUENCE		28A5	86	-	6.049 MS
START		2841	00		0 US
+01		2842	9B	+	4.0 US
+02		0001	03	+	8.0 US
+03		2842	9B	+	481.9 US
+04		0001	03	+	485.9 US
+05		2842	9B	+	959.9 US
+06		0001	03	+	963.9 US
+07		60F0	FF	+	1.079 MS
+08		60F1	FF	+	1.087 MS
+09		60F2	FF	+	1.095 MS
+10		2864	60	+	1.099 MS
+11		60F3	FF	+	1.103 MS
+12		60F4	FF	+	1.111 MS
+13		60F5	FF	+	1.119 MS
+14		60F6	FF	+	1.127 MS
+15		60F7	FF	+	1.135 MS
+16		60F8	FF	+	1.145 MS

Fig. 5–42. Time interval displayed in the absolue mode shows the time between the trace position and the acquired state

mode, all states occurring prior to the start are shown as minus (–). Similarly, the beginning time of all the segments is shown referenced to the end of the program (or start of the trace).

Figure 5–46 gives the time interval in relative mode. (The count measurement is done simultaneously with the trace of data. Selecting either absolute or relative merely changes the output display and does

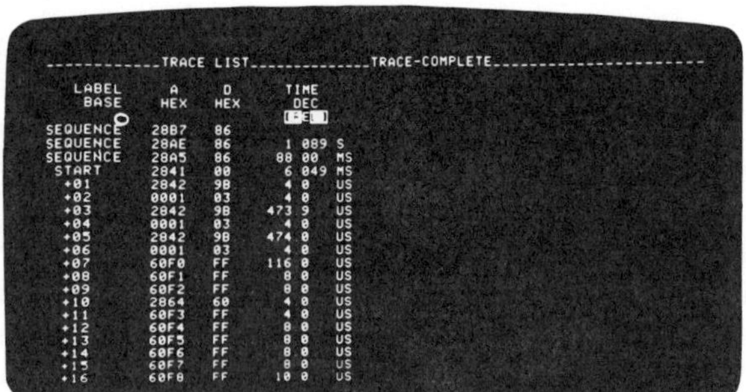
------------TRACE LIST-------------TRACE-COMPLETE--------------------

LABEL BASE	A HEX	D HEX	TIME DEC
SEQUENCE	28B7	86	
SEQUENCE	28AE	86	1 089 S
SEQUENCE	28A5	86	88 00 MS
START	2841	00	6 049 MS
+01	2842	9B	4 0 US
+02	0001	03	4 0 US
+03	2842	9B	473 9 US
+04	0001	03	4 0 US
+05	2842	9B	474 0 US
+06	0001	03	4 0 US
+07	60F0	FF	116 0 US
+08	60F1	FF	8 0 US
+09	60F2	FF	8 0 US
+10	2864	60	4 0 US
+11	60F3	FF	4 0 US
+12	60F4	FF	8 0 US
+13	60F5	FF	8 0 US
+14	60F6	FF	8 0 US
+15	60F7	FF	8 0 US
+16	60F8	FF	10 0 US

Fig. 5–43. Time interval in the relative mode shows the time between each state and the previously acquired state

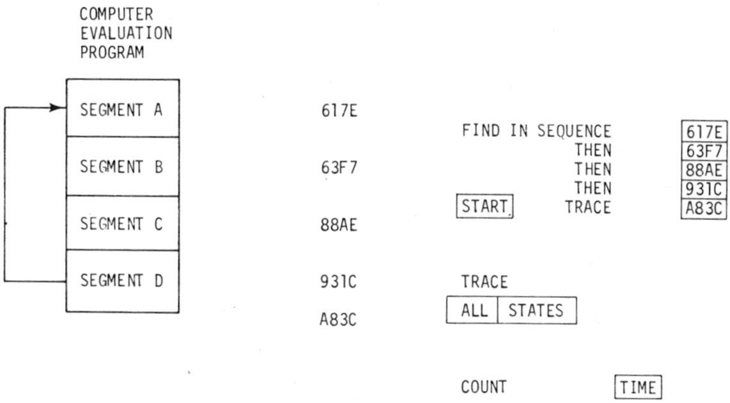

Fig. 5–44. Trace specification for a benchmark test that evaluates the time for two systems to execute the same program

-----------TRACE LIST-----------------TRACE COMPLETE------------

LABEL BASE	A HEX		TIME DEC ABS
SEQUENCE	617E	-	2.168 s
SEQUENCE	63F7	-	75.89 ms
SEQUENCE	88AE		7.395 ms
SEQUENCE	931C	-	87.0 us
START	A83C		.0
+01			
+02			
+03			

Fig. 5–45. Trace list of a benchmark showing a time interval measurement of specific states referenced to the start of the trace (absolute mode)

----------------------TRACE LIST---------------TRACE COMPLETE----------------

LABEL BASE	A HEX	TIME DEC REL
SEQUENCE	617E	
SEQUENCE	63F7	2.092 s
SEQUENCE	88AE	68.53 ms
SEQUENCE	931C	7.272 ms
START	A83C	87.0 us
+01		
+02		
+03		

Fig. 5–46. Trace list of a benchmark showing a time interval measurement of specific program segments; the interval is referenced to the previously acquired state (relative mode)

not require rerunning the measurement.) In relative mode, the individual elapsed time of each segment is displayed. Here the interval is between each state and the previous state.

5–4.6 Detecting Program Errors

Being able to analyze the amount of time spent between two successive states in a microcomputer has proved to be invaluable in rapidly spotting errors or conditions leading to errors. Examination of Fig. 5–43 shows some interesting activity at states +03, +05, and +07. The elapsed time between these states and the previous state (which always had address = 0001_{16} and data = 03) is 473.9, 474.0, and 116.0μs, respectively. The question could immediately be asked as to why it took so much more time to go from state 0001_{16} to 2842_{16} (474.0 μs) than it did to go from 0001_{16} to $60F0_{16}$ (116.0 μs)? A detailed examination of the program coding is required to answer this question specifically, but it only requires a brief look at relative elapsed time to locate the apparent problem.

5–4.7 Verification of Program Activity

Once a program has been written to perform a task, the next step is to run the program and verify that the program actually does the task. It is sometimes possible to be fooled by a program. For example, a program may eventually perform its task, but may also perform other nondesired activities. By analyzing the program states using a state count in the absolute and relative modes, the programmer can easily verify the program coding.

An example of this is found in the nested loop program of Fig. 5–36. To verify that the program actually executed the number of loops that were specified, count the number of occurrences of state 2840_{16}, and then compare this count to what was programmed. Figure 5–47 shows the calculation of how many times a state (2840_{16}) of the innermost loop should occur before the trace (as specified) begins. The resultant trace list of a relative count of state 2840_{16} is shown in Fig. 5–48. As shown, the count is exactly as calculated. That is, 1287 counts of state 2840_{16} occurred between $28B7_{17}$ and the ninth occurrence of $28AE_{16}$, and 104 counts of 2840_{16} occurred between the ninth occurrence of $28AE_{16}$ and the eighth occurence of $28A5_{16}$, and so on.

However, Fig. 5–49 shows the same data displayed in the absolute mode. Here the number of states of 2840_{16} between $28B7_{16}$ and 2841_{16} (the total before the trace starts) is shown to be 1398 (exactly as calculated in Fig. 5–47).

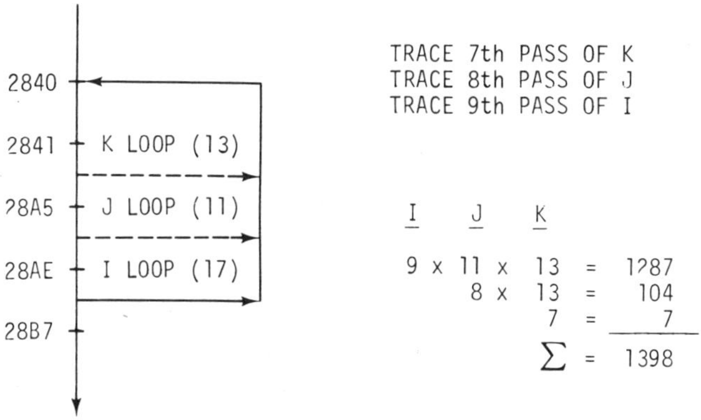

Fig. 5–47. Calculation of how many times state 2840_{16} of the innermost loop should occur before the specified trace should begin

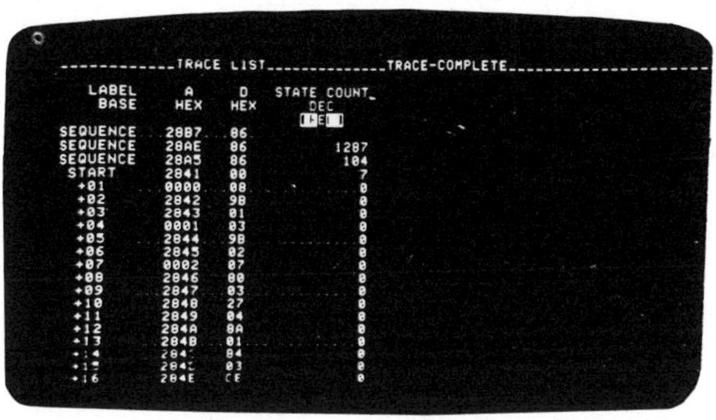

Fig. 5–48. Resultant trace list of a relative count of state 2840_{16} as defined in Fig. 5–47

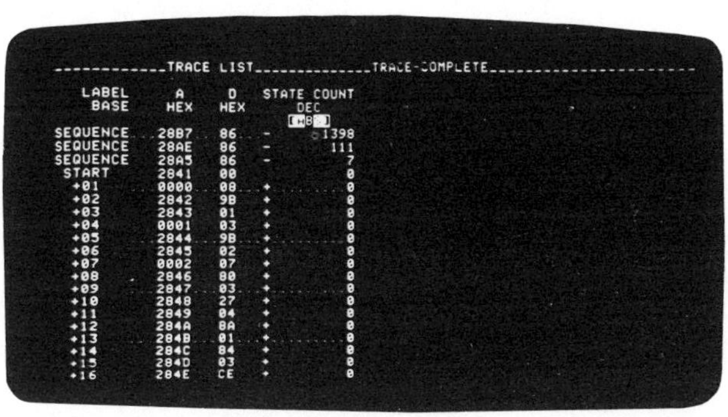

Fig. 5–49. Resultant trace list in the absolute count mode shown to be as calculated in Fig. 5–47

5–4.8 System Overview Using a State Flow Graph

The ability to monitor the general activity of certain areas in a system is a fundamental logic analysis tool. Many analyzers use mapping for such monitoring. (Mapping is discussed further in Sec. 5–5.) The 1610A uses a different graph display that allows the user additional help in monitoring general or overall activity of a microcomputer.

There are four criteria that must be satisfied to permit a rapid, meaningful overview of program state flow: (1) relative state magnitude, (2) state-to-state directional flow, (3) dynamic and static monitoring, and (4) locating specific areas for detailed analysis.

The chart of Fig. 5–50 shows the differences in implementation between a graph and a map, and how each satisfies the four basic requirements. However, use of a graph provides the following additional features: (1) user-defined limits (using the *y*-axis for magnitude expression), (2) selectable labels for examination of several areas without having to relocate probes, and (3) redefinable time base (*x*-axis) for data contraction. Let us consider some examples of these additional features.

Consider a program such as the nested loop of Fig. 5–36. A trace specification of Fig. 5–51 is defined, and data are acquired with the resultant trace graph shown in Fig. 5–52. Normally, the lower and upper limits would be 0000_{16} and $FFFF_{16}$ (for a typical map function), respectively. These limits would show a line near the bottom of the graph with very little vertical displacement. However, by using the increment and decrement keys, or by direct entry from the keyboard, the upper and lower limits were changed to $285C_{16}$ and 2847_{16}, respectively.

As shown in Fig. 5–52, the program is cycling (looping) through four iterations before jumping to memory locations above the upper

	MAP	GRAPH
Relative state magnitude	Positions (X-Y) of dot on CRT	Vertical displacement of dot on CRT (Y-Axis)
State-to-state directional flow	Interconnecting arrows between states	Left to right displacement of dots (X-axis)
Dynamic and static monitoring	Repetitive mode and static mode	Run continuous or single trace
Location of specific areas for detailed analysis	Movable cursor	Movable intensified dots

Fig. 5–50. Differences in implementation between a graph and a map display

-------------TRACE SPECIFICATION------------TRACE COMPLETE-----------

	LABEL BASE	A HEX	D HEX
START	TRACE	2848	XX

TRACE

ALL STATES

COUNT OFF

Fig. 5–51. Trace specification for examining a specific area of a nested loop

limit. The intensified dots have been moved using the roll keys to the area of the large jump. Now, by pressing the list key, the detailed list of the intensified dot area can be examined, as shown in Fig. 5–53. Note that the program was looping from 2852_{16} to 2855_{16} (positions +35

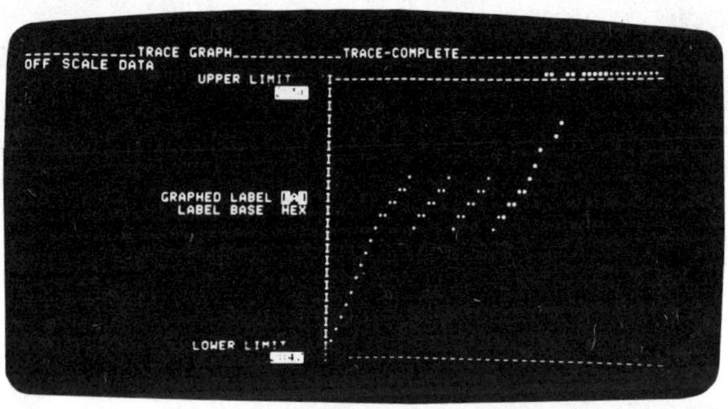

Fig. 5–52. Resultant trace graph of the trace specification of Fig. 5–51.

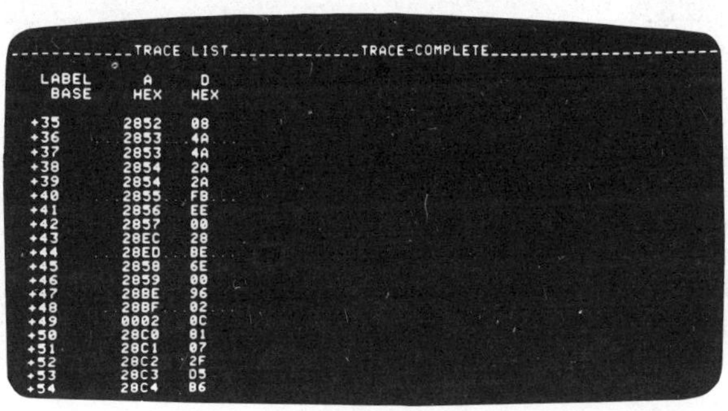

TRACE LIST — TRACE-COMPLETE

LABEL BASE	A HEX	D HEX
+35	2852	08
+36	2853	4A
+37	2853	4A
+38	2854	2A
+39	2854	2A
+40	2855	FB
+41	2856	EE
+42	2857	00
+43	28EC	28
+44	28ED	BE
+45	2858	6E
+46	2859	00
+47	28BE	96
+48	28BF	02
+49	0002	0C
+50	28C0	81
+51	28C1	07
+52	28C2	2F
+53	28C3	D5
+54	28C4	B6

Fig. 5–53. Resultant trace list of the intensified dots in the trace graph of Fig. 5–52

to +40) prior to jumping off scale to $28EC_{16}$ (position +43). By use of the definable limits, the graph was expanded to show meaningful information. Through the ability to move the intensified dots to an interesting area and the recalling of the list of the intensified dots, a detailed examination of states is possible.

The graph can be monitored dynamically (by entering the *trace continuous* mode, or statically (by using a single-trace mode). The graphed information represents all 64 states being stored in memory. It is possible to enlarge the apparent size of memory by changing the sample of data. Figure 5–54 shows the same graph as in Fig. 5–52, but the upper limit has now been changed to 2888_{16}. This has the effect of reducing the vertical magnitude of the state changes.

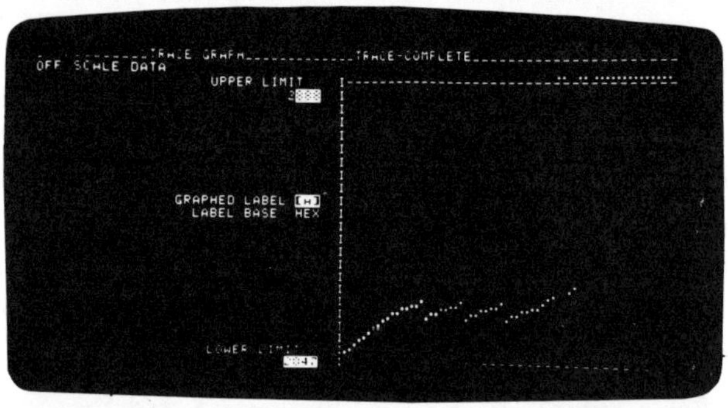

Fig. 5–54. Upper limit of the graph in Fig. 5–52 changed to 2888_{16}, which reduced the vertical magnitude of state changes

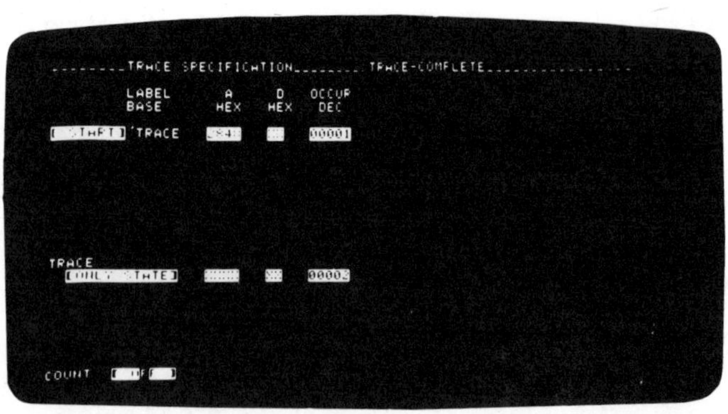

Fig. 5–55. Multiple occurrence counter of the trace only state set to capture one of every two states, effectively doubling the state flow viewing window

The horizontal time scale has not been affected in the display of Fig. 5–54. If it is desired to reduce the horizontal time base by a factor of 2 (and thus double the viewing "window" of state flow), the multiple occurrence counter of the trace only state can be changed from 1 to 2, as shown in Fig. 5–55. Now, when a new trace is performed, the 1610A acquires one state every two samples (if the counter were set to 5, one state would be acquired every five samples). The resultant graph for the trace specification of Fig. 5–55 is shown in Fig. 5–56. Note that the time base is one-half that of the previous graph, and that the loop cycles contain less states. In effect, the graph now provides an overview of the program form for 128 states.

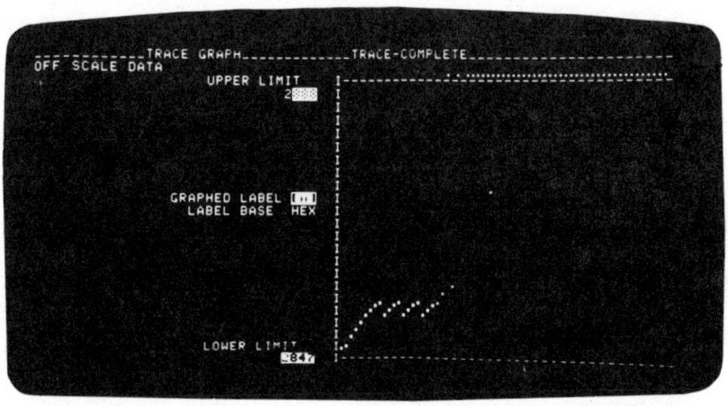

Fig. 5–56. Resultant graph of the trace specification of Fig. 5–55 shows that the graph provides an overview of program form for 128 states

5-4.9 Comparing Dynamic Data Versus Stored Data

The trace compare function is useful in detecting differences or similarities among data. Quite often, it is necessary to monitor for intermittent state changes, or to compare the contents of one memory unit relative to another. The 1610A can be used to constantly monitor incoming data and compare it with known stored data. When a non-equality or equality (of all 32 by 64 bits) is detected, the acquisition of data stops, and the difference is indicated in a listed display.

An example of a possible situation is indicated in Fig. 5–57. The format specification shows two labeled data fields of A and D with both in a display code of binary. A trace specification is then defined, and information acquired by executing a trace. All 2048 bits of acquired data are then placed in memory A. These data bits are transferred to an internal memory by pressing the *store* key. Both memories then contain the same information. By pressing the *compare verus store* key, a list

```
---------FORMAT SPECIFICATION-----------TRACE COMPLETE-------------

CLOCK SLOPE          +

(+,-)

                     POD      POD4      POD3      POD2      POD1
                     PROBE    7--0      7--0      7--0      7--0

LABEL ASSIGNMENT             [AAAAAAAA][AAAAAAAA][DDDDDDDD][XXXXXXXX]
(A,B,C,D,E,E,F,X)              !! !     !!!!!!!!  !!!!!!!
                                        ACTIVE CHANNELS

                     LABEL               A         D
LOGIC POLARITY
   (+,-)                                [+]       [+]

NUMERICAL BASE                          [BIN]     [BIN]
   (BIN,OCT,DEC, HEX)
```

Fig. 5–57. Format specification of two labeled data fields for comparing dynamic versus stored data

of the exclusive-OR results between A and D memories is shown. Any differences are indicated and decoded according to the display code selected for the fields.

The trace compare menu has a selectable field that allows the acquisition of data to stop when the comparison with store data is either equal (=) or not equal (≠). In addition, the stopping of acquired data can be turned off so that the 1610A can free-run while indicating the dynamic mismatch of incoming versus stored data.

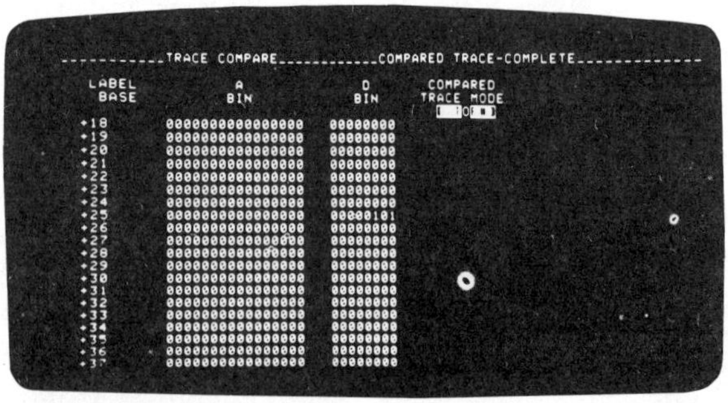

Fig. 5–58. Results of a trace compare shows a mismatch in position +25; in binary format the differences are indicated by ls

The results of a trace compare when the *stop when not equal* mode was selected is shown in Fig. 5–58. In this example, the 1610A was continuously comparing the incoming data with stored data; when a mismatch was found (position +25 in the D label), the acquisition of data stopped and the difference was indicated by the 1s in the appropriate channels.

5–5. USING THE TEKTRONIX 7D01 LOGIC ANALYZER

This section describes use of the 7D01 logic analyzer for microcomputer troubleshooting. As discussed in Sec. 3–11, the 7D01 features 16-channel data acquisition and word recognition, 4K formattable memory, pre-, center, or posttrigger, and synchronous and asynchronous timing. Data may be *mapped,* formatted as *state tables,* or presented in timing diagram format. All three formats feature readout in binary, hex, or octal notation. The addition of a WR501 *word recognizer* provides up to 32 channels of word or pattern recognition, plus digital delay capability. Formatting is done with the DF1 *formatter* also described in Sec. 3–11.

The following paragraphs take you through a typical microcomputer troubleshooting sequence, from mapping to state tables to timing diagrams. Every step can be performed with the 7D01/DF1/WR501 package described here. We start with a review of mapping.

5–5.1 Review of Mapping

With mapping, the entire contents of the 7D01 memory are displayed at once, and a unique *dot pattern* is generated. This unique pattern greatly simplifies such procedures as checking program flow or obtaining a software signature.

When 16-bit words are mapped, the inputs from channels 8 to 15, representing the most significant byte, are inputted to a D/A converter, which drives the vertical deflection circuitry of the CRT; the inputs from channels 0 to 7, representing the least significant byte, are inputted to another D/A converter, which drives the horizontal deflection circuitry. Thus, each combination of 1s and 0s in a word deflects the beam to a particular position on the CRT.

With 16 bits (2^{16}), 65, 536 unique memory locations are displayed in a 256 by 256 matrix. What happens is that we take the 254 words (each 16 bits wide) stored in the 7D01 memory and display all 254 of them as dots at the position defined by the combination of 1s and 0s that makes up each word. If some of the 254 words are identical, they will be displayed in the same spot, making that location brighter than the others. This can result in a pattern similar to that shown in Fig. 5–59.

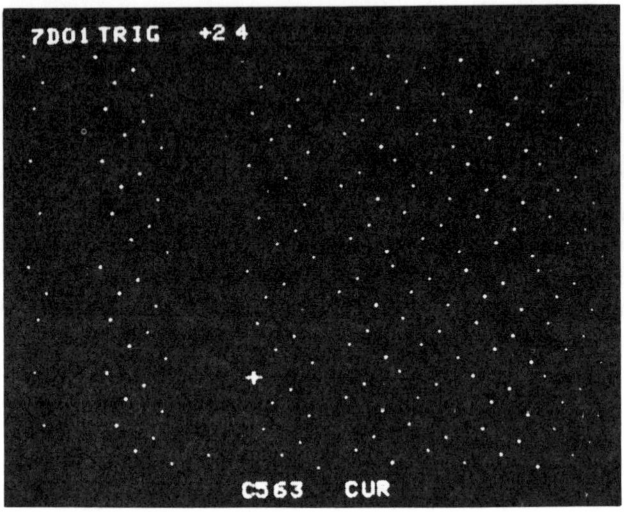

Fig. 5–59. Typical 7DO1 dot pattern

5–5.2 Advantages of Mapping

Mapping enables you to quickly look at all 254 words and compare their relative numerical values. Thus, in a microcomputer, you might want to analyze an address bus that is 16 bits wide. The pattern of 1s and 0s on that bus tells us which device (and which location in that device) takes data from or puts data onto the data bus. So if we know the address, we know what device the microprocessor is operating on at that point.

The total number of addresses available is broken into blocks for the supporting memory and I/O. For example, hex addresses 0000 to 00FF might be reserved for a 256- by 8-bit RAM (where the data that the microprocessor works on is kept). Addresses 0100_{16} to 0900_{16} might be assigned to a 2K by 8-bit PROM, where the instructions that make up the program are stored. Addresses $FFOO_{16}$ and $FEFC_{16}$ might be the addresses of two 8-bit-wide I/O ports that communicate with a terminal. If the microcomputer is talking with a terminal, you would expect to see some dots at the locations defined by $FFOO_{16}$ and

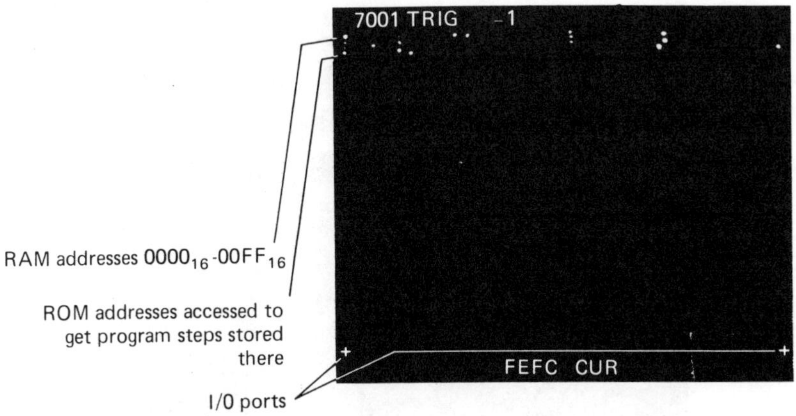

Fig. 5-60. Dot pattern when microcomputer is talking with a terminal.

$FEFC_{16}$, as well as some in the RAM address space (where the microcomputer stored what the terminal sent to it, such as shown in Fig. 5-60).

Now, rather than tediously going through all 254 words stored in the 7D01 and looking for $FF00_{16}$ or $FEFC_{16}$, you could easily see at a glance whether the microcomputer ever went to the I/O port during a program. That is the main advantage of mapping.

A larger microcomputer system might have much more program memory. By mapping the address line activity, you will quickly get an idea of which routines the microcomputer is performing. For example, a block data transfer routine might produce a display as shown in Fig. 5-61. But suppose that you find a display more like Fig. 5-62. Obviously,

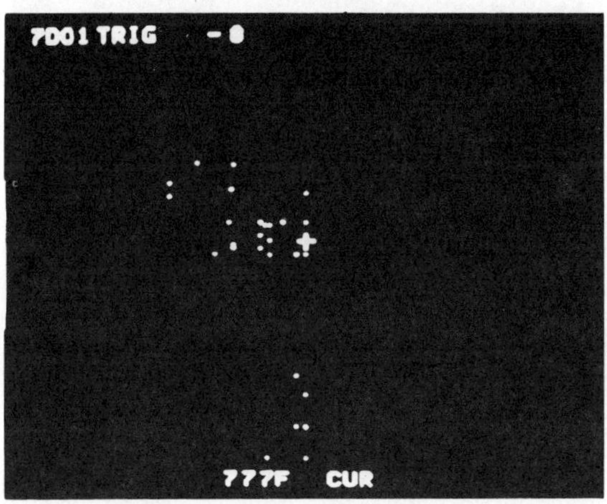

Fig. 5-61. Typical block data transfer dot pattern

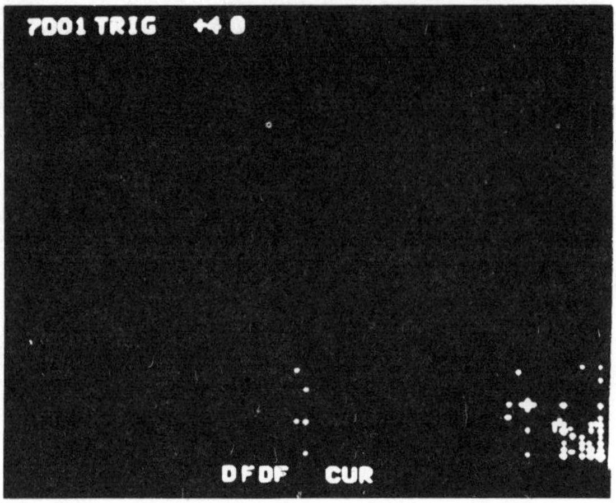

Fig. 5–62. Incorrect dot pattern (does not follow that of Fig. 5–61)

the microcomputer is doing something other than what you had in mind.

By locating the address of one of these invalid points with the *cursor* (shown as a + in Figs. 5–61 and 5–62), you can quickly set up a trigger on the built-in (16-bit) 7D01 word recognizer. Then you can restart the microcomputer and wait for the 7D01 to trigger. When the trigger occurs, you will have a picture of how the microprocessor got to those invalid addresses. By using the cursor, you can then track the addresses in sequence and see at just what location the address jumped, as shown in Fig. 5–63.

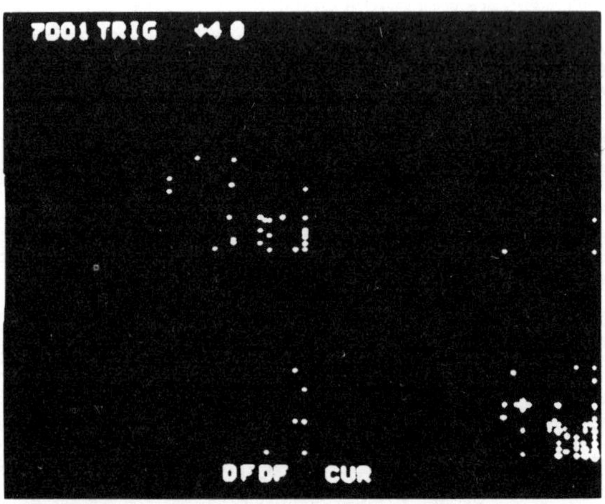

Fig. 5–63. Tracking the location where address jumped (using the cursor)

5–5.3 State Table Displays

State table displays are important aids for debugging software. Once you have located a problem area with mapping, you can go on to the next step, locating the faulty bit or bits in the program itself.

In a binary system, high voltage level might mean a 1, and a low voltage level might mean a 0. The parallel combination of 1s and 0s on a group of lines at a given instant will represent a word or state. For example, as shown in Fig. 5–64, the top line in binary is 1111111011111100. This is a 16-bit word displayed in binary. The same word in hex is represented by FEFC, as shown in Fig. 5–64. You might recognize FEFC as the address of an I/O port (Fig. 5–60), but it is difficult to recognize the same word in binary. This is the value of hex (or octal) decoding; masses of data are reduced to an easy-to-use form. However, no matter what coding or form is used, the state table display is a means of looking at the program, as stored in the 7D01 memory (just as is the mapping display).

Like mapped data, the state tables differ from timing diagrams in that the data bytes are stored using the same clock as the microcomputer system. That is, the data bytes are stored synchronously. The microprocessor system ignores the voltages present on a bus between active clock edges. In other words, the voltages on a bus are sampled by the microprocessor only at certain times, and it is to our advantage to use the same samples that the microprocessor uses so that we store only what the microprocessor "sees."

As an example, take the map of address lines (Fig. 5–63) as discussed in Sec. 5–5.3. The map is incorrect, indicating that you have

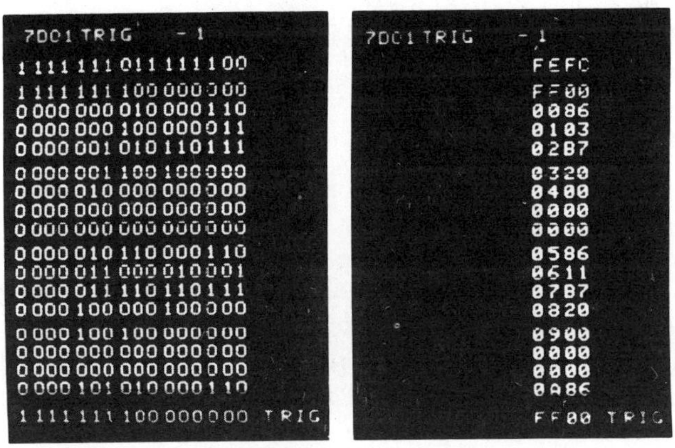

Fig. 5–64. Sixteen-bit word displayed in binary

stored an incorrect block of addresses. You then switch over to the state table mode, which shows the address word at the cursor location and the next 16 words stored (17 of 254 words total that have been captured). Then, using the cursor control, you can locate the illegal address area. In this case, the suspect address is $DFDF_{16}$ toward the bottom of the table shown in Fig. 5–65.

Once you have displayed the suspected area in state table form (Fig. 5–65), it is a relatively easy matter to see what devices in the microcomputer were being accessed by the microprocessor just before the fault occurred. For example, if the fault occurs when the ROM (or PROM) is being addressed, you can check the program listing of the ROM contents and see exactly what the microcomputer is supposed to do at that point.

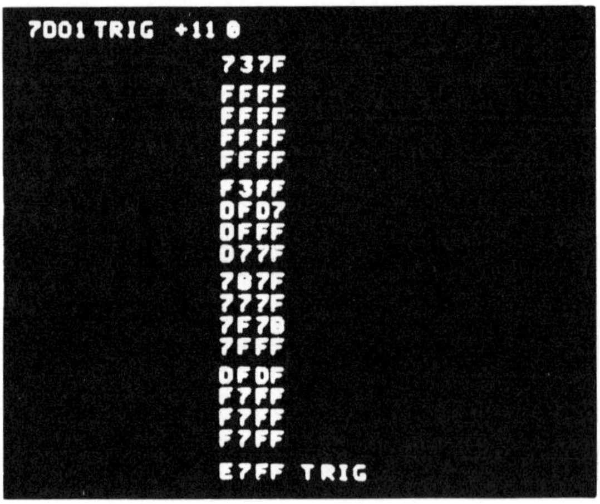

Fig. 5–65. Locating an illegal address area

5–5.4 Expanding the Word Recognition Capability

With the WR501 as part of the 7D01 package, you have 34-channel word or pattern recognition, with 16 channels stored and displayed. The digital delay feature allows you to delay inputs from the word recognizer by words or clock pulses. With word recognition and digital delay both, it is possible to word-recognize on word or pattern A, then on B, then to delay; or to word-recognize on A, delay for a certain count, then recognize on B.

5–5.5 Advantages of Expanded Word Recognition

To understand the advantages of word recognition, let us continue our example from the discussion on state table displays (Sec. 5–5.3). You now know that the microcomputer was accessing the PROM just before it went bad. By attaching the address bus probes to the WR501, setting up the WR501 word recognizer for the *first illegal address,* and attaching the 7D01 to the data bus, you can record data bus activity around the point of failure.

Now assume that an examination of the state tables shows that the microprocessor received the code for a jump instruction and, in the next two lines, received DFDF as the address. However, DFDF is the first address in the illegal block of code. It appears that the PROM has been incorrectly programmed. The WR501 has triggered the 7D01, allowing you to store the area of operation that you were looking for on the data bus, and so to locate the fault.

5–5.6 7D01 Reference Memory

The 4K reference memory of the 7D01 is separate from the working memory. When a block of data has been stored in the 7D01 and is found to be correct by your analysis, it can be "set aside" as a reference. You can then specify that data gathered on subsequent storage be ignored *if they match* a 17-word table that you select with the cursor, or if they match the entire 254-word reference memory. The 7D01 will count the number of correct matches, generate an external TTL reset pulse, and reset itself until a mismatch occurs. Then it will hold the erroneous data and intensify them in the display so that you know immediately where and what they are. As shown in Fig. 5–66, there is a mismatch on the tenth line (0001 compared to 0041) indicated by the intensified 0.

As an example of how this feature can be used, suppose that a microcomputer must perform a given sequence upon restart, but suppose that it *fails intermittently* (a not uncommon problem in microcomputers). First you capture a good sequence restart, designate that as your reference, and, using the 7D01 external reset pulse to restart the microcomputer, you activate the *reset if* mode. Then you go home for the night. Upon your return in the morning, you find that the 7D01 is holding the record of the thirty-sixth restart sequence (Fig. 5–66), which is obviously incorrect. As you can see from this example, the reference memory with intensified exclusive-OR comparison can be a real time saver.

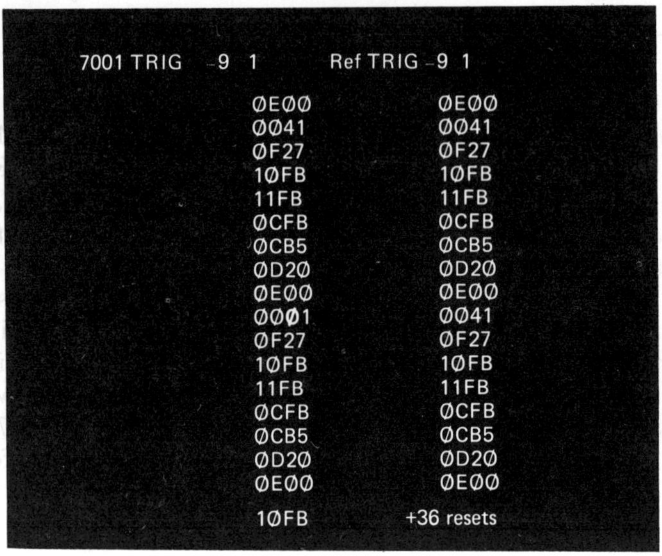

Fig. 5–66. Display showing a mismatch on the tenth line

5–5.7 Using the Timing Display

Timing diagrams may be generated by using the internal time base of the 7D01. In this way, 16 channels may be sampled at up to 50-ns intervals, 8 channels at up to 20-ns intervals, or 4 channels at up to 10-ns intervals. The channels can then be displayed as pseudowaveforms in the familiar timing diagram format, such as shown in Fig. 5–67.

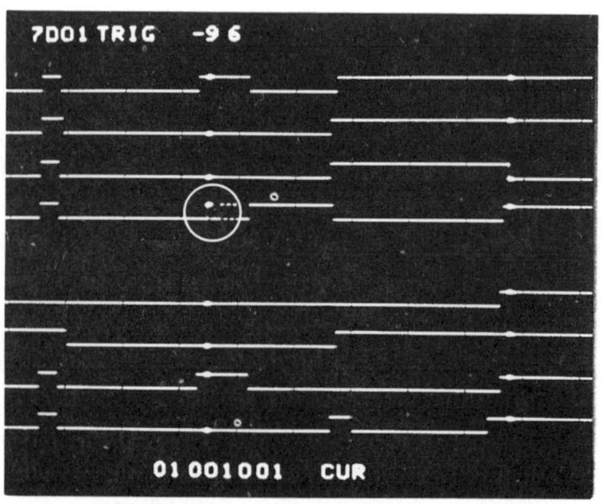

Fig. 5–67. Typical 7DO1 timing display

As an example of how timing diagrams can be used in troubleshooting, suppose that the fault described in the state table discussion (Sec. 5–5.3) has been traced to an I/O port instead of to a PROM. Incorrect data are being presented to the microprocessor by the I/O port. Are they incorrect data coming from the I/O port or the hardware (probably a peripheral) on the other side?

By using the 7D01 internal time base as an asynchronous clock, the keyboard-generated waveforms on the "outside world" side of the I/O port can be examined in detail. (And they can only be examined asynchronously.) In our example, the I/O port is found to be good. The trouble is traced to a faulty pull-up resistor on the switch input to the keyboard encoder, or to a race condition in the keyboard debounce circuitry, or to a faulty Schmitt trigger (as shown in the circled area of Fig. 5–67), or to any number of internal or external problems.

To sum up, the map and state table formats of the 7D01 package should be used for checking the internally clocked, or synchronous, portions of the microcomputer (such as the bus structure). The timing diagram format of the 7D01 should be used for troubleshooting circuits of the "outside world," as well as the linkage between the microcomputer and the outside world or peripherals.

5–6. SERIAL PATTERN RECOGNITION PROBLEMS

Most of the circuits within a microcomputer operate with parallel data bits. The microprocessor, ROM, RAM, and I/Os are interconnected with parallel data and address buses. This is not always true with the "outer world" circuits, which often use serial data transmission. The floppy disk and typewriter are classic examples of peripherals using serial data. In use, the I/O converts the serial data into parallel form for use in the microcomputer, and then converts parallel microcomputer data for use by the peripheral.

This situation creates an obvious problem in troubleshooting. Suppose that there is an apparent fault with a peripheral. The letter A has been recorded on a floppy disk at some point in a program, but the letter B appears on the data bus inside the microcomputer at that point. Is the output from the floppy disk truly an A? Or was it recorded improperly? Or is the I/O at fault? Your first step is to monitor the floppy disk output to the I/O. However, if you use an oscilloscope for monitoring, *all the serial bits* that make up the character must be displayed and checked for a unique digital pattern (typically ASCII bits). This means that the oscilloscope must be *triggered at exactly the correct* point to view the full pattern. On the other hand, if you use a logic analyzer to monitor serial peripheral (floppy disk) output, you must have some means for converting to parallel (since present-day analyzers operate with parallel data).

A *serial pattern word recognizer,* such as the Hewlett Packard 1620 can be used to solve the oscilloscope monitoring problem. A *serial-to-parallel converter,* such as the Hewlett Packard 10254, can be used to solve the logic analyzer monitoring problem. The following paragraphs describe operation and use of both devices in troubleshooting.

5–6.1 Using the HP1620A Pattern Analyzer in Troubleshooting

The pattern analyzer, such as shown in Fig. 5–68, generates a pattern trigger output (PTO) pulse when it recognizes, in the serial data flow, the same serial data bit arrangement (or trigger word) that has been selected by the settings on the analyzer's trigger word switches (TWS). This trigger word can be recognized at operating speeds up to 20 MHz (such as on a high-speed disk system). In addition, a digital delay feature can generate a digital delayed trigger output (DTO). The DTO display may be delayed any number of clock pulses (up to 999,999) past trigger word recognition. As a result, two display trigger pulses occur with each pattern recognition, enabling the operator to view activities associated with the selected PTO, both at the time of recognition (PTO) and at some predetermined time after pattern recognition (DTO).

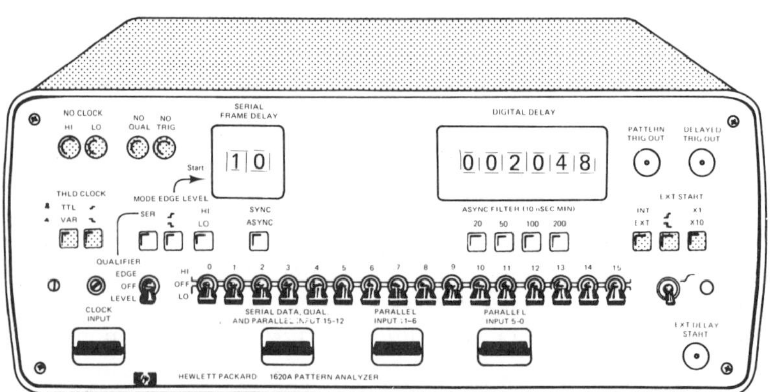

Fig. 5–68. Hewlett Packard 1620A pattern analyzer

5–6.2 Review of ASCII codes

As discussed in Chapter 1, one of the more common serial codes in use is the ASCII. The major use of ASCII is the transfer of information between a microcomputer and some of its peripherals such as typewriters and floppy disks. Figure 5–69 shows what a basic teleprinter system block diagram might look like, as well as the data format between the microcomputer and peripheral. The interface card inserts a start bit (always a 0) and two stop bits (always 1s) to make an 11-bit serial word with a parity bit of 0 for even parity.

There are several other signals of interest when transmitting ASCII characters in the serial mode. These are the clock and framing pulses (the framing pulse is sometimes called an STC or set control pulse). Figure 5–70 shows the relationship of these waveforms.

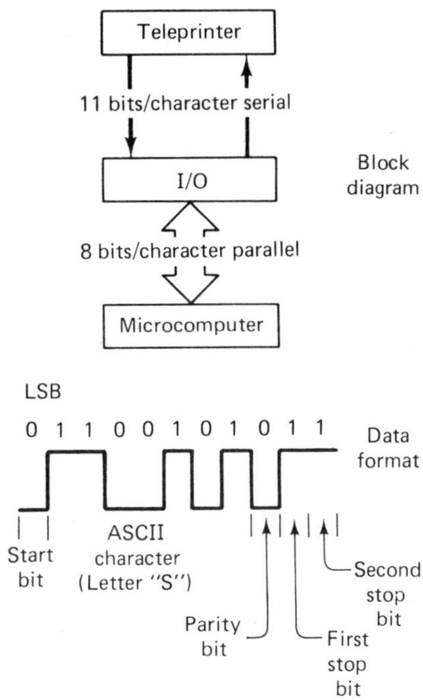

Fig. 5–69. Basic teleprinter system block diagram and data format

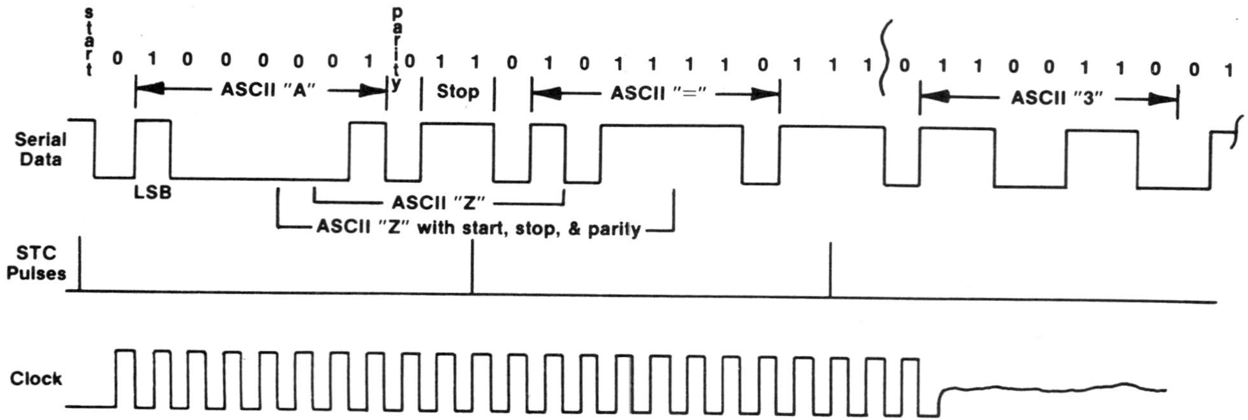

Fig. 5–70. Relationship of waveforms when transmitting ASCII characters in the serial mode (timing format)

5–6.3 Pattern Recognition

Figure 5–71 shows the basic connections between the pattern analyzer and microcomputer system, as well as the trigger word switch settings required to trigger on an ASCII 3. Note that the LSB is at the right on the 1620A front panel, and is on the left in the timing diagram (Fig. 5–70). Also, recognition of the 11 bits is set to occur on switches 15 through 5 rather than 10 through 0. This is because data are loaded with the LSB first starting at bit 15 on the 1620A. If the switches 10 through 0 are used, trigger recognition will occur 5 bits later, and you will not be able to view 5 bits of the character following the recognition character.

To be certain that you trigger on the desired character, the *serial qualifier* must be used to identify specific characters in a long string. As an example, suppose that it was desired to trigger on an ASCII Z. Without serial qualification, the 1620A will trigger on the Z bit pattern, as shown in Fig. 5–70. The pattern looks like a Z (including parity, start, and stop pulses) when it is actually a combination of A and =. The STC pulse is the serial qualifying or framing pulse that occurs once per serial character and allows positive identification of any specific character.

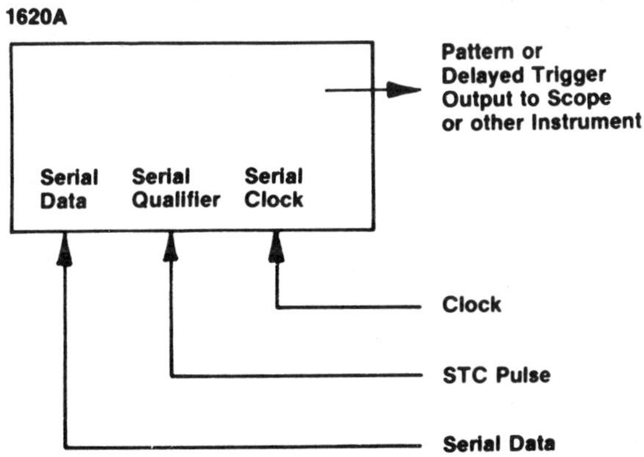

SWITCH NO.	15	14	13	12	11	10	9	8	7	6	5	4	3	2	1	0
SWITCH POSITION	1	1	0	0	1	1	0	0	1	1	0 (LSB)	OFF	OFF	OFF	OFF	OFF

Trigger Word Switch Settings for ASCII '3'

Fig. 5–71. Basic connections between the pattern analyzer and microcomputer system, as well as the trigger word switch settings for an ASCII 3

To set up serial qualification, set the 1620A *qualifier* switch to edge, and set the *serial frame delay* to 10. Notice that the serial frame delay is set to 10 and not 11. This is because the 1620A starts counting at 0 and not 1, and there are actually 11 counts when set to 10.

Once a character has been recognized, *digital delay* can be used to generate a trigger to an oscilloscope (or other instrument) a selected number of bits downstream up to 999,999. For example, if the message is

1 → 12
A = 35 MICROSECONDS

and you want to look at the D in MICROSECONDS, trigger on the 3 and set digital delay to 132 bits (12 characters) (11 bits/character) = 132 bits.

5–6.4 Troubleshooting Example with the 1620A

An actual troubleshooting example of the 1620A serial triggering capability occurred with a teleprinter terminal that occasionally generated unassigned ASCII characters. (The teleprinter does not have a complete ASCII character set. Thus, unassigned characters show up as spaces when transmitted back to the teleprinter. The unassigned characters can be recognized by the microcomputer, however, since it has a complete ASCII character set.)

Using a storage oscilloscope triggered by the 1620A, the bit patterns were examined, and it was noted that a hard press on the space bar occasionally generated unassigned ASCII characters. A close visual examination of the space bar reed relay switch revealed that its damping pad had worked up on its shaft. This permitted the switch to bounce and generate characters that were not assigned in the terminal. After replacing the damping pad, the system operated properly.

5–6.5 Using the 1620A with Disk Systems

Information bits are written onto or read from disk platters by analog signals, which are driving (or being driven by) read/write recording heads, as discussed in Sec. 2–8. Adjustment of these signals is extremely critical to accommodate interchangeability of platters, magnetic surface quality variation, head-to-track alignment, and other factors. Examination of the parameters of these analog signals with an oscilloscope is frequently complicated by display jitter, causing difficulty in interpreting the waveform. Display jitter is introduced when the oscilloscope trigger is not fully synchronized with data under investigation.

Some disk platters are designed in such a way that data on the platter are synchronous with the index pulse or the sector pulse, or with both. Stable oscilloscope displays are relatively easy to obtain in these types of systems. Oscilloscopes with a delayed sweep, especially a digital delay, enhance the stable display capability when examining analog signals at the read/write head.

Other disk systems are designed in such a way that data on the platter are not necessarily synchronous with index or sector pulses. Instead, data are phase locked to the clock pulses in such a way that the analog waveform on the platter contains both clock and data information. This design method permits higher disk system performance characterized by increased density of data on the platter and a higher rate of data transfer. Higher rates of data transfer are made possible by faster clocking synchronous with data information. Systems of this type generate index pulses and sector pulses mechanically, and usually cause unstable display of read/write head analog signals when used to trigger an oscilloscope.

5–6.6 Typical Disk System Data Formats

The HP7900A is a high-performance disk system with a moving head, phase-lock loop, two-platter disk, operating at 2400 RPM. Each side of each platter (four sides) has 200 + 3 tracks with 24 sectors per track. Data in each sector is positioned and has a fomat as shown in Fig. 5–72. Figure 5–72 also illustrates the manner in which data pulses and clock pulses are combined for entry onto the data track with data bits inserted between clock pulses. Because the clock pulse rate is 2.5 MHz, a string of 1s in the data stream presents the equivalent of a 5-MHz pulse rate in the track format, while a string of 0s in the data stream presents the 2.5-MHz pulse rate in the track format. When reading the disk head information track, the read head, synchronized with the clock pulses, separates the clock pulses from the data bits. The write head, on the other hand, transfers clock and data pulses to the disk head in the track format. Figure 5–72b illustrates how the separated clock is combined with, or separated from, the data 11001010 into the track format.

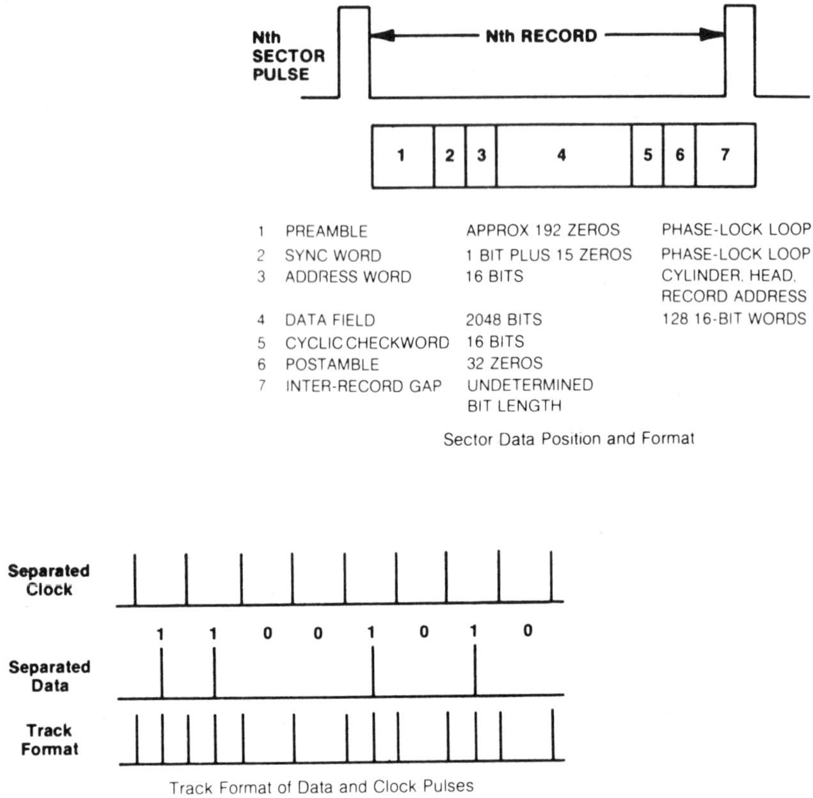

Fig. 5–72. Sector data position and format, together with track format of data and clock pulses

5–6.7 Synchronizing to Disk Data with the 1620A

Clock pulses and data bits are synchronized within each loop only from the start of the sync word to the beginning of the interrecord gap, as shown in Fig. 5–72a. An oscilloscope trigger point taken from a point outisde this region will almost certainly result in a jittery display. Within this region, however, is an address word containing cylinder, head, and sector coding. The address word defines a unique sector among some 19,000 sectors. Using qualifier, frame delay, digital delay,and pattern recognition features, the 1620A can be set up to recognize any desired unique address word within that sector. On recognition, the 1620A generates a reliable PTO pulse and displays a stable waveform on an oscilloscope. Figure 5–73 illustrates this concept.

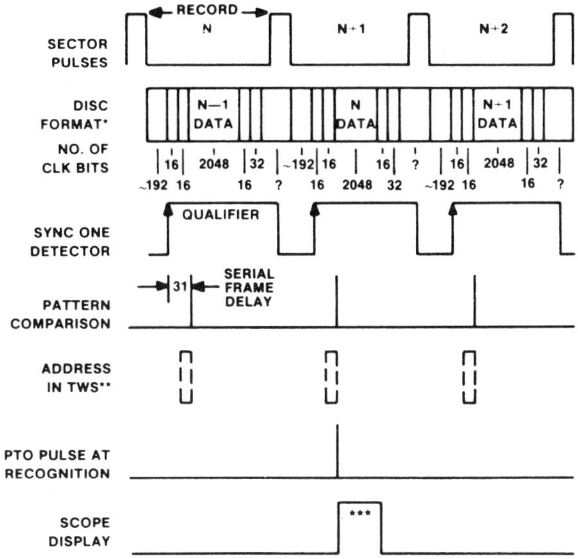

**TWS MEANS TRIGGER WORD SWITCHES ON THE ANALYZER
***TIME DEPENDS ON SWEEP SPEED

Fig. 5–73. Disk system data and control signal format, and pattern analyzer functional relationship

Three adjacent and active records at the disk read head are shown in Fig. 5–73. Separated data (detailed in Fig. 5–72) are clocked continuously through the trigger word shift register in the pattern analyzer. Output of the *sync one* detector from the disk interface board goes high with the 1-bit in the sync word of each active record (Fig. 5–72a). The sync one signal remains high during the synchronized area of the record, and then goes low during the interrecord gap. The 16-bit address word ends 32 clock pulses after the sync one signal goes high. Therefore, with the pattern analyzer serial frame delay set for 31, and qualified from the positive edge of the sync one output, you are assured that address pattern recognition occurs only when the address in the TWS shift register matches the address pattern of the desired record.

5–6.8 Synchronizing the Oscilloscope Display

Upon address pattern recognition, a PTO is generated for synchronizing an oscilloscope. Stable display of head analog signals, separated data, separated clock pulses, and other waveforms in the sector can be achieved using the DTO and appropriate digital delay. Without changing any of the connections to the pattern analyzer, the operator is able to sync the oscilloscope display from any sector of the disk system memory simply by positioning the TWS to recognize and capture the address of the sector of interest.

5–6.9 Setting the Trigger Word Switches to the Sector Address

Most disk system handbooks show the address format for the sectors in a manner similar to Fig. 5–74. The HP7900A, for example, uses the address pattern shown in Fig. 5–74 to indicate cylinder 97, head 1, sector 5, unprotected. However, note that this format is generated serially starting with the LSB of the cylinder coding and continuing for the next 15 address bits. Because the serial (address) word is shifted into the pattern analyzer TWS serial register from its most significant bit, the pattern analyzer TWS must be set to reflect the mirror image of the address format, or

0101001001100001

To further confuse the issue, most disk systems (HP7900A for example) are so designed that when the sector pulse for sector (N + 1) occurs, the data for sector (N) appears. Thus, if you use the switch settings shown in Fig. 5–74, you would get data written in sector 4, to be read by head 1, from cylinder 97.

Bit No.	16	15	14	13	12	11	10	9	8	7	6	5	4	3	2	1
Code	1	0	0	0	0	1	1	0	0	1	0	0	1	0	1	0
Address For	lsb CYLINDER								lsb HEAD		SECTOR				lsb	PROTECT

Fig. 5–74. Address coding for locating a desired sector

5–6.10 Analyzing Oscilloscope Displays

Most pattern analyzer user manuals and application notes contain elaborate descriptions of how to analyze the oscilloscope displays obtained from serial data systems using the analyzer. This information will not be duplicated here. However, there are some points to keep in mind. A common problem that contributes to disk reading errors is analog signal quality from the read head. Poor-quality analog signals

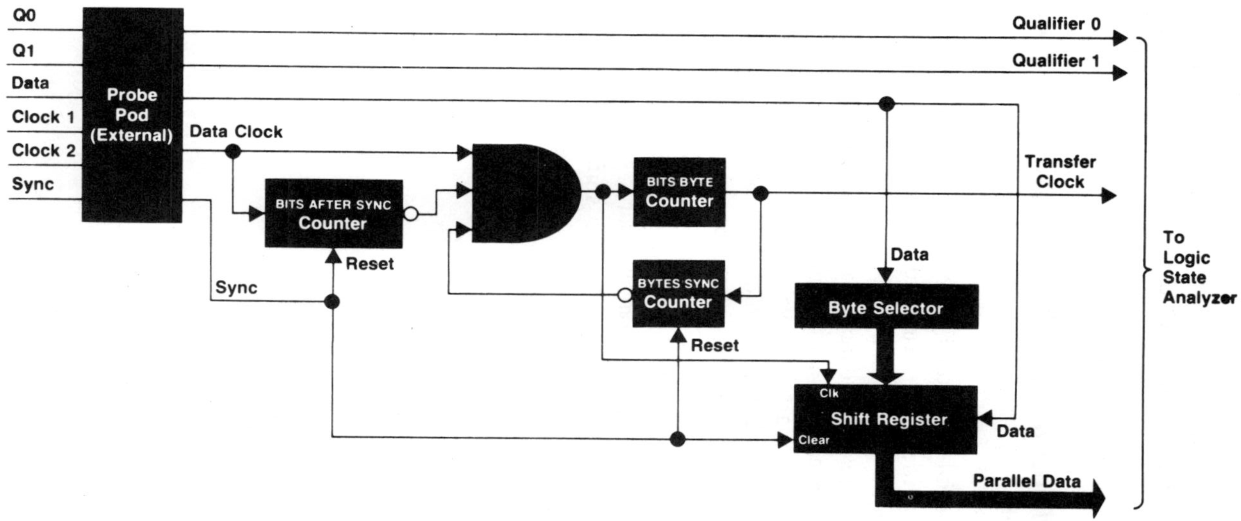

Fig. 5–75. Simplified block diagram of Hewlett Packard 10254A serial-to-parallel converter

can be caused by head-to-track alignment, quality and uniformity of the magnetic oxide, coating, and disk surface velocity. However, as the head moves from outside to inside tracks of a disk, the amplitude of the read signals will vary, even with a properly performing disk system.

5–6.11 Using the HP10254A Serial-to-Parallel Converter

The serial-to-parallel converter, such as shown in Fig. 5–75, accepts data in serial form and formats it into a parallel word for presentation on a logic analyzer. Once in parallel form, the data can be analyzed in the normal manner. Just as with other parallel data, the logic analyzer can be set to capture and display the data sequence beginning with a particular word, or data leading up to the word, or data at some point downstream from the word, enabling the user to search out and find the part of the program where malfunctions occur. Operation of the converter is described fully in the user manuals. The key point to remember is that the converted serial data can be analyzed in the same way as normal parallel data. As shown in Fig. 5–75, serial-to-parallel conversion occurs in the shift register. The other blocks control the timing and direction of shift register loading and the timing of data transfer to the logic state analyzer.

INDEX

Accumulators, 31
Adder circuits, 11
Addition, binary, 6
Address
  bus, 24
  label, 82
  microprocessor, 24
  register, 76
  selection, 47
Addressing, 72, 235
  counting sequence, 325
Alphanumeric codes, 20
ALU (arithmetic logic unit), 10, 40
Analyzer, logic, 156
Architecture, 42
ASCII, 21
  codes 373
Assemblers, 70
Assembly, 70
  code, 82
  language, 3, 80
Asynchronous, I/O, 94

Baud rate generator, 247, 289
BCD (binary coded decimal), 20
Benchmarks, logic analyzer, 353
Bidirectional, 24
Binary
  addition, 6
Binary (*cont.*)
  codes, 20
  complements, 8
  division, 11
  fractions, 5
  multiplication, 11
  numbers, 3
  numbers vs. electrical signals, 22
  subtraction, 7
  to decimal conversion, 5
  to hex conversion, 19
  to octal conversion, 13
  values, 4
Bits, 3
Block diagram, microprocessor, 43
Branch instructions, 75
Breaking the microprocessor loop, 323
Breakpoint, 156
Buffer, 36
Buffer state control, 46
Bus, 24
  enable, 37
  fight, 321
  interface, 207
  logic, 216
Bytes, 3

Call, subroutine, 75
Cassette recording, 113
Character generator, 100

Character generator circuits, 268
Character-at-a-time printer, 106
Checkerboard, 121
Clip, logic, 150
Clock, 206
  circuits, troubleshooting, 323
  period, 66
  pulses, 27
Comparator, logic, 151
Conditional assembly, 83
Conditional branch, 76
Constant check, tape read/write, 118
Control circuit, microprocessor, 40
Count measurement, logic analyzer, 353
Counters, 31
  circuits, 285
  program, 71
Counting, binary, 4
Counting sequence on address line, 325
CPU (control or central processor unit), 2
CRC (cyclic redundancy check), 119
Crosstalk, 321, 326
Crowbar circuits, 225
CRT/keyboard terminal, 99
Current loop, 20-mA, 287
Current tracer, 146
  in digital troubleshooting, 318
  problems, 321
Cursor, logic analyzer display, 161

Daisy-chain interface, 124
Data
  access, 126
  block tape, 117
  bus, 24
  bus, microprocessor 59
  communications, 133
  display, 157
  processing, peripherals, 92
  records, tape, 117
  selection, 237
  selector, 246
  set, 135
Debugging, 26, 333
Decimal
  to binary conversion, 6
  to binary conversion with octal, 14
  to hex conversion, 17
  to octal conversion, 13
Decoders, 36
Decoding, 237
Decremented, 32
Development stage troubleshooting, 321
Diagnostic routines, 314
Digital delay, logic analyzer, 350
Digital IC failure, 310
Digital IC troubleshooting, 307
Digital troubleshooting examples, 314
Disk troubleshooting, 376
Diskette drive, 127
Diskette recording, 122
Diskette recording format, 129
Display formatter DFI, 183
Division, binary, 11
DMA (direct memory access), 216
Drivers, 36, 38
Drum printer, 106
Dual recording, tape, 118
Dumping, counters/registers, 34
Dynamic data vs. stored data, 361
Dynamic vs. static RAM, 49

EAROM (electrically alterable ROM), 54
EIA (Electronic Industries Association) I/O, 287
Electronic address, tape, 121
Emulators, 88
Enable signal, 37
Encoders, 36
EPROM (erasable PROM), 52
Erasure, ultraviolet, 53
Evaluation of expressions, 83
Evaluation kit, 88
Execution phase, 76

Failure, IC, 310
Fetch phase, 76
Fetch (instructions), 41
Firmware, 41

Flag signal, 33, 96
Floppy disk recording, 122
Flow chart, 70, 86
Format specification, logic analyzer, 340
Four-bit system, 20
Fractions, binary, 5
Front panel controls, 226

Gate-to-gate faults, 148
Gate testing, 144
Graph display, analyzer, 160
Groundplanes, testing, 319

Halt instruction, 28
Handshake bus, 24
Hard sectoring, 133
Hardware, I/O, 54
Hardware, memory, 45
Hardware, microcomputer, 68
Hardware, microprocessor, 41
Hardware, system, 86
Heathkit H9 Video Terminal, 248
Heathkit H10 Paper Tape Reader/Punch, 292
Heathkit H11 Computer System, 200
Hewlett Packard 1602A Logic State Analyzer, 180
Hewlett Packard 1610A Logic State Analyzer, 169
Hewlett Packard 1611A Logic State Analyzer, 162
Hex, 14
  number manipulation, 19
  to binary conversion, 17
  to decimal conversion, 16
High voltage power supply, video terminal, 263
Highway, 24
Horizontal sweep circuits, 262
H9 Video Terminal, 248
H10 Paper Tape Reader/Punch, 292
H11 Computer System, 200
HP1610A Logic State Analyzer, 339
HP1620A Pattern Analyzer, 372
HP10254A Serial-to-Parallel Converter, 382

IC (integrated circuit)
  failure, digital, 310
  troubleshooting, digital, 307
Incremented, 32
Index recording, 133
Indirect addressing, 72
Initializing, counters/registers, 34
Input, peripheral, 94
Instruction
  microprocessor, 22
  phase or cycle, 76
  program, 75
  register, 77
  set, microprocessor, 22
Interblock gaps, tape, 117
Interface, 207
  I/O, 240
  memory, 60
  microprocessor, 59
  parallel, 236
  peripheral, 62
  serial, 242
Interfacing, 55
  diskette, 124
Interrecord gaps, tape, 117
Interrupt, 41, 60, 79, 96, 211, 241, 246
Intersect, matrix, 39
I/O (input/output), 208, 240
  bus, 202
  circuits, 285
  hardware, 54
  turning on, 330

Jumps, program, 40

KD11-F Microcomputer, 204
Keyboard circuits, 279
Keyboard video terminal, 251

Language, assembly and machine, 80
Latches, 36
  I/O, 241
LENKMICROCOMP, 67
Libraries, 78
Line-at-a-time printer, 106
Loading, 76
  counters/registers, 34

Logic
  analyzer, 156, 162, 169, 180, 183
  clip, 150
  comparator, 151
  gate testing, 144
  microprocessor, 40
  probe, 140
  pulser, 143
  signals, 226
  state analyzer, 162, 169, 180
Loop, program, 83

Machine cycle, 67
Machine language, 80
Macro assembly, 84
Magnetic recording basics, 110
Map display, 195
Mapping, 363
Mapping display, analyzer, 160
Matrix, 38
Matrix printer, 109
Memory, 203, 218
  expansion circuits, 233
  hardware, 45
  microprocessor, 24
  microprocessor system, 59
Microcomputer
  analysis with logic analyzer, 191
  basics, 1
  circuits, 199
  hardware, 68
  KD11-F, 204
  operation cycle, 76
  system production, 89
  troubleshooting approaches, 307
  troubleshooting, basic approach, 152
  troubleshooting equipment, 137
  typical system operation, 67
Microcontroller, 2
Microprocessor, 1, 204
  addresses, 24
  architecture, 42
  block diagram, 43
  circuit functions, 30
  controls, 63
  development of system, 84
Microprocessor (*cont.*)
  hardware, 41
  loop breaking, 323
  memories, 34
  program model, 44
  to ROM link, 327
Minicomputer, 2
Mnemonic, 71
Model 1602A Logic State Analyzer, 180
Model 1610A Logic State Analyzer, 169
Model 1611A Logic State Analyzer, 162
Modem, 135
Motor (tape) timing, 294
MPU (microprocessor unit), 2
M6800 system response, 338
Multiple gate input problems, 149
Multiplexer, 36
Multiplication, binary, 11

Nesting, 78, 348
Nibbles, 3
NRZL (non return to zero level), 115
NRZM (non return to zero mark), 115
Number identification, 4
Number systems, 2

Octal numbers, 12
Octal-to-binary conversion, 13
Octal-to-decimal conversion, 13
Off-line, 93
One's complement, 8
On-line, 93
Op-codes (operation codes), 70
Opens, testing, 317
Operand, 74
Oscilloscope, synchronizing displays with, 379
Output
  peripheral, 97
  printer, 105
Overcurrent circuits, 225
Overvoltage circuits, 225

Paper-tape reader/punch, 102, 292

Parallel
  data, 27
  interface, 236
  I/O, 55
  operation of counters/registers, 33
Parity
  bits and checks, 29
  option, 96
  vertical, 119
Pattern analyzer, serial, 372
Pattern recognition, 375
Peripherals, 57, 203
  equipment, 68
  equipment, introduction to, 91
  interface, 62
  prioritizing, 79
PIA (parallel interface adapter), 60
Pointers, 31
Polled method (peripherals), 79
Port, 24
Postamble bits, 121
Power supply, 28, 220
  reader/punch, 298
  video terminal, 256
Powers of 2, 7
Preamble bits, 121
Printer, output, 105
Prioritizing peripherals, 79
Probe, logic, 140
Probes, logic analyzer, 163, 171
Process control, peripherals, 93
Program
  basic, 69
  code, 87
  counters, 31, 71, 76
  errors, detecting, 356
  flow, 358
  flow, analyzing, 334
  instructions, 75
  listing vs. tabular display, 159
  model, microprocessor, 44
  trace, 153, 325, 334, 367
Programming example, 72
Programming PROM, 52
PROM (programmable ROM) circuit, 51
Pulses, 27
Pulse activity, checking, 316
Pulse packing or density, 116
Pulse tracing, point-to-point, 309
Pulser, logic, 143
Punch, paper-tape, 104
Punch timing, 299

Radial interface, 124
Radio Shack TRS-80 Printer, 109
RAM (random access memory), 2
  circuits, 45, 285
  dynamic, 49
  static, 49
  turning on, 329
  volatile, 49
Read cycle, 236
Reader, paper-tape, 102
Real time, 93
  analysis 143
Recording
  diskette, 133
  format, diskette, 129
  magnetic, 110
  tape, 112
Registers, 31
Regulator circuits, 222
Reset, 211
  circuit troubleshooting, 323
  instruction, 28
RMM (read mostly memory), 54
ROM (read only memory), 2
  checking, 326
  circuits, 49
RZ (return to zero), 115

Safety precautions in microcomputer troubleshooting, 138
Screen printer, 110
Sector recording (disk), 133
Seek and restore operation, 125
Seiko printer, 108
Select signal, 37
Serial
  data, 27
  data transmission, 95
  interface, 242
  I/O, 56, 287

Serial (*cont.*)
- operation of counter/register, 31
- pattern recognition, 371
- to-parallel converter, 382

Service request (peripheral), 41
Service routine, 94
Servicing peripherals, 79
7D01 Logic Analyzer, 363
Shift register, 11
Shifting counters/registers, 34
Shorts, testing for, 317
Signature, mapping, 160
Signed-binary numbers, 5, 9
Simulators, 88
Single stepping, 153
Software, 41
- design aids, 89
- developing, 333

Solder bridge/cable problems, 148
Source code, 82
Stack, program, 75
State table displays, 367
Static vs. dynamic RAM, 49
Storage register, 77
Stored data vs. dynamic data, 361
Strobe signal, 37
Stuck line, 319
Subroutines, 78
Subtraction, binary, 7
Subtraction, two's complement, 10
Synchronization, system, 65
System overview, logic analyzer, 358

Tabular data display, analyzer, 157
Tabular display, 195
Tape
- coding, 114
- control, 117
- data records, 117
- punch, 298
- read/write constant check, 118
- reader/punch, 102, 292
- recording, basic, 112
- records, accuracy and safety, 117
- records, locating data, 121

Tektronix DF1 Display Formatter, 183
Tektronix 7D01 Logic Analyzer, 183, 363
Three-state buffers, 38
Time sharing, 135
Timer pulses, 27
Timing
- circuits, 285
- diagram, 193
- diagram display, 195
- diagrams and display, analyzer, 156
- digital IC, 308
- display, 370
- problems, 155
- system, 65

Trace, program, 153
Trace specification, logic analyzer, 343
Track formats, diskette, 130
Training courses, 85
Trigger words, pattern analyzer, 380
Troubleshooting, 26
- by analyzing program flow, 334
- approaches, microcomputer, 307
- character generator circuits, 284
- circuit, 199
- in development stage, 321
- digital IC, 307
- disk systems, 376
- equipment, 137
- example, 191
- examples, digital, 314
- H11 circuits, 230
- I/O circuits, 292
- keyboard circuits, 284
- memory, 236
- microcomputer, 220
- microcomputer (basic), 153
- parallel interface, 242
- power supply, 231
- reader/punch circuits, 304
- serial interface, 247
- with HP1620A, 372

TRS-80 Printer, 109
TTL (transistor-transistor logic) I/O, 289
TTY (typewriter) terminals, 94

20-mA current loop, 287
Two's complement, 8
Two's complement subtraction, 10
Typewriter terminals, 94

UART (universal asynchronous receiver transmitter), 243
Unconditional branch, 76
Universal I/O, 94
UV (ultraviolet) erasure procedure, 53

Vector, matrix, 39
Vertical sweep circuits, 257
Video amplifier circuits, 263
Video circuits, 257
Video terminal, 99, 248
Volatile RAM, 49

Waveforms, checking, 325
Wired-AND problems, 147
Word recognition, 369
Words, 3
Write cycle, 235
Writing sample programs, 85